the
CONNECTICUT
FARM TABLE
COOKBOOK

Maria –
Happy Cooking!
Enjoy,
Tracey Medeiros

the CONNETICUT FARM TABLE COOKBOOK

150 Home-Grown Recipes

from the Nutmeg State

TRACEY MEDEIROS
AND CHRISTY COLASURDO

Photographs by **Oliver Parini**

THE COUNTRYMAN PRESS

WOODSTOCK, VERMONT

Interior photographs by Oliver Parini unless otherwise specified.

BOOK DESIGN BY Michelle Farinella

INTERIOR COMPOSITION BY Eugenie S. Delaney

FRONTISPIECE: Cato Corner Farm

Published by The Countryman Press, P.O. Box 748, Woodstock, VT 05091

Distributed by W.W. Norton & Company, Inc., 500 Fifth Avenue, New York, NY 10110

Printed in the United States of America

The Connecticut Farm Table Cookbook

ISBN: 978-1-58157-256-8

10 9 8 7 6 5 4 3 2 1

The Countryman Press

Woodstock, Vermont

www.countrymanpress.com

Waldingfield Farm

We dedicate this book to the Connecticut farmers, fishermen, cheese makers, beekeepers, foragers, and food producers who take great pains—and pride—in bringing us fresh, wholesome local foods, while serving as responsible stewards of our natural resources. Neither drought, nor rain, nor heat, nor pests can keep these hardy souls from their appointed rounds. We salute you for your commitment to providing us with a colorful array of locally grown edibles that nourish our health, our ecosystem, and our communities. We are enduringly grateful.

ACKNOWLEDGMENTS

As we started visiting small farms across the state, we were heartened to meet so many farmers who are still in the trenches, fighting the good fight and turning out the region's most delicious edibles—despite all odds. With this book, we set out to celebrate Connecticut's food and farms, and we dedicate these pages to our hardworking farmers and food producers—for waking at sunrise every morning and toiling through the wee hours to carry on a rich agricultural tradition that has true meaning. As our farmers tend to fields and flocks, they are nurturing our health, our regional landscapes, our soil, and our communities through sustainable practices and old-fashioned grit.

It's a beautiful thing to tour one's own state and discover a thriving green foods scene in every corner, with pick-your-own operations; rustic roadside farm stands and clam shacks; community-centered farmers' markets in the cities and suburbs; and gorgeous farms, vineyards, and orchards. From Norwalk to Niantic, we met restaurateurs and chefs forging relationships with sustainable farmers, fishermen, cheese makers, butchers, bakers, and canners. We salute each individual who strives to keep these wonderful New England food traditions alive for future generations, and wish we could have included each and every one of you in this book!

We thank our entire team at The Countryman Press, particularly editor Ann Treistman, designer Michelle Farinella, copyeditor Iris Bass, compositor Eugenie Delaney, Countryman's production manager Fred Lee, production editor Doug Yeager, and publicist Devorah Backman for bringing our vision to life. Our heartfelt thanks go to Oliver Parini, our talented photographer, who wielded his trusty Canon across the state, brilliantly capturing the essence of the Connecticut food and farm scene in poignant imagery. Thank you to Sarah Strauss, our indefatigable recipe tester, for tirelessly testing and tweaking recipes so to ensure that they are easily replicated by the home cook. Thank you to Justin Molson for jumping in to help test recipes. Thank you to Winter Caplanson, of Connecticut Food & Farm, for inviting us to the Coventry Farmers' Market and the Connecticut Farmers' Market Trail, and plugging us into a circuit of small farmers and photographers, and to Lori Cochran, market director of the Westport Farmers' Market, for introducing us to wonderful local farmers and creating a go-to destination in the heart of the suburbs where farmers, foodies, chefs, and soccer moms converge for a taste of the local green foods scene. Thank you to Jennifer Balin, of Sugar & Olives in Norwalk, for letting us turn her space into a photography studio. And last but not least, we thank all the farm and restaurant contributors who share their stories, images, and recipes.

Finally, we express heartfelt gratitude to our families, for their endless patience, love, and support as we took this book from concept to fruition.

A portion of the proceeds from the sale of this book will be donated to the Connecticut Farmland Trust.

LEFT: *Matt and Jess at Speckled Rooster Farm*

FOREWORD

The Connecticut Farm Table Cookbook beautifully captures the profound shift in tastes and attitudes that have transformed the Connecticut restaurant scene into one with a purpose beyond pleasing our palates. Chefs were the first to champion the work of our farmers and artisan food producers, enticing us with fresh, seasonal foods enhanced by culinary alchemy into meals so deliciously memorable we had to tell all our friends about them and couldn't wait to return for another visit. Word spread, more eaters came, and ever-increasing numbers of chefs were inspired to source vegetables, fruit, meat and poultry, cheese, bread, honey, maple syrup, and even wine and spirits from small Connecticut farms and producers. In less than a decade, the most exciting and delicious food in Connecticut is now crafted with ingredients grown and raised close to home.

Eaters were so strongly influenced by such pioneering chefs as Michel Nischan, Bill Taibe, and Tim LaBant, that we began frequenting farmers' markets and buying into community supported agriculture (CSA) programs in pursuit of sustainably grown, local flavors for our own tables. Demand for food grown by our farmers and artisans has become so regular that Fairfield County alone boasts seven winter farmers' markets and more than 30 spring/summer farmers' markets. From spring's first asparagus to frost-sweetened parsnips in winter, our farms provide us with sustenance throughout all four seasons. Consumers who find farmers' market schedules inconvenient rely on farm-to-door delivery services to stock their refrigerators and pantries. One does not have to travel far, or at all, to find green garlic in the spring, sweet corn in the summer, freshly dug potatoes in the fall, and celeriac in the winter.

The Connecticut Farm Table Cookbook pays homage to the passionate work of our chefs, farmers, and artisan food producers while providing home cooks with the gift of re-creating favorite restaurant meals at home. Simplicity is the hallmark of the recipes found in this cookbook, ensuring at least a handful will become regulars in weeknight dinner rotations. Restaurant, chef, farmer, and artisan food producer profiles take readers on a journey of food discovery through Connecticut, while spotlighting annual events to bookmark as road trips and farm dinners with celebrated chefs to plan with friends. Touring farms, visiting wineries for tastings, picking your own fruit in orchards, learning how farmstead cheese is made and aged, and tasting honey straight from the hive are powerful catalysts for changing the way we think about food. Taste trumps all and is therefore the ultimate arbiter in our decision to adopt the philosophy of eating locally and sustainably.

The local food web is incomplete without eaters like you and me who have come to appreciate the impact our food choices have on our health, our community, and the environment. Enjoy this cookbook as you lovingly prepare and share restaurant-quality meals with friends and family that reflect the Connecticut seasons, connect us to the land, and strengthen our communities.

Every meal crafted from locally grown and raised ingredients is an investment in a more sustainable future.

Analiese Paik

Local-sustainable food advocate
and founder of the Fairfield Green Food Guide

LEFT: *Chef/restaurateur Bill Taibe at Farahs' Farm*

Contents

Breakfast

March Farm 17
Sugary Apple Muffins 18
Rose's Berry Farm, LLC 19
Blueberry Muffins 20
Blackberry River Baking Co. 21
Blackberry River Scones 21
Red Flannel Hash 22
Freund's Farm Market & Bakery, LLC 23
Pumpkin Bread 24
Farm to Hearth 25
Baked French Toast 26
Arethusa al Tavolo 27
Eggs "Manolo Blahnik Style" 28

Soups and Salads

Barberry Hill Farm 31
Pistou Soup 32
Blue Lemon Restaurant 33
Arugula and Endive Salad with Apples,
    Celeriac, Caramelized Walnuts,
    and Cider Vinaigrette 33
Thompson Street Farm, LLC 35
Carrot and Sunflower Sprout Salad
    with Basil Vinaigrette 36
Heirloom Restaurant and Lounge 37
Starlight Farm's Kale Salad with Sour
    Cherry Vinaigrette 38
The Wharf Restaurant at Madison
    Beach Hotel 39
Heirloom Tomato and Burrata Salad 40
Mediterranean Pasta Salad with Fennel,
    Basil, and Fresh Mozzarella 41
The Oak Room, Copper Beech Inn 42
Baby Kale "Caesar" with Fried Capers, Anchovies,
    and Herbed Crostini 42
Lobster, Tomato, and Burrata Salad 44
White Gate Farm 45
Moroccan Chickpea and Carrot Salad 46
Holcomb Farm 47

Beet and Carrot Slaw with Raspberry
    Vinaigrette 48
Bread Salad 49
Holbrook Farm 50
Smoked Chicken, Apple, and Walnut Salad 51
Union League Cafe 52
Salad of Mixed Baby Greens and Beltane
    Farm Goat Cheese 53
Plum Luv Foods 54
Late Summer CT Heirloom Tomato Salad 54
West Street Grill 55
Mixed Greens with a Sherry Shallot
    Vinaigrette 56
South End 57
Farmers' Salad 58
Napa & Co. 60
Saunder's Farm Arugula Salad with Orange
    Vinaigrette and Harvest Moon Cheese 60
Roìa 62
Crispy Poached Egg Salad 63
Massaro Community Farm 64
Vegan Cream of Carrot Soup 64
Carole Peck's Good News Café 66
Chilled Green Gazpacho 67
Zinc 68
Chilled Pea and Leek Soup with Salmon
    Gravlax and Pickled Shallots 69
Claire's Corner Copia 71
Fresh Corn Soup 72
G-Zen Restaurant 73
Squash Almond Bisque 74
Golden Lamb Buttery 75
Country Cottage Soup 76
River Tavern 77

Vegetables

Roasted Root Vegetable and Artisan
    Handcrafted Sausage Stuffing 80
Métro Bis 82
Curried Brussels Sprouts with Bacon
    and Honey 83

LEFT: *Sub Edge Farm*

Gilbertie's Herb Gardens and Petite Edibles 84
Brussels Sprouts and Petite Edibles 85
Tarry Lodge Enoteca Pizzeria 86
Rosa Bianca Eggplant alla Caponata 87
Jacques Pépin 88
Peas à la Française 89
Wakeman Town Farm 90
Chipotle Veggie Chili 91
Terrain Westport Garden Café 92
Salt-Roasted Beets with Blood Oranges,
    Pistachios, and Goat Cheese Salad 93
Cafémantic 94
Curried Roasted Opo Squash 94
Caseus Fromagerie Bistro 96
Roasted Potatoes with Raclette Cheese 97
Farming 101 98
Green Tomato Fritters 99
Waldingfield Farm 100
Grilled Swiss Chard Roll-ups 101
Fried Green Tomatoes with Hot and
    Sweet Aioli 101
Fat Cat Pie Co. 103
Roasted Potato and Heirloom Tomato
    Tower 104
Sub Edge Farm 105
Old South Collard Greens with Pot Likker
    (a.k.a. "Mess o' Greens") 106
Riverbank Farm 108
Garlic-Cilantro Slaw 109
Sautéed Delicata Squash with Kale,
    Raspberry Balsamic Vinegar, and Toasted
    Walnuts 109
Schoolhouse at Cannondale 110
Fennel-Parmesan Fritters with Greens in
    Buttermilk-Bacon Dressing 111
Barcelona Wine Bar & Restaurant 113
Roasted Carrots al Andaluz 114
Beltane Farm 116
Swiss Chard and Fresh Ricotta Cheese 117
Paci 118
Grilled Violetta di Firenze Topped with Heirloom
    Tomatoes, Fresh Burrata, and Basil 119

Millwright's Restaurant 120
Carrot Terrine and Quinoa Garnished with
    Soubise and Carrot Top–Cashew Pesto 122
Millstone Farm 124
Roasted Jerusalem Artichokes, Brussels
    Sprouts, and Carrots 125
Baked Shiitake Caps 125

Sandwiches, Flatbread, Savory Pies, and Crostini

The Farmer's Cow 127
Spinach and Feta Frittata 127
Skinny Pines, LLC 128
Artisan Italian Sausage, Onion, and Kale
    Frittata 128
Sixpence Pie Company 131
Cottage Pie 132
Cinnamon Chicken with a Mashed Potato
    Crust Topped with Tomme Cheese
    (Shepherd's Pie Style) 133
Dish Bar & Grill 134
Heirloom Tomato Pie 134
Chamard Vineyards Farm Winery
    Bistro 136
Flatbread with Roasted Fig-Olive Tapenade,
    Goat Cheese Ricotta, "Prosciutto-Style"
    Duck Breast, and Arugula 137
Sport Hill Farm, LLC 139
Kugelis 140
Marinated Grilled Tofu Medallions 141
Butter-Poached Lobster Sandwich 142
Grants Restaurant and Bar, Restaurant Bricco,
    and Bricco Trattoria 144
Homemade Whipped Ricotta Crostini with
    Local Honey and Sage 145

Pasta, Grains, and Beans

Parallel Post 147
Homemade Tagliatelle Pasta with
    Norm Bloom & Son CT Lobster 148
G. W. Tavern 150
Pasta with Beef and Veal Bolognese 151

Spicy Rabbit Ragù with Pappardelle Pasta 152
Darling Farm 153
Autumn Pasta Sauce of Cauliflower
    and Apples 154
Macaroni and Cheese 155
Caseus Mac' N Cheese 156
Ricotta Gnocchi 158
Truelove Farms 160
Millet and Lacinato Kale with Dried Sour
    Cherries, Pistachios, and Chèvre 161
Winivan Relais & Châteaux 162
Lentils with Chorizo and Bacon 163
Sugar & Olives 164
Quinoa Paella 165
Community Farm of Simsbury 167
Seasonal Quinoa Salad 168

Poultry

Ekonk Hill Turkey Farm, LLC 171
Slow Cooker Turkey Chili 172
Billings Forge Community Works & Firebox
    Restaurant 173
Cast-Iron Duck Breast 174
The Max Restaurant Group 176
MarWin Farm's Duck with Corn Bread Stuffing
    and Strawberry Sauce 178
The Mill at 2T 181
Duck and Foie Gras Poutine 182
Bistro Seven Restaurant 184
Organic Duck Breast with Ginger-Carrot
    Puree and Ginger-Orange Sauce 184
Muse by Jonathan Cartwright 186
Pan-Roasted New England Pheasant Breast
    with Shallot-Cranberry Puree, Braised
    Red Cabbage, and Madeira Sauce 187
Buttermilk Fried Chicken 189
CT Valley Farms, LLC 191
Chicken Ginger Stir-fry 192
Mountaintop Mushrooms 193
Chicken and Blue Oyster Mushrooms
    with Sherry Cream Sauce 193
The Spread 195

Barcelona Wine Bar and Restaurant

Chicken Under a Brick 196
Oven-Roasted Chicken with Stuffing-Style
    Frittata, Pickled Green Beans, and Poached
    Cranberries 197
Infinity Music Hall & Bistro 199
Quail with Yam Puree and Microgreens 199

Fish and Seafood

Coriander Café & Country Store 202
Atlantic Cod with Wild Rice and Corn Griddle
    Cakes and Garlicky Kale 202
Match Restaurant 205
Bacon-Jalapeño Oysters 206
LeFarm and the Whelk 208
Deviled Eggs with Cornmeal Fried Oysters
    and Pickled Red Onion 210

Bailey's Backyard

Connecticut River Shad 222
Calamari with Eggplant Chutney 224
Swordfish Pizzaioli 225
La Belle Aurore 226
Stonington Royal Red Shrimp over
    Root Vegetable Cakes 226
Walrus + Carpenter 229
Stonington Royal Red Shrimp and
    Heirloom Grits with Smoked Tasso Pork 230
Spicy Littleneck Clams 232

Meat

Local Lamb Burgers with Wasabi Aioli 234
Polpette alla Napoletana (Meatballs) 235
Community Table 236
Swedish Meatballs G. Swenson Style
    (G. Swenson's Köttbullar) 237
Grass-Fed Beef and Root Vegetable
    Meat Loaf 238
Four Mile River Farm 239
Four Mile River Farm Burgers 240
Skirt Steak over Roasted Butternut Squash,
    Rainbow Swiss Chard, Topped with
    Caramelized Onions 240
Saugatuck Craft Butchery (The Kitchen) 242
Dry-Aged Steak Tartare Crostini with Pickled
    Garden Turnips 243
Slow-Roasted Porchetta with Cilantro
    and Smoked Paprika 244
Ox Hollow Farm 245
Oxen Driver's Short Ribs 246
Bailey's Backyard 247
Balsamic-Glazed Short Ribs with Gilfeather Turnip
    Puree and Rainbow Carrots with Orange-
    Blossom Honey and Fresh Sage 248
Nutmegger's Lamb Chops 250
Sepe Farm Lamb Meat Loaf with Goat Cheese 250
Truck 252
Green Chile Stew 253
Grilled Berkshire Pork Chops Topped with Braised
    Pork Belly and Baked Asian Pear Stuffed with
    Blue Cheese 254
Pork-Belly–Stuffed Tomatoes 257

Seared Scallops with Corn and Purslane 212
Mystic River Oysters with Grace Cocktail
    Mignonette 213
Grilled Tuna with White Bean and
    Arugula Salad 214
Mama's Boy Southern Table & Refuge 215
Low Country Bouillabaisse 216
Estia's American 218
Cioppino Verde 219
Figs Wood Fired Bistro 221
Maple-Glazed Salmon 221

Bar Sugo 258
Antipasto Platter 259
Oyster Club and Engine Room 260
Pork Ciccioli Terrine Served on Rustic Bread
    Topped with Soft-Boiled Duck Eggs and Mustard
    Pickled Ramps 260
3B Ranch 262
Farmer's Pork Special 262

Pesto, Condiments, and Sauces

Urban Oaks Organic Farm 264
Arugula and Sunflower Seed Pesto over Sliced
    Heirloom Tomatoes 265
Fort Hill Farm 266
Garlic Scape and Basil Pesto 266
Averill Farm 267
Quince Paste (Membrillo) 267
Green Tomato Salsa Verde 268
Cato Corner Farm 269
Fondue with Farmstead Cheeses 269
Chef Scott Quis's Kimchee 270
Northfordy Farm 271
Fresh Pickled Ginger 271

Drinks

Hidden Vegetable Smoothie 273
Green Pear Smoothie 273
The Stand Juice Company 274
Summer Garden Mojito Smoothie 274
Sweet Curry Juice 274
The Willows 275
Garden Fresh Bloody Mary 276
Infused Vodka 276
Miya's Sushi 278
Knot Your Mother's Lemonade 279

Desserts

Wave Hill Breads Bakery 281
Maple Bread Pudding 282
Honey Black Walnut Tart 284
Blueberry Tea Cake with Crumble Topping 285
Blueberry Sour Cream Coffee Cake 286

Strawberry Shortcake 287
Fresh Peach Tart 287
Bloodroot Restaurant 289
Macerated Summer Fruit Tart 290
The SoNo Baking Company & Café 292
Caramel-Apple Tart 293
Strawberry Frangipane Tartlets 295
Pâte Sucrée 296
Simon Pearce Restaurant 296
Individual Pumpkin Cheesecakes with a
    Gingersnap Cookie Crust and Citrus-Cranberry
    Compote 297
Maple Pecan Bourbon Pie 300
Dirt Road Farm 301
Maple-Cardamom Pots de Crème with Crème
    Fraîche and Fleur de Sel 301
Baked Bishop's Orchard Gala Apples with Whipped
    Caramel Cream and Apple Cider Sauce 302
Ashlawn Farm Coffee and Lyme Farmers'
    Market 304
Cold Brew Infused Irish Coffee Cupcakes
    with Bittersweet Whiskey Ganache 305
Fort Hill Farms 306
The Quintessential Lavender Cookies 307
Zest Fresh Pastry 308
Chocolate-Orange Five-Spice Bundt Cake 308
Lemon-Lavender Coconut Macaroons 309

Connecticut Farm Table Cookbook Directory 310

Photography Credits 315

Index 316

People and Places 324

BREAKFAST

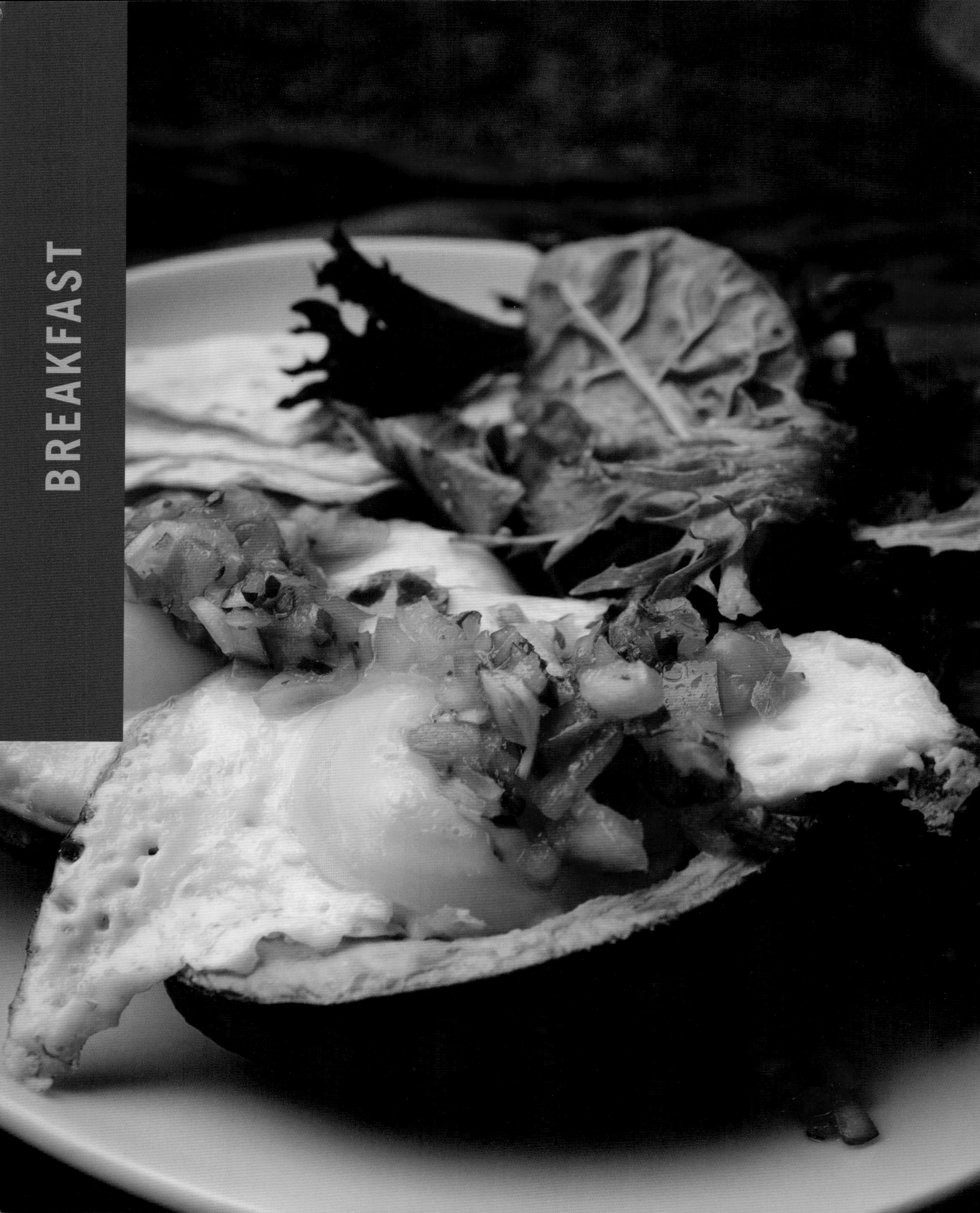

MARCH FARM

March Farm is a fourth-generation family farm set on 150 acres in northwest Connecticut. In addition to operating the area's most popular pick-your-own (PYO) fruit and berry operation, the March family has created a thriving agritourism destination. Ben March says, "We understand the importance of keeping people connected with where their food comes from and strive to create a hands-on farm experience for all ages. We offer many PYO crops (strawberries, blueberries, cherries, peaches, apples, and pumpkins), seasonal activities, such as corn mazes and hayrides, as well as a free playscape and animal yard."

The year-round parade of visitors comes for more than apples, fruit pies, and cider donuts. They travel to Bethlehem to experience the tranquil beauty of the Litchfield County farm and to interact with the March family, which has worked this land for more than 100 years.

Purchased in 1915 by Thomas and Rose Marchukaitis, the farm originally consisted of 114 acres with 15 cows and two horses. In 1937, Thomas and Rose's son, Matthew, and his wife, Anastasia, bought the farm; they operated it for many years. In 1976, the farm was purchased by Matt and Anastasia's son, Tom, and his wife, Sue, who continue to run it with the help of their son, Ben, and Sue's brother and nephew.

During the 1940s, the family added 50 cows and about 600 chickens. In the 1950s, they purchased 14 acres of adjoining land and planted apples, which would become a star attraction. Over the next three decades, the farm grew to 100 dairy cattle, 40 acres of fruit trees, 5 acres of blueberries, and many acres of sweet corn, cabbage, potatoes, squash, pumpkins, other vegetables, and hay.

The March family also helped launch the Litchfield Hills Farm-Fresh Market held on Saturday mornings. Recently, the farm was celebrated in *March Farm: Season by Season on a Connecticut Family Farm*, a pictorial homage authored by Bethlehem resident Nancy McMillan.

Sugary Apple Muffins

MAKES 12 MUFFINS

These muffins are light and airy with a nice crunchiness from the sugary topping that is not overly sweet or cloying.

Muffins

2 1/4 cups all-purpose flour

3 1/2 teaspoons baking powder

1/2 teaspoon ground cinnamon

1/2 teaspoon ground nutmeg

1/2 teaspoon kosher salt

1/4 cup vegetable shortening

1/2 cup granulated sugar

1 large egg, lightly beaten

1 teaspoon pure vanilla extract

1 cup milk

2 cups peeled, cored, and chopped apples
    (about 2 large apples)

Topping

2 tablespoons granulated sugar

1/4 teaspoon ground cinnamon

1/8 teaspoon grated nutmeg

1. Preheat the oven to 425°F. Spray a 12-cup muffin tin with nonstick cooking spray or line with paper liners. Set aside.

2. To make the muffins: In a medium-size bowl, sift together the flour, baking powder, cinnamon, nutmeg, and salt.

3. Using an electric mixer on medium speed, cream together the shortening and sugar. Add the egg and vanilla and beat until well combined. While the mixer is running, alternately add the flour mixture and milk to the egg mixture and mix until smooth. Fold in the apples. Spoon or scoop about 1/3 cup of batter for each muffin into prepared muffin cups.

4. To make the topping: In a small bowl, combine the sugar, cinnamon, and nutmeg.

5. Sprinkle each filled cup with 1/2 teaspoon of the sugar mixture. Bake the muffins until a toothpick inserted into the center of a muffin comes out clean, about 25 minutes. Let the muffins cool in the pan for 15 minutes, then invert onto a cooling rack to cool completely.

Anastasia March of March Farm

PICK-YOUR-OWN-FARMS

There's something nostalgic about visiting Connecticut's pick-your-own farms in the heat of the summer, when fields of berries and orchards laden with peaches are ripening in the sun. Or how about the time-honored fall leaf-peeping expedition to an orchard, where you'll pick (and eat) your way through so many fat Jonagold, Macoun, and Honeycrisp apples that your stomach aches.

Winter through fall, Connecticut offers a true New England pick-your-own-farm experience—whether it's fruit or pumpkins or Christmas trees. Many local PYO farms go out of their way to provide a fun family experience, with such attractions as corn mazes, hayrides, and petting zoos. In the farm markets, watch cider being made on the premises, stock up on home-baked fruit pies and hot cider donuts, plus local maple syrup, honey, jams, candies, and specialty items, as well as just-picked flowers and vegetables.

ROSE'S BERRY FARM, LLC

A 20-acre fruit farm established in 1908, Rose's Berry Farm is now a 100-acre family destination farm, as well as a vendor at 14 weekly farmers' markets statewide. Rose's also sells its fruit through wholesale partners, such as Freshpoint, Whole Foods Markets, Highland Park Markets, and Big Y, and supplies berry and vinegar products to local chefs.

Through the hard work and guidance of the late Henry Rose (third generation) and the marketing savvy of his wife, Sandi, the farm promotes "Keeping Connecticut Green and Growing" year-round with a variety of locally grown products. These include strawberries, blueberries, raspberries, blackberries, currants, pears, apples, pumpkins, and Christmas trees, grown in the Tuscan-like countryside of South Glastonbury. It is the largest blueberry farm in Southern New England, and was one of the first PYO farms, starting in the late 1960s.

At its farm stand in Glastonbury, Rose's sells the majority of its vegetables (20 acres) and some strawberries. Locals anxiously await the stand's opening every May on one of the town's main thoroughfares.

The Rose "family" extends beyond Sandi to farm manager Michael Draghi; summer student help; Debbie Cofiell and her "Jam Ladies"; the breakfast wait staff; and dedicated seasonal farmhands, who leave their families behind in season for a chance to make a better living.

On Sundays in season, fans flock to the farm's Breakfast with a View (typically June–October) for pancakes, waffles, or French toast with fresh berry toppings, served atop the elevated deck with sweeping vistas of the fields.

Rose's Berry Farm has been a vendor at farmers' markets for over 10 years and is a "cornerstone" farm at such markets as City-Seed in New Haven since 2004. The farm follows GAP (Good Agricultural Practices) and IPM (integrated pest management) measures. Rose's also works closely with the USDA and UConn agriculture researchers to keep up with the latest developments in sustainable crop production.

Blueberry Muffins

MAKES 18 MUFFINS

These blueberry muffins are a classic. Plump, fresh-picked blueberries make all the difference.

2 1/4 cups all-purpose flour

2 1/2 teaspoons baking powder

1/2 teaspoon kosher salt

1/2 cup (1 stick, 4 ounces) unsalted butter, at room temperature

1 1/4 cups granulated sugar, or to taste

2 large eggs

1 cup milk

1 1/2 teaspoons freshly grated lemon zest

2 1/2 cups fresh or frozen blueberries, picked over, divided

1 1/2 tablespoons turbinado sugar, or to taste

1. Preheat the oven to 375°F. Spray one 6-cup and one 12-cup muffin tin generously with non-stick cooking spray or line with paper liners. Set aside.

2. In a medium-size bowl, sift together the flour, baking powder, and salt.

3. Using an electric mixer on medium speed, cream together the butter and granulated sugar. Add the eggs, one at a time, and beat until well combined. While the mixer is running, alternately add the flour mixture and milk to the egg mixture and mix just until smooth. Do not overmix. Fold in the lemon zest and 2 cups of the blueberries. Fill the prepared muffin cups three-quarters full with batter. Sprinkle the remaining 1/2 cup of blueberries over the top of the batter, pressing the berries gently down. Sprinkle the turbinado sugar evenly over the top.

4. Bake the muffins, rotating the pans halfway through the baking time, until the tops are golden brown and a toothpick inserted into the center of a muffin comes out clean, about 25 minutes. If not using paper liners, let the muffins cool in the pan for 15 minutes before unmolding. Transfer the muffins to a cooling rack and allow to cool completely. Serve.

Rose's Berry Farm, LLC

BLACKBERRY RIVER BAKING CO.

Blackberry River Baking Co. is a charming little breakfast and lunch restaurant with a full bakery tucked inside. The young owners, Sam and Audrey Leary, made their way from hipster Brooklyn, New York, to sleepy Canaan to create an inviting gathering spot with a cool and homey point of view.

Audrey, who trained at the French Culinary Institute in Manhattan and honed her skills at Baked in Red Hook and the Annex in Fort Greene, Brooklyn, decided that all Blackberry River's breads would be made from scratch, and all of its pastries, from French macarons to hot cinnamon-sugar donuts to traditional éclairs, with real butter from local farms. Its fresh restaurant fare, created by chef Johannes DeVries, follows a similar philosophy. It is made with simple, good, high-quality local ingredients, and from scratch as much as possible. We love the curried carrot and butternut squash soup and the quinoa salad with cubed chicken, feta, tomatoes, peanuts and arugula.

In this charming roadside bakery/café, breakfast is served all day—pancakes loaded with fresh berries, vanilla cream, and granola; eggs any way you like 'em; and all sorts of Benedicts on the weekends. Everything here is made with love: The sandwiches are served on Blackberry River's own delicious breads, the café slices its meats and cheeses to order and makes its own dressings, and the menu features changing house-made soups (made in small batches) and blackboard specials daily.

Blackberry River Scones

MAKES 8 SCONES

"This is probably the most popular breakfast pastry I make, and it receives the most unlikely raves—people don't expect much from a scone, but these are moist and really pack a punch with the berries; they aren't overly sweet, but the vanilla sugar gives a nice crunch to the top. I hope you enjoy them as much as our regulars do!" —Audrey Leary

2 cups all-purpose flour
3 tablespoons granulated sugar
1 tablespoon baking powder
1/4 teaspoon kosher salt
5 tablespoons unsalted butter, chilled, cut into pieces
1 cup fresh blackberries
1 cup plus 2 tablespoons heavy cream, divided
Vanilla sugar, for sprinkling

1. Preheat the oven to 350°F. Lightly grease a baking sheet with butter and cooking spray. Set aside.

2. Process the flour, sugar, baking powder, and salt in a food processor until combined. Add the butter and pulse until pea-size pieces form, then transfer to a medium-size bowl.

3. Fold the blackberries into the dough. Add 1 cup of the cream and mix gently until the dough comes together and forms a ball.

4. On a lightly floured surface, flatten the dough into an 8-inch circle about 1 1/2 inches thick. Using a floured knife, cut into eight triangles. Place the scones on the prepared baking sheet.

5. Brush the tops of the scones with the remaining 2 tablespoons of cream, then top with the vanilla sugar. Bake until golden brown, 20 to 25 minutes. Transfer the scones to a cooling rack and let cool a bit before serving.

Blackberry River Baking Co.

Red Flannel Hash

SERVES 4

"This is a spin-off of an old classic. I love goat cheese and add it to everything I can! I love this with runny eggs and sourdough toast to sop up the yolks." —Audrey Leary

Top each serving with a poached egg and a side of toast, if desired.

3 large potatoes, such as Yukon Gold, peeled and cut into 1/2-inch cubes (about 2 pounds potatoes)

3 large beets, greens removed, peeled and cut into 1/2-inch cubes (about 2 pounds beets)

1 tablespoon chopped fresh rosemary, plus more for sprinkling (optional)

2 tablespoons extra-virgin olive oil

Kosher salt and freshly ground black pepper

2 tablespoons unsalted butter

1 small onion, diced

1 teaspoon minced garlic

2/3 cup fresh goat cheese, crumbled, plus more for sprinkling (optional)

1. Preheat the oven to 400°F. Lightly oil a baking sheet.

2. Place the potatoes, beets, and rosemary in a large bowl. Drizzle the oil over the vegetables and toss to combine, making sure to coat all the vegetables well.

3. Spread the vegetable mixture onto the pre-pared baking sheet. Season with salt and pepper to taste. Roast, stirring every 15 minutes, until the vegetables are fork-tender and golden brown, 40 minutes. Set aside.

4. Melt the butter in a medium-size sauté pan over medium heat. Add the onion and cook, stirring occasionally, until golden brown, about

8 minutes. Add the garlic and sauté for 1 minute. Add the potatoes and beets and cook, stirring occasionally, until heated through, about 1 min-ute. Stir in the goat cheese and cook until the cheese has melted. Season with salt and pepper to taste. Garnish with additional rosemary and goat cheese, if desired.

Blackberry River Baking Co.

FREUND'S FARM MARKET & BAKERY, LLC

The backdrop to Freund's Farm in East Canaan is picturesque Canaan Mountain dotted with a herd of 300 Holstein milking cows. Brothers Matthew and Ben Freund run the dairy farm, while Matt's wife, Theresa, is doyenne of the classic country farm market, which overflows with home-grown tomatoes, corn, peas, beans, and squash, as well as a selection of freshly made pies, breads, pastries, jams, cheeses, smoked meats, maple syrup, and honey.

Theresa reflects, "This is where I started 35 years ago as a college kid milking cows and doing chores to help pay for college. A sweet corn stand was part of the summer landscape since the 1960s. This is really how I got into retail sales. If I could sell sweet corn, I knew that I could sell anything that I grew in the family garden. We have expanded through the years to include greenhouse production of tomatoes, high-tunnel production of early crops, as well as growing vegetable seedlings for home gardeners. We grow a wide variety of crops on 10 to 12 acres."

Sweet corn is still a major crop, as are tomatoes. Theresa recalls, "At first, customers were skeptical that a greenhouse-produced tomato could be so good. I now have well-trained customers who come to expect tomatoes that are vine-ripe to perfection by the beginning of June." Because the farm had tomatoes so early, the Freunds started planting earlier crops of lettuce, summer squash, green beans, and cucumbers in the high tunnel, extending their growing season.

They also grow an assortment of lesser-known crops, such as kohlrabi, along with the typical summer crops of eggplants, peppers and herbs. They finish out the season with a great variety of winter squashes and pumpkins.

The farm maintains permanent plantings of treats such as rhubarb, raspberries, asparagus, and red currants. Theresa says, "We also harvest the Chinese chestnuts from the trees that we planted around our home. Our daughter, Rachel, started a laying hen project, 'Rachel's Radiant Eggs,' which has become popular with customers. She has an assortment of laying hens that produce a beautiful mix of blue-green and brown eggs."

Regulars love the Freunds' prepared foods, including homey chicken pot pie and quiches.

Pumpkin Bread

MAKES 2 (8 X 4-INCH) LOAVES

Lovely, golden loaves!

1 pie pumpkin (about 3 pounds; see note)
3 1/2 cups all-purpose flour
2 teaspoons baking soda
1 teaspoon ground cinnamon
1/2 teaspoon ground nutmeg
3/4 teaspoon kosher salt
2 cups granulated sugar
2/3 cup vegetable shortening
1 teaspoon pure vanilla extract
4 large eggs, lightly beaten
1/2 cup dried coarsely chopped tart cherries
1/2 cup coarsely chopped pecans

1. Preheat the oven to 450°F. Lightly grease a baking sheet and set aside.

2. Cut the pumpkin in half lengthwise; scoop out the seeds and strings and discard them. Place the pumpkin, cut side down, on the prepared baking sheet. Roast until fork-tender, about 40 minutes. Set aside to cool. When the pumpkin is cool enough to handle, scoop out the flesh, transfer to a food processor, and process until smooth.

3. Preheat the oven to 350°F. Spray two 8 x 4-inch loaf pans with nonstick cooking spray and dust lightly with flour. Set aside.

4. In a large bowl, sift together the flour, baking soda, cinnamon, nutmeg, and salt.

5. Using an electric mixer on medium speed, mix together the sugar, shortening, vanilla, eggs, and 2 cups of the pumpkin puree, scraping down the sides of the bowl as needed. Add the flour mixture and beat until smooth. Fold in the cherries and pecans. Pour into the prepared pans and bake until a toothpick inserted into the center of the bread comes out clean, about 1 hour.

6. Let the bread cool in the pans for about 15 minutes, then turn out the loaves onto a cooling rack. Let cool completely before serving.

Notes:
You can store the remaining pumpkin puree in an airtight container in the refrigerator for up to 5 days or in the freezer for several months.

You can substitute 2 cups of organic canned pure pumpkin puree (just be sure not to use pie filling, which is spiced and sweetened).

Freund's Farm Market & Bakery, LLC

FARM TO HEARTH

Melissa Marchant and Todd Solek at Farm to Hearth, in Haddam, have a particular philosophy about crafting bread. Todd says, "We bake out of a retained-heat, custom-designed, wood-fired masonry oven. Our breads are leavened by a natural wild yeast culture using regionally sourced, organically grown grains and stone-milled flours. We utilize long, slow fermentation to unlock the fullest flavor and maximum nutrition from the grain."

Melissa and Todd make all of their breads by hand with a sense of passion, and often, their two small children, Lilah, four, and Liam, two, like to get into the act. Todd says, "We believe this gives our bread 'soul.' Our focus is bringing real bread to our community, and bringing a warming sense of comfort to those who enjoy our breads."

The breads change all the time, but some of our favorites include the Country, a naturally leavened rustic table bread that uses a blend of organic wheat and stone-milled whole-grain wheat, as well as the Struan, a hearty bread that combines toasted sunflower seeds, flax, sesame seeds, cracked oats, cracked corn grits, sprouted amaranth, red quinoa, and millet.

Farm to Hearth breads can be found at numerous dining establishments, retail establishments, and farmers' markets in Connecticut.

Baked French Toast

SERVES 4

Custard

4 large eggs, lightly beaten

1 1/2 cups raw milk or organic whole milk

3 tablespoons granulated sugar

1 teaspoon ground cinnamon

1/4 teaspoon ground nutmeg

1 teaspoon pure vanilla extract

1/4 teaspoon kosher salt

Toast

8 (1-inch-thick) slices day-old country bread

1/4 cup (1/2 stick, 2 ounces) unsalted butter, plus more for serving (optional)

Pure Connecticut maple syrup

Confectioners' sugar (optional)

1 cup fresh berries (optional)

1. Lightly grease a 15 x 10-inch baking dish. In a large bowl, whisk together the eggs, milk, granulated sugar, cinnamon, nutmeg, vanilla, and salt.

2. Place the bread slices in a single layer in the prepared baking dish. Pour the custard mixture evenly over the bread, and gently press on the bread, allowing it to absorb some of the liquid. Cover with plastic wrap and refrigerate for 30 minutes. Using a slotted spatula, turn the slices over, allowing the bread to soak in the liquid. Refrigerate for another 30 minutes.

3. Preheat the oven to 350°F. Lightly grease a baking sheet and set aside.

4. Melt 2 tablespoons of the butter in a large cast-iron skillet over medium heat. Shake off the excess liquid and, working in batches, add the bread slices in a single layer. Cook until golden brown on both sides, about 3 minutes per side. Repeat this step with the remaining 2 tablespoons of butter and bread slices.

5. Transfer the fresh toast to the prepared baking dish and bake for 15 minutes, or until the desired texture is reached. Serve with butter, maple syrup, confectioners' sugar, and blueberries, if desired.

Note: For a firmer, crisper texture, cook the French toast a bit longer.

Farm to Hearth

ARETHUSA AL TAVOLO

Next time you're planning a day trip, consider a visit to Arethusa Farm and Dairy in historic Litchfield, capped off by dinner at Arethusa al Tavolo, a casual yet urbane Bantam eatery celebrating local agriculture, using only the best and freshest of the season.

Arethusa is a flourishing, 325-acre farm, with 350 head of cattle and 150 hens of various breeds, saved from the wrecking ball in 1999 by an unlikely duo—Tony Yurgaitis and George Malkemus—the fashion force behind the Manolo Blahnik brand, the hand-crafted, Italian stilettos famously coveted by *Sex and the City*'s Carrie Bradshaw.

We were lucky enough to get the grand tour from Tony and George themselves. Traversing bumpy dirt roads and rolling pastures in their silver pickup, we were struck by their genuine passion, as they pointed out heifer and calf barns, explained how each cow is named for her lineage, and stopped to chew the fat with farmhands.

For the well-heeled leaders of one of fashion's most iconic brands, they are refreshingly hands-on and down-to-earth (apparently comfortable with mud on their shoes). It's clear that they relish their roles in reviving the dairy culture in the sleepy hamlets of Bantam and Litchfield.

In 2013, inspired by their trips to Puglia, home to what Tony calls "the original farm-to-table," the pair set out to create their own farm-to-table bistro/wine bar called al Tavolo ("to the table"), with indoor and alfresco seating. They hit the jackpot with talented young executive chef Dan Magill, who trained under Daniel Boulud and is known for his culinary artistry. *Connecticut Magazine* gave the restaurant three and a half out of four stars straight out of the gate and the *New York Times* rated it Very Good.

Eggs "Manolo Blahnik Style"

SERVES 12

These decadent brunch treats or hors d'oeuvres are just right when you have guests to impress.

"At Arethusa al Tavolo, we have the access to all the great products that Arethusa Farm Dairy produces. Located right next door to the restaurant, the dairy produces great milk, cream, cheese, and ice cream with milk from Arethusa Farm. I created this dish using the products from our farm, including milk and cream. The eggs are from our laying hens. Adding truffles, lobster, and osetra caviar takes the dish to another level . . . like, say, the Manolo Blahnik level!"
—Executive Chef Dan Magill

Custard (makes 3 cups)

12 large eggs
1 cup milk
1 cup heavy cream
1 tablespoon granulated sugar
1 1/2 teaspoons truffle oil
1 tablespoon chopped black truffles
1/2 cup lobster meat, cut into 1/4-inch pieces
Kosher salt and finely ground white pepper

Grey Goose Cream (makes 2 cups)

1 cup heavy cream, chilled
2 1/2 teaspoons vodka, such as Grey Goose, chilled
1 tablespoon minced fresh chives
1 ounce osetra caviar, or to taste

1. To prepare the eggshells (see note): Tap the top of each egg gently on the counter. Using an egg-top cutter or serrated knife, carefully cut off the tops of each egg. Transfer four whole eggs (whites and yolks) and four egg yolks to a bowl,

reserving the remaining whites and yolks for another use.

2. Run cold water into the inside of the 12 empty eggshells, then hold an eggshell in one hand and gently work a finger around the inside of the shell to peel out and discard the membrane. Set the eggshells aside in the bottom half of an empty paper egg carton (reserve the other half of the carton).

3. To make the custard: Using a blender on medium speed, blend the four eggs, four egg yolks, milk, cream, sugar, and truffle oil until the yolks are pale yellow. Add the truffles and pulse for 30 seconds. Cover tightly with plastic wrap, and refrigerate for 1 hour.

4. Preheat the oven to 375°F.

5. Using a spoon, gently skim any foam from the top of the egg mixture, then carefully stir until well combined.

6. Place the egg carton with the eggshells in a small roasting pan. Evenly distribute the lobster meat among the eggshells. Fill each eggshell three-quarters of the way up with the custard. Add enough water to the roasting pan to come halfway up the sides of the eggshells. Bake, covered with foil, until the custard is set, about 40 minutes. Do not let the eggs "soufflé," or the texture will be like scrambled eggs. Carefully remove the eggs from the roasting pan and place in the clean remaining half of the egg carton.

To make the cream: While the custards are baking, whip the cream until stiff peaks form. While whipping, add the vodka. Fold the chives into the cream. Transfer the cream to a pastry bag fitted with a small star tip.

To assemble: Place the filled eggshells in egg cups. Top the custard with the whipped cream and a dollop of caviar. Serve at once.

Notes:

In a pinch, you can substitute twelve 6-ounce greased ramekins for the 12 eggshells.

The eggs can be served hot or cold, depending on your preference; at the restaurant they are served cold, which requires the custards to be refrigerated for at least 1 hour. Top with the cream and caviar just before serving.

At the restaurant, the eggs are served in a small porcelain bowl with wet salt underneath to help keep the eggs upright.

Arethusa al Tavolo

SOUPS AND SALADS

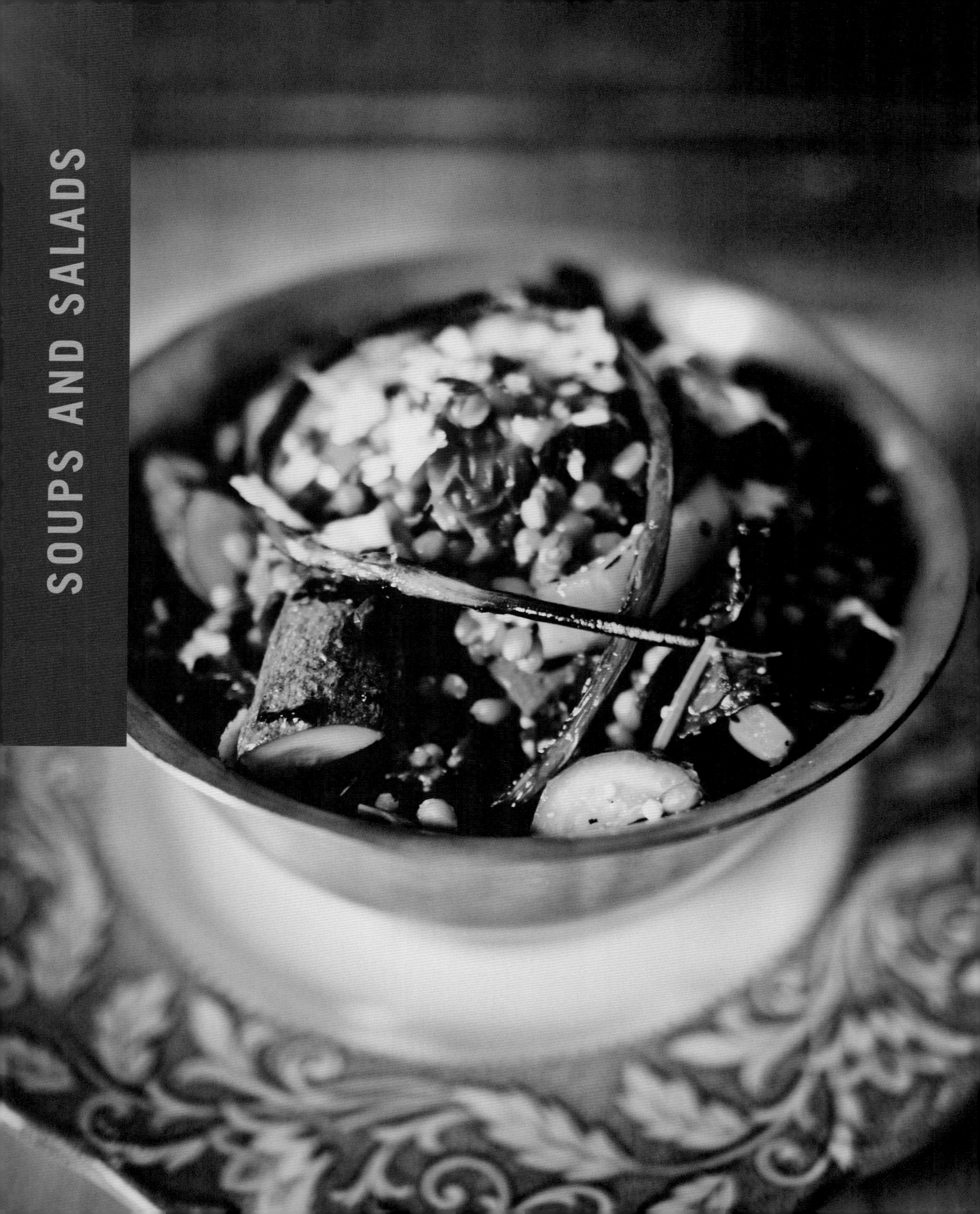

BARBERRY HILL FARM

Barberry Hill Farm is a family farm established in 1909 in the hills of Madison. Perched along a winding knoll, the verdant farm, now owned by Kelly and Kingsley Goddard, is the scenic backdrop for weddings and plein air painters, and serves as one of the host sites for the past nine years of Dinners at the Farm, New England's original farm dinner benefit series (see sidebar, page 78).

Barberry Hill grows vibrant cut flowers (including the long-lasting Sunbright Supreme), as well as fruits and vegetables, specializing in varieties of heirloom tomatoes and hard-to-find, or old-school, vegetables, such as Blue Hubbard squash. The Goddards also raise sheep, chickens and ducks on the property, and practice sustainable growing techniques using leaf mulch. They do not use pesticides, herbicides or fungicides. They host a CSA, a self-serve farm stand and participate in farmers' markets across the state.

Pistou Soup

SERVES 8 TO 10

"Pistou Soup (a vegetable soup from Provence with a swirl of pistou [pesto]) is one of our favorites on the farm. As with so many dishes, the fresher the vegetables the better. This is a great way to use what is in your CSA box or whatever greens and veggies look best at the farmers' market." —Kelly Goddard, Barberry Hill Farm

Soup

2 tablespoons olive oil

1 large onion, chopped

2 large carrots, scrubbed and cut into 1/4-inch cubes

3 medium-size leeks, white part only, halved lengthwise, cleaned and julienned crosswise

1 large zucchini, cut into 1/2-inch dice

2 medium-size red potatoes, scrubbed and cut into 1/4-inch cubes

8 cups low-sodium chicken stock or water, hot, plus more as needed

3/4 cup dried pasta, such as orzo or elbows

1 cup green beans, trimmed and cut into 1/2-inch pieces

1 (15-ounce) can navy or cannellini beans, drained and rinsed

1 bunch Swiss chard, stems and center ribs removed, sliced into 1-inch pieces

2 cups chopped tomatoes with juice

Pistou

1/4 cup coarsely chopped garlic (6 to 8 large cloves)

2 cup chopped fresh basil leaves

1 cup grated Parmigiano-Reggiano cheese, plus more for serving (optional)

1/2 cup extra-virgin olive oil

Kosher salt and freshly ground black pepper

1. To make the soup: Heat the oil in a large stockpot over medium heat. Add the onion, carrots, leeks, zucchini, and potatoes and cook, stirring occasionally, until the onion and leeks are soft and translucent, about 14 minutes. Whisk in the stock and bring to a boil over medium-high heat, about 18 minutes. Lower the heat to a simmer and add the pasta, green beans, navy beans, and Swiss chard. Cook until the potatoes are fork-tender and pasta is al dente, about 8 minutes. Add the tomatoes and cook for 2 minutes.

2. To make the pistou: Puree the garlic, basil, cheese, and oil in a blender or food processor until smooth. Add half of the pistou to the stockpot with the soup; if necessary, add extra water to thin the soup to the desired consistency and continue to cook until heated through, about 1 minute. Season with salt and pepper to taste. Serve with the remaining pistou dolloped on top, if desired. Sprinkle with additional cheese, if desired, and serve.

Note: Save the extra pesto and use on bruschetta, or as a spread on sandwiches or toss with vegetables instead of butter.

Barberry Hill Farm

BLUE LEMON RESTAURANT

An unassuming little restaurant tucked into Sconset Square in Westport, Blue Lemon has been a quiet contender on the downtown scene for more than a decade. Chef-owner Bryan Malcarney, who also owns Rory's Restaurant in Darien, has a good handle on what he calls "Modern American" cuisine.

Although not a true farm-to-table restaurateur, Malcarney does a commendable job of integrating local and seasonal elements into his menus. A weekly shopper at the Westport Farmers' Market, he uses fresh herbs, fruits, vegetables, and locally sourced fish, poultry, and meats to great advantage. And in fact, many of the freshest vegetables that appear in daily specials are picked that morning from his own organic garden.

Malcarney says, "I have been known to use homegrown arugula from my garden or my mother's garden. For the arugula salad, just-picked arugula makes all the difference."

Arugula and Endive Salad with Apples, Celeriac, Caramelized Walnuts, and Cider Vinaigrette

SERVES 6 AS A MAIN DISH OR 8 TO 10 AS A SIDE

This is a colorful, elegant, and crunchy salad. The caramelized walnuts, blue cheese, and cider vinaigrette are the perfect finishing touches.

Caramelized Walnuts

6 tablespoons unsalted butter
5 tablespoons granulated sugar
12 ounces (3 cups) walnut halves
2 tablespoons fresh lemon juice
1/8 teaspoon hot sauce

Vinaigrette (makes 1 cup)

1/4 cup cider vinegar
1 teaspoon Dijon mustard
3/4 cup olive oil
Kosher salt and freshly ground black pepper

Salad

1/2 small celeriac root (about 1/3 pound), peeled and cut into matchsticks (about 1 cup)
3/4 pound (12 cups) unpacked baby arugula
2 large apples, such as Northern Spy, peeled, cored, and diced
1/4 pound (1 cup) blue cheese, crumbled, plus more for garnish (optional)
2 Belgian endives, trimmed, washed, dried, and leaves separated

1. To make the caramelized walnuts: Preheat the oven to 350°F. Lightly grease a baking sheet with nonstick cooking spray and set aside.

2. In a medium-size skillet, melt the butter and sugar over medium heat, stirring frequently, until the sugar dissolves, about 4 minutes. Add the walnuts, lemon juice, and hot sauce and toss to coat evenly. Transfer the walnut mixture to the prepared baking sheet.

3. Bake until the walnuts are a deep brown, stirring occasionally, about 15 minutes. Remove from the baking sheet and transfer to a cooling rack to cool completely, breaking the nuts apart before using.

4. To make the vinaigrette: In a small bowl, whisk together the vinegar and mustard. Whisking vigorously, add the oil in a slow, steady stream. Season with salt and pepper to taste.

5. In a large bowl, combine the celeriac, arugula, apples, blue cheese, and walnuts and add the vinaigrette to taste. Season with salt and pepper to taste.

6. To assemble: Divide the salad mixture among six to eight plates. Top with the endive leaves and sprinkle with additional blue cheese, if desired. Serve at once.

Note: The caramelized walnuts can be made several days ahead; store in an airtight container at room temperature.

Blue Lemon Restaurant

THOMPSON STREET FARM, LLC

Proving that good things come in small packages, Brenda Sullivan has turned her 1.3 acres in South Glastonbury into a thriving micro farm, Thompson Street Farm LLC, Connecticut's first SPIN (small plot intensive farming) farm. Sullivan specializes in growing small leafy greens, herbs, and vegetables in 22 raised beds and in various types of containers. She also designed and built several greenhouses for microgreens, which she sells to local restaurants as well as to caterers and farmers' markets.

Sullivan says, "I grow a lot of arugula and microgreens that are very popular with local restaurants here in Glastonbury. Early this summer, my greens got the honor to be served to rocker Dave Matthews and his crew while here in Hartford on tour. That was fun!"

One of great thing about microgreens, besides their high nutrient profile, is their variety. Thompson Street Farm sells everything from arugula to Red Russian kale, pea shoots, purple radishes, Bull's Blood beets, sunflower shoots, haricots verts, wasabi, horseradish, and broccoli to white popcorn.

In addition to her own property, Brenda leases a 0.75-acre plot where she grows such produce as tomatoes, potatoes, onions, green beans using the SPIN method. Sullivan tills and maintains Thompson's rich, fertile soil by hand to limit its carbon footprint, and signed on as Pledge Farm through CT-NOFA (Northeast Organic Farmers Association), following the guidelines for organic growers, farming without chemicals and/or pesticides.

Carrots and Sunflower Sprouts Salad with Basil Vinaigrette

SERVES 4 TO 6

With nutrient-rich microgreens becoming more readily available at farmers' markets and health food stores, it is getting easier to find ready-to-eat sunflower sprouts, which are a tasty topper for salads, sandwiches, or smoothies. Fresh, crunchy, and slightly nutty, they can also be grown indoors as a year-round source of fresh greens.

If you cannot find sunflower sprouts, you can substitute daikon radish sprouts in their place. Daikon sprouts have a similar taste but without the spiciness. Sunflower greens will also work well; just remove the little shells and rinse.

Basil Vinaigrette

1/2 teaspoon minced garlic
2 tablespoons minced fresh basil
1/4 cup extra-virgin olive oil
2 tablespoons red wine vinegar
Kosher salt and freshly ground black pepper

Carrot and Sunflower Sprout Salad

2 cups shredded carrots (3 to 4 carrots)
4 ounces sunflower sprouts (about 2 cups)
1 small head radicchio, chopped into bite-size
    pieces
1/2 cup chopped dried cranberries or cherries

1. To make the vinaigrette: In a small bowl, whisk together the garlic, basil, oil, and vinegar. Season with salt and pepper to taste. Let sit at room temperature for at least 1 hour before serving.

2. To make the salad: In a large bowl, combine the carrots, sunflower sprouts, radicchio, and cranberries. Pour half of the vinaigrette over the salad and toss to coat, adding more dressing to taste. Season with salt and pepper to taste. Serve.

Thompson Street Farm, LLC

HEIRLOOM RESTAURANT AND LOUNGE

In downtown New Haven, on a city block lined with Thai restaurants, coffee bars, and funky retail shops, you'll find a soothing, mod oasis known as the Study at Yale. Within the urbane, refurbished boutique hotel, just past the cushy lobby, lies Heirloom, an equally stylish eatery, with floor-to-ceiling glass windows, a refuge where professors, doctors, hipsters, and foodies linger over breakfast, lunch, and dinner.

Under the guidance of chef Carey Savona, Heirloom draws upon the heritage growers and artisan suppliers of Connecticut and other New England states to create what he calls "Farm + Coastal" cooking. He says, "Our kitchen showcases an ingredient- and flavor-focused cuisine that is redefining what it means to eat and dine in New Haven." Taking inspiration from the New England coast and fields, Savona pays homage to his venue's current stable of farmers and provisions on the restaurant's dining room chalkboard.

Savona earned his stripes working alongside talented chefs and restaurateurs in San Francisco, Connecticut, south Florida, and New York City, where, with Drew Nieporent and the Myriad Restaurant Group, he earned two stars from the *New York Times* for Mai House.

He says, "I grew up around food. My dad was a great cook from a family of Italian fisherman and fishmongers; he owned a bar and tavern in Connecticut. We shucked local oysters together, cooked side by side, and ate honest, heartfelt food." Using locally sourced and heirloom provisions, Savona's menu is a celebration of East Coast bounty, from local oysters, to tempura squash blooms, simple farm greens, burrata, poultry, and grass-fed beef.

While Savona draws on regional sources for the cuisine, he draws on Heirloom's relationship to campus and downtown city life to create a relaxed yet hip neighborhood gathering place, as well as a destination spot for travelers and businesspeople who come for good, seasonal food and drink and to watch the comings and goings on Chapel Street.

Starlight Farm's Kale Salad with Sour Cherry Vinaigrette

SERVES 2 TO 3 AS A MAIN DISH OR 4 AS A SIDE

Kale can be woody and tough, but here's a tip: After adding the oil and vinegar, give the kale a quick massage. That's right: Get your (clean) hands in there and knead or "massage" the kale leaves until they go from looking raw to soft and glistening—you're breaking down the cell walls in the leaves so they'll be more tender.

Note: The cherry-infused vinegar must steep for at least four days, so prepare accordingly.

Sour-Cherry Vinaigrette (makes about 1 3/4 cups)

1 cup pitted sour cherries (see note), crushed
1/2 cup granulated sugar
1/2 cup white wine vinegar
1 cup water
1/8 teaspoon kosher salt

Kale Salad

1/4 cup hazelnuts, toasted
1 bunch red kale, stemmed and cut into
    bite-size pieces
2 tablespoons hazelnut oil
1/4 cup grated ricotta salata or feta cheese,
    plus more for garnish (optional)
1/4 cup bread crumbs, toasted (see note),
    plus more for garnish (optional)
Kosher salt and freshly ground black pepper

1. To make the sour-cherry vinaigrette: Combine the cherries, sugar, vinegar, water, and salt in a medium-size saucepan and bring to a boil over medium-high heat, stirring often. Lower the heat to a simmer and cook for 1 minute. Let cool to room temperature. Pour into a 16-ounce glass jar with a tight lid and seal. Let the vinegar sit at room temperature for 5 days. Strain the vinegar through a fine-mesh strainer into a clean jar. Before discarding the cherries, press them against the strainer with the back of a spoon. Cover and refrigerate for up to 2 weeks.

2. To make the salad: Preheat the oven to 350°F. Place the hazelnuts in a single layer on a small baking sheet. Roast, stirring occasionally, until fragrant and light golden brown (the skins will begin to split), about 7 minutes. Set aside to cool. When the hazelnuts are cool enough to handle, transfer to a dry dish towel and rub the nuts together until most of the skins come off. Coarsely chop the nuts and set aside.

3. In a large bowl, combine the kale, oil, and 1/4 cup of the vinegar. Here's where you can give the leaves a quick massage. Next, add hazelnuts, cheese, bread crumbs, and more vinegar to taste. Season with salt and pepper to taste. Top with additional bread crumbs and cheese, if desired. Serve at once.

Notes:

Feel free to use sweet cherries in place of sour.

In a small, dry skillet over medium heat, toast the breadcrumbs until golden.

Heirloom/The Study at Yale

THE WHARF RESTAURANT AT MADISON BEACH HOTEL

Although the Long Island Sound is the jewel of the Connecticut coast, there are surprisingly few places along the shoreline to dine with a waterfront vista. But the Wharf, at the Madison Beach Hotel, is one such venue.

On a private stretch of pristine beach in Madison, the Wharf rolls out chef Brendan Dion's modern interpretation of regional classics, which include everything from a succulent raw bar medley to scallops with cherrywood-smoked bacon, local honey, and arugula—farm-to-table cuisine inspired by classic Atlantic Northeast fare. Expect to enjoy local littlenecks, farm-raised roasted beets with local chèvre and classic New England clam chowder, as well as fine executions of seasonal fish and tuna tartare to a simple yet satisfying burger.

With upholstered banquettes, chandeliers, and French doors with views out to the Sound, the renovated resort restaurant is almost a tad too formal a backdrop for a restaurant perched over a beach. No matter. The space is comfy, with a toasty fire warming up the space in winter and an open-air patio in warmer weather.

Chef Dion's menu incorporates fresh local estate-grown ingredients and local organic produce. He notes, "Our philosophy is to use the highest-quality ingredients with focus on proper techniques and seasoning, and keep it simple to allow the food to speak for itself."

Heirloom Tomato and Burrata Salad

SERVES 4

Summer on a plate!

1/4 cup extra-virgin olive oil plus more as needed

1 teaspoon aged balsamic vinegar, plus more as needed

2 tablespoons thinly sliced fresh basil leaves, plus 1 large whole fresh leaf (see note)

Kosher salt and freshly ground black pepper

1 1/4 pounds large, ripe heirloom tomatoes, cored and sliced into 1/2-inch-thick wedges

8 ounces fresh burrata cheese (see note)

4 slices rustic bread, such as ciabatta, cut into thick slices and grilled or toasted

1. In a small bowl, stir together the olive oil, vinegar, and 2 tablespoons of basil with a fork.

2. Place the tomato wedges in a medium-size bowl and gently toss with the vinaigrette.

3. To arrange the salad: Place the basil leaf in the center of a large plate. Top with the burrata cheese round and fan the tomatoes around the cheese. Drizzle the cheese and tomatoes with the vinaigrette. Season with salt and pepper to taste. Serve with toasted ciabatta.

Notes: Feel free to use a few of the larger leaves to make a little pad for the plating.

If you can't find burrata cheese, substitute fresh mozzarella cheese; however, it will not have the same creamy interior.

The Wharf at Madison Beach Hotel

THE BARONS OF BURRATA

Around for decades in Italy, this delicious cousin to mozzarella di bufala only gained a foothold locally the past decade, thanks, in large part, to promotion by the Food Network. Today, you'll find this "it" cheese on the menus of top restaurants.

The soft, white homemade mozzarella ball looks no different than traditional round bufala mozzarella: the surprise is inside the decadent, tangy, soft center, which contains a shredded mozzarella and cream, giving it a unique texture—"like buttah." (*Burrata* means "buttered" in Italian.)

LiuzziAngeloni Cheese in Hamden is the tristate's favorite producer of handmade burrata. The founders, Pasquale and Nick Liuzzi, came to this country in 1969 from Puglia, Italy, the home of burrata, with a dream to produce premium cheeses and fine foods reminiscent of those made by the Liuzzi family for five generations.

Lino Liuzzi and the Liuzzi family began making it for their retail location back in the 1980s. Since then, Liuzzi burrata has evolved into a consistent medal winner in the annual competition sponsored by the prestigious American Cheese Society.

It takes two teams of 10 to 15 people to make the 4,000 pounds of burrata per week that is sold at the Liuzzi Gourmet Market in North Haven, and via distributor to restaurants and customers along the Northeast corridor as well as at their gourmet specialty foods market in North Haven. That's between 10,000 and 15,000 individual burrata balls per week. "It's as popular now as bufala mozzarella was at its height," says Ralph Liuzzi.

One of the main producers of burrata in the Northeast, the Liuzzi family makes the burrata the old-fashioned way, making their own cultured cream from the milk of Vermont cows on the premises of their Hamden cheese plant. After the cream ferments and develops, it is combined with thinly pulled mozzarella strands, called stracciatella, hand shredded, pulled into tiny pieces, then stuffed into balls, tied with string, and immersed in a liquid bath to retain freshness.

Mediterranean Pasta Salad with Fennel, Basil, and Fresh Mozzarella

SERVES 4 AS A MAIN DISH OR 6 TO 8 AS A SIDE

This recipe celebrates the marriage of fresh basil and mozzarella in early summer while we await the first tomatoes of the season. The fennel adds a little twist on the traditional pasta salad.

Salad (makes 2 3/4 quarts)

1/2 pound fusilli or rotini pasta

2 tablespoons extra-virgin olive oil

1 medium-size fennel bulb, fronds removed and reserved, bulb quartered and cut into 1/4-inch dice (about 9 ounces)

1 small sweet onion, such as Ailsa Craig, Walla Walla, or Vidalia, minced

1/2 pound fresh mozzarella cheese, chopped into 1/4-inch pieces

2 cups cooked chickpeas, or 1 1/2 (15.5-ounce) cans, drained and rinsed

1 (12-ounce) jar artichoke hearts, drained and sliced into 1/4-inch wedges

Vinaigrette

1/4 cup white balsamic vinegar or other mild white vinegar

1 tablespoon fresh lemon juice

7 tablespoons extra-virgin olive oil

1/2 teaspoon kosher salt, or to taste

1/4 teaspoon freshly ground black pepper, or to taste

Garnishes

1/3 cup fresh basil, finely chopped

1/4 cup fennel fronds, finely chopped

1. To make the salad: Bring a medium-size pot of salted water to a boil. Add the pasta and cook until al dente, about 8 minutes. Drain the pasta, transfer to a large bowl, and toss with the 2 tablespoons of olive oil. Stir in the fennel, onion, cheese, chickpeas, and artichoke hearts.

2. To make the vinaigrette: Whisk together the vinegar and lemon juice. Slowly whisk in olive oil until well combined. Season with salt and pepper. Add the vinaigrette to the pasta and stir to coat. Adjust the seasonings with salt and pepper to taste. Garnish with the basil and fennel fronds, and serve.

Fort Hill Farm, New Milford

THE OAK ROOM, COPPER BEECH INN

If you're in the mood for romance, or are celebrating a special occasion, consider a getaway to the Copper Beech Inn, an intimate country hotel situated in the hamlet of Ivoryton, one of three small villages within the historic town of Essex on the Connecticut River. Locals and weekend warriors flock here for dinner in the Oak Room, a cozy barside dining spot with a roaring fire; larger parties converge on the inn's elegant main dining room; both serve the culinary creations of award-winning chef Gaspar Stantic, executed by chef de cuisine Carlos Cassar.

Chef Stantic, a Switzerland native, is the master chef and visionary, constantly searching for meaningful food experiences to bring to the table. His focus is to create simple yet flavorful meals using locally grown products from the farms that dot the countryside, as well as mushrooms foraged by local mycological gurus. He says, "Simple elements create great things."

Cassar aims for excellence, whether it is in bar snacks or four-course meals, relying on the freshest seafood, cheeses, meats, and vegetables plucked from shoreline fields and waterways. At the Oak Room, it's all about updated classes, such as prime beef tenderloin with potatoes au gratin and seasonal vegetables and Pan-Seared Day Boat Scallops with lobster sweet corn risotto. Be sure to avail yourselves of the first-rate wine cellar.

Baby Kale "Caesar" with Fried Capers, Anchovies, and Herbed Crostini

SERVES 2 AS A MAIN DISH OR 4 AS A SIDE

This recipe updates the Caesar salad of yesteryear, substituting baby kale for romaine, herbed crostini for croutons, and adding fried capers and anchovies for a salty kick.

Caesar Dressing (makes about 1 cup)

3 garlic cloves, peeled
1 large egg yolk (see note)
1 1/2 teaspoons Dijon mustard
1 teaspoon Worcestershire sauce, or to taste
1 tablespoon white wine vinegar
1/2 cup extra-virgin olive oil
1/3 cup grated Parmesan cheese, plus more for garnish
2 tablespoons fresh lemon juice, or to taste
Kosher salt and freshly ground black pepper

Herbed Crostini

4 (1/2-inch-thick) slices rustic farm bread
2 1/2 tablespoons olive oil
1 1/2 teaspoons chopped fresh thyme
Kosher salt and freshly ground black pepper

Fried Capers

1 tablespoon olive oil
1 tablespoon capers, drained, rinsed, and patted dry

Fried Anchovies

2 cups vegetable oil

3 tablespoons all-purpose flour

Freshly ground black pepper

4 fresh anchovy fillets

6 cups packed (about 5 ounces) baby kale
(see note)

1. To make the Caesar dressing: Pulse the garlic in a food processor until minced. Add the egg yolk, mustard, Worcestershire sauce, and vinegar and pulse until well combined. While the machine is running, gradually add the oil, cheese, lemon juice, and salt and pepper to taste. Serve immediately, or transfer to a container with a lid and refrigerate. (The dressing will keep for 2 days.)

2. To make the herbed crostini: Preheat the oven to 350°F. Arrange the bread slices in a single layer on a baking sheet. Drizzle the slices with olive oil and season with the thyme, and salt and pepper to taste. Bake until golden brown, about 16 minutes. Set aside.

3. To make the fried capers: Heat the oil in a small skillet over medium-high heat until hot but not smoking. Add the capers and fry, stirring often, until golden brown, about 2 minutes. Using a slotted spoon, remove the capers and drain on paper towels.

4. To make fried anchovies: Heat a 2-inch depth of oil to 350°F in a heavy-bottomed 4-quart saucepan over medium-high heat. In a small bowl, stir together the flour and pepper. Dredge each anchovy in the flour mixture. Drop the anchovies into the hot oil and fry until golden brown, turning occasionally to brown on all sides, about 1 minute. Using a slotted spoon, remove the anchovies and drain on paper towels.

5. To assemble: Place the kale in a large bowl and combine with half of the dressing. Using tongs, massage the kale until it is bright green and slightly softened, 2 minutes, adding more dressing to taste. Top with the fried capers, anchovies, and Parmesan cheese. Serve with the crostini on side.

Notes: Use only fresh, clean, properly refrigerated eggs with intact shells.

If you can't find baby kale, feel free to use curly green kale, stemmed and cut into bite-size pieces.

The Copper Beech Inn

Lobster, Tomato, and Burrata Salad

SERVES 4

This elegant appetizer is a study in simplicity. The lobster meat lends a sweetness to the dish. It is bright with citrus notes from the orange segments, as well as a mild peppery flavor from the watercress.

6 to 8 grape or cherry tomatoes

2 (4-ounce) mozzarella balls or burrata cheese, cut into quarters

6 ounces lobster meat, cut into chunks

Zest from 1 lemon

2 tablespoons chopped fresh basil leaves

Extra-virgin olive oil

Watercress, radish sprouts, or baby arugula (about 6 sprigs or sprouts per portion, or to taste), optional

1 orange, peeled, white pith removed, and segmented

1. Score each tomato by cutting an X on the underside. Set aside. Bring just enough water to cover the tomatoes to a boil in a medium-size pot. Fill a medium-size bowl halfway with ice water. Working in batches if necessary, using a slotted spoon, carefully place the tomatoes in the boiling water and blanch until the skins begin to crack, about 20 seconds. Carefully remove the tomatoes and place them in the ice water for 1 to 2 minutes. Remove the tomatoes from the water and peel off the skins. Set aside.

2. Adjust an oven rack to the top position and heat the broiler. Coat four 6-ounce soufflé cups with butter. Evenly divide the cheese quarters into the center of each cup. Evenly arrange the tomatoes and lobster meat around the cheese. Place the dishes on a baking sheet and broil until the cheese just begins to melt, about 4 minutes. Sprinkle with lemon zest and basil. Drizzle with olive oil and season with salt and pepper to taste. Top with watercress, if using, and orange segments.

The Copper Beech Inn

WHITE GATE FARM

Situated in East Lyme on 100 picturesque acres, White Gate Farm provides many reasons to visit.

The appealing on-site farm stand, open year round, features home-grown organic produce, roasting chickens, eggs, and turkeys, as well as an array of salads, pizzas, preserves, and pastries. Check the website for hours of operation and seasonal offerings.

Customers are welcome to explore the farm grounds, and especially invited to admire baby chicks and turkeys when they arrive, or to go looking for tadpoles in the pond. There's always something to see at the farm: In April, it's the large swaths of daffodils; in August, the towering sunflowers; in October, the maple trees; in January, the expanse of glittering snow. Summer season is perfect for picnics.

Other farm occasions include cooking classes, Dinners at the Farm (see page 78), and weddings. White Gate also sells produce to local retail outlets and restaurants.

The quintessential New England landscape displays its origins in rocky ledges and the deposits of glaciers. Stone walls edge and crisscross the property. The earliest were built in the 1700s to contain livestock. An ice house perches on the shore of Lake Pattagansett. First used to store blocks of ice to sell for local iceboxes, it is now a charming guest house.

In the mid-1900s White Gate was a dairy farm and grew hay for its own cows and to sell. In 1975, Ruth Lord purchased the property; in 2000, her daughter and son-in-law, Pauline Lord and David Harlow, moved from California to establish the organic farming business. The couple count themselves lucky to be stewards of White Gate Farm while building community and supporting the health of their customers and the environment.

Moroccan Chickpea and Carrot Salad

SERVES 4 TO 6

This easy-to-prepare salad with the flavors of Morocco pairs well with grilled meat and fish.

Spice Mixture

1 tablespoon ground cumin

1/2 teaspoon ground ginger

1 1/2 teaspoons ground coriander

1 teaspoon ground cinnamon

2 teaspoons Hungarian sweet paprika

2 teaspoons sea salt

Salad

2 pounds carrots, peeled and thinly sliced into half-moons (about 4 cups)

3 (15.5-ounce) cans chickpeas, drained and rinsed

Moroccan Dressing

1/4 cup extra-virgin olive oil plus more as needed

2 cups minced onion

2 small jalapeños, halved, stemmed, seeded, and minced

2 tablespoons minced garlic

3 tablespoons white or red wine vinegar

5 scallions, sliced thinly diagonally (white and green parts)

3/4 cup chopped fresh cilantro

1/2 cup chopped fresh parsley

Juice of 1 lemon

Honey (optional)

1. Fill a medium-size bowl with ice water and set aside.

2. For the spice mixture: In a small bowl, combine the cumin, ginger, coriander, cinnamon, paprika, and salt. Set aside.

3. To make the salad: Bring a medium-size pot of salted water to a boil. Add the carrots and cook until crisp-tender, about 7 minutes. Drain the carrots in a colander and transfer to the bowl of ice water and immerse, stirring occasionally, until completely cooled, about 5 minutes. Drain in a colander, then pat dry with paper towels. Place in a large bowl with the chickpeas; set aside.

4. For the Moroccan dressing: Heat the olive oil in a medium-size skillet over medium-high heat until hot but not smoking. Add the onion and cook, stirring often, until soft and translucent, about 5 minutes. Add the jalapeños and cook, stirring often, until soft, about 3 minutes. Add the spice mixture and cook, stirring often, until fragrant, about 1 minute. Stir in the garlic and cook for 30 seconds. Stir in the vinegar, scraping up the browned bits from the bottom of the pan, and cook for 1 minute. Let cool to room temperature.

5. Add half of the dressing to the carrot mixture, tossing to combine. Fold in the scallions, cilantro, parsley, and lemon juice. Adjust seasonings with more dressing, lemon juice, and honey, if desired. Season with salt and pepper to taste. Cover, refrigerate, and allow to marinate for at least 3 hours or up to 24 hours before serving.

White Gate Farm

HOLCOMB FARM

Decades ago, Laura and Tudor Holcomb generously donated their beautiful 367-acre property to be used for agriculture, educational research, passive recreation, and wildlife sanctuary. Over 20,000 visitors annually enjoy this legacy.

Holcomb is a working farm and a community gathering place, operated between the Town of Granby and a dedicated board of directors composed of local citizens. The board is dedicated to preserving, promoting, and protecting the agricultural heritage of the farm and legacy of Laura and Tudor Holcomb.

Holcomb Farm CSA grows over 100 different varieties of produce, using sustainable growing practices. This produce is grown for 450 summer share members, 75 winter share members, select area restaurants, and Fresh Access, the farm's extensive food donation program that provides healthy fresh produce to seniors and families throughout the region.

Every week during growing season, Fresh Access supplies 125 pounds of produce to its partner organizations—that's more than 6 tons of fresh produce to over 1,300 people every year. Current Community Partners include Granby Senior Center and the Waste Not Want Not Community Kitchen, Granby (South Congregational Church); Hispanic Health Council; and Hartford Food System, Hartford.

Holcomb is a place for visitors to enjoy nature and to gather, brimming with activities year-round—from folk concerts to festivals to art and yoga classes.

Beet and Carrot Slaw with Raspberry Vinaigrette

SERVES 4

"As a CSA member and blogger, the challenge each week is to find unique ways to utilize the ever-changing variety of produce harvested from the farm. This recipe was developed in the height of the season when beets and carrots were still plentiful and the raspberries were bursting from the late-summer bushes." —Julie Wern

Raspberry Vinaigrette (makes 3/4 cup)

1/2 cup fresh raspberries
1 teaspoon orange zest, plus 2 tablespoons
    fresh orange juice
1 tablespoon red wine vinegar
1 teaspoon Dijon mustard
2 teaspoons honey
1/4 cup extra-virgin olive oil
Kosher salt and freshly ground black pepper

Beet and Carrot Slaw

14 small carrots, peeled and shredded
3 large beets (red, golden, or a combination),
    stemmed, peeled, and shredded
1/3 cup hulled sunflower seeds
1 tablespoon chopped fresh mint, or to taste
Kosher salt and freshly ground black pepper

1. To make the vinaigrette: Pulse the raspberries in a food processor until minced. Add the orange zest and juice, vinegar, mustard, and honey and pulse until well combined. With the processor running, gradually add the oil and process until smooth. Season with salt and pepper to taste.

2. In a large bowl, combine the carrots and beets. Drizzle with the vinaigrette to taste and toss to coat. Top with the sunflower seeds and mint. Season with salt and pepper to taste, and serve at once.

Julie Wern for Holcomb Farm

Bread Salad

SERVES 6

This salad is a wonderful use of locally grown bounty and some leftover bread as a fresh and substantial accompaniment to a meal.

Croutons

1/2 loaf of day-old country bread (about 9 ounces), cut into 1-inch cubes (about 4 cups)
2 tablespoons extra-virgin olive oil
2 tablespoons melted unsalted butter
1 dried Thai chile pepper, crushed
Kosher salt and coarsely ground black pepper

Dressing (makes 1 1/2 cups)

Zest and juice of 2 lemons
8 oil-packed anchovy fillets, drained and minced
4 garlic cloves, minced
1 cup extra-virgin olive oil
1 teaspoon kosher salt
1 teaspoon freshly ground black pepper

Salad

1 (8-ounce) bag salad greens, such as mesclun
1 pint cherry tomatoes, halved
1 cucumber, skinned, seeded, and cut into 1/3-inch-thick half-moons
1/2 cup diced red onion
Freshly grated Parmesan cheese

1. To make the croutons: Preheat the oven to 350°F. In a large bowl, toss the bread cubes with the olive oil, butter, and chile pepper and season with salt and pepper to taste. Spread out the bread in a single layer on a baking sheet and bake, tossing occasionally, until golden brown, about 15 minutes. Let cool to room temperature.

2. To make the dressing: In a medium-size bowl, whisk together the lemon zest and juice, ancho-

vies, and garlic. Whisking vigorously, add the olive oil in a slow, steady stream. Season with salt and pepper to taste and set aside.

3. In a large bowl, combine the salad greens, tomatoes, cucumber, onion, and croutons and toss with 1/2 cup of the dressing, or to taste. Season with salt and pepper to taste. Top with the Parmesan cheese and serve.

Farm to Hearth

HOLBROOK FARM

Holbrook Farm is not the traditional version of a farm that has been tilled by the same family for generations. Although Lynn and John Holbrook have lived on the 13-acre property for more than 35 years, they didn't start out as farmers. In fact, Lynn and John met at Procter & Gamble in Cincinnati, where Lynn worked in market research and John in marketing. When they moved to work in Westport, they found a lovely old house in Bethel where there was room for animals and gardens and where their children could enjoy growing up with a taste of the country.

It was after their children were grown that they seriously considered expanding from a family farm selling flowers and produce from a roadside stand, to a thriving retail operation that welcomes visitors, to a farm market and bakery. The changes evolved as a way to secure their retirement and keep the farm thriving.

Inside the red-barn market, you'll find an array of in-season produce, spanning to the traditional to the exotic, coming from Holbrook's grounds and greenhouses, as well as fragrant fresh-baked pies, scones, cookies and breads, homemade jams, jellies, pickles, honey, and, a customer favorite, fresh eggs from the Holbrook's 400 or so free-range chickens.

Lynn explains, "Farmers have to have savvy business plans today to stay suc-

cessful, so we've innovated, now growing vegetables in the winter. And growing more ethnic varieties, such as pac choi and komatsuna, and bringing in products from other farmers."

"What we don't grow we buy from other local sources," Lynn says, including raw milk from Stonewall Dairy in Cromwell; Goat's milk, artisan cheeses, yogurts and even lotions.

One thing that hasn't changed is the way they treat the land. Holbrook Farm has been clean of pesticides and herbicides for the past 30-plus years that the Holbrooks have owned the property. "We don't spray with pesticides; we try to use beneficial insects and companion plants," John says, "and we don't use herbicides. Weeds have a place in the ecological mix as long as they are controlled."

Smoked Chicken, Apple, and Walnut Salad

SERVES 3 TO 4

This crunchy chicken salad is a Holbrook family lunch favorite.

Dressing (makes 1/2 cup)

3 tablespoons fresh lemon juice

1 teaspoon Dijon mustard

1/2 teaspoon minced garlic

1 1/2 teaspoons chopped fresh rosemary

6 tablespoons extra-virgin olive oil

Kosher salt and freshly ground black pepper

Salad

2 medium-size tart apples, such as Granny Smith, cored and diced

1 cup packed watercress, thin stems and leaves

1 cup packed baby tender lettuce, such as red oak leaf, leaves separated and torn into bite-size pieces if large

1 cup packed romaine lettuce, trimmed and torn into bite-size pieces

2 celery ribs, diced

1 large red sweet bell pepper, seeded and cut into thin strips

1/2 cup toasted walnuts, coarsely chopped

Kosher salt and freshly ground black pepper

1/2 pound deli sliced smoked chicken breasts, sliced on the bias into thin slices

1. To make the dressing: Whisk together the lemon juice, mustard, garlic, and rosemary. Whisking vigorously, adding the oil in a slow, steady stream. Season with salt and pepper to taste.

2. To make the salad: In a large bowl, combine the apples, watercress, lettuces, celery, red pepper, and walnuts. Add the dressing and toss to coat evenly. Season with salt and pepper to taste.

3. Arrange the salad on plates. Place the chicken slices on top and serve at once.

Holbrook Farm

UNION LEAGUE CAFE

So much has been written about Union League Cafe, one of Connecticut's most enduringly romantic and lavishly lauded restaurants, that there's not much more add, except: *Go!* The quintessential special occasion restaurant is sited in an historic former men's club near the Yale campus, with a dazzling Beaux-Arts interior accented by the soaring ceiling and intricate woodwork of a bygone era. The venue is highly rated by the *New York Times*, *Connecticut Magazine*, *Zagat*, and *Travel and Leisure*, and is consistently identified as one of Connecticut's best. If you haven't been yet, put it on your bucket list, but don't wait for a special occasion.

Whether you walk in off the street for a more casual lunch in the handsome Club Room or plan an impressive dinner with top clients in the Beaux-Arts dining room, you will enjoy the divine French cuisine and the lavish attentions of chef-owner Jean-Pierre "JP" Vuillermet and an impeccably trained staff.

What you may not know is that local and organic produce, fish, meats, and artisanal cheeses are the foundation of Vuillermet's award-winning cuisine. JP explains, "Sourcing from local farms and suppliers goes back to my roots in France. You had to have this network if you wanted to work with fresh ingredients and feature what was truly seasonal from the region. I've sourced farms like Cole's from the time I arrived in the United States, but back in

the 1980s it was far more difficult and not common. It is great to see this movement become popular and appreciated in this country; it has tremendous benefits for the farmers and local suppliers, for the environment, for chefs and for the overall quality of food we prepare for our customers. We are fortunate to be surrounded by so many wonderful family farmers."

When it comes to dessert, Union League makes it worth the calories, whether it's for a traditional crème brûlée or profiteroles, or a seasonal specialty, such as the Tarte aux Fraises, a tart made with local strawberries, Brittany cookie crust, strawberry emulsion, and vanilla Chantilly or the Schuss Figue-Cerise, a Connecticut farm ricotta mousse, with lavender honey, roasted Black Mission figs, black cherry jam, and a pistachio biscuit.

Salad of Mixed Baby Greens and Beltane Farm Goat Cheese

SERVES 4

This refreshing salad has a nice lingering tangi-ness from the goat cheese croutons.

Dressing

1 tablespoon fresh lemon juice

Pinch of salt

Freshly ground pepper

1/4 cup extra-virgin olive oil plus 2 tablespoons, divided

1 tablespoon chopped fresh basil leaves

1 baguette

2 tablespoons extra-virgin olive oil, plus more for serving

8 ounces goat cheese, such as Danse de la Lune

2 (5-ounce) bags mesclun greens

2 tablespoons chopped black olives

1. Preheat the broiler.

2. To make the dressing: In a small bowl, mix the lemon juice, salt, and pepper to taste. Whisk in the 1/4 cup of olive oil. Add the basil. Set aside.

3. Cut the baguette into 1/4-inch-thick slices (three slices per person). Place on a baking sheet and brush each slice with the remaining 2 table-spoons of oil.

4. Slice the goat cheese into 1/4-inch-thick rounds and place on top of each baguette slice. Place under the broiler and broil until the cheese starts to brown, about 5 minutes.

5. In a large bowl, toss the mesclun mix with the olives and dressing.

6. To serve: Arrange the salad in the middle of a large plate or platter. Place the goat cheese

"croutons" around the plate. Finish with a drizzle of extra-virgin olive oil. Serve at once.

Union League Cafe

PLUM LUV FOODS

If you watch food TV, you'll likely catch a glimpse of gregarious Chef Plum, a Virginia-born chef and Culinary Institute of America graduate and chef-owner at Plum Luv Foods in Newtown, bringing cooking to life on the small screen, as host of the Allrecipes.com segment on the nationally syndicated *Better* show on The Hallmark Channel (191 in Connecticut). Recently, Plum was the winner of episode 2 of Guy Fieri's *Guy's Grocery Games* on the Food Network. Closer to home, as a private chef and caterer, Chef Plum brings his farm-sourced foods to families, small parties, Broadway actors, and executives through Plum Luv Foods, a Connecticut-based catering outfit.

Chef Plum has a passion for simple, easy-to-make farm foods, believing great food doesn't need gimmicks. His latest brainchild, Dinner Underground, has brought a series of pop-up farm-inspired dinners to a variety of venues in Newtown and Danbury. More recently, Chef Plum was the first chef to ever host a pop-up restaurant inside the walls of a Williams Sonoma retail store.

Chef Plum shares two tomato-based recipes from a recent farm dinner; his Pork Belly–Stuffed Tomatoes can be found on page 257 of this book.

Late Summer CT Heirloom Tomato Salad

SERVES 4

Diverse heirloom varieties make this colorful salad a thing of beauty that literally bursts with summer flavors.

2 pounds mixed heirloom tomatoes, such as Black Prince, German green, or Kellogg's Breakfast, cut into 1/4-inch-thick slices (larger tomatoes) or halved (smaller tomatoes)

2 tablespoons young or green garlic cloves thinly sliced lengthwise

1 tablespoon minced fresh oregano leaves

Sea salt and freshly ground white pepper

2 tablespoons extra-virgin olive oil, for drizzling

Crusty bread, for serving

Arrange the tomatoes on a 10-inch platter. Sprinkle the tomatoes evenly with the garlic, oregano, and salt and pepper to taste. Drizzle the olive oil over the tomatoes. Serve with crusty bread.

Note: Do not refrigerate. Serve at once.

Plum Luv Foods

WEST STREET GRILL

Restaurateur James O'Shea grew up on a farm in Ireland, so when he and Charles Kafferman opened Litchfield's West Street Grill in the '90s, they wanted to do the kind of simple, "perfect food" that could only be accomplished with the freshest farm ingredients.

For decades, the restaurant's top-selling item in season has been its simple fresh tomato salad, featuring flavorful, just-picked, peak-season tomatoes, a sprinkle of fleur de sel (hand-harvested sea salt), a few sprigs of basil, and a drizzle of imported aged balsamic vinegar. Although this salad is ubiquitous today, its sheer simplicity was a revelation in an era that celebrated rich sauces, huge portions, and overwrought cuisine.

After banishing relish trays and iceberg lettuce salads, O'Shea began working with local farmers, fishermen, and foragers long before the concept of using local, organic, and wild became fashionable. He recalls, "In came breads baked fresh daily on the premises, and fresh fish from off the docks . . . often served rare, and shocking at the time."

The Grill began drawing celebs, authors, and captains of industry who owned country homes in the Litchfield Hills, for what O'Shea calls "Modern American" cuisine. It wasn't long before the *New York Times* awarded the Grill an "Excellent." Years later, Danny Meyer, CEO of Union Square Hospitality Group, aptly summed it up by

saying: "It is notable not just for serving notables, but even more so for serving destination-worthy food with unparalleled consistency and hospitality for the past 20 years."

The restaurant's longevity proves the premise of letting top-quality ingredients do the talking. The kitchen, presided over by head chef James Cosgriff, bakes its own bread twice daily, makes his own mozzarella and burrata, shops local markets, and imports specialty ingredients—from Spanish olive oil to fleur de sel from Mormarge, France, and maintains an organic herb garden of 25 years. They feed their kitchen garden with organic fertilizer and compost from the restaurant. O'Shea notes, "We grow our own rhubarb, garlic, chives, mint, multiple basil varieties, oregano, rosemary, and several summer annual crops." In addition, he says, "We have a 'picker' from Tara Farm, who goes around to the local Connecticut farms and brings us back great quantities of the freshest of products."

Mixed Greens with a Sherry Shallot Vinaigrette

MAKES 2/4 CUP VINAIGRETTE

This West Street Grill staple is simple, simple, simple and fresh, fresh, fresh. The vibrant vinaigrette is just as good as a poultry marinade.

1 1/2 tablespoons chopped shallots

2 to 3 tablespoons good-quality sherry vinegar

1 teaspoon Dijon mustard

1/4 teaspoon honey, or to taste

1/2 teaspoon chopped fresh herbs, such as basil or thyme, or to taste

1/4 teaspoon sea salt, or to taste

1/4 teaspoon freshly ground white pepper, or to taste

1/2 cup vegetable oil

Serve over: organic gem, baby romaine, Lola Rosa and Lola Biondo, or baby red leaf lettuce, or any local organic mixed greens

Pulse the shallots in a food processor until they are finely chopped. Add 2 tablespoons of the vinegar, mustard, honey, herbs, and salt and pepper to taste and pulse until well combined. While the machine is running, gradually add the oil. Adjust the seasonings with honey and/or mustard, if desired, up to 1 more tablespoon of sherry vinegar, and salt and pepper to taste. Drizzle over a bed of mixed greens.

West Street Grill

SOUTH END

Chef Nick Martschenko's vision to create a modern tavern and neighborhood gathering spot sourcing from local farmers has caught on—so much so that it can be a tricky weekend reservation to score.

A Culinary Institute of America graduate, Nick began his career with two-time James Beard Award–winner Melissa Kelly at the Old Chatham Sheepherding Company Inn and Restaurant in upstate New York and Primo in Rockland, Maine, and worked up to executive sous chef with chef-owner Tom Colicchio at Gramercy Tavern in New York City, among notable posts, before pouring his heart into his own restaurant, South End, in downtown New Canaan.

South End's food is approachable, flavor-filled, and inspired by farmers and producers in the area. Fueled by Nick's unrelenting passion, the *New York Times* gave South End a "Very Good" rating in a March 2014 review, for a "stimulating gustatory experience."

Nick and the team are focused on serving up seasonal comfort food and creative libations in an open floor plan that is casual and befitting a small, urbane town like New Canaan. The decor is rustic-chic, with reclaimed barn wood beams, innovative lighting, linen-upholstered banquettes, and moody prints of the countryside and farm animals, referencing Martschenko's appreciation for the local farming community.

Sit by the bar and make a meal of the starters, such as burrata served with charred peas and tendrils, shaved Speck, burnt onion vinaigrette, and grilled bread; the Spicy Tuna Poke; and of course, Nonna's meatballs, stuffed with pork, veal, and ricotta cheese. Be sure to try the artisanal meats and delicious farmstead cheeses sourced from small Connecticut and Vermont farms.

South End's pastas, such as Maccheroncini with Braised Rabbit, are all homemade, and do Nick's Nonna proud. The kitchen has a special knack for meats, from the Spring Chicken Cooked Under a Brick to the Pork Chop Scarpariello. The menu also offers options from the sea. Whether it's Caramelized Diver Scallops or East Coast Halibut, each entrée is amped up with seasonal accoutrements, such as English peas, sour cream onions, romaine, red-veined sorrel, and crispy ham.

Peruse the "Ruffage" or "It's Not Every Day" sections of the menu, where local farms make a star turn in dishes like the Crispy Duck Confit Salad: a honey-hazelnut glazed duck leg, adorned with baby turnips, green beans, and pickled spring vegetables in a hazelnut vinaigrette.

South End set out with a simple food philosophy—create foods that are uncomplicated, seasonal, and flavorful. Clearly, they've nailed it.

Farmers' Salad

SERVES 4

"This is one of my favorite seasonal recipes that we offer in the late spring and early summer. These simple few ingredients pack a bright crisp punch of flavor sourced from four of our local farmers—all within ten miles of our restaurant."
—Chef Nick Martschenko

Vegetables

1/2 pound yellow wax beans, trimmed and cut in half
1/2 pound green beans, trimmed and cut in half
1 bunch breakfast radishes, trimmed and peeled
8 ounces frisée greens

Walnut Pesto

1/2 cup walnuts, toasted and coarsely chopped
2 1/2 tablespoons walnut oil, divided
Kosher salt and freshly ground black pepper

Duck Eggs

4 duck eggs
4 cups canola oil, or as needed
1/2 cup all-purpose flour
2 large eggs, lightly beaten
1 cup panko bread crumbs, pulsed in a food processor
1 1/2 teaspoons grated Parmesan cheese
Kosher salt and freshly ground black pepper

For Assembly

Juice of 1/3 lemon, or to taste
1 ounce fresh chervil leaves, chopped
1 ounce fresh shungiku (Garland chrysanthemum leaves; see note), chopped
Olive oil

1. To make the vegetables: Fill a large bowl with ice water and set aside. Bring a medium-size saucepan of salted water to a simmer over medium-high heat. Add the beans and cook until tender, about 5 minutes. Using a slotted spoon, transfer the beans to the prepared ice-water bath and let cool completely, about 3 minutes. Remove the beans and place in a bowl; set aside.

2. Cut the radishes crosswise into 1/8-inch-thick slices with a slicer or sharp knife. Add the radishes and frisée greens to the bowl with the beans. Set aside.

3. To make the walnut pesto: Combine the walnuts and 2 tablespoons of the walnut oil in a food processor and pulse to a coarse paste. Season with salt and pepper to taste; set aside.

4. To make the duck eggs: Fill a medium-size bowl with ice water and set aside. Place the duck eggs in a medium-size pot and add at least 1 inch of water to cover. Bring water to a boil over medium-high heat. Turn off the heat, cover, and let the eggs stand for 2 minutes. Using a slotted spoon, transfer the eggs to the ice-water bath and let cool completely, about 3 minutes. Remove the eggs and carefully peel; discard the shells.

5. Fill a deep, heavy-bottomed pot with about 4 inches of canola oil. Heat the oil to 350°F, using a candy thermometer.

6. Place the flour in one bowl, the lightly beaten eggs in a second bowl, and the bread crumbs with cheese, salt, and pepper in a third bowl. Dredge the duck eggs in the flour, making sure they are well coated, then in the beaten eggs, and then in the bread crumb mixture. With a slotted spoon, gently drop into the hot oil until golden brown, 2 to 3 minutes.

7. To assemble: Add the walnut pesto, remaining 1 1/2 teaspoons of walnut oil, lemon juice, and herbs to the green beans and stir to coat well. Adjust the seasonings with additional walnut oil and lemon juice. Season with salt and pepper

to taste. Divide the salad among four plates and place one duck egg in the center of each salad. Drizzle with olive oil. Serve immediately.

Note: You can find shungiku at your local Asian market. Or substitute spinach.

South End

NAPA & CO.

It wasn't long after Napa & Co. opened in downtown Stamford that the restaurant, designed to transport patrons to a Napa Valley state of mind, became the hottest ticket in town. It was soon listed among the top 100 American Restaurants (*Zagat*), voted Best Overall Restaurant in the State (*Connecticut Magazine*), and earned an "Excellent" rating (*New York Times*).

Napa has garnered praise for innovative cuisine with a local influence, and has kept true to its mission to offer "great wine and food made simple." The clean flavors of Mediterranean-influenced cuisine have always been at the menu's core. At the helm, chef Adam Truelove is bringing exciting new twists to the table. After graduating from the French Culinary Institute, he honed his skills at Esca in New York, then in Fairfield County, where he made a name for himself at Tarry Lodge, Sole, and the J House's Eleven14 Kitchen.

The award-winning fare at Napa & Co. is based on the philosophy "From the farm to the plate." Truelove explains: "What does this mean, exactly? We want to let the ingredients reach you and speak to you. We do not want to manipulate [process] our ingredients. It is our mission to provide you with the freshest seasonal ingredients possible while continuing to support our local purveyors and farms. In doing this, the rewards are two-fold for all involved: You will receive the freshest ingredients possible and you will never get bored."

Saunder's Farm Arugula Salad with Orange Vinaigrette and Harvest Moon Cheese

SERVES 4

The citrus vinaigrette is the perfect complement to peppery arugula and a nutty cheese.

Vinaigrette (makes about 3/4 cup)

1/4 cup plus 2 tablespoons extra-virgin olive oil
1/4 cup fresh orange juice
4 teaspoons honey, or to taste
4 teaspoons red wine vinegar
Kosher salt and freshly ground pepper

Salad

1 pound arugula
Kosher salt and freshly ground pepper
1/2 cup toasted chopped walnuts
1 (4-ounce) wedge hard, nutty-flavored Spanish-style cheese, such as Harvest Moon (Beltane Farm) or Chèvre Noir (Quebec)
1/4 cup coarsely chopped fresh flat-leaf parsley
1 teaspoon finely grated orange zest

1. To make the vinaigrette: In a small bowl, whisk together the oil, orange juice, honey, and vinegar. Season with salt and pepper to taste.

2. To make the salad: Combine the arugula and vinaigrette in a large bowl. Season with salt and pepper to taste and toss to combine. Divide the salad among four plates and scatter the walnuts evenly over the top. Using a vegetable peeler, shave the cheese over the top of the salad. Garnish with the parsley and orange zest. Serve at once.

Adam Truelove for Napa & Co.

ROÌA

If you're seeking a bite after a show at the Shubert Theater, or have a yen to check out the revamped Taft Hotel Restaurant, head on over to Roìa, a bustling New Haven hotspot.

Chef Avi Szapiro and his wife, Meera, fell in love with the historic space, once home to the Taft Hotel's grand two-story restaurant, and agreed to come onboard with partner Francis Moezinia—provided they restore the hallowed halls to their Gilded Age glory. A two-year renovation stripped away layers of linoleum, carpet, and paint, unearthing the original mosaic tile floor, oak paneling, and period details, including the ornate plaster ceiling best seen from the mezzanine. Then they added contemporary touches, such as the red leather banquettes, dark wood paneling, and masculine lighting, to make the massive space less fussy and more relevant.

Avi, a talented 35-year-old chef originally from Colombia, combines his love of French and Italian cuisines, and his training in Paris, London, Italy, and California to create the menu at Roìa, aptly named for a river that runs through the border of France and Italy. Flavors of these countries are in evidence in the ingredients: olives, wine reductions, branzino, octopus, homemade pastas.

The Euro-local current flows through many signature dishes, such as the handmade black pepper–and–rosemary pappardelle with a hen ragù, made with the

meat from local hens, and Castelvetrano olives from Sicily, or the Raw Stonington Fluke with toasted pine nuts and truffle-lime vinaigrette. Avi picked up his penchant for local sourcing while working with Paul Bertolli (of Chez Panisse) at Oliveto Restaurant and Café.

You'll find organic chicken, grass-fed beef, local baby beets, carrots, artichokes, and greens, and plenty of sustainable and seasonal surprises woven into the menu. Avi says, "I'm looking forward to heirloom tomatoes, local corn, eggplant, and cucumbers. The local produce we get from the farms allows us to get creative and have a lot of fun."

Crispy Poached Egg Salad

SERVES 6

This is a great recipe to have up your sleeve the next time you are hosting brunch. The crispy poached egg is what provides the "wow" factor to a salad of peppery fresh greens.

Vinaigrette (makes 1 cup)

3/4 cup extra-virgin olive oil
1/4 cup balsamic vinegar
Honey
Kosher salt and freshly ground black pepper

Poached Eggs

2 tablespoons white wine vinegar
6 large eggs

Dredge

1 cup all-purpose flour
1 tablespoon kosher salt
1 tablespoon freshly ground black pepper
2 large eggs, lightly beaten
1 1/2 cups panko bread crumbs
2 tablespoons extra-virgin olive oil, or as needed

Greens

4 cups red watercress
4 cups arugula
Kosher salt and freshly ground black pepper
Coarse salt

1. To make the vinaigrette: In a small bowl, whisk together the oil, vinegar, and rosemary. Adjust the seasonings with honey and salt and pepper to taste. Set aside.

2. To poach the eggs: Prepare an ice-water bath and set aside. Crack an egg into a small cup and set aside. Fill a small saucepan with 3 inches of water, add the vinegar, and bring to a boil over medium-high heat. Lower the heat to a bare simmer; then gently slide the egg into the saucepan, swirling the water with a spoon to help the egg to form into a solid shape. Cook the egg until the white is firm but yielding to the touch and yolk is soft and runny, about 3 1/2 minutes. Using a slotted spoon, transfer the egg to the prepared ice-water bath. Return the water to a boil and repeat the process with the remaining eggs.

3. To make the dredge: In a medium-size bowl, stir together the flour and salt and pepper to taste. Place the eggs in a second bowl and the bread crumbs in a third bowl. Gently dip each egg in the flour mixture, then in the egg, and then in the bread crumbs. Set the eggs on a baking sheet lined with parchment paper.

4. Heat 2 tablespoons of oil in a large skillet over medium-high heat until hot but not smoking. Add the dredged eggs, in batches, and cook until the crust is nicely browned on both sides, 2 to 3 minutes per side. Using a slotted spoon, transfer the eggs to paper towels to drain.

5. To make the greens: Combine the greens in a large bowl, drizzle with 1/2 cup of the vinaigrette, and toss to coat, adding more vinaigrette as needed. Season with salt and pepper to taste. Top with the eggs. Sprinkle with coarse salt and serve at once.

Roìa Restaurant

MASSARO COMMUNITY FARM

Organized in 2008, Massaro Community Farm, Inc. is a 57-acre, nonprofit, certified organic farm providing vegetables and flowers to customers, as well as open space for hands-on education for all ages.

Committed to sustainable farming methods, the farm is a place where everyone is welcome to be a part of building a legacy for future generations.

Each year, the farm produces enough organic vegetables to support a 175-member CSA, a weekly booth at a local farmers' market, and select area farm-to-table restaurants. Farm manager Steve Munno says, "We believe in engaging all the senses in the process of protecting the natural landscape. We endeavor to provide experiences that will connect us to each other and to the land that sustains us."

The farm offers summer camp programs and school visits, as well as seasonal workshops for adults on beekeeping, organic land care, composting, home food preservation, and more. In addition to workshops, camps, and tours, the farm hosts annual events open to the community, including Celebrate Spring, Dinner on the Farm, and Family Fun Day.

Vegan Cream of Carrot Soup

MAKES 5 SERVINGS (ABOUT 1 1/2 CUPS EACH)

"We love our carrots at the farm, which are a favorite of our farm manager. They are especially sweet if they've come through a frost, which allows the sugars to concentrate in the root and make them exceedingly sweet. Enjoy this simple soup any time of year!" —Katy Pool, executive director

2 pounds carrots, peeled and chopped (about 4 1/3 cups chopped)
4 cups vegetable stock
3 tablespoons olive or grapeseed oil
1 cup chopped onion
3 garlic cloves, minced
1 cup soy milk
1 teaspoon grated fresh ginger
2 teaspoons chopped fresh thyme
3 tablespoons chopped dill fronds, plus more for garnish
2 tablespoons dry sherry, plus more as needed
3/4 tablespoon kosher salt
Freshly ground black pepper
Crusty bread, for serving (optional)

1. Place the carrots and vegetable stock in a stockpot. Bring to a boil over medium-high heat. Lower the heat and simmer until the carrots are fork-tender, about 12 minutes. Set aside to cool.

2. Meanwhile, heat the oil in a medium-size sauté pan over medium heat. Add the onion and sauté until soft and translucent, about 8 minutes. Add the garlic, stirring often, and cook until fragrant, about 1 minute. Add the onion mixture to the stock.

3. Transfer the soup to a blender and puree in batches until smooth. Return the soup to the

stockpot and slowly whisk in the soy milk. Cook over medium heat until heated through. Add the ginger, thyme, dill, sherry, and salt. Thin with additional stock, if necessary. Adjust the seasonings with sherry, salt, and pepper to taste. Garnish with dill and a drizzle of sherry, if desired, and serve with crusty bread.

Massaro Community Farm

CAROLE PECK'S GOOD NEWS CAFÉ AND RESTAURANT

If you ask who pioneered the concept of farm-to-table cuisine in Connecticut, plenty of folks give a nod to trailblazer Carole Peck, who set out to create a new venue based on local organic foods in 1992. At the eponymous Carole Peck's Good News Café in Woodbury, acolytes continue to praise Carole's fresh and inventive fare, inspired by local farm products, all served by a friendly staff in sunny, upbeat digs, with a rotating selection of original art.

One of the first female chefs to graduate from the Culinary Institute of America in the '70s, Peck forged her reputation for culinary excellence early on, relying on nearby Litchfield County farms for seasonal inspiration, devoid of the deprivation previously associated with healthy, organic fare. But whereas other early farm-to-table chefs petered out, Peck turned up the heat, putting together bright and novel flavor combinations—from the citrusy spring salad of Ruby Red grapefruit, orange, pomegranate, avocado, and watercress to the savory tagine of lamb with winter squash, calypso beans, artichokes, onions, carrots, and pearl couscous. Her dishes are novel and delicious.

Creative without being stuffy (think: killer burgers and crispy onion bundles with homemade ketchup), Good News attracts the gamut—Litchfield locals to foodies to such politicos as Hillary and Bill Clinton, who celebrated Hillary's birthday lunch here with their daughter, Chelsea, and her husband, Marc Mezvinsky.

Peck and Bernard Jarrier, her husband and business partner, have imbued Good News Café with a casual European vibe that is reflected in the menu, the wine list, and the ambience, thanks to frequent trips abroad to Europe.

Indeed, they are living the dream—carving out a culinary empire that includes a travel business based on cooking trips to their home in Provence, a line of gift items, and Ici La Press (a cookbook publishing business). At the end of the day, though, the beating heart of the operation is still Peck's Good News Café. If you haven't visited yet, put it on your must-try list.

Chilled Green Gazpacho

**MAKES 3 1/2 QUARTS SOUP;
SERVES 7 (2 CUPS EACH)**

A twist on the classic Spanish gazpacho, this no-cook soup is a cool addition to the lunch table in the heat of July and August.

Soup

1 large sweet onion, such as Vidalia, peeled and coarsely chopped (about 3 1/3 cups)

1 jalapeño pepper, stemmed, seeded, and minced

3 cups seedless green grapes, halved

1 cup coarsely chopped celery (about 5 ribs)

2 (about 1 pound each) European or hothouse cucumbers, peeled, halved, seeded, and coarsely chopped

2 garlic cloves, peeled and chopped (about 2 tablespoons)

2 (5.5-ounce) cans pineapple juice

Water as needed to reach desired consistency

1 cup extra-virgin olive oil, plus more as needed

Kosher salt and freshly ground black pepper

Garnishes

1/2 cup peeled and diced sweet onion, such as Vidalia

1/2 cup peeled and diced celery root

1 cup diced celery (about 5 ribs)

1 cup diced fennel (reserve fronds for garnish)

1 cup peeled, halved, seeded, and diced cucumber (about 1/2 cucumber)

8 fresh tomatillos, husked, rinsed and diced

1 cup seedless green grapes, diced

Croutons

2/3 (6-ounce) loaf baguette, day old, cut into 3/4-inch cubes (about 3 1/2 cups)

2 tablespoons extra-virgin olive oil

Kosher salt and coarsely ground black pepper

1. To make the soup: Working in batches, puree the onion, pepper, grapes, celery, cucumbers, and garlic in a blender or food processor, adding the pineapple juice and water a little bit at a time, until smooth. While the machine is running, slowly add the olive oil and pulse until well combined. Using a coarse sieve or a food mill, strain the soup into a large bowl; discard any seeds and skins.

2. Add the garnishes: Stir the onion, celery root, celery, fennel, cucumber, tomatillos, and grapes. Season with salt and pepper to taste. Cover and refrigerate until the soup is chilled, about 1 hour.

3. To make the croutons: While the soup is chilling, preheat the oven to 350°F. In a large bowl, toss the bread cubes with the olive oil and season with salt and pepper to taste. Spread out the bread in a single layer on a baking sheet and bake, tossing occasionally, until golden brown, about 15 minutes. Let cool to room temperature.

4. Ladle the soup into bowls and garnish with a drizzle of olive oil, if desired, and top with croutons. Garnish with the reserved fennel fronds and serve.

Note: The longer the gazpacho soup sits in the refrigerator, the more flavors will develop.

Carole Peck's Good New Café

ZINC

In the heart of downtown New Haven, across from the historic New Haven Green, Zinc has been dishing up an innovative seed-to-plate menu with a focus on sustainability for more than 15 years. Head chef Denise Appel's fare features regionally farmed produce and cheeses, hormone- and antibiotic-free beef, veal, poultry, and fresh (nonendangered) line-caught fish.

Denise uses a "seed-to-plate" approach that has earned many honors, including *Edible Nutmeg*'s 2008 Local Hero Award for Chef/Restaurant, and Best New Restaurant in New Haven County, and Best American Restaurant in Connecticut from *Connecticut Magazine*, among others.

Denise and co-owner Donna Curran employ the same fresh ingredient philosophy at Kitchen Zinc, a casual artisan pizzeria and bar with a killer outdoor patio.

The owners don't leave their all-important produce selection up to chance, planning what they want with local farms at the growing and development stage. Denise says, "We understand the importance of harvesting amazing, vibrant ingredients, so we start at seed selection stage. In essence, our farmers help us write our menus. Staying local also allows us to ease the stress on the surrounding environment and promote a thriving community of farmers, chefs, and diners."

Zinc is deeply connected to many local partner farms, most of which are proudly featured within these pages. Donna notes, "We're also involved with CitySeed, which engages the community in growing an equitable, local food system. Our restaurant is passionately associated with Connecticut's Farm-to-Chef program, which connects local chefs and food service professionals with growers, producers, and distributors of Connecticut-grown products. Zinc also supports Connecticut Grown, a collaboration of Connecticut farm and food organizations working together."

Denise says, "We love to see what is fresh each week at the local farmers' market, then get creative on a new menu and include the new recipes on our blog. And to make it a little more fun, we include original cocktails on each week's Market Menu as well."

Chilled Pea and Leek Soup with Salmon Gravlax and Pickled Shallots

SERVES 5 (2 CUPS EACH)

Note: Cure the salmon three days and pickle the shallots one day before you intend to serve the soup.

Salmon Gravlax

1/2 teaspoon fennel seeds

2 whole star anise, broken into pieces

6 juniper berries, crushed

2 bay leaves, broken into pieces

1/2 cup granulated sugar

1/2 cup sea or kosher salt

1 tablespoon coarsely ground black pepper

1 pound skin-on fresh wild salmon fillet or char (thinner tail section is best), pin bones removed

3 tablespoons minced fresh parsley

1 teaspoon freshly ground black pepper

1/4 cup vodka

Pickled Shallots

3 whole fresh shallots, thinly sliced

5 tablespoons sherry vinegar

1/4 cup granulated sugar

Freshly ground black pepper

1/8 teaspoon red pepper flakes

Chilled Pea and Leek Soup

1/4 cup extra-virgin olive oil, divided

4 cups fresh spinach

1 spring onion, cut into small dice

1 small fennel bulb, cut into small dice

3 leeks, washed, white and pale green parts only, chopped into medium dice

2 tablespoons minced fresh garlic

1/4 cup dry white wine, such as sauvignon blanc

4 cups vegetable stock

2 pounds fresh or frozen shelled English peas

1 tablespoon fresh lemon thyme, chopped

2 tablespoons fresh tarragon, chopped

For Assembly

Crème fraîche

Sherry vinegar

Olive oil

Minced chives

1. To make the salmon gravlax: In a small bowl, combine the fennel seeds, star anise, juniper berries, bay leaves, sugar, salt, and coarsely ground pepper; set aside.

2. Rinse the salmon under cold running water and pat dry with paper towels. In a glass baking dish (just big enough to hold the salmon), spread half of the parsley, pepper, and fennel seed mixture on the bottom of dish. Place the salmon, skin side down, on the mixture. Sprinkle the remaining parsley, pepper, and fennel seed mixture evenly over the fish.

3. Slowly pour the vodka over the fish, gently smoothing out the salt-sugar mixture evenly over the fish. Place a sheet of parchment paper over the salmon and set a second baking sheet atop the fish; top with several cans to weight down. Place in the refrigerator; turn and baste the fish with the accumulated juices every 10 to 12 hours. The fish will be ready to slice when the flesh is opaque, about 3 days, depending on the thickness of the fish.

4. To make the pickled shallots: Place the shallots in a 16-ounce glass mason jar with a tight lid. Combine the vinegar, sugar, pepper, and red

pepper flakes in a small saucepan. Cook, stirring often, until the sugar has dissolved, over medium-high heat, about 3 minutes. Remove from the heat and pour over the shallots and gently stir to evenly distribute the vinegar and seal. Let sit at room temperature for 24 hours.

5. Rinse the salmon under cold running water; removing all the salt mixture. Pat dry with paper towels. Transfer to a cutting board, skin side down, and using the palm of your hand carefully

run a knife along the bottom, slicing parallel to and as close as possible to the cutting board to remove the skin. Discard the skin. Thinly slice on the bias into 1/4-inch slices, then into small cubes. Transfer the cubes to a medium-size bowl and toss with the chives.

6. To make the chilled pea and leek soup: Heat 2 tablespoons of the oil in a large skillet over medium-high heat. Add the spinach and cook until just wilted; set aside.

7. Heat the remaining 2 tablespoons of oil in a large saucepan over medium heat. Add the onion, fennel, and leeks and cook, stirring often until the vegetables are soft but not browned, about 8 minutes. Add the garlic and cook until fragrant, about 1 minute. Stir in the wine and deglaze the pan, scraping up the bits from the bottom of pan. Stir in the stock and bring to a simmer. Add the peas and continue to cook until the peas are just tender, about 8 minutes. Add the lemon thyme and tarragon and continue to simmer for 1 minute. Remove from the heat and transfer to a blender or food processor, in batches, if necessary, along with the wilted spinach, and puree until smooth. Season with salt and pepper to taste. Place the soup in a large bowl and transfer to the refrigerator; allow to cool completely.

8. To assemble: Ladle the soup into soup bowls, top each with 2 tablespoons of salmon gravlax, 1 tablespoon pickled shallots, or to taste, a dollop of crème fraîche, a drizzle of sherry vinegar and olive oil, and a sprinkle of chives.

Note: Save the extra salmon gravlax and serve on top of cucumber slices or mini pumpernickel or brioche toasts.

Zinc

CLAIRE'S CORNER COPIA

Claire LaPia, a registered nurse, and Frank Criscuolo, a musician, were married in 1975, and opened Claire's Corner Copia in New Haven that year as a way to spend time together. Both excellent cooks, they were inspired to follow in the footsteps of their Italian-American ancestors, particularly Claire's mother, Anna Bigio LaPia, who was "obsessed" with eating delicious, fresh homemade food, with lots of fruits and vegetables, grains, and beans. Her mantras were: "Eat this, it's good for you" and "We don't eat foods with ingredients I can't pronounce."

After 40 years, Claire's remains true to these family values, bringing healthy, organic foods to the masses, and doing it in a way that is sustainable—always using paper, rather than plastic, for its take-out bags; making its own natural kitchen cleaners for windows and floors; and switching to compostable cups and take-out boxes made from corn and printed with soy ink.

In 2004, the Criscuolos went on to open Basta Trattoria next door, serving organic, wild, line-caught fish and seafood; organic and free-range chicken; prime grass-fed beef; handmade Italian cheeses, and wines from small family-owned vineyards throughout Italy. Although Frank passed away unexpectedly in 2012, chef Eduardo Saldana-Pena and Claire are keeping his spirit alive at Basta.

Claire's stays true to the principles that continue to earn accolades, such as being named one of the 10 Best Heart-Healthy Restaurants in America by MSNBC, and voted Best Quiche by *Connecticut Magazine* and Best Vegetarian, Soups & Desserts by the *New Haven Advocate*.

CLAIRE'S SOUP TIPS:

- Use a heavy pot, stainless steel with a thick aluminum core for even heating and to help prevent sticking or burning.

- Sort your beans for any stones or foreign matter, leaves, and such, and rinse before using to be sure no dirt remains.

- Use the best oils, beans, grains, herbs, and vegetables for your soups—the results are only as good as the ingredients.

- Consider sharing your soup with a neighbor, particularly an elderly neighbor. It's rewarding knowing that you are sharing something good.

Fresh Corn Soup

SERVES 5 TO 6 (1 1/2 TO 2 CUPS EACH)

"This 'creamy' soup is so simple to prepare and is the essence of summer's end, made using freshly harvested corn and potatoes, both grown in Connecticut by our farmers . . . We buy as much [corn] as we can use, and then we shuck and strip the kernels and freeze them for the months when we don't have fresh corn—for a taste of summer." —Claire Criscuolo

8 cups fresh corn kernels (cut from 10 to 13 ears of corn; depending on the size), cobs reserved

1 tablespoon vegan buttery spread or unsalted butter

4 medium-size red-skinned potatoes, scrubbed, peeled, and cut into 1/4-inch cubes

Kosher salt and freshly ground black pepper

Crème fraîche

1 medium-size red or yellow bell pepper, seeded and finely chopped

Chopped fresh basil

Fresh lime juice (optional)

1. In a large stockpot, bring 12 cups of lightly salted water to a boil over medium-high heat. Carefully add the reserved cobs and buttery spread, cover, and cook, stirring occasionally, for 30 minutes. Using tongs, carefully remove the cobs and discard. Leave 7 cups of the cob water in the pot. Add the potatoes and corn kernels, cover, bring to a simmer, and cook until the potatoes are tender, about 15 minutes. With a slotted spoon, remove 1/2 cup of the corn kernels; set aside.

2. Working in batches, puree the soup in a blender or food processor, until smooth. Return the soup and the reserved 1/2 cup of corn kernels to the stockpot and cook until heated through. Season with salt and pepper to taste. Ladle the soup into cups and serve with a dollop

of crème fraîche and a sprinkling of bell pepper, basil, and lime juice, if desired.

Claire's Corner Copia

G-ZEN RESTAURANT

G-Zen is located in downtown Branford, just a short walk from the Green. The restaurant (and food truck) represent the vision of chefs Mark and Ami Beach Shadle. Together, they take the concept of "farm to table" to a whole new level, by growing their organic ingredients, serving them fresh at the restaurant and through their mobile truck, and then composting everything back at Shadle Farm, their sustainable 1730s farm in Durham (see sidebar, page 141).

The youthful duo, with model-perfect healthy looks, are both deeply "in the power" of a plant-based diet, and both have been following a vegetarian and vegan lifestyle for more than 20 years.

At G-Zen, the Shadles have managed to make vegan eating fun, serving fresh, delicious, and healthful food in a relaxed setting. Ami notes, "This philosophy extends to our drinks. We don't stray from these ideals where saki-tini elixirs or sangrias are concerned. We use all organic ingredients—everything from the fruit to the wine, and use a natural low-glycemic sweeter, raw agave nectar, instead of simple sugar or brandy."

G-Zen was named one of Top Ten Upscale Vegan Restaurants in America by *SHAPE* magazine. In 2013, G-Zen was featured in *Travel + Leisure Magazine*'s "Best Vegetarian Restaurants in USA," received the "Nature's Plate Award" from the Nature Conservancy, as Connecticut's Most

Sustainable Restaurant, for running on 100-percent solar power, serving organic ingredients, supporting local farmers, and installing composting programs.

The menu is entirely plant-based and sourced from organic, sustainable, and local ingredients whenever possible. The food is scratch-made daily. Executive chef Mark Shadle is a world-renowned vegan chef and culinary Olympic gold winner and has more than 25 years experience in the natural foods movement and vegetarian cuisine.

Squash Almond Bisque

SERVES 5 (1 1/2 CUPS EACH)

"The inspiration behind this G-Zen favorite is the bountiful butternut squash harvest that we are blessed to have at our Shadle Farm. The unique twist of almond butter and cinnamon takes this extra-creamy and spicy classic squash bisque to another level." —Ami Shadle

2 tablespoons canola oil
1 cup diced carrot (about 1 very large carrot)
1 cup diced celery
1 cup diced onion (about 1 large onion)
4 cups diced butternut squash (about 2 pounds)
1 tablespoon dried basil
1 teaspoon sea salt
1 tablespoon minced garlic (about 2 large cloves)
1 tablespoon minced fresh ginger (about
    2-inch piece)
4 cups vegetable stock, plus more as needed
2 teaspoons ground cinnamon
1 cup almond butter
Kosher salt and freshly ground black pepper
5 slices baguette, toasted (optional)
Chopped fresh cilantro, for garnish

1. Heat the oil in a large stockpot over medium heat. Add the carrot, celery, onion, squash, basil, and salt and sauté until the onion is translucent and tender, about 8 minutes. Add the garlic and ginger and sauté until the garlic is fragrant, about 1 minute. Stir in the stock and bring to a boil over medium-high heat. Lower the heat to a simmer and cook until the squash is fork-tender, about 20 minutes. Stir in the cinnamon and almond butter and remove from the heat. Working in batches, puree the soup in a blender, food processor, or with an immersion blender until smooth. Return the soup to the pot and add stock, if necessary, to achieve the desired consistency. Season with salt and pepper to taste.

2. Place one baguette slice, if using, in the bottom of each bowl. Ladle the soup into the bowl. Garnish with cilantro and serve at once.

G-Zen/Shadle Farm

GOLDEN LAMB BUTTERY

Opened in the '60s by Bob and Virginia "Jimmie" Booth, the Golden Lamb Buttery, located in Brooklyn, is a destination venue, tucked away in the "quiet corner" of Connecticut, a trip in and of itself, and one of the state's most memorable dining experiences.

A Connecticut treasure, the Golden Lamb restaurant is set on a family farm—the backdrop for countless proposals, anniversaries, and weddings over more than 50 years.

Serving locally sourced meats, seafood, and provisions, the Golden Lamb's chef pulls fresh vegetables and herbs right from the farm's gardens. But these are no mere kitchen cutting gardens. Hillandale Farms comprises 1,000 acres of open pastures, beautiful stone walls, woods, and a pond. The farm has been in the Booth family since the early 1940s, and is protected farmland. Guests are invited to stroll or even tour the property by hayride, serenaded by an acoustic guitarist.

In recent years, granddaughter Katie Bogert took the reins as proprietor and host. She relishes the idea of continuing the family tradition for the next generation, and recently published an anniversary cookbook, *The Golden Lamb Buttery*.

Guests are welcomed with cocktails in the old red barn, a space brimming with antiques and memorabilia, which spills out onto a deck that provides a bucolic vista of the pond and the sheep, horses, and cows grazing in the pastures.

At dinner, guests are led into the restaurant through a tiny kitchen, where a four-course, prix-fixe extravaganza of choices, such as roast duckling, honey-balsamic-glazed rack of lamb, and chateaubriand, is being prepared. Inside, guests are shown to one of three charming dining rooms and are invited to dine, linger, and relax "until the candles burn down" to the sounds of live music.

Country Cottage Soup

MAKES ABOUT 2 3/4 QUARTS SOUP

This is an old family recipe, made with love . . . and a bit of lovage.

"One of Jimmie's (my grandmother's) favorites was lovage, a yellow-flowered perennial that tastes a bit like spicy celery. It gives great flavor to soups and pairs well with fish." —Katie Bogert

2 tablespoons unsalted butter

1 cup diced onion

2 cups coarsely chopped leek, white parts only

1 1/2 cups diced celery

2 tablespoons minced garlic

1 (2-pound) cauliflower head, green leaves discarded and broken into florets (about 4 cups)

3 cups low-sodium chicken stock, or as needed

1 pound cream cheese

2 cups milk, or as needed

2 tablespoons lovage leaves or celery leaves

1/2 teaspoon lemon pepper, or to taste

Kosher salt

2 tablespoons chopped fresh chives

2 tablespoons chopped fresh dill

1. Melt the butter in a large, heavy stockpot over medium heat. Add the onion, leek, and celery and cook, stirring often, until the onion is soft and translucent, 8 minutes. Add the garlic and cook, stirring often, until fragrant, about 1 minute.

2. Add the cauliflower and stock. Increase the heat to a simmer, cover, and simmer until cauliflower is fork-tender, about 20 minutes. Lower the heat to low. Stir in the cream cheese in batches until melted. Remove from the heat and allow the soup to cool for 20 minutes. Slowly stir in the milk and lovage leaves. Transfer the soup to a blender and puree in batches until smooth. Return the soup to the saucepan and add the lemon pepper and salt to taste. Thin with additional stock, if necessary. Serve immediately, garnished with chives and dill.

Golden Lamb Buttery

RIVER TAVERN

Jonathan Rapp's River Tavern has been a locavore mainstay in the heart of the charming riverside town of Chester for more than a dozen years—well before the term *locavore* was coined. The creative New American menu changes daily and features seasonal ingredients sourced from Connecticut's best local farms, underscored by a stellar wine list. In addition to spearheading Dinners at the Farm (see page 78), chef-owner Rapp takes pride in being among the early organizers of the Connecticut Department of Agriculture's Farm-to-Chef program; and even offers a $10 Children's Menu on Sundays, in which proceeds support Get Fresh 4 School, a healthy school lunch initiative for Region 4 schools in the Chester, Deep River, and Essex area.

The interior of the quaint 19th-century building puts one in the mind of a Brooklyn, New York, art gallery, hung with an array of bright, geometric pieces by American conceptual artist Sol LeWitt, who once resided in Chester. There's a perennially packed bar, with weekly half-price wine and cocktail specials, an open kitchen, and a wall of windows overlooking picturesque Pattaconk Brook.

On the dinner menu, you'll find imaginative local fare, such as Grilled Stonington Swordfish with jasmine rice, cabbage, red turnips, eggplant and cilantro; or the Fried Soeltl Farm Chicken with summer vegetables, coleslaw, spicy corn bread, and sweet-and-sour gravy. There's also a fun bar menu with lighter options. Feeling decadent? Be sure to save room for River Tavern's seasonal desserts, especially its signature baked-to-order Date Pudding with Dark Rum Caramel Sauce and fresh whipped cream.

DINNERS AT THE FARM

In 2007, Jonathan Rapp, of River Tavern, created Dinners at the Farm, Connecticut's first farm dinner benefit series, in partnership with Drew McLachlan of the former Feast Gourmet Market in Deep River and Chip Dahlke of Ashlawn Farm. They started the series to bring people to local farms and to generate awareness of the local farming community and the delicious, wholesome and abundant food it provides. The dinners provide a wonderful opportunity to meet and talk with local farmers whose food you will be enjoying.

The multicourse feasts feature spontaneous menus based on what's available that day. The convivial, open-air meals are served to guests seated at beautifully dressed tables, smack dab in the fields at select local farms. The food is cooked from scratch fresh off the back of the team's signature, red, vintage cook truck—a 1955 Ford F-600. Guests dine by candlelight under a large tent, and there is always plenty of wine flowing.

Each of the 10 to 24 dinners highlights local farming traditions, and the often forgotten value of eating fresh food that was just harvested by a local farmer.

At the end of the day, Dinners at the Farm also raises funds for local agricultural and humanitarian nonprofit organizations. Over the past nine seasons, Dinners at the Farm has fed over 10,000 guests at 88 dinners, donated $105,000, and directly purchased more than $180,000 worth of food and wine from Connecticut producers. In 2014, the organization donated $20,000 toward the critical work of beneficiaries CitySeed, Connecticut Farmland Trust, Working Lands Alliance, Region 4 Schools and the New Connecticut Farmer Alliance, a group of emerging farmers working to grow and sustain new farms in Connecticut, ensuring a viable agricultural future. Clearly, Dinners at the Farm has made a significant contribution to celebrating and promoting Connecticut-grown products.

Roasted Root Vegetable and Artisan Handcrafted Sausage Stuffing

SERVES 12 TO 14

This rustic stuffing is all about subtle layers of flavor. It has a creamy tang from the goat cheese and a sweet earthiness from the roasted ruta-baga, red beets, carrot, and onion. The citrus notes from the lemon zest provide an extra punch of brightness, which is the perfect counterpoint to the savory artisan handcrafted sausage. Serve this stuffing with beef, pork, roast chicken, or turkey.

Roasted Vegetables

1 (2-pound) rutabaga, ends trimmed, peeled and cut into 1-inch pieces

1 pound red beets, scrubbed, ends trimmed and cut into 1-inch pieces

1 large carrot, peeled and cut diagonally into 1/2-inch pieces

1 small onion, cut into 1/3-inch-wide wedges

5 garlic cloves, peeled

1 1/2 teaspoons minced fresh rosemary

1 1/2 teaspoons minced fresh sage or thyme

Kosher salt and freshly ground black pepper

1/4 cup extra-virgin olive oil

1 tablespoon Connecticut honey, or to taste

1 (1- to 1 1/2-pound) loaf artisan bread, cut into 1-inch cubes

1 pound artisan handcrafted sausage, such as red wine and garlic pork sausage, casings removed

3 large eggs, at room temperature, lightly beaten

1 (4-ounce) log chèvre cheese

Zest of 1/2 lemon

1 tablespoon chopped fresh parsley

2 cups low-sodium chicken stock, or as needed

1. Preheat the oven to 400°F. Lightly oil a baking sheet and set aside.

2. Place the rutabaga, beets, carrot, onion, garlic, rosemary, and sage in a large bowl. Season with salt and pepper to taste. Drizzle with the olive oil and honey and toss to combine, making sure to coat all the vegetables well.

3. Spread the vegetable mixture on the prepared baking sheet. Roast, stirring occasionally, until the vegetables are just fork-tender, about 45 minutes. Set aside.

4. Place the bread cubes on an ungreased baking sheet and toast in the oven, tossing occasionally, until crisp and golden brown, about 15 minutes. Remove from the oven and let cool.

5. While the bread cubes are toasting, cook the sausage. Heat a nonstick skillet over medium heat. Add the sausage and cook, crumbling with a fork, until just browned and slightly pink in the center, about 7 minutes. Remove from the heat and set aside.

6. Lightly butter a 9 x 13-inch baking dish. Place the bread cubes in a large bowl. Mash the garlic with the back of a fork or spoon. Add the vegetable mixture, including the mashed garlic, to the bread cubes. Using a slotted spoon, transfer the sausage to the bread stuffing. Stir in the eggs, chèvre, lemon zest, and parsley. Gently mix all the ingredients together; do not overmix. Season with salt and pepper to taste. Pour the stuffing into the prepared baking dish. Pour the stock over the surface of the stuffing. If the mixture seems too dry, add more stock until the desired consistency is achieved.

7. Lightly coat the dull side of a sheet of foil with nonstick cooking spray and cover the baking dish. Bake for 30 minutes. Uncover the stuffing and continue to bake until the top is crisp and golden brown, about 15 minutes. Let the stuffing rest for 5 minutes before serving.

Tracey Medeiros

MÉTRO BIS

Métro Bis restaurant moved to the charming Simsbury 1820 House in September 2013 after 15 years in a snug bistro just to the north. Chef Chris Prosperi and his wife and co-owner, Courtney Febbroriello, are proud to welcome guests to the new location in the heart of town, a more spacious 74-seat eatery with dining on the porch for 20 and an additional 100 seats for parties and events. Because the present location is a historic B&B, you can wrap a weekend or overnight around your visit.

Longtime customers were pleased that the duo integrated elements of the original restaurant's decor into the new design, including the Paris Métro train doors, as well as the lights from a different Métro station. In addition, the owners added a sycamore "cookbook bar," a cocktail nook lined with cookbooks from favorite chefs. True to form, Prosperi retained his penchant for using local, farm-fresh ingredients to create his changing menus. A tip: One of the best ways to sample the sublime cuisine is via the Tasting Menu, a four-course feast, paired with wines, for $70 ($50 without wines).

Clearly, Chris's longtime dedication to serving innovative local cuisine has paid off. *Zagat* ranked Métro Bis among the top five restaurants in the state for American food, The *New York Times* declared, "Métro Bis is worth a detour" and *Chef Magazine* nominated Chris as one of five national finalists for the Chef of the Year Award.

He is a weekly recipe columnist for the *Hartford Courant* and he's visible across the country via radio, TV, cooking series, food festivals, and appearances.

"Connecticut has so much to offer with each season, and a dish featuring a flavorful foundation requires little effort to truly shine," Chris says.

Curried Brussels Sprouts with Bacon and Honey

SERVES 2 TO 3 AS A MAIN COURSE OR 4 AS A SIDE

Chris loves Brussels sprouts and looks forward to autumn, when the farm he purchases from begins the harvest. A member of the cabbage family, Brussels sprouts are the little "heads" growing on stalks that can hold dozens of sprouts. If picked in early fall, before the frost, they have a bitter, nutty taste. Harvested after a couple of chilly nights, the sprouts will actually sweeten with the freeze. Chris developed this recipe at the Litchfield Farm Fresh Market, using early harvest Brussels sprouts that he sweetened with local honey. As the season progresses, simply adjust the amount of honey, depending on the bitterness of the vegetable. Be sure to visit a neighborhood farm, weekend market, or grocery store for some locally grown Brussels sprouts and honey to enjoy this seasonal favorite.

1 tablespoon olive oil

5 ounces (about 5 slices) smoked bacon, minced

1 medium-size onion, diced

1 medium-size carrot, peeled and minced

1 pound Brussels sprouts, trimmed and halved
    lengthwise

1 cup water, plus more as needed

1 1/2 teaspoons rubbed dried sage (see note)

1 teaspoon curry powder

2 tablespoons honey, plus more as needed

1 1/2 teaspoons red wine vinegar, plus more
    as needed

Kosher salt

1. Heat the oil in a large skillet over medium-high heat. Add the bacon and sauté, stirring frequently, until the bacon is crisp, about 4 minutes. Using a slotted spoon, remove the bacon and set aside to drain on paper towels.

2. Add the onion and carrot and cook, stirring frequently, until the onion is light golden brown, about 4 minutes.

3. Add the Brussels sprouts and sauté, stirring frequently, for 5 minutes. Stir in 1 cup of water and bring to a simmer.

4. Lower the heat to medium-low, cover, and cook until Brussels sprouts are fork-tender, stirring occasionally, adding more water as needed, about 8 minutes.

5. Stir in the reserved bacon, sage, and curry powder until well combined. Remove from the heat and stir in the honey and vinegar. Season with additional honey and/or red wine vinegar, if desired, and salt to taste.

Note: If you cannot find rubbed dried sage, you can substitute ground sage. Ground sage is more potent; therefore you should use half of the amount.

Métro Bis

GILBERTIE'S HERB GARDENS AND PETITE EDIBLES

Gilbertie's Herb Gardens was established in 1922 as a cut-flower operation.

For over 90 years, Gilbertie's has grown high-quality herbs and vegetables, and, in 2008, prompted by concerns about pesticides, consumer health, and the environment, transitioned into organic growing and became certified by the USDA.

When Gilbertie's started growing herb plants for kitchen gardens, it was one of the first to do so. Today, Gilbertie's is the largest certified organic grower in New England, offering over 300 varieties of herbs, vegetable plants, and cut greens in the family's 20-plus greenhouses in Easton, still run by the Sal Gilbertie and the Gilbertie family, now in its fourth generation.

Although his plants are shipped to more than 800 garden centers, nurseries, and farms, Sal is dedicated to the local green foods movement, running classes, speaking at farm conferences, and hosting the Westport Winter Farmers' Market at the Westport location.

He and his team are constantly innovating. For example, Gilbertie's now plants and maintains custom organic raised garden beds for local chefs, restaurants, and markets in Easton.

In another development, Sal has expanded into the "Petite Edibles" category. These tender microgreens provide both chefs and home cooks with a range of colorful organi-cally certified cut greens and herbs year-round in a variety of mixes, such as Asian (tatsoi, shungiku, red pac choi), Citrus (lemon basil, sorrel, red amaranth), and Mediterranean (kale, basil, and arugula). The microgreens are grown in a custom soil mix, as opposed to hydroponically, making them more flavorful and nutritionally dense. They are harvested two to three weeks after sowing (at their peak of flavor and nutrition), and are used as both a garnish and as a flavor boost, adding a dash of color and zing to salads, soups, sandwiches, and entrées. They are available at local food markets and specialty stores in Connecticut and Westchester.

Brussels Sprouts and Petite Edibles

SERVES 4 AS A SIDE DISH

1 pound organic Brussels sprouts, rinsed, ends trimmed, dark outer leaves removed and discarded

2 1/2 tablespoons extra-virgin olive oil, plus more as needed

2 large organic garlic cloves, minced

Salt and freshly ground black pepper

1/4 cup freshly grated Parmigiano-Reggiano cheese

2 ounces microgreens, such as arugula or mizuna, or radishes (about 1 cup packed)

1. Preheat the oven to 350°F. Lightly oil a rimmed baking sheet; set aside.

2. Cut the sprouts in half, lengthwise. Arrange the sprouts, in a single layer, cut side down, on the prepared baking sheet, and bake for 15 minutes. Remove from the oven and drizzle the olive oil over the sprouts. Sprinkle with the garlic and season with salt and pepper to taste. Toss to coat evenly. Return the sprouts to the oven and roast until browned and tender, about 15 more minutes. Add the cheese, microgreens, and additional oil, if desired, and toss to combine well. Season with salt and pepper to taste. Serve at once.

Gilbertie's Petite Edibles

MOOREFIELD HERB FARM

Moorefield Herb Farm is a relatively small farm on just 6 acres in Trumbull. It is over 45 years old. Nancy Moore has a green thumb, cultivating approximately two of those acres and growing 35 varieties of heirloom tomatoes, 200 varieties of herbs, everlasting flowers, perennials, greens, gourds, pumpkins, and succulents.

In the summer, Moorefield Herb Farm participates in eight farmers' markets, primarily in lower Fairfield County. In the winter, the farm team is busy giving talks on garden topics to garden clubs and other local green organizations.

On the property, there is a small greenhouse where the farm's plants are started. One of Moorefield's specialties is helping home gardeners get started with flats of unique heirloom vegetables, such as American Tondo pumpkins, round zucchini, yellow straightneck squash, Fordhook zucchini, Valenciano (white) pumpkins, several varieties of nasturtiums, pickling cucumbers, and Marketmore cukes. Nancy notes, "Although we are not certified organic, we grow all of our plants using organic methods."

TARRY LODGE ENOTECA PIZZERIA

When Tarry Lodge Enoteca Pizzeria touched down in Westport, locals swarmed to the pizzeria and wine bar to sample celebrity chef Mario Batali's thin-crust pies (e.g., the killer burrata, pancetta, and chili oil), paired with imported Italian wines.

Soon they learned that the team of Mario La Posta, Andy Nusser, and Nancy Selzer, all from the Port Chester venue, was also turning out an array of more sophisticated seasonal offerings, such as beer-braised pork shoulder with butternut squash and charred Brussels sprouts, roasted root vegetables, hen-of-the-woods (maitake) mushrooms, Gorgonzola with Bibb lettuce and walnuts, black fettuccine with rock shrimp, quail with delicata squash, polenta with portobello mushroom, whole branzino, pumpkin fiore, and venison with lentils and chanterelles.

What customers might not know is that Tarry Lodge, part of the Batali & Bastianich Restaurant Group, with venues around the world, is a green pioneer, sourcing locally and launching a number of green initiatives, such as food-waste composting, alternative fuel sources, energy benchmarking programs, sustainable food purchasing plans, Green Seal Certified cleaning products, and corporate-wide participation in both Meatless Monday and a no-bottled-water policy.

We love that the restaurant is Certified Green and sources its ingredients as much as possible from the Westport Farmers' Market, almost as much as we love some of chef La Posta's homespun Italian classics, such as the addictive Polpette (tiny meatballs) that disappear as soon as they are brought to the table, and the hearty Eggplant alla Caponata, both of which recipes he shares with us.

Rosa Bianca Eggplant alla Caponata

SERVES 14 (2 SLICES EACH)

Note: This recipe is best made one day ahead. If cooled completely before storing, the caponata can be refrigerated up to four days in an airtight container.

3 tablespoons plus 1/2 teaspoon olive oil, divided

2 pounds heirloom eggplants, such Rosa Bianca (see note), trimmed, peeled, and cut into 1/2-inch dice

1 medium-size red onion, minced

2 cups (about 1 pound) red bell peppers, stemmed, seeded, and minced

1 teaspoon dried oregano, or to taste

3 large garlic cloves, thinly sliced

1 teaspoon red pepper flakes, or to taste

1/4 cup red wine vinegar

4 heirloom plum tomatoes (see note), seeded and finely chopped

1/4 cup coarsely chopped pitted black Italian olives, such Gaeta or Kalamata

2 tablespoons salt-packed capers (see note), drained and rinsed

1/2 cup golden raisins

1 teaspoon pure maple syrup, plus more as needed

1/4 cup pine nuts, lightly toasted

Kosher salt and freshly ground black pepper

Chopped fresh parsley

16 (1/4-inch-thick) diagonal slices baguette, toasted

1. Heat 2 tablespoons of the oil in a 12-inch skillet over medium-high heat until hot but not smoking. Add the eggplant and lower the heat to medium. Season with salt and pepper to taste. Cook, stirring often, until the eggplant is tender, about 8 minutes. Using a slotted spoon, transfer to paper towels to drain. In the same skillet, heat 1 tablespoon of the oil over medium heat. Add the onion, peppers, and oregano and cook, stirring often, until the onion is soft and translucent, about 8 minutes. Add the garlic and red pepper flakes and cook, stirring often, for 1 minute. Stir in the vinegar and bring to a gentle boil over medium-high heat until the liquid is reduced by half, about 2 minutes.

2. Add the eggplant, tomatoes, olives, capers, raisins, and maple syrup. Lower the heat to medium-low and cook, stirring often, until the vegetables are fork-tender and the mixture is thick, about 10 minutes. Transfer to a bowl and season with salt and pepper to taste. Cover and refrigerate for at least 5 hours or overnight.

3. To toast the pine nuts: Place the pine nuts and the remaining 1/2 teaspoon of oil in a small skillet and toss to coat. Toast over medium heat until the nuts turn light brown, about 3 minutes. Remove from the pan and set aside on paper towels.

4. Serve at room temperature. Just before serving, fold in the pine nuts. Season with salt and pepper and additional maple syrup, as desired. Garnish with parsley.

Notes:

Rosa Bianca is a Sicilian heirloom eggplant variety with a mild taste, no bitterness, and very few seeds. You can substitute Italian purple or Bianca Oval eggplant in its place.

If you cannot find heirloom plum tomatoes, you can substitute a nonheirloom variety, such Roma, which is commonly found in supermarkets.

If you cannot find salt-packed capers, feel free to substitute regular vinegar capers and rinse well before using.

Tarry Lodge Enoteca Pizzeria

JACQUES PÉPIN

Farm-sourced fare is in Jacques Pépin's blood. Born in France in 1935, Pépin first apprenticed in a kitchen at the age of 13, where the notion of visiting the local markets for the freshest catch and the ripest plums was de rigueur. After training in Paris, he moved to the United States, where he worked as a chef in top restaurants, and later as a food research director and a restaurant owner. An award-winning chef who has collaborated with Julia Child and other top chefs around the world, written more than 20 books, and continues to host PBS cooking shows, Pépin is a local treasure on the Connecticut Shoreline. For more than 40 years, he has lived with his wife, Gloria, in Madison, where he shops the local markets, dines at local restaurants, and plays boules with friends.

Nearing 80, Pépin hasn't slowed down. In June 2013, he teamed up at Millstone Farm in Wilton with celebrated local chefs Bill Taibe of LeFarm and the Whelk and Tim LaBant, of the Schoolhouse at Cannondale, to film an episode of *A Moveable Feast*, a PBS special with *Fine Cooking* magazine. Connecticut food bloggers Dan and Kristien Del Ferraro described the show on their blog, *OmNom*, reporting: "The Holy Trinity of culinary awesomeness spontaneously whipped up an amazing meal based exclusively on the bounty gleaned from what was available at Millstone that afternoon. Pépin and granddaughter, Storey, using eggs from the farm's heritage hens to create a dish served in lettuce cups, Taibe slow-roasting a pork shoulder, and LaBant turning baby turnips and greens into a lovely fennel fritter salad. Each dish was sourced on the grounds, and prepared right in the Millstone Farm kitchen."

Here, Pépin shares a favorite spring dish—a study in simplicity—with fresh peas and baby lettuce from just down the road. This version is adapted from a recipe in his *Essential Pépin*.

Peas à la Française

SERVES 4 AS A SIDE DISH

"In this classic dish, small, young lettuce and tiny pearl onions are cooked with a dash of oil and water, and then fresh peas are added and cooked for a little longer. Fresh Bibb or Boston lettuce is best for this recipe; it remains slightly crunchy, with a hint of bitterness that goes well with the onions and peas. I wait the whole year to make this dish when the peas are available in late spring. Cole Farm on Horse Pond Road, right here in Madison, calls me when the peas are ready and I get small pearl onions at the farm as well. I usually have fresh, tender lettuce in my garden at that point. When prepared with these fresh ingredients—especially the peas—this is a dish for the gods." —Jacques Pépin

6 ounces small pearl onions (11 to 16, depending on size), peeled

1 sprig thyme, leaves removed and stem discarded

1 teaspoon granulated sugar

1 teaspoon kosher salt

1/4 teaspoon freshly ground black pepper

2 tablespoons extra-virgin olive oil

1/2 cup water

2 pounds unshelled fresh peas (2 1/2 to 3 cups shelled; see note)

2 heads fresh lettuce (8 ounces), such as Boston, washed, cored, and cut into 2-inch pieces

2 tablespoons unsalted butter

1. Combine the onions, thyme leaves, sugar, salt, pepper, oil, and water in a large saucepan and bring to a boil over medium-high heat, then boil for 4 minutes. Lower the heat to low, cover, and simmer for 5 minutes.

2. Add the peas and cook, covered, over medium heat for 4 minutes. Add the lettuce and cook, covered, for 4 minutes. Boil gently, covered, until the peas are tender but not mushy (adjusting the timing as required, based on the size of the peas). Mix in the butter until melted and serve.

Note: If fresh peas are not available, frozen peas may be used.

Jacques Pépin

WAKEMAN TOWN FARM

In its heyday, Wakeman Farm was a thriving family farm with 41 acres of chickens, cows, and vegetables in the heart of Westport, selling 5,000 ears of corn across the tristate area every weekend for 15 years.

Built in 1905 by John Wakeman, the farmhouse and its property were run by members of the Wakeman family for more than 65 years.

Today, it's owned by the Town of Westport and called Wakeman Town Farm and Sustainability Center, a demonstration farm, a community gathering spot, a CSA drop-off, and an educational center.

An all-volunteer board (including Bill Constantino, Ike and Pearl Wakeman's grandson) oversees the farm, where junior farmers learn the ins and outs of organic farming and sustainability and adults learn composting, canning, chicken-keeping, and other homesteading skills. At the helm (and the farm's heart) is environmental science teacher Mike Aitkenhead, with his wife, Carrie, and two young children by his side.

Today, Wakeman Town Farm teems with life—goats, sheep, chickens, alpacas, bunnies, and bees (as well as a few pesky, crop-eating groundhogs).

To stay self-sustaining, WTF hosts educational farm programs and camps, apprentice programs, workshops and cooking classes, and family-friendly events, such as pancake breakfasts, farm-to-table dinners, and green-foods and environmental advocacy programs. The farm's motto is "Grow your food, know your food": WTF strives to teach kids not only where their food comes from, but also that farming takes patience, collaboration, and perseverance.

Chipotle Veggie Chili

SERVES 8 (1 1/2 CUPS EACH)

This chili has been a consistent crowd-pleaser. Created by chef Craig Charlton, the chili won second place in a local chili cook-off and is now a staple served at community events. Chef Craig likes to serve it with corn bread.

1/4 cup extra-virgin olive oil

1 cup chopped red onion

1 cup diced carrot

1 cup seeded and diced green bell pepper

1 cup seeded and diced red bell pepper

3 medium-size garlic cloves, chopped

2 tablespoons chili powder

1 tablespoon ground cumin

2 (28-ounce) cans diced tomatoes

1 (15-ounce) can black beans, drained and rinsed

1 (15-ounce) can red kidney beans, drained and rinsed

1 (15-ounce) can hominy, drained and rinsed

1/4 to 1/2 cup pureed chipotle peppers in adobo (see note)

Vegetable stock, as needed

Kosher salt and freshly ground black pepper

2 limes, quartered

Plain yogurt (optional)

Shredded cheese, such as Monterey Jack or Cheddar (optional)

Heat the oil in a Dutch oven or large pot over medium heat. Add the onion, carrot, and bell peppers and sauté, stirring often, until the onion is soft, about 8 minutes. Add the garlic and sauté for 1 minute. Stir in the chili powder, cumin, diced tomatoes with juice, beans, hominy, and chipotle peppers. If the chili is too thick, add vegetable stock as needed. Bring to a boil, stirring occasionally, then lower the heat, cover, and simmer for 1 hour, stirring occasionally. Season with salt and pepper to taste. Serve with lime wedges and a dollop of yogurt and/or a sprinkle of cheese, if desired.

Note: Cutting back on the pureed chipotle pepper in adobo can reduce the spiciness to your preferred level of heat.

Chef Craig Charlton for Wakeman Town Farm

TERRAIN WESTPORT GARDEN CAFÉ

Terrain is a 17,500 square-foot home and garden fantasyland, complete with a farm-inspired garden café, a curated collection of home goods, books, jewelry, and accessories, plus design gurus to help you create a dream landscape at home.

For farm dining, the outdoor garden patio is one of Westport's hidden gems. A verdant oasis, tucked behind the Post Road, the patio is flanked by a nursery bursting with fragrant perennials and garden plants. It's a fashionable setting for farm-style drinks and nibbles, at lunch and at dinner.

Farmers, foodies, and local food purveyors celebrated the arrival of executive chef Jared Frazer, who came armed with more than 13 years of culinary experience, including as executive chef and chef de cuisine at Supper in Philadelphia and at Perry's in Washington, DC. He has also worked with chefs José Andrés and Michel Richard, in several top restaurants throughout Washington, DC, New Jersey, and Pennsylvania. After getting things rolling, Frazer returned to the Terrain flagship in Philadelphia, and now Alissa Svorka, his talented former sous chef, is at the helm, carrying out her own farm-to-table cooking vision.

Here, the drinks and portions are ample, the dishes are unfussy, the bread is baked and served in terra-cotta pots, and the drinks arrive in mason jars, festooned with basil, mint, and other fresh herbs.

At a recent spring lunch, we enjoyed pickled beet salad with grapefruit, chèvre, candied pistachios, and spicy greens tossed in an orange vinaigrette, and a hefty grilled portobello sandwich, topped with roasted red pepper and blue cheese and served on a ciabatta roll, accompanied by crispy, house-cut fries. There are delicious options at lunch, dinner, and weekend brunch.

Svorka is continuing to forge relationships with area purveyors and farmers, so you'll note that many of the cheeses, produce, meats, and other ingredients on the menu hail from a radius of small farms in Connecticut and New York.

Salt-Roasted Beets with Blood Oranges, Pistachios, and Goat Cheese Salad

SERVES 4

The assortment of colored baby beets makes this vibrant salad a beautiful presentation. Roasting beets on a bed of sea salt keeps them moist and seasoned from the outside in.

5 ounces sea salt, plus more for dressing

2 large red beets, scrubbed, greens removed, cleaned, and reserved (see notes)

2 tablespoons extra-virgin olive oil, divided

6 baby beets, preferably assorted colors (see note), trimmed and scrubbed

1 blood orange, peeled and cut into segments, plus juice of 1 orange

3 pink peppercorns, coarsely ground, or to taste

4 ounces (about 1/2 cup) goat cheese, softened, plus more

1 ounce (about 1/4 cup) shelled roasted pistachios

1. Preheat the oven to 300°F. Pour the salt into a small baking dish and arrange the two large red beets upright in the salt. Drizzle the beets with 1 tablespoon of the olive oil. Cover with foil and roast the beets until soft and tender, about 1 hour 50 minutes. Add the baby beets to the baking dish for the last 50 minutes of cooking time. Remove the beets from the pan and set aside to cool in the refrigerator.

2. When the beets are cool enough to handle, use a paper towel to gently rub off their skins. Dice the large beets into 1/2 inch cubes, and place in a large bowl along with the orange segments; set aside. Slice the reserved beet greens into thin strips lengthwise; set aside. Cut the baby beets in half and set aside in a separate bowl.

3. To make the dressing: In a medium-size bowl, whisk together the orange juice, remaining 1 tablespoon of olive oil, and the ground pink pepper. Season with sea salt to taste. Pour over the diced beets and orange segments and let sit for 5 minutes, stirring occasionally.

4. Using an electric mixer on low speed, beat the goat cheese until smooth; set aside.

5. Using a spice grinder, blender, or food processor, pulse the pistachios into a powder.

6. To assemble the salad: Spread the goat cheese onto a small platter with the back of a spoon. With a slotted spoon, remove the beets and orange segments from the bowl, reserving the dressing, and place on top of the goat cheese. Add 1 1/2 cups of the beet greens to the reserved dressing and toss until well combined. Using tongs, remove the beet greens from the bowl, reserving the dressing, and place on top of the beets and orange segments. Place the baby beets in the bowl with the reserved dressing, tossing until well combined. Place the baby beets on top and drizzle the salad with the remaining dressing. Garnish with the pistachio powder and additional crumbled goat cheese, if desired, and orange juice, if desired. Serve.

Notes:

Using an assortment of different colored baby beets will make this salad more vibrant.

Stemmed Swiss chard is a good substitute for beet greens.

Wash the beet greens in a sink filled with cold water.

Terrain Westport Garden Cafe

CAFÉMANTIC

Sensing that every college town needs a coffee shop/gathering space, Andrew Gütt, who went to Eastern State in Willimantic, decided to open Cafémantic in the heart of his college stomping grounds. Drawn to the architecture and main drag location in downtown Willimantic, Gütt created the venue to match his vision.

Cafémantic is the type of café/restaurant/espresso-wine bar that would be welcome in any town. It's cozy, welcoming, and cool—with consistently above-par, farm-sourced fare, served at breakfast, lunch, and dinner. Since opening, the café/American "small-plate" restaurant has garnered multiple "Best of" awards, recognizing the cooking chops of chef Jonathan Hudak.

Although the restaurant serves as a community hangout and café during the day, the ever-changing seasonal local menu keeps serious foodies coming back at lunch and dinner. In winter, you might find herb-roasted New York State duck breast, served with duck confit hash, braised winter greens and a bacon emulsion. In summer, you'll dip into butter-and-sugar corn soup and smoked prosciutto and cantaloupe with cape gooseberries, arugula, and wildflower honey.

As the restaurant has grown in popularity, so have its offerings. The team recently added a late-night menu and built a patio out back that overlooks the river. Outside, under twinkling lights, Cafémantic hosts twice-monthly jazz jams and even al fresco summer movies.

Curried Roasted Opo Squash

SERVES 4

The opo squash is also known as calabash, bottle gourd, Italian edible gourd, or long melon. It has a very mild flavor similar to that of zucchini. If you cannot find opo squash, you can substitute zucchini. Serve alone or over rice. A lovely aromatic dish that pairs nicely with rice.

2 tablespoons extra-virgin olive oil

4 cups opo or zucchini squash, unpeeled, large seeds removed and cut into 1-inch cubes (about 18 ounces)

2 tablespoons minced fresh ginger, or to taste

1 tablespoon minced fresh lemongrass (lower bulbous portion of the stem only)

2 tablespoons minced garlic (about 8 peeled cloves)

1/4 cup minced shallot (2 bulbs)

1 hot pepper, such as habanero or jalapeño, stemmed, seeded, and finely chopped

2 tablespoons green curry paste

2 cups unsweetened coconut milk

Juice of 1/2 lime

1 tablespoon chopped fresh cilantro

2 scallions, thinly sliced

Salt and freshly ground black pepper

1. Heat the oil in a large, heavy saucepan over medium-high heat. Add the squash and cook, stirring frequently, until the squash is soft, about 15 minutes. Add the ginger, lemongrass, garlic, shallot, and hot pepper and cook, stirring constantly, for 1 minute.

2. Stir in the curry paste and coconut milk and simmer until the liquid has slightly reduced and thickened, about 15 minutes. Stir in the lime juice, cilantro, and scallions. Adjust the seasonings with salt and pepper to taste.

Cafémantic

CASEUS FROMAGERIE BISTRO

Yale students, professors, and New Haven neighbors all sing the praises of Caseus Fromagerie Bistro, a small local cheese shop and bistro/bar that strives to cook honest food highlighting the efforts that farmers and artisans put into the ingredients. Owner Jason Sobocinski, who wrote the *Caseus Fromagerie Bistro Cookbook* and hosts *The Big Cheese* on the Cooking Channel, believes in sustainability of both the environment and of his community. He says, "We give back at every opportunity we can, to better the lives of our friends and family who are our valued customers."

At the red-brick bistro, an award-winning gastropub, cheese shop, and foodie hangout in the heart of downtown New Haven, "Cheese is, of course, a major focus, but more so food in general," Sobocinski notes,

"with a story that can be told, so that when dining at Caseus, you leave with both a full stomach and your mind filled with a taste of a place and all that went into a dish."

Chef John Naughright puts a little local love into every creation. A recent lunch special tells the story: local pan-roasted Rohan duck sliced over beluga lentils, dried apricots, macadamia nuts, topped with cheese and finished with pickled cherry vinaigrette and greens.

Devotees also flock to the Caseus Cheese Truck, a mobile kitchen that drives the streets of New Haven, selling killer grilled cheese sandwiches, tomato soup, salads, and more.

Roasted Potatoes
with Raclette Cheese

SERVES 6

"Raclette is the name of the cheese, the name of the dish, and the name of the piece of equipment that is used traditionally to melt the cheese right off the wheel. This recipe is a way to melt your cheese with just your oven. Be sure to ask about the different types of Raclette your local cheese shop might carry. At the Caseus cheese shop, we often have French Raclette, Swiss Raclette, and a version from Vermont called Reading Raclette. All are exceptional for this recipe."
—Jason Sobocinski

Serve with a green salad.

3 pounds fingerling potatoes, unpeeled

4 1/2 ounces (1/2 cup plus 2 tablespoons) rendered duck fat (see note)

Kosher salt and freshly ground black pepper

8 ounces Raclette cheese, cut into 1/8-inch-thick square slices

6 slices Speck, prosciutto, or serrano ham, thinly sliced and chopped

6 tablespoons thinly sliced sour cornichon pickles (sliced into rounds)

6 tablespoons finely chopped red onion

Coarse-grain or Dijon mustard

1. Preheat the oven to 400°F. Lightly oil a 9 x 13-inch baking dish or a large rimmed baking sheet and set aside.

2. Place the potatoes in a large bowl. Add the duck fat and salt and pepper to taste, and toss to combine, making sure to coat all the potatoes.

3. Spread the potatoes into the prepared baking dish. Roast, stirring every 15 minutes, until the potatoes are fork-tender and golden brown, about 55 minutes. When cool enough to handle, cut the potatoes in half lengthwise. Divide the potatoes, cut side up, evenly among six 9-ounce cast-iron oval serving dishes. Arrange the cheese evenly over the potatoes in a single layer.

4. Preheat the broiler. Broil until the cheese has melted, about 3 minutes. Season with salt and pepper to taste. Garnish with the Speck, cornichons, and onion. Serve with the mustard on the side.

Note: In a pinch, you can substitute bacon fat for the duck fat.

Caseus Fromagerie Bistro

FARMING 101

Farming 101 is a small farm and homestead run by Jennifer and Trout Gaskins in Southwest Hills region of Connecticut in an area once known as the Western Uplands. The farm has been growing fresh produce for Fairfield County since 2008, and became certified organic in 2010.

The fields, ringed with traditional stone walls, have been farmed almost continuously since the 1700s. The barns and the Gaskins' home were built roughly 150 years ago. Still a 75-acre farm in the 1950s, the land was finally subdivided in the 1980s, and the Gaskins took possession of the original homestead in 2007.

As a small-scale, owner-producer farm, Farming 101's summer product selection includes 40-plus varieties of certified organic heirloom tomatoes, okra, garlic, fresh herbs, and vibrant fresh flower bouquets. In the cooler months, it produces tasty Asian and traditional salad greens, as well as other tempting surprises in its seasonal high tunnel (unheated greenhouse). Its flock of heritage Barred Rock and Buff Orpington hens is truly cage-free and free-range, and provides fresh eggs all year long.

In addition to produce, the Gaskins proudly offer lamb that is born and hand-raised on the farm and is currently featured in restaurants throughout Fairfield County, as well as used by private local chefs and caterers. You can also find their products at the Greenwich Farmers' Market in season.

Green Tomato Fritters

MAKES ABOUT 26 FRITTERS

1 tablespoon olive oil

1/2 cup cored, seeded, and finely chopped red
  bell pepper (about 1/2 large pepper)

1/3 cup finely chopped sweet onion, such as
  Vidalia (about 1/3 large onion)

2 cups cored, seeded, and finely chopped
  green tomato

1/3 cup crumbled feta cheese (about
  2 3/8 ounces)

1/4 cup corn flour

1/4 cup all-purpose flour

1/2 teaspoon baking powder

1/2 teaspoon kosher salt

1 large egg, lightly beaten

1 cup panko bread crumbs

1/4 teaspoon cayenne pepper

3 cups oil, such as peanut or grapeseed

1. Line a baking sheet with parchment paper or spray with nonstick cooking spray; set aside.

2. Heat the oil in a small sauté pan over medium-high heat. Add the bell pepper and onion and cook, stirring often, until soft and translucent, about 5 minutes. Transfer to a medium-size bowl; set aside to cool. Add the tomato and cheese, stirring until well combined. Sprinkle the vegetable mixture with the flours, baking powder, and salt, stirring until fully incorporated. Add the egg and stir gently until just combined.

3. Mix the bread crumbs and cayenne in a small bowl.

4. Scoop 1 1/2 tablespoons of the vegetable mixture and form into a ball. Roll the ball into the bread crumb mixture and place on the prepared baking sheet. Repeat with the remaining balls. Freeze the fritters for 1 hour.

5. Fill a 9-inch-diameter, deep, heavy-bottomed pot with the oil. Heat the oil to 350°F. Working in batches, fry the fritters until golden brown, turning occasionally to brown on all sides, 2 to 3 minutes. Using a slotted spoon, remove the fritters and drain on paper towels. Serve immediately.

Farming 101

WALDINGFIELD FARM

Mr. C. B. Smith, a New York lawyer, purchased Waldingfield Farm at the beginning of the last century; it was for many years a working dairy farm, as well as a summer retreat for the family. But the onset of World War II and the declining dairy industry in New England put an end to the farm's milking operation. For the next 50 years, the farmland was worked by neighboring farmers.

In 1990, Daniel Horan, great-grandson of C. B. Smith, began the process of reclaiming Waldingfield as a working farm—but with a difference. Waldingfield was to farm organic vegetables. Dan started on a small, half-acre plot and recruited his younger brothers, twins Quincy and Patrick, to help with the daily work. Since then, Waldingfield has been a family affair.

Waldingfield Farm is one of the largest certified organic operations in Connecticut (Baystate Organic Certifiers). The team cultivates roughly 20 to 25 acres and runs an active CSA program. Patrick says, "The CSA model, we believe, is the wave of the future for smaller farms like ours." The farm also serves numerous top Litchfield County restaurant clients, participates in seven farmers' markets (one winter, five summer), distributes via wholesale, and runs a roadside stand.

Quincy and Patrick, along with operations manager Jed Borken, now manage the daily workings of the farm, while Dan and the Horan parents sit on the farm board and help with strategy and land management. Patrick says, "All of us at the farm thank our supporters for believing in the goals of organic farming. It remains our passion, and we will work as hard as we can to bring the highest quality produce to our customers. See you in the fields!"

Grilled Swiss Chard Roll-ups

MAKES 14 ROLL-UPS

A tasty summer treat!

14 large fresh Swiss chard leaves (from 2 to 3 bunches)

8 ounces cheese, such as smoked mozzarella, fresh mozzarella, or goat, cut into 1/4-inch cubes

1/2 cup dried fruit, such as apricots, golden raisins, or dates, cut into 1/4-inch pieces

3 tablespoons chopped toasted walnuts or pine nuts

3 tablespoons extra-virgin olive oil, plus more for brushing

1. Using a sharp knife, remove the thick stem from the center of each chard leaf, reserving stems for another dish, such as a stir-fry or quiche. Create a row of cheese—about 1 to 1 1/2 tablespoons of it (depending on the leaf size)—on the end of the widest part of each leaf, leaving a 1-inch border. Add 1 to 3 teaspoons of dried fruit (depending on the leaf size) and 1/2 to 1 teaspoon of walnuts (depending on the leaf size) on top of the cheese row.

2. Working one at a time, fold up the bottom of each leaf over the filling and roll into a tight cylinder, folding in the sides as you go. Using a toothpick, spear each roll-up to keep it closed.

3. Heat the oil in a large skillet over medium-high heat or heat a grill to medium-high. Brush each roll-up with olive oil and cook, seam side down first, constantly turning them, for about 4 minutes, or until the cheese has begun to soften and the Swiss chard is tender.

Waldingfield Farm

Fried Green Tomatoes with Hot and Sweet Aioli

MAKES ABOUT 18 TOMATOES; SERVES 4 AS AN APPETIZER OR SIDE DISH

Hot and Sweet Aioli (makes about 1 cup)

1 large egg yolk

3/4 cup extra-virgin olive oil

2 tablespoons light brown sugar

1 teaspoon hot sauce, such as sriracha

2 tablespoons fresh lemon juice

Kosher salt and freshly ground black pepper

Fried Green Tomatoes

2 large eggs, lightly beaten

2 tablespoons milk

1 cup all-purpose flour or cornmeal

1 teaspoon celery salt

1 teaspoon ground ginger

1 teaspoon dry mustard

Kosher salt and freshly ground black pepper

3 pounds firm green tomatoes (about 6 tomatoes), cut crosswise into 1/3-inch slices

4 cups vegetable oil

1. To make the aioli: Place the egg yolk in a small bowl. While whisking constantly, add the oil in a slow, steady stream. Whisk in the brown sugar and hot sauce until well combined. Whisk in the lemon juice, and salt and pepper to taste. Place in the refrigerator.

2. Place the eggs and milk in a small bowl and whisk until well combined; set aside. In a separate small bowl, stir together the flour, celery salt, ginger, mustard, and salt and pepper; set aside.

3. Place the tomatoes in a single layer on two parchment-lined baking sheets.

4. Fill a 5 1/2-quart, heavy-bottomed pot with about 1 inch of oil. Heat the oil to 350°F. Working in batches of four or five tomatoes at a time, dredge the tomatoes first in the egg mixture, then the flour mixture, making sure they are well coated. With tongs, gently drop into the hot oil and cook until golden brown on both sides, about 2 minutes. Using a slotted spoon, remove the tomatoes and drain on paper towels. Season with salt and pepper to taste. Serve with the aioli at once.

Waldingfield Farm

FAT CAT PIE CO.

Celebrating more than a decade in Norwalk, Fat Cat Pie Co. is a unique community-based wine pub featuring small-production wine, thin-crust organic pizza, generous organic salads, artisanal cheese and charcuterie, house-made desserts, and a true espresso bar.

Housed in the historic Twin City Building, a former theater, Fat Cat was founded by brothers Mark and Anthony Ancona and their father, Stephen, as a familial wine bar in which to showcase their own imports. Almost immediately upon introducing their thin-crust pies, Fat Cat Pie became a cult classic. These days, Tony and Suzanne Ancona manage the day-to-day operations, while Mark continues to develop the ever-expanding wine portfolio, featuring 300-plus bottles on the main wine list, with over 15 verticals and more than 30 wines by the glass. Michael Pelletier (wine "searcher") and Robert Herlihy (chef) complete the culinary/vinous team, joined in spirit via a long history of friendship, food, and wine.

Fat Cat's menu is simple —thin-crust pies, tasty salads cobbled together from the best of what is delivered that day from local farms, artisanal cheeses/charcuterie, and killer desserts. Before it was fashionable, Fat Cat raised the bar, relying on organic and local ingredients and partnerships with authentic producers and purveyors of food and drink.

Several local farms provide most of the produce for Fat Cat's vegetarian-focused menu and inspiration. In the spring of 2012, the Fat Cat crew, under the guidance of in-house gardener David Tullio, planted 10 garden plots at historic Fodor Farm (see sidebar below) in Norwalk. Since that first season, the Fat Cat garden has flourished, as has the alliance between Fat Cat and Fodor Farm in their efforts to continue the development and preservation of the farm and its buildings, both new and historic.

FODOR FARM

On the edge of an urban/suburban section of Norwalk, Fodor Farm comes as a welcome surprise. When you drive up to the historic, 200-year-old farm property, which the city acquired with the help of a state open-space grant in 1997, you'll notice that it's not only the beehives that are buzzing with action. On the rambling, 9-acre plot, you see families tending their individual garden plots in the 300-plot community garden, moms strolling the apple orchard and picnicking with kids under the pavilion, gardeners from Norwalk's Fat Cat Pies tending their restaurant garden plots, and various workers tinkering in the greenhouses and toolsheds, and on the new tree farm.

The revival of the farm was the brainchild of Mike Mocciae, director of Norwalk Recreation and Parks, who envisioned a renaissance that would open the space up to town organizations and to the public.

At the historic homestead, tradesmen are faithfully reconstructing both the caretaker's quarters and the main house. These will add to the historic enrichment and public service as an education center and a space for Norwalk-based nonprofit organizations. A caretaker will live in one portion.

Near the house, a newly constructed post-and-beam "barn" is being used for pottery making, cooking, events, and classes.

The restoration of this agrarian treasure is one of the city's proudest accomplishments.

Roasted Potato and Heirloom Tomato Tower

SERVES 4

"The genesis of this late summer love salad came from our close relationship with Riverbank Organic Farms in Roxbury and our own Norwalk Fodor Farm community garden initiative. The key is the supreme quality of the raw materials used, a mantra that resonates through the Fat Cat Pie Co. ethos, whether it be vegetables, artisanal cheese, or our signature wines. The salad has a bit of a Greek feel, with the addition of a good feta and a touch of fresh oregano and thyme."
—Suzanne Ancona

Vinaigrette

3 tablespoons extra-virgin olive oil

1 1/2 tablespoons white wine vinegar

1 garlic clove, crushed

1/2 teaspoon kosher salt

1 teaspoon freshly ground black pepper

1 tablespoon minced mixed fresh herbs, such as thyme, oregano, or rosemary

Roasted Vegetables

8 to 10 fingerling potatoes, cut into batons 1 inch wide or halved, depending on the size

2 slices fennel, chopped (about 1/2 cup)

1 shallot or small onion, finely chopped

1 garlic clove, minced

1/4 cup fresh oregano leaves, coarsely chopped

2 tablespoons fresh thyme leaves, coarsely chopped

3 tablespoons extra-virgin olive oil

Salt and freshly ground black pepper

1 head coarsely chopped red leaf lettuce

2 large heirloom tomatoes, cut horizontally into 1/2-inch-thick slices, tough core removed

1 cup coarsely grated feta cheese

1 cup Kalamata olives, pitted and coarsely chopped

1 cucumber, such as Burpless, thinly sliced

1. To make the vinaigrette: In a small bowl, whisk all the ingredients together. Set aside for at least 1 hour.

2. Preheat the oven to 350°F. Lightly oil a 9 x 13-inch baking dish and set aside.

3. To make the roasted vegetables: Place the potatoes, fennel, shallot, garlic, oregano, and thyme in a large bowl. Drizzle the oil over the vegetables and toss to combine, making sure to coat all the vegetables well. Spread the vegetable mixture in the prepared baking dish. Season with salt and pepper to taste. Roast, stirring every 15 minutes, until the vegetables are fork-tender and golden brown, about 50 minutes.

4. To make the salad: Tosss lettuce with the vinaigrette until well coated.

5. To assemble: Place about 1/2 cup of lettuce in the center of each plate. Begin the tower with a slice of tomato and season with salt. Top with the roasted vegetable mixture. Gently press and repeat with a second layer.

6. Top with the cheese and olives so they spill down the sides of the tower. Garnish with cucumber slices and serve at once.

Fat Cat Pie Co.

SUB EDGE FARM

Sub Edge Farm comprises 289 acres in the heart of the Farmington River Valley. The farm dates back 20,000 years, to when the last glaciers retreated from Connecticut, leaving behind a rich, sandy, and loamy soil, ideal for growing vegetables.

The Tunxis Native Americans once farmed the nearby riverbanks; then, in postcolonial times, the Tillotson family raised dairy cattle on the property. Next came female architect and teacher Theodate Pope Riddle, who named the farm "Sub Edge" and used it to teach agriculture to students at her Avon Old Farms School.

For many years, the farm, which straddles Farmington and Avon, was known as Fisher Farm. In 2002, the towns jointly purchased it from the Fisher family, agreeing to preserve it as farmland in perpetuity. The 27 acres that include the farmhouse, barn, and other buildings reside in Farmington, while 317 acres that are used as open space and fields for crops, hay and grazing are in Avon.

In 2013, Isabelle and Rodger Phillips signed on to lease the property. Isabelle grew up in a small farm town in rural Quebec, and Rodger in suburban Connecticut. They fell in love with farming while working on a small organic farm and, after almost a decade of toiling for others, they are now raising their four kids on their own farm—and sharing their passion for foods raised the old-fashioned way.

Rodger recalls, "Our family had been searching for a piece of land to start a community supported agriculture [CSA] farm on for five years. We looked at hundreds of properties, and were so happy to land in a spot so close to our friends and family."

Sub Edge is a sustainable community farm rooted in tradition, selling heirloom vegetables, herbs, and flowers mainly through CSA shares and a farm market. Visitors will find chicks hatching, cows and sheep grazing, and the four Phillips kids frolicking. Rodger notes, "We love to be able to talk to the community about our belief in the importance of family farm raised, healthy, local food. We also work hard to foster responsible stewardship of the land by using exclusively organic methods."

Old South Collard Greens with Pot Likker (a.k.a. "Mess o' Greens")

SERVES 4 TO 6

Collards are high in vitamins A, B$_6$, C, E, and (especially) K. High in fiber and low in fat, collards also provide riboflavin, calcium, iron, manganese, thiamine, niacin, magnesium, phosphorus, and potassium. That's all good, we like collards because they are so darned tasty.

Serve with corn bread, biscuits, or crusty bread on the side, if desired.

4 bunches collard greens, thoroughly washed, tough stems and ribs removed, and cut or torn into wide 1-inch strips (about 2 pounds)

1 1/2 pounds smoked turkey parts, such as legs or wings (see notes)

1 cube vegetable bouillon

1 large tomato, coarsely chopped

1 fresh bay leaf

1 1/2 teaspoons red pepper flakes, or to taste

1/4 cup cider vinegar, or as needed

4 to 5 tablespoons honey

1 white onion, finely chopped

2 tablespoons olive oil

2 large garlic cloves, minced

Kosher salt and freshly ground black pepper

1. Fill an 8-quart pot with 1 inch of water and bring to a simmer over medium heat. Add the collards and steam, covered, until the greens are just wilted, about 5 minutes. Using a slotted spoon, remove the greens and set aside.

2. Add 4 cups of water and the turkey, bouillon cube, tomato, bay leaf, red pepper flakes, vinegar, and honey to the steaming liquid. Bring to a boil over medium-high heat, then lower the heat to a simmer.

3. Meanwhile, heat the olive oil in a large sauté pan over medium heat. Add the onion and cook, stirring occasionally, until soft and translucent, about 10 minutes. Add the garlic and cook until fragrant, about 1 minute. Add the greens and season with salt and pepper to taste.

4. Add the collard mixture to the pot with the turkey, cover, and simmer until the turkey and greens are tender, stirring occasionally, about 45 minutes. If the pot becomes too dry, add water as needed to keep the greens just covered.

5. Using tongs, remove the turkey. When cool enough to handle, about 20 minutes, pull off and shred or dice any meat attached to the bones. Discard the skin and bones. Stir the meat into the greens until well combined. Adjust the seasonings with vinegar, additional honey, if desired, and salt and pepper to taste. Using a slotted spoon, transfer the collard greens, meat, and some of the juice to a bowl.

Notes:

For a vegetarian version, substitute 2 teaspoons of smoked paprika for the turkey.

Feel free to substitute a ham bone or ham hocks for the smoked turkey parts.

Kelley Lanahan for Sub Edge Farm

RED BEE HONEY

Marina Marchese is changing the way people taste and think about honey. The founder and visionary behind Red Bee Honey, Marina visited a neighbor's apiary on a trip to Italy during her previous career as an international designer. Her first taste of fresh honey from the beehive changed the course of her life. She quit her job, built a beehive, and acquired some Italian honeybees to become a beekeeper. It was on a visit to Montalcino, Italy, "la citta del miele," that Marina became passionate about single-origin honeys. Compelled by the philosophy of terroir and the diverse flavor profiles of honey determined by the type of nectar gathered by the honeybees, Marina launched a collection of single-origin crafted honeys under the Red Bee brand. In

2013, Marchese coauthored *The Honey Connoisseur* with Kim Flottum, editor of *Bee Culture* magazine. Her internationally best-selling memoir, *Honeybee Lessons from an Accidental Beekeeper*, chronicles Marina's journey into beekeeping, plus everything you ever wanted to know about honeybees.

Marina studied the sensory analysis of tasting honey in Guspini, Italy, and honey judging at the UGA and the American Apitherapy Society. She is the founder of the American Honey Tasting Society, created to protect the quality and character of this noble food and educate through her signature Honey Tasting Laboratory Workshops. Marina's Red Bee Honey was honored with a Snail of Approval from Slow Food Metro North.

RIVERBANK FARM

Since colonial times, Riverbank Farm has passed through the hands of four different families that raised crops and milked cows. Currently, Riverbank grows a diversity of certified organic vegetables, cut flowers, and hay on its picturesque 45 riverside acres, including three large greenhouses (great for propagation and for tomatoes). Nourished by the fertile bottomland soil of the Shepaug River, the farm uses no herbicides, synthetic fertilizers, or synthetic pesticides.

David Blyn moved to the Roxbury farm in 1989 in hopes of running a carpentry business. He was drawn to the landscape and river bordering the farm. As David worked on the barn, he also planted a half-acre of vegetables, which increased each year, until David began farming full-time in 1991. He continued to farm solo, jumping from tractor to tractor, as he managed his small, diversified operation with old equipment and farm machinery.

In the summer of 1996, while delivering produce on Long Island, David met Laura. She had come east after finishing sustainable agriculture studies in Santa Cruz, California. Their love for farming and each other blossomed. Through hail storms, deer damage, late work nights, frosts, unpredictable weather, and bug and weed outbreaks, they built a resilient farming operation, and a family with three young farm gals, daughters Lily, Alice, and Stella.

Riverbank's produce is sold at farmers' markets from Greenwich to New Haven, natural food stores, and local restaurants. The Blyns make hay on the farm and adjoining farms. They also have a small apple orchard and keep bees, chickens, and goats. They also turn out an array of seasonal, vegetarian-prepared soups, salads, and sauces, and canned goods (amazing pickles!).

They pay it forward through an apprentice program, in which four to five apprentices per year learn about managing a successful market farm, including propagation, cultivation, record keeping, farm management, harvesting, and marketing. Laura says, "Here are two of our crews' favorite recipes. They are both simple and delicious!"

Garlic-Cilantro Slaw

SERVES 3 TO 4

Unlike a traditional ho-hum mayonnaise slaw, this spicy, zippy slaw literally wakes up your taste buds—thanks to the addition of chiles, ginger, garlic, and lime juice. It makes a crunchy and welcome addition to almost any meal.

3 to 4 cups finely shredded cabbage, such as napa, savoy, or red (about 13 ounces)

4 Purplette onions (see note), or 1 small red onion, or 1 bunch scallions, thinly sliced

1/4 cup roasted, salted peanuts or almonds

3 garlic scapes or 2 large garlic cloves, coarsely chopped

3 cups fresh cilantro, coarsely chopped

2 medium-size fresh green chiles, such as Hatch or Anaheim, stemmed, seeded, and coarsely chopped

1 (1-inch) piece fresh ginger, peeled and coarsely chopped

1 teaspoon kosher salt

1 tablespoon pure maple syrup

5 tablespoons fresh lime juice

1/4 cup extra-virgin olive oil

1. In a large bowl, combine the cabbage and half of the Purplette onions.

2. Place the nuts in a food processor and pulse until coarsely chopped. Add the remaining ingredients and pulse until just smooth with a slight texture. Adjust the seasonings with salt and pepper to taste. Drizzle over the cabbage mixture and toss to coat. Cover, and refrigerate for 30 minutes before serving.

Note: Purplette onions are small, purple-red skinned bulbs with a mild flavor.

Riverbank Farm

Sautéed Delicata Squash with Kale, Raspberry Balsamic Vinegar, and Toasted Walnuts

SERVES 4

This is a great reason to love fall vegetables. Enjoy!

2 medium-size unpeeled delicata squash

1 tablespoon extra-virgin olive oil

1 small onion, such as Vidalia, minced

1 medium-size garlic clove, minced

1 teaspoon chopped fresh rosemary leaves

3/4 cup low-sodium chicken stock

1 1/2 teaspoons raspberry balsamic vinegar

Kosher salt

5 medium-size kale leaves, such as Red Russian, stemmed and cut into thin strips

Freshly ground black pepper

2 tablespoons toasted chopped walnuts

1. To prepare the squash: Using a sharp knife, slice off both ends and discard. Cut the squash in half lengthwise. Using a spoon, remove and discard the seeds and strings. Cut each piece of squash in half lengthwise once more, then crosswise into 1/2-inch-wide slices.

2. In a large skillet, heat the oil over medium heat. Add the onion and cook, stirring occasionally, until soft and translucent, about 6 minutes. Add the garlic and cook until fragrant, about 1 minute. Add the squash and rosemary. Stir in the stock, vinegar, and 1 teaspoon of salt.

3. Cook, covered, stirring occasionally, over medium heat, until the squash is fork-tender, 8 to 10 minutes. Add the kale and cook until wilted, about 1 minute. Adjust the seasonings with vinegar, if desired, and salt and pepper to taste. Garnish with the walnuts and serve at once.

Riverbank Farm

THE SCHOOLHOUSE AT CANNONDALE

If you can find The Schoolhouse, you're in for a treat (hint: head north on Rte. 33 in Wilton and follow signs for Cannondale Train Station to the quaint little restaurant housed in a former schoolhouse). Classically trained chef-owner Tim LaBant and his wife, Julie, along with chef de cuisine Nick Verdisco and pastry chef Jessie Fila are favorites on the Fairfield County farm-to-table scene, sweeping numerous awards, including Best Special Occasion Restaurant and Best Chef Runner Up (*Westport Magazine*), Best of New England (*New England Magazine*), and Best Pastry Chef (*Connecticut Magazine*). But they're perhaps most proud of the OpenTable Awards, winning Best Overall, Best Food, Best Service, Best Ambiance, Fit for Foodies, and so on, as one of the Top 50 American Restaurants in the US and Top 10 in the Tri-State, including Manhattan.

One customer opined, "Hands-down the best chef in Connecticut and a top contender in New York. Beautiful presentation, freshest hyper-local ingredients and best service. Oh, and a well-chosen drink list."

The Schoolhouse has teamed up with nearby Millstone Farm (page 124) for a perennially sold-out Farm-to-Fork series, and makes sourcing from sustainable Connecticut farms a priority, whether in the restaurant or at offsite catering gigs.

The selections are elegant and artistic, and, as such are not inexpensive. That said, the Thursday prix fixe menu is great value. On it, you'll find four show-stopping courses, such as buffalo hanger steak with confit potatoes, broccoli rabe, and hen-of-the-woods (maitake) mushrooms, or Millstone Farm's heritage pork, a half-black, half-Tamworth breed that is simply some of the best pork you'll ever taste.

On Wednesdays, they've rolled out a weekly vegetarian menu that is so good that you won't miss the meat.

Fennel-Parmesan Fritters with Greens in Buttermilk-Bacon Dressing

SERVES 8

Fennel has become more popular than ever, and this is an easy, yet interesting, recipe you can use to incorporate this versatile vegetable into your repertoire and wow your friends. Best served family style.

Dressing (makes about 1 1/3 cups)

3 slices thick-cut bacon (4 ounces), cut into 1/4-inch-thick pieces

1/2 cup buttermilk, well shaken

1/2 cup mayonnaise

1 medium-size garlic clove, minced and mashed to a paste with a pinch of salt

1 small scallion, trimmed and finely chopped

Kosher salt and freshly ground black pepper

Fritters (makes about 25)

1 teaspoon kosher salt, plus more as needed

1 pound fennel bulbs, stalks and fronds removed, bulbs halved and cored

1 (6-inch-long) piece of baguette, cut into 1-inch pieces

2 ounces Parmigiano-Reggiano cheese, finely shredded (about 1 cup)

4 large eggs, lightly beaten

2 garlic cloves, finely chopped

1/4 teaspoon freshly ground black pepper, plus more as needed

2 tablespoons olive oil for frying each batch of fritters, or as needed

Greens

8 ounces mixed greens (8 cups)

1. To make the dressing: In a heavy 10-inch skillet, cook the bacon over medium heat, stirring occasionally, until crisp, about 8 minutes. Using a slotted spoon, transfer the bacon to a paper towel–lined plate to drain. Coarsely chop the bacon and set aside.

2. In a medium-size bowl, whisk together the buttermilk, mayonnaise, garlic, scallion, 1/2 teaspoon of salt and 1/2 teaspoon of pepper. Fold in the bacon. Cover and chill in the refrigerator for at least 1 hour and up to 8 hours.

3. To make the fritters: Bring 5 cups of water to a boil in a 3-quart saucepan. Add the teaspoon of salt. Using the large holes of a box grater, or the shredding blade on a food processor, coarsely grate the fennel (about 3 cups grated fennel). Add the fennel to the boiling water and cook for 2 minutes. Drain in a fine-mesh strainer and rinse under cold running water until completely cool. Using a large spoon, press out as much water as possible from the fennel while in the strainer, and then transfer to a paper towel–lined plate. Place another paper towel over the fennel and press to remove more excess water.

4. Place the bread in a food processor and process until coarse crumbs form (about 2 cups). Transfer the crumbs to a large bowl. Add the fennel, cheese, eggs, garlic, and pepper. Mix gently to combine.

5. Heat the oil in a 10-inch cast-iron or nonstick skillet over medium heat until shimmering. Drop a heaping tablespoonful of the batter into the oil. Press down lightly onto each fritter to form a 2-inch patty. Cook the fritters in batches, five per batch, until golden and crisp, 2 to 3 minutes per side. Transfer to a paper towel–lined plate to drain briefly.

6. To assemble: Arrange the greens on six serving plates. Place three fritters over each and drizzle with some of the dressing. Serve immediately with the remaining dressing on the side.

The Schoolhouse at Cannondale

AMBLER FARM

Ambler Farm is a 200-year-old working farm dedicated to celebrating the community's agrarian traditions through hands-on learning programs, sustainable agriculture, responsible land stewardship, and historic preservation.

When you roam the 18 acres of organic vegetable and flower gardens, meadows, seasonal farm stand, live farm animals, and the Raymond-Ambler Farmhouse, you will see a true community hub.

Jonathan Kirschner is the farm's director of agriculture and manages the organic garden and greenhouse and harvesting produce for the weekly seasonal farm stand, Wilton Farmers' Market, and local restaurants. Jonathan also helps develop agricultural-related programs with

Kevin Meehan, a master science teacher, who is responsible for planting the seeds for future generations of farmers. "Mr. Meehan," as the kids call him, has created signature programs, including apprentice programs, Maple Syrup Tap-a-Tree for families, Adventures at the Farm (summer program), and Fright Night. He also built and maintains the educational gardens with the assistance of the Ambler apprentices.

On any given day, you'll find apprentices cleaning out the chicken coop, whacking weeds, harvesting vegetables, picking (and eating) berries, and driving the tractor. In many ways, the apprentices run the gardens, and through real responsibilities, develop a lifelong connection to the land.

BARCELONA WINE BAR & RESTAURANT

If you haven't been to Barcelona, you've been missing the fiesta. Tasty tapas, a sexy bar scene and festive tunes have been hallmarks of Barcelona Wine Bar & Restaurant since 1996, when Andy Pforzheimer and Sasa Mahr-Batuz took South Norwalk by storm. Today, Barcelona is the largest Spanish restaurant group in America, with six locations in Connecticut: Fairfield, Greenwich, New Haven, South Norwalk, Stamford, and West Hartford, as well as venues in Atlanta, Georgia; Brookline, Massachusetts; and Washington, DC.

After reveling in the cuisine and culture of Spain for years, Sasa and Andy decided to re-create the fantastic flavors, hip design, and the easygoing lifestyle that they had so enjoyed. At Barcelona, star chefs from top kitchens in America and Europe turn out tapas both simple and elegant, specials using the finest seasonal picks, and specialties from Spain and the Mediterranean. The flavors are bold and the ingredients—including produce and meats sourced from Wilton farmer and forager Farah Masani—speak for themselves.

Barcelona was ahead of the curve in farm sourcing, planting gardens on the hills outside its Fairfield venue, and taking the staff on "field" trips to visit the farms where the restaurant's vegetables are grown. On a recent outing, Easton farmer Patti Popp walked 30-plus Barcelona employees—servers, chefs, bartenders, sous chefs, and managers—through fields of lettuce and broccoli that was going to seed due to high temps. Visiting the farm enhances the farmer-chef connection, allowing chefs to see firsthand why a vegetable might not be available due to excessive heat, rain, pests, or other variables.

Roasted Carrots al Andaluz

SERVES 3 TO 4 AS A MAIN DISH OR 5 AS A SIDE

This is a very pretty dish with lots of color and flavors, from the tart, slightly bitter tasting olives to the mildly sweet roasted carrots. The chef notes, "We have done this dish very successfully with carrots from Farah's Farm in Wilton and Cherry Grove Farm in Newtown."

Carrots

3 pounds baby to midsize carrots, including greens (the carrots should be 5 inches long), tops trimmed to 1 inch, peeled

2 tablespoons extra-virgin olive oil

3 tablespoons fresh thyme leaves

3 tablespoons fresh rosemary leaves

Kosher salt and freshly ground black pepper

Garlic

1/4 cup extra-virgin olive oil, divided

2 tablespoons thinly sliced garlic

1 cup Manzanilla olives, pitted and quartered, 1/4 cup of the juice reserved

1/2 cup Medjool dates, pitted and cut to the same size as the olives

1 cup toasted almonds, coarsely chopped, divided

Kosher salt and freshly ground black pepper

1 cup fresh flat-leaf parsley, leaves removed and stems discarded

1. To make the carrots: Preheat the oven to 425°F. Place the carrots, oil, thyme, and rosemary in a large bowl. Season with salt and pepper to taste and toss to combine, making sure to coat all the carrots well.

2. Spread the carrots on a baking sheet. Roast, stirring occasionally, until the carrots are browned and just fork-tender, about 30 minutes.

3. To make the garlic: In a large sauté pan, heat 3 tablespoons of the olive oil over medium-low heat. Add the garlic and cook, stirring often, until fragrant and just golden brown, about 3 minutes. Add the carrots and olives and cook until the carrots are heated through, about 3 minutes. Add the dates and cook until just heated through, about 2 minutes. Add the reserved olive juice and allow to reduce until most of the juice has evaporated, about 3 minutes.

4. Remove from the heat and fold in 1/2 cup of the almonds. Adjust the seasonings with salt and pepper to taste.

5. Stir in the parsley and the remaining 1 tablespoon of oil. Arrange on a platter and sprinkle the remaining 1/2 cup of almonds over the top. Serve at once.

Chef Adam Halberg, Barcelona Restaurant

FARAH'S FARM

Farah Masani, a local homesteader and food forager in Wilton, is a long way from home. Growing up in Bombay, she enjoyed escaping the city to spend weekends at her family's countryside properties.

Along the way, Farah grew wheat and rice, worked side alongside goat herders in the Himalayas, learned canal and terrace farming, and water management. In the '90s, she moved to Texas and earned degrees in economics, social work, and therapy, and rolled out farm-based curriculums and small workable gardens into her jobs at schools in Vermont and New Hampshire.

Eventually, Farah moved to Connecticut with the goal of full-time farming. She began at a Wilton farm, and four years later, branched off on her own.

Farah is master juggler. She runs Farah's Farm, a three-acre homestead that teems with heirloom ducks, chickens, and bees, and also oversees a few local satellite farms. For her day job, Farah is chief food purchaser for Barteca (owner of Bar Taco and Barcelona restaurants). This job suits her—young, outgoing, and intrepid, Farah has established relationships with local farmers and restaurateurs, and sources from local farms as much as possible. She also makes frequent jaunts to Spain, building relationships with the farmers who provide the restaurants' olive oil, cheeses, and meats.

"One of the great things about this job is that we do a lot of volume, so we can ask a farmer to plant an entire field of fingerlings or purple potatoes. It's rewarding to be a part of this movement of making high-quality food affordable to the public, and I love it while respecting the land."

BELTANE FARM

Paul Trubey, the owner of Beltane Farm, has been making goat milk cheeses since the spring of 1998, when he set up a commercial dairy and small cheese plant at a friend's farm in South Glastonbury. A few years later, he and his partner moved to Lebanon, where he started Beltane Farm with 12 Swiss goats. In what Trubey calls "beginner's luck," his first year's fresh chèvre won a blue ribbon from the American Cheese Society, and Trubey knew he was on to something (the chèvre is still his most popular). Today, in addition to the award-winning chèvre (plain or rolled in herbes de Provence, black pepper, dill, or chives), Beltane turns out a variety of delectable dairy products, including Greek-style yogurt, feta, ricotta, blue cheese, and several unique specialty cheeses, such as Danse de la Lune, Harvest Moon, and Vespers.

Trubey loves caring for his 100-plus goats of different breeds (Oberhasli, Nubian, LaMancha, and Saanen), which are raised on the farm and milked twice a day to supply milk for Beltane's cheeses and yogurt. The cheese is part of the offerings of various local CSAs, and is featured at many farm dinners in Connecticut. Beltane cheese is available at farmers' markets around the state, at variety of specialty markets and co-ops, and directly at the farm in certain months. Each May, Trubey opens the farm on Sundays for cheese tastings and tours, and then again in October through December each Sunday afternoon (check for hours). Beltane Farm cheese is also featured on the menus at many local restaurants.

Swiss Chard and Fresh Ricotta Cheese

SERVES 8

"At Beltane Farm, we enjoy this dish from spring to early winter, since Swiss chard has such a long growing season. We use the bacon from Ladies of Lebanon Dairy right down the dirt road from our farm and apples from Glastonbury. You can also substitute spinach and kale, if you prefer, for some seasonal variation." —Paul Trubey

4 ounces (about 4 slices) smoked bacon, roughly chopped

2 bunches Swiss chard, stems and leaves separated, stems chopped and leaves sliced into 1-inch pieces

2 tablespoons extra-virgin olive oil

1 tablespoon sherry vinegar

Sea salt and freshly ground black pepper

2/3 cup crisp red apples, cored and cut into 1/2-inch pieces

1/2 cup fresh ricotta cheese, such as Beltane's Ricotta Fresca, or to taste

3 tablespoons chopped fresh parsley or basil

1. Cook the bacon in a medium-size skillet over medium-high heat, stirring frequently, until crisp, about 5 minutes. Using a slotted spoon, transfer to paper towels to drain. Set aside.

2. Meanwhile, fill a medium-size saucepan with water and bring to a boil over medium-high heat. Fill a large bowl with ice water. Add the chard stems to the boiling water and blanch for 4 minutes. Using a slotted spoon, transfer the stems to the ice-water bath and let cool completely. Drain the stems and set aside. Heat the olive oil in a large skillet over medium heat. Add the chard leaves. Cover and cook until just wilted, stirring occasionally, about 4 minutes. Add the chard stems, vinegar, and salt and pepper to taste and continue to cook until stems are just tender, about 4 minutes. Transfer to a platter and scatter the bacon, apples, and ricotta over the top. Garnish with the parsley and serve.

Beltane Farm

PACI

When Robert Patchen and his wife, Donna, opened Paci at the Southport train station in 1996, their vision was to bring a fresh concept to fine dining. Patchen, the chef-owner, says, "Our mantra was that good food begins at the market." Their upscale seasonal Italian eatery set the benchmark for "farm-to-table" long before that term became part of the vernacular in Connecticut. Patchen attributes Paci's longevity and popularity to "the simplicity and authenticity of our dishes."

Patchen explains of his restaurant, which has won a James Beard Restaurant Design Award and the *Wine Spectator* Award of Excellence, "Sourcing and networking go hand in hand. Reaching out to the local farms and their concession stands is the beginning process. Over the years, we've established a relationship with local purveyors, farmers, fish mongers, bread makers, and so forth, who produce the best quality of products that, in turn, make it possible for us to prepare the dishes that our customers have come to both expect and enjoy."

Patchen goes through his mental Rolodex to share some of his best local purveyors. "Our favorite fish monger is BonTon Fish Market in Greenwich. Tony knows exactly the quality that Paci serves, and selects nothing less for us. The other local markets are many—Lloyd's (Double L Market, Westport), Gilbertie's Herbs (Easton), Sport Hill Farm (Easton)

and local farmers' markets. Our meat source in Manhattan provides us with Amish chickens, Muscovy duck, prime sirloin from Kansas, and lamb from a family owned ranch in Lava Lake, Idaho." After 17 years ahead of the curve, Patchen admits that it's a challenge to stay ahead of the pack, but he is driven by his need to put out top quality.

Grilled Violetta di Firenze Topped with Heirloom Tomatoes, Fresh Burrata, and Basil

SERVES 6 (2 EGGPLANT ROUNDS EACH)

This recipe is a study in simplicity, incorporating local Purple Florentine eggplant, colorful heirloom tomatoes, and fresh burrata into a sophisticated starter.

7 tablespoons extra-virgin olive oil, or as needed, divided

1 pound eggplant, such as Violetta di Firenze, trimmed and cut into 1/2-inch-thick rounds (about 13 slices)

Kosher salt and freshly ground black pepper

3 medium-size to large heirloom tomatoes, cut into 1/2-inch-thick slices (about 1 1/4 pounds)

1 pound burrata cheese cut into quarters (four 4-ounce balls)

1/3 cup fresh basil leaves, cut into thin strips

Heat a gas or electric grill to medium heat and generously brush the cooking grate with oil. Brush both sides of the eggplant slices with olive oil and season with salt and pepper to taste. Grill until grill marks form, about 5 minutes. Using a large spatula, carefully flip the eggplant slices over and grill until fork-tender, about 5 more minutes. Transfer to a small platter. Place the tomato slices over the eggplant. Drizzle with the remaining 2 tablespoons of olive oil, or to taste, and season with salt and pepper to taste. Top with the cheese. Garnish with the basil.

Note: If you do not own a grill, heat the olive oil in a large nonstick skillet or grill pan over medium heat. Add the eggplant rounds in batches, and the oil as needed, and cook, turning once, about 5 minutes per side, then continue as directed.

Paci

MILLWRIGHT'S RESTAURANT

When chef Tyler Anderson left Copper Beech Inn to open his own show, expectations were high. At Millwright's, housed in a 17th-century mill, reviewers have run out of accolades. *Connecticut Magazine* voted it Best New Restaurant in 2013, the *New York Times* rated it "Don't Miss," and *Harford Magazine* gave it five stars.

Anderson treats diners to inventive New England cuisine "that both dazzles and delights," per the *New York Times*. The rustic setting, with an outdoor deck by the waterfall and a cozy, underground tavern with fireplace, sets the stage for a spectacular food and wine experience with a wait staff so well trained that their movements often seem synchronized.

Diners fawn over can't-eat-just-one hot cornmeal biscuits, made from corn grown nearby at Stonington's Stanton-Davis Farm, Connecticut's oldest working farmstead (1654) and ground at a Pawtucket mill (1654) and now served at the renovated Hopbrook Mill (1680). Slathered with honey butter flecked with sea salt and poppy seeds, they presage the experience about to unfold. Other surprises include a seasonal amuse-bouche and an inventive aperitif.

Tyler Anderson, Jesse Powers, and Niles Talbot, and the entire culinary team use local ingredients—grown, raised, produced, foraged, and prepared—whenever possible. Anderson is committed to buying 80 percent of his ingredients from

purveyors in New England and upstate New York. He is once again crop planning with farmer Eloise at Geo Roots Farm in Canton and says, "We are also planting at a new farm at my home, a very special piece of land that borders the Farmington River in Avon. We will dedicate the entire 2.5-acre property to heirloom vegetables and greens for our use at Millwright's. Planting, growing, tending to and harvesting the product will create a special bond between cooks and product, and just as New Englanders before us, we will pickle, jar, can, and preserve as much as possible,

keeping the season 'fresh' in our heads and dishes through the winter months."

The team turns out works of art, whether it's a well-plated foie gras, a colorfully layered carrot terrine, delicate squash blossom fritters, or a perfectly pink duck breast or lamb loin. And they know when to let a classic stand on its own, offering a hefty "duo of prime beef" featuring a New York strip steak and short ribs, twice-baked potato, and carrots.

At Millwright's, Anderson has found his groove. In 2014, he, along with Joel Viehland of Community Table, made the list of semifinalists for Best Chef: Northeast in the prestigious James Beard Awards. In addition, he won Chef of the Year from the Connecticut Restaurant Association for 2014.

Carrot Terrine and Quinoa Garnished with Soubise and Carrot Top–Cashew Pesto

SERVES 6

The inspiration for this dish was "ultra-sweet, snowed-over carrots from one of our local farms," explained executive chef Tyler Anderson, of this rustic terrine first made at an "Inspired New England Dinner" at the James Beard House in New York. "The carrots were slowly roasted in the hearth at Millwright's, then simply set in carrot juice with gelatin. We wanted to take a very earthy dish and present it in a technique-driven way that didn't look too contrived." The terrine is a handsome, make-ahead dish, plated with quinoa, soubise, and carrot-top pesto.

Note: The carrot terrine and pesto need to be made 1 day before they are served.

Carrot Terrine

30 small to medium-size rainbow carrots, assorted colors (see note), scrubbed, tops and bottoms trimmed, tops reserved for pesto
1 tablespoon extra-virgin olive oil
Kosher salt and freshly ground black pepper
1 2/3 cups carrot juice
2/3 tablespoon cider vinegar
1/4 teaspoon xanthan gum
1 1/3 envelope unflavored gelatin

Pesto

2 1/2 cups packed carrot tops, leaves only, no stems, thoroughly cleaned, plus more for garnish
1 scant cup toasted cashews
Zest and lemon juice of 1 lemon
1 1/2 tablespoons extra-virgin olive oil
Kosher salt and freshly ground black pepper

Soubise (onion-cream sauce)

1 yellow onion
1 1/4 cups heavy cream
3 cardamom pods
Scant 2 tablespoons cider vinegar
3 tablespoons apple cider
1 sprig thyme
1 fresh bay leaf

Quinoa

3 tablespoons extra-virgin olive oil, divided
1 1/2 cups onion, cut into small dice
2 3/4 cups red quinoa, rinsed
4 1/4 cups or 1 liter water
1 bouquet garni (2 garlic cloves, 8 sprigs thyme, 8 sprigs parsley, 2 bay leaves)
2 tablespoons fresh lemon juice

1. To make the carrot terrine: Preheat the oven to 350°F. Lightly oil a baking sheet. Spread the carrots onto the prepared baking sheet. Drizzle the oil over the carrots. Season with salt and pepper to taste. Toss to combine, making sure to coat all the carrots well. Roast, stirring occasionally, until the carrots are fork-tender, about 40 minutes. Line the carrots lengthwise on a parchment-lined quarter size baking sheet. In a blender, combine the carrot juice, cider vinegar, and xanthan gum.

2. Meanwhile, pour 1 inch of water into a saucepan and bring to a simmer over medium heat. Place half of the carrot juice and the gelatin in a heatproof bowl and mix until well combined; let stand for 3 minutes or until the gelatin blooms. Add the remaining carrot juice. Place the bowl with the gelatin over (but not touching) the simmering water and bring the juice to a near boil, stirring frequently, about 8 minutes, then pour over roasted carrots and refrigerate overnight.

3. To make the pesto: Combine the carrot tops, cashews, and lemon zest and juice in a food processor and pulse to a puree. While the motor is

running, slowly add the oil. Season with salt and pepper to taste. Spread the pesto in the bottom of a glass dish and smooth the top with a rubber spatula and place in the freezer overnight. Once frozen, allow the pesto to thaw slightly. Using a small circular cookie cutter, cut into coin shapes.

4. To make the soubise: Heat a grill to medium-high. Slice the onion into quarters and then skewer each quarter. Grill the onion until charred. Remove from the grill and chop into 1-inch pieces. Combine all the ingredients in a sauce-pan and simmer over medium-low heat for 30 minutes. Discard the thyme and bay leaf. Transfer to a food processor and process until smooth. Strain through a sieve. Set aside.

5. To make the quinoa: Heat 2 tablespoons of the oil in a 3-quart pot over medium heat. Add the onion and sauté, stirring frequently, until soft and translucent, 8 minutes. Add the quinoa and toast lightly, about 3 minutes. Add the water and bouquet garni and bring to a boil. Cover, lower the heat to low, and simmer until tender, about 15 minutes. Drain in a fine-mesh strainer. Return the quinoa back to the pot, cover, and let sit for 15 minutes. Fluff with a fork and season with the lemon juice and the remaining 1 tablespoon of olive oil, and salt and pepper to taste.

6. To assemble: Slice the terrine and dot the soubise around the terrine. Top with a few coins of pesto. Mound some of the quinoa alongside the terrine. Garnish with the reserved carrot tops.

Note: Any tender, farm-fresh carrot will also work well for this dish.

Millwright's Restaurant

MILLSTONE FARM

Millstone Farm is a 75-acre working farm nestled in the rolling hills of upper Wilton. Owners Betsy and Jesse Fink pursue a mission to rebuild the local food community through small-scale agriculture, educational activities, and events.

Farm manager Johnny Cameron raises pastured, heirloom-breed sheep, Tamworth pigs, and rare, heritage chicken breeds, such as the mop-topped Golden Polish, feather-footed Sultans, and Cuckoo Marans. And under the guidance of master farmer Annie Farrell, the farm also grows vegetables for a CSA, local chefs, and family-owned markets in the area.

When Millstone was founded in 2006, the team began building the market for heirloom varieties, preserving genetic diversity, and working with pioneer chefs in the space, including Michel Nischan (Dressing Room), Brian Lewis (Elm) Tim LaBant (The Schoolhouse at Cannondale), and Bill Taibe (LeFarm and The Whelk).

In 2010, Millstone partnered with the Wilton's The Schoolhouse at Cannondale Restaurant to host festive farm-to-table dinners that include farm tours and incorporate the farm's freshest products. In 2014, Elm chef Brian Lewis debuted a dinner series at Millstone as well.

Millstone Farm grows a variety of vegetables and herbs, consulting with its partner chefs and piloting new varieties every year. It also offers a small, working, seasonal CSA that is focused on creating

community and teaching members how to grow food sustainably. The farm also holds educational workshops on related topics, such as canning, composting, and juicing.

In 2013, Millstone added a pig CSA to its popular meat chicken CSA to provide the farm's highly sought, pasture-raised pork. The farm also harvests honey and maple syrup, and is testing recipes for healthy, value added-products, such as salsa, tomato sauce, and pickles.

The Millstone Farm Glean Team, a volunteer effort, also started helping southern Connecticut farmers reduce the amount of produce that goes to waste in their fields by gleaning and donating their excess crops to a local food bank—a creative means to get fresh food to the state's hungry.

Roasted Jerusalem Artichokes, Brussels Sprouts, and Carrots

SERVES 4

This savory roasted vegetable dish incorporates mildly sweet and earthy sunchokes into the mix.

1 pound Jerusalem artichokes (sunchokes), scrubbed, left unpeeled, and sliced 1/4 inch thick
1 pound Brussels sprouts, cut in half lengthwise
1 pound carrots, peeled and sliced 1/4 inch thick
3 tablespoons extra-virgin olive oil
Kosher salt and freshly ground black pepper
2 teaspoons fresh lemon juice, or to taste
1 teaspoon finely grated lemon zest
2 tablespoons chopped fresh flat-leaf parsley

1. Preheat the oven to 400°F. Lightly oil two rimmed baking sheets; set aside.

2. Place the artichokes, Brussels sprouts, and carrots in a large bowl. Add the oil and season with salt and pepper to taste. Toss until well combined. Arrange the artichokes and sprouts, cut side down, and carrots, on the prepared baking sheets, and bake until fork-tender, about 25 minutes. Transfer the vegetables to a serving bowl and drizzle with the lemon juice. Add the lemon zest and parsley and toss until well combined. Season with salt and pepper to taste and toss once more. Serve.

Millstone Farm

Baked Shiitake Caps

SERVES 5

These luscious, fragrant mushroom caps make a great appetizer or simple vegetarian entrée, or serve on top of pasta.

1 tablespoon olive oil
2 tablespoons sesame oil
1 tablespoon soy sauce
3 tablespoons white wine
1 garlic clove, minced
1 pound whole shiitake mushrooms (about 38) trimmed, stems removed and discarded
Shredded Manchego cheese (optional)

1. Preheat the oven to 350°F. Lightly oil a baking sheet and set aside.

2. In a small bowl, whisk together the oils, soy sauce, wine, and garlic.

3. Using a pastry brush, coat the mushroom caps with the oil mixture. Spread out the mushrooms in a single layer, gill side up, on the prepared baking sheet. Bake for 15 minutes. Carefully flip the mushrooms over and bake until they are evenly browned, about 15 more minutes. Let cool slightly and sprinkle with shredded Manchego, if desired.

Notes:

For an appetizer: Lightly toast five slices of rustic farm bread under the broiler. Arrange about seven mushroom caps on top of each slice. Sprinkle with Manchego cheese, and serve.

For shiitake sandwiches: Arrange about six mushroom caps on one side of a toasted slice of rustic farm bread, place caramelized onions over the mushroom caps, and top with heirloom tomato slices and a handful of baby arugula. Cover with a second slice of bread and serve.

Mountaintop Mushrooms

THE FARMER'S COW

This recipe is from John Turenne, founder and president of Sustainable Food Systems, a national leader in sustainable food practices based in Wallingford, recognized for his role as executive chef at Yale University and in the creation of the Yale Sustainable Food Project, as well as bringing healthy local foods into schools and institutions in Connecticut, Massachusetts, and Maine.

Turenne says, "To me, using the right ingredients when working with school kids is not just about quality and taste. It's about good stories behind those ingredients. The Farmer's Cow exemplifies both of these attributes. Not only does their product taste great, it represents a connection to a local group of farmers who are committed to our environment, our local economies, humane animal husbandry and good nutrition. And when you throw in the brand's marketing appeal to kids, you have a home run!"

This frittata uses local eggs from The Farmer's Cow.

Spinach and Feta Frittata

SERVES 4 TO 6

This frittata makes a delicious brunch dish or dinner, served with a tossed green salad and a crusty baguette.

8 large eggs, lightly beaten
1 teaspoon chopped fresh oregano leaves, plus more for garnish
Kosher salt and freshly ground black pepper
2 tablespoons unsalted butter
2 small onions, peeled and thinly sliced
2 garlic cloves, minced
5 ounces fresh baby spinach leaves, rinsed, dried, and coarsely chopped
4 ounces feta cheese, crumbled (about 3/4 cup)

1. In a medium-size bowl, whisk together the eggs, oregano, and salt and pepper to taste. Set aside.

2. Adjust an oven rack to the top position and heat the broiler. Melt the butter in a broiler-proof 12-inch nonstick or cast-iron skillet over medium heat. Add the onions and cook until soft and translucent, about 10 minutes. Add the garlic and cook until fragrant, about 1 minute. Add the spinach and cook until just wilted, about 2 minutes.

3. Spread the vegetables evenly over the bottom of the pan. Pour the egg mixture over the vegetables. Using a spatula, gently lift up the vegetable mixture along the sides of the skillet to allow the egg mixture to flow underneath. Sprinkle with the cheese. Lower the heat to medium-low and cook until the frittata is almost set but still slightly runny.

4. Place the skillet under the broiler and broil until the frittata is puffed and golden brown, about 3 minutes. Let rest for 5 minutes, then, using a rubber spatula, loosen the frittata from the skillet and carefully slide onto a platter. Cut into wedges, sprinkle with oregano, and serve.

John Turenne, Sustainable Food Systems

SKINNY PINES, LLC

What's better than a perfectly cooked brick oven pie? A perfect thin-crust pie that is created largely out of local, seasonal ingredients that reflect the local landscape. That's why fans line up for Skinny Pines, a mobile, wood-fired brick oven that turns out Neapolitan-style pizzas and wood-fired creations at both private events and weekly farmers' market appearances in Fairfield County. Easton-based owner Jeff Borofsky carefully considers sustainability in each aspect of his business, from sourcing through local and organic farmers and producers (many from the Westport Farmers' Market) to using biodegradable tableware and recycled pizza boxes.

Believing food should be simple and fresh, Borofsky sources flour, local cheeses, kale, heirloom tomatoes, and meats from farm purveyors in Connecticut and New York. We're partial to the "Bianca" pie, which has endless variations, but our favorite version of this white pizza begins with a blend of mozzarella and provolone, rosemary, oil-cured Taggiasca olives, and extra-virgin olive oil. The "Two Guys from Woodbridge," pie, also called the "Magic," is an often requested pizza topped with a combination of shiitake mushrooms, bacon, onion, sage, and mozzarella.

Artisan Italian Sausage, Onion, and Kale Frittata

SERVES 4

Serve this savory, protein-rich dish with a green salad and a crusty baguette for the perfect country lunch or dinner.

6 large eggs, lightly beaten

1/2 cup grated Parmigiano-Reggiano cheese, plus more for garnish

1 tablespoon chopped fresh basil, plus more for garnish

1/2 pound sweet or hot artisan Italian sausage, casings removed

1 tablespoon unsalted butter

1 small onion, minced

3 large kale leaves, stems and inner ribs removed and discarded, leaves cut into 1-inch strips

1/2 cup shredded mozzarella cheese

Salt and freshly ground black pepper

1. Adjust an oven rack to the top position and heat the broiler.

2. In a medium-size bowl, whisk together the eggs, Parmigiano-Reggiano, and basil.

3. Heat a broiler-proof 10-inch nonstick skillet over medium heat. Add the sausage and cook, crumbling with a fork, until browned, about 8 minutes. Using a slotted spoon, transfer to a bowl. In the same skillet with the reserved sausage drippings, melt the butter over medium heat. Add the onion and cook, stirring occasionally, until soft and translucent, about 6 minutes. Add the kale and cook until just wilted, about 2 minutes. Return the sausage back to the skillet. Spread the onion, kale, and sausage evenly over the bottom of the pan. Pour the egg mixture over the onion mixture. Using a spatula, gently lift up the onion mixture along the sides of the skillet to allow the egg mixture to flow underneath. Sprinkle with the mozzarella. Lower the heat to medium-low and cook until the frittata is almost set but still slightly runny.

4. Place the skillet under the broiler and broil until the frittata is puffed and golden brown, about 2 minutes. Let rest for 5 minutes, then, using a rubber spatula, loosen the frittata from the skillet and carefully slide onto a cutting board. Season with salt and pepper to taste. Cut into wedges, sprinkle with Parmigiano-Reggiano and basil, and serve hot or warm.

Skinny Pines Brick Oven Caterer

WESTPORT FARMERS' MARKET

In 2005, the original Westport Farmers' Market (WFM) sprung to life with an A-list cast. Lori Cochran, the market director, recalls, "The late, great Westporter Paul Newman, chef Michel Nischan of Dressing Room restaurant, and the Town of Westport wanted access to local food. So they started the market in the Dressing Room's parking lot."

Since then, the market has grown into a year-round community hub that centers around a thoughtfully curated selection of more than 40 local vendors who adhere to WFM's high bar for being organic, local, and GMO-free. You won't find jobbers (farmers who buy produce for resale and try to pass it off as their own) here.

WFM is a town meeting spot where friends stop and chat over organic coffee and kombucha or linger for a lunch of tamales or pizzas topped with locally farmed cheeses and produce, in the warmth of a greenhouse at Gilbertie's Herb Gardens in winter or alfresco in summer, where a rotating roster of food trucks also make an appearance.

Cochran has kicked up the programming, creating Fork It Over, a series of themed offsite dinners—from a New England clambake to a pig roast—using ingredients from local producers prepared by top chefs. WFM also introduced a series of cooking competitions, judged by local chefs, challenging residents to prepare their best recipe with market veggies.

The market's partnership with the Gillespie Center (a local shelter) and Staples High School Culinary Team is a model for how farmers' markets can forge community bonds. Once a month, students prepare a meal with fresh ingredients from market vendors and serve it to the recipients at the Gillespie Center.

Cochran also assisted in starting an RSA (restaurant supported agriculture) program that makes it easier for chefs to purchase fresh local foods, so it's good bet you'll run into at least a few culinary rock stars shopping the market.

SIXPENCE PIE COMPANY

Sixpence Pie Company's savory meat and sweet pies are retro comfort food. Hand-crafted and wholesome, the pies are made with ingredients that are sourced directly from local growers and producers. Owners Kara More and Lisa Totten got their start at a small array of farmers' markets, and are sticklers for fresh and local ingredients. The proof is in the pies, which fans still line up for at local farmers' markets. Today, they're also available at quality Connecticut grocers, as well as the two Sixpence Pie Company locations.

Kara says, "Initially, we set out to craft the most delicious and wholesome variety of savory pasty and sweet pies from local growers. We were on to something. Blending classic, old-world pies with our creative ingredients came so naturally, but was exactly what set us apart."

The pies, with such fillings as cider-braised pulled pork with caramelized onion or chicken, spinach, artichoke, and blue cheese béchamel, hearken back to a simpler time, when home cooks created scratch pies based on the practicality of sourcing everything from fresh eggs and vegetables from their own gardens, or the neighboring farm. To simulate the experience, Sixpence uses only locally grown produce and meats that are natural and humanely raised.

Sixpence is proud to serve up hearty pies, quiches, soups, and salads in a kicked-back café. Both the Southington and New Haven

locations offer an intimate café setting and a great variety for takeout. The larger pies and quiches are great for family dinners to go, the handheld pastries make great after-school snacks for hungry kids and the minis are a fun homespun hors d'oeuvres for parties.

Cottage Pie

MAKES 2 PIES (6 SERVINGS EACH)

Cottage refers to the modest means of those who originally put this tasty dish together. They used whatever meat they had available. Owners Kara More and Lisa Totten use grass-fed beef. Lucky us!

Crust (makes enough for 2 piecrusts)

2 1/2 cups unbleached all-purpose flour

1/4 teaspoon kosher salt

1 cup (2 sticks, 8 ounces) salted butter, frozen, cut into 1/2-inch cubes

1/2 cup ice water

Cottage Pie Filling

1 tablespoon olive oil

1 large sweet onion, chopped

4 carrots, chopped

4 celery ribs, chopped

2 pounds ground beef, preferably grass-fed

2 teaspoons minced fresh thyme

1 teaspoon minced fresh sage

Kosher salt and freshly ground black pepper

1/4 cup all-purpose flour

1 1/2 cups homemade or high-quality low sodium beef stock

1/4 cup tomato paste

1/4 cup Worcestershire sauce

2 Turkish bay leaves

Potato Topping

2 pounds Yukon Gold potatoes, peeled and diced

Kosher salt

1/2 cup (1 stick, 4 ounces) salted butter, cut into 1-inch cubes

1/2 cup half-and-half, warmed

Chopped fresh parsley, for garnish

Sweet Hungarian paprika, for garnish

1. To make the crust: Process the flour and salt in a food processor for 10 seconds. Add the butter and pulse until small lumps form. While the food processor is running, slowly drizzle in the ice water until the dough just comes together. The dough should still be crumbly. Turn the dough out onto a lightly floured surface and form into two equal-size disks. Wrap the disks in plastic wrap and refrigerate for at least 1 hour.

2. On a lightly floured surface, roll out the one disk of dough into a 12-inch round. Transfer to a 9-inch pie plate, trim the excess dough, leaving a 1/2-inch overhang, and crimp the edges. Repeat with second disk. Place the crusts in the refrigerator and chill for at least 30 minutes.

3. To make the filling: Heat the oil in a large sauté pan over medium heat. Add the onion, carrots, and celery and cook, stirring occasionally, until the onion is soft and translucent, about 10 minutes. Add the beef, thyme, and sage and increase the heat to medium-high. Cook, breaking up with a fork, until the meat is browned. Season with salt and pepper to taste. Stir in the flour and cook, stirring frequently, for 2 minutes. Stir in the beef stock, scraping up the brown bits from the bottom of the pan. Stir in the tomato paste and Worcestershire sauce. Add the bay leaves and lower the heat to low. Simmer, uncovered, stirring occasionally, for 30 minutes. Remove and discard the bay leaves. Season with salt and pepper to taste.

4. To make the potato topping: While the pie filling is simmering, combine the potatoes and 1/2 teaspoon of salt in a large pot, cover with water, and bring to a boil over medium-high heat. Lower the heat and simmer until the potatoes are very tender, about 15 minutes. Drain the potatoes and transfer to a large bowl. Add the butter and half-and-half. Mash with an old-fashioned masher or immersion blender until smooth, then season with salt and pepper to taste.

5. Preheat the oven to 375°F.

6. Pour the pie filling evenly into the piecrusts. Spread the potato topping evenly over the filling and smooth the top with a rubber spatula. Place the pies on a baking sheet and bake for 35 to 40 minutes, or until the potatoes are lightly browned and the pies are heated through. Sprinkle with parsley and paprika, and serve.

Sixpence Pie Company

Cinnamon Chicken with a Mashed Potato Crust Topped with Tomme Cheese (Shepherd's Pie Style)

SERVES 4 TO 6

This dish is a nice departure from the traditional shepherd's and cottage pies.

Potato Crust

1 1/2 pounds Yukon Gold potatoes, peeled and diced
1/2 teaspoon salt
2 tablespoons salted butter, cut into 1-inch cubes
1/4 to 2/3 cup milk, warmed
1/8 teaspoon ground cinnamon, or to taste
Kosher salt and freshly ground black pepper

Pie Filling

1 tablespoon olive oil, or as needed
1 1/2 medium-size sweet onions, thinly sliced
1 teaspoon minced garlic
1 tablespoon all-purpose flour
1 cup low-sodium chicken stock
1 pound skinless, boneless chicken breast, cooked and cut into medium dice, about 2 1/2 cups
3/4 cup frozen peas
1 teaspoon Dijon mustard
1 tablespoon chopped chives

Kosher salt and freshly ground black pepper
1/4 pound Tomme-style cheese, such as Tomme De Savoie or Tomme de Manigodine, grated (about 1 cup)
Chopped fresh parsley, for garnish

1. Preheat the oven to 375°F. Lightly grease an 8 x 8-inch baking dish.

2. To make the potato crust: Combine the potatoes and 1/2 teaspoon of salt in a large pot of water, and bring to a boil over medium-high heat. Lower the heat and simmer until the potatoes are very tender, about 15 minutes. Drain the potatoes in a colander and transfer to a large bowl. Add the butter, milk, and cinnamon. Mash with an old-fashioned masher or immersion blender until smooth; season with salt and pepper to taste.

3. Spread half of the mashed potatoes evenly over the bottom of the prepared baking dish and smooth with a rubber spatula to form a crust. Bake until the crust is lightly golden brown, about 20 minutes.

4. While crust is baking, make the pie filling: Heat the oil in a large sauté pan over medium-high heat. Add the onions and cook, stirring often, until the onions are golden brown, about 15 minutes. Add the garlic and cook until fragrant, about 1 minute. Stir in the flour and cook, stirring frequently, for 30 seconds. Whisk in the chicken stock and cook, stirring often, until thickened, about 2 minutes. Remove the sauté pan from the heat and stir in the chicken, peas, mustard, and chives. Season with salt and pepper to taste.

5. Place the baking dish on a baking sheet. Pour the pie filling evenly over the crust. Spread the remaining mashed potatoes evenly over the filling and smooth the top with a rubber spatula. Sprinkle the cheese over the top. Bake the pie until heated through, about 25 minutes. Season with salt and pepper to taste. Sprinkle with parsley, and serve.

Carole Peck's Good News Café

DISH BAR & GRILL

Dish Bar & Grill is located in the space occupied formerly by the Sage Allen department store on Main Street in downtown Hartford. A cool urban setting and a boisterous bar scene are the backdrop to the food, which is a carnivore's dream. In addition to an array of juicy filets, New York strips, rib eyes, and gargantuan porterhouses, chef Bill Carbone, who is also the chef-partner at Dish 'n Dat in Canton and the recently opened Sorella, across the street, in Hartford, is focused on using local ingredients and serving upscale comfort food "with a twist."

Just when you think the menu is at its finest with simple classics, such as grilled lamb loin chops, lobster pot pie, or short ribs braised in red wine, Carbone will surprise you with a sophisticated terrine of Hudson Valley foie gras, a bright hamachi crudo, or a dish of perfectly seared Maine diver scallops with Asian-braised pork belly, drizzled with carrot-mango puree and soy caramel.

Carbone thinks so much of his farm suppliers that he lists his local farm sources and ingredients—from peaches and pork to oysters and clams to grits—front and center on his menu.

Heirloom Tomato Pie

SERVES 8

At Dish, the heady, ripe heirloom tomatoes for this recipe come from the gardens of farmer David Zemelsky, of Starlight Gardens, Durham. This dish is the quintessential midsummer crowd-pleaser, great when there's a bumper crop of ripe heirlooms from your garden or at your local farmers' market.

Tomatoes

5 medium-large mixed heirloom tomatoes (about 2 1/2 pounds), tough cores removed and cut into 1/2-inch slices
3 tablespoons extra-virgin olive oil
Kosher salt

Crust

1 1/4 cups all-purpose flour, plus more for rolling
1/4 teaspoon kosher salt
6 tablespoons (3/4 stick) unsalted butter, chilled, cut into small cubes
4 tablespoons ice water or as needed

Filling

1/2 cup mayonnaise
1/4 cup chopped fresh basil, plus more for garnish
1 1/2 cups (about 5 ounces) shredded fontina cheese
Kosher salt and freshly ground black pepper

1. Preheat the oven to 200°F. Line one or two large baking sheets with parchment paper.

2. To make the tomatoes: Place the tomatoes on the prepared baking sheet. Sprinkle with oil and salt to taste, and bake for 2 hours. Set aside to cool.

3. Meanwhile, to make the crust: Combine the flour and salt in a large bowl. With a pastry blender or fork, cut the butter into the flour until just crumbly. Add the water, 1 tablespoon at a time, and mix until the dough just comes together. Turn out the dough onto a lightly floured surface and form into a disk. Wrap the disk in plastic wrap and refrigerator for at least 1 hour.

4. On a lightly floured surface, roll out the disk into a 12-inch round. Transfer to a 9-inch deep-dish pie plate or 9-inch tart pan with 2-inch sides and a removable bottom. Using your fingers, press back into the crust any pieces of dough that may have fallen off. Trim the excess dough just at the level of the edge of the pie plate. With a fork, pierce the bottom of the crust. Place the crust in the refrigerator and chill for at least 30 minutes.

5. Preheat the oven to 350°F. Place the piecrust on a baking sheet, line the dough with foil, and fill with dried beans. Bake the crust until the edges are golden brown, about 20 minutes. Remove the foil and beans and continue to bake until the crust is golden brown all over, about 10 minutes. Remove from the oven and allow to cool slightly.

6. To add the fillings: Increase the temperature to 375°F. Gently pat the tomatoes dry with paper towels. Arrange a layer of the tomato slices; overlapping as needed, in the bottom of the pie shell. Spread a thin, even layer of the mayonnaise over the top; then sprinkle evenly with about 1 1/2 tablespoons of the basil and about 1/2 cup of the cheese. Repeat the layering with the remaining ingredients, ending with any leftover cheese.

7. Bake until the tomatoes, cheese, and the crust are golden brown, about 1 hour. Let rest for 1 hour. Garnish with basil. Add salt and pepper to taste. Cut into slices and serve warm.

Note: This pie can also be made using a double crust.

Dish Bar & Grill

CHAMARD VINEYARDS FARM WINERY BISTRO

If find yourself shopping at the Clinton Crossing Outlets or in the vicinity of the shoreline towns of Clinton, Madison, or Westbrook, plan a pit stop at Chamard Vineyards for a delightful lunch or dinner among the grapes. The Farm Winery Bistro at Chamard is a charming little eatery set in a stone winery building adjacent to a cozy tasting room, situated on Chamard's 40-acre vineyard that produces wines influenced by Bordeaux and Burgundy. Every day, the chefs pick fresh herbs and produce from the farm's large kitchen garden plot, and incorporate fare from fellow farmers and fisheries into their contemporary casual cuisine.

Chefs Brad Stabinsky and Matthew Bouffard explain, "Our style of cooking is rooted in classic French technique, but using modern and contemporary approaches to our dishes. Ultimately, we develop our recipes to best highlight our wines produced at Chamard Vineyards. The basic philosophy is: 'If it grows together, it goes together.'"

In addition to tours and tastings, Chamard is the backdrop to many a fabulous event, such as the 2012 Harvest Dinner to benefit the Connecticut Farmland Trust, featuring special guest chef Michel Nischan, and a mouthwatering menu highlighting local ingredients.

Established in 1983, Chamard Vineyards is one of the Connecticut Wine Trail's originals (read about the trail on page 256).

Tucked between the Long Island Sound and the Connecticut River, Chamard enjoys a unique marine microclimate that is ideal for growing European varietals, such as chardonnay, Riesling, Gewürztraminer, cabernet sauvignon, cabernet franc, merlot, and pinot noir. Chamard's mission has been to produce French inspired wines from the Connecticut Shoreline and pair the wines with locally sourced fare.

Flatbread with Roasted Fig-Olive Tapenade, Goat Cheese Ricotta, "Prosciutto-Style" Duck Breast, and Arugula

SERVES 3 TO 4

The saltiness of the prosciutto-style duck breast and olive tapenade is balanced by the mildness of the ricotta.

Note: The duck breast prosciutto must be started seven days before it is served. The result is well worth the time and effort; however, for a quick version of this recipe, you can use a good-quality prosciutto, such as prosciutto di Parma.

Note as well that you will need to macerate the figs in sugar one day before you intend to serve the flatbread.

Prosciutto-Style Duck Breast

1 pound skin-on duck breast, trimmed
4 ounces (1/2 cup) kosher salt
1 teaspoon freshly cracked white pepper

Figs

6 Mission figs, stemmed and quartered, plus 2 whole
2 tablespoons light brown sugar

Roast Fig-Olive Tapenade

2 ounces black olives such as Niçoise or Greek, rinsed, pitted, and sliced (about 1/2 cup)
1 teaspoon orange zest
1 teaspoon capers, rinsed, drained, and squeezed dry
1 medium-size garlic clove, peeled
1 tablespoon chopped fresh flat-leaf parsley
3 tablespoons extra-virgin olive oil

Sherry Vinegar Glaze (makes about 1/4 cup)

4 ounces (1/2 cup) sherry vinegar
2 tablespoons granulated sugar

Goat Cheese Ricotta

4 ounces (1/2 cup) goat cheese or cow's milk ricotta
1 teaspoon extra-virgin olive oil

For Assembly

3 tablespoons cornmeal, or as needed
1 pound pizza dough
1 1/2 teaspoons olive oil, or as needed
1.5 ounces baby arugula

1. To make the prosciutto-style duck breast: Arrange a large sheet of plastic wrap, a little larger than the size of the breast, on a clean work surface. Rinse the duck breast and pat dry with paper towels. Spread 2 ounces of the salt in the center of the wrap and top with the duck breast. Spread the remaining 2 ounces of the salt and pepper over the top of the meat. Tightly wrap the breast and place on a plate, fat side down, and cure in the refrigerator for 7 days. Unwrap the duck and scrape off the residual salt (do not rinse) and pat dry with paper towels. Using a meat slicer or a long- and thin-bladed knife, thinly slice the meat against the grain, trimming away most of the excess fat (see note).

2. To macerate the figs: Place the fig wedges in a small bowl and sprinkle with the brown sugar. Stir, and place in the refrigerator overnight.

3. To make the roast fig-olive tapenade: Preheat the oven to 350°F. Position the oven racks in the upper third and lower third of the oven and place a baking stone (see note) on the upper rack. Spread out the figs on a small baking sheet, reserving the juice, and roast on the lower oven rack, until the figs are fork-tender, 6 minutes.

Place the roasted figs, olives, orange zest, capers, garlic, and parsley into a food processor and pulse until a thick paste forms. Add the olive oil and continue to pulse until chunky-smooth. Thin with the reserved fig juice, if necessary. Set aside.

4. Preheat the oven to 450°F. The baking stone should preheat for 45 minutes.

5. To make the sherry vinegar glaze: Combine the vinegar and sugar in a medium-size saucepan and bring to a simmer over medium heat, stirring often, and cook until reduced by half and the sauce coats the back of a spoon, about 13 minutes.

6. To make the ricotta: Place the ricotta cheese in a small bowl and stir in the olive oil.

7. To assemble: Sprinkle the cornmeal onto a pizza peel and place the dough on the peel. Using your hands, stretch the dough into a rectangle about 12 x 10 inches and 1/4 inch thick. Lightly brush the dough with the olive oil. Spread a very thin layer of the tapenade evenly over the dough, leaving a 1-inch border, then evenly spread the ricotta over the top, leaving a 1-inch

border. Arrange about 25 slices of the prosciutto evenly over the dough, leaving a 1-inch border. Thinly slice the remaining two figs and sprinkle over the top.

8. Slide the pizza onto the baking stone and bake until the edge of the crust is lightly crisp and the cheese is lightly browned, 15 to 20 minutes.

9. Transfer the pizza to a platter. Arrange the arugula in the center of flatbread. Drizzle the flatbread with the sherry vinegar glaze to taste, and serve.

Notes:

Ask a deli, specialty market, or restaurant to slice the duck breast wafer thin for you.

If you don't own a baking stone, you can use a flat or upside-down rimmed baking sheet. A baking sheet or cutting board can also stand in for a pizza peel.

Save the extra prosciutto and add to pasta, or wrap around sweet dates or melon balls.

Chamard Vineyards Farm Winery Bistro

SPORT HILL FARM, LLC

If you visit any of the farm-to-table venues in Fairfield County, chances are at least part of your meal—from kohlrabi and kale to pasture-raised eggs—will be fresh from the fields of Sport Hill Farm in Easton.

The small family farm, established in 2001, is the labor of love of Patti Popp, a self-taught "farm gal," and her husband, Al, who owns a landscaping company while farming in his "spare time." In an era when many established farms were selling land to developers, Patti says, "My husband and I took a gamble to see if we could make a difference." Slowly, a thickly wooded lot became workable, sustainable farmland. Today, Sport Hill has 20 acres under cultivation, including neighboring farmland that is leased, producing crops for a large CSA, an onsite farm market, restaurants as well as The Westport Farmers' Market and the new Black Rock Farmers' Market. Patti says, "We grow and nurture our produce from seed to harvest. No GMOs are ever planted. Crop rotation, green manure, and compost help to replenish depleted nutrients and organic matter back into the soil after each harvest."

Patti was one of the first farmers in the area to recognize the value of both education and community outreach to keep sustainable farming methods alive for future generations. Early on, she teamed up with the Unquowa School in Fairfield to offer a farm camp, introducing kids to the tactile process of farming. Today, she runs

this and other farm education programs, including classes for adults on everything from organic farming to canning and preserving the harvest.

She also was one of the first farmers in the region to offer a CSA. Her 20-week CSA program now serves 150 families, and is available at Wakeman Town Farm in Westport and in Black Rock, Bridgeport. Recently, she began a novel crop cash program, which allows customers to pay up front (which helps keep the farm self-sustaining), then come to the farm market to purchase seasonal fruits and vegetables à la carte, as well as an array of stellar local products, such as cheese, breads, and ice creams from local farms and small, artisanal producers.

Kugelis

SERVES 12

"Kugelis, otherwise known as potato pudding, pulls from my Lithuanian roots. It's a tradition for us, which my family looks forward to every holiday." —Patti Popp

10 large potatoes, such as russet, peeled and grated
3 medium-size onions, peeled and grated
1 cup whole milk, heated to a simmer
5 slices thick-cut bacon, cut into thin strips
8 large eggs, lightly beaten
Kosher salt and freshly ground pepper
Sour cream
Fresh parsley, minced

1. Preheat the oven to 400°F. Lightly coat a 9 x 13-inch baking dish with cooking spray. Set aside.

2. Wrap the grated potatoes and onions in a clean dish towel and squeeze out the excess moisture; then transfer to a large bowl. Pour the hot milk over the potato mixture and stir until well combined. Set aside.

3. Meanwhile, heat a medium-size skillet over medium-high heat. Add the bacon and cook, stirring often, until fully crisp and fat is rendered, about 7 minutes. Add the bacon and the bacon fat to the potato mixture and stir until well combined. Pour the eggs over the potato mixture, stirring until well combined. Season with salt and pepper to taste. Transfer to the prepared baking dish and bake for 15 minutes. Lower the oven temperature to 375°F and continue to cook until the top is golden brown, about 45 minutes.

4. Let rest for 15 minutes. Cut into squares and top with a dollop of sour cream and a sprinkle of parsley, and serve.

Sport Hill Farm

Marinated Grilled Tofu Medallions

SERVES 2 (3 SLICES EACH)

"We wanted to create a knockout dish to prove that tofu is delicious, and can be as satisfying as any other entrée. It a great staple vegan recipe for all skill levels." —Ami Shadle

Note: The tofu must be prepared 12 hours before it is served.

Serve with a salad or as a part of a sandwich (bánh mi style) with other ingredients, such as pickled veggies.

1 pound firm tofu

Marinade

1/4 cup extra-virgin olive oil
1 1/2 teaspoons chopped garlic
2 tablespoons chopped onion
2 tablespoons chopped fresh basil
1 teaspoon chopped fresh tarragon
6 tablespoons cider vinegar
6 tablespoons water

1. To make the tofu: Preheat the oven to 350°F. Line a baking sheet with parchment paper. Set aside.

2. Pat the tofu dry with paper towels. Place the tofu on a paper towel–lined plate. Set a small plate on top of the tofu and weigh it down with a heavy can or brick for 30 minutes. Remove the weight and discard any liquid from the tofu. Cut the tofu into six slices lengthwise. Arrange the tofu slices in a single layer on the baking sheet. Bake, flipping the slices occasionally, until the outside of the tofu is a pale golden brown and slightly puffed, about 20 minutes.

3. Let cool completely on the baking sheet, about 30 minutes; then transfer the slices to a medium-size bowl.

4. Make the marinade: In a small bowl, whisk together the oil, garlic, onion, basil, tarragon, vinegar and water. Pour over tofu and toss until well coated. Cover with plastic wrap, and place in the refrigerator for at least 12 hours.

5. Drain the tofu (the marinade can be reserved, and used as a dipping sauce for sandwiches or for another recipe). When ready to use, either grill or broil the tofu slices until heated through, about 4 minutes. Serve with reserved marinade.

G-Zen Restaurant

SHADLE FARM

Shadle Farm is 270-year old historic farm in Durham that is a couple's home and sanctuary.

Mark and Ami Shadle, of G-Zen Restaurant, have been restoring the property and slowly turning it back into active farmland by planting a wide array of organic fruits, herbs, medicinal plants, and vegetables after 30 years of its lying dormant.

The farm, commercial kitchen, and entire property all are run exclusively on solar-powered energy, and are the hub of much of the inspiration of the life work that the Shadles share.

Many of the organic ingredients for the restaurant and its food truck are grown and harvested at the farm and are incorporated into the seasonally inspired menu. The couple also composts all of the organic waste material from both the restaurant and truck, which in turn creates a nutrient-dense soil for the gardens and growing beds. The restaurant, truck, and farm are an examples of full sustainability and green business practices.

Butter-Poached Lobster Sandwich

SERVES 4

To regulars at the West Street Grill, the lobster sandwich is a summer ritual. Due to the gentle cooking process, the lobster is more tender, moist, and flavorful than in other lobster rolls. James O'Shea jokes, "This is how to properly cook lobster. Call me when you are on your third bite."

4 (1 1/4- to 1 1/2-pound) live, locally caught lobsters

Beurre Monté

3 ounces premade or homemade lobster stock (recipe follows) or water

1 1/2 cups (3 sticks, 12 ounces) unsalted butter, cut into chucks

2 sprigs tarragon

1/8 teaspoon white pepper

French sea salt

Buns

4 buns, such as potato, brioche, Parker House, or hot dog

2 tablespoons butter, melted

Chopped fresh tarragon, for garnish (optional)

1. Prepare a large ice-water bath. Bring a large pot of salted water to a boil. Plunge the lobsters headfirst into the pot, and cook for 3 minutes. Using tongs, plunge the lobsters into the ice-water bath for 5 minutes, then drain.

2. Twist off the lobster tails and claws (including knuckles) from the carapace and remove the meat. Cut the tails in half lengthwise. Pat the meat dry with paper towels and set aside and let come to room temperature before poaching in the beurre monté. Reserve the body of one lobster for stock or discard.

3. To make the beurre monté: In a large saucepan, bring the stock to a boil over medium heat. Lower the heat to low and whisk in the butter, one piece at a time. The temperature of beurre monté should be between 180° and 190°F. Add the lobster meat, tarragon, and white pepper and poach, basting the meat with the sauce, until cooked through, about 4 minutes. Salt to taste.

4. Meanwhile, heat a large skillet over medium heat. Brush the insides of the buns with melted butter and grill until crisp and golden brown.

5. To assemble: Line the bottom of each bun with lobster meat and pour a little of the sauce over the top. Garnish with tarragon, if desired. Top the sandwiches with the remaining bun tops. Serve, passing the remaining sauce at the table.

Note: Save the extra beurre monté and serve over steamed green beans or asparagus.

Lobster Stock

MAKES ABOUT 1 1/2 CUPS STOCK

1 tablespoon extra-virgin olive oil

Shells from 1 cooked lobster

1/2 cup dry white wine

1 large carrot, coarsely chopped

1 tablespoon tomato paste

1 sprig tarragon

1 bay leaf

4 cups cold water

Heat the oil in a medium-size saucepan over medium heat. Add the lobster shells and brown lightly, stirring often, for 15 minutes. Add the wine, carrot, and tomato paste, and continue to cook, stirring often, for 5 minutes. Add the tarra-

gon, bay leaf, and water, and simmer for 1 hour. Strain and discard the carrots, tarragon, and bay leaf before using.

Note: Freeze the extra lobster stock for up to 3 months.

West Street Grill

GRANTS RESTAURANT AND BAR, RESTAURANT BRICCO, AND BRICCO TRATTORIA

Though you might not consider Billy Grant's restaurants among the traditional farm-to-table milieu, Billy has long walked the walk when it comes to local sourcing and supporting the Hartford community. The chef-owner of the popular Grants Restaurants, Billy and his chefs can be found walking the fields at Gutt Family Farm in Glastonbury, picking out tomato varietals every morning, or hosting farm dinners at local farms over the summer.

Along with his brothers, Tony and Michael, Billy Grant created two sophisticated eateries in the heart of the revitalized West Hartford Center: Restaurant Bricco, serving seasonal Italian food, and Grants, the bustling flagship restaurant serving "scratch fare" featuring updated American classics. They go out of their way to use a range of local and seasonal ingredients, including Stonington scallops, New England oysters, and locally farmed fruits and vegetables. In 2010, they launched Bricco Trattoria, a more casual eatery in Glastonbury, which won Best New Restaurant from *Hartford Magazine* in 2013 and a "Don't Miss" from the *New York Times*. All three restaurants have received numerous awards by *Connecticut Magazine*, the *Hartford Advocate*, and *Hartford Magazine*, including Best Chef; and BG Catering won Best Caterer from *Hartford Magazine*.

Whatever you order at any of Billy's restaurants, it's a good bet that it is made from scratch with local components. Billy says, "Our customers know the products we buy. We don't take shortcuts. We buy the best local products we can and we treat 'em right. It's our job to balance the best things and use them at the height of the season. You're getting things that are really honest and really well done. That's been our secret to success."

After 11 years, Grants recently underwent a facelift, though still using local and seasonal ingredients. Along with a team of talented chefs, Billy brought back many classics, such as rack of lamb, signature filet mignon, and popular raw bar selections. He also added a slew of homey "Blue Plate Specials," including Truffled Chicken Potpie, Mom's Meatloaf, and a new, well-priced Tavern menu that includes a great American Burger and an array of delicious "share" plates.

Homemade Whipped Ricotta Crostini with Local Honey and Sage

SERVES 8 TO 10

1 gallon whole milk

2.5 fluid ounces distilled white vinegar

2 teaspoons kosher salt, divided, plus more
   for seasoning

1 cup heavy cream

1 loaf crusty loaf bread, cut into 1/2-inch-thick
   slices (about 20 crostini)

Drizzle of extra-virgin olive oil

Drizzle of local clover honey

Sage Sea Salt

1/2 cup sea salt flakes, such as Maldon

2 tablespoons coarsely chopped fresh sage
   leaves, or to taste

1. Combine the milk, vinegar, and 1 teaspoon of the salt in a heavy, nonreactive stockpot and cook, stirring frequently, over medium-low heat, until the mixture reaches an internal temperature of 180° to 185°F, about 50 minutes. Remove from the heat and let rest for 5 minutes.

2. Line a fine-mesh strainer with two layers of cheesecloth. Ladle the curds into the prepared strainer and let drain at room temperature for about 2 hours.

3. Transfer the ricotta to a bowl and whisk in the cream and the remaining 1 teaspoon of the salt.

4. Preheat the oven to 350°F. Arrange the bread slices in a single layer on a baking sheet. Drizzle the slices with olive oil and season with salt and pepper to taste. Bake until golden brown, about 10 minutes. Set aside.

5. To make the sage sea salt: combine the sea salt flakes and sage in a food processor for 1 minute. Set aside.

6. To assemble: Just before serving, generously spread the ricotta on each bread slice and drizzle with honey. Sprinkle the sage sea salt to taste over the top. Serve at once.

Notes:

Save the extra ricotta and add to your favorite risotto dish.

Save the extra sea salt and sprinkle over chicken or pork. If stored in an airtight container, the salt will keep for 2 weeks.

Grants Restaurant and Bar

PASTA, GRAINS, AND BEANS

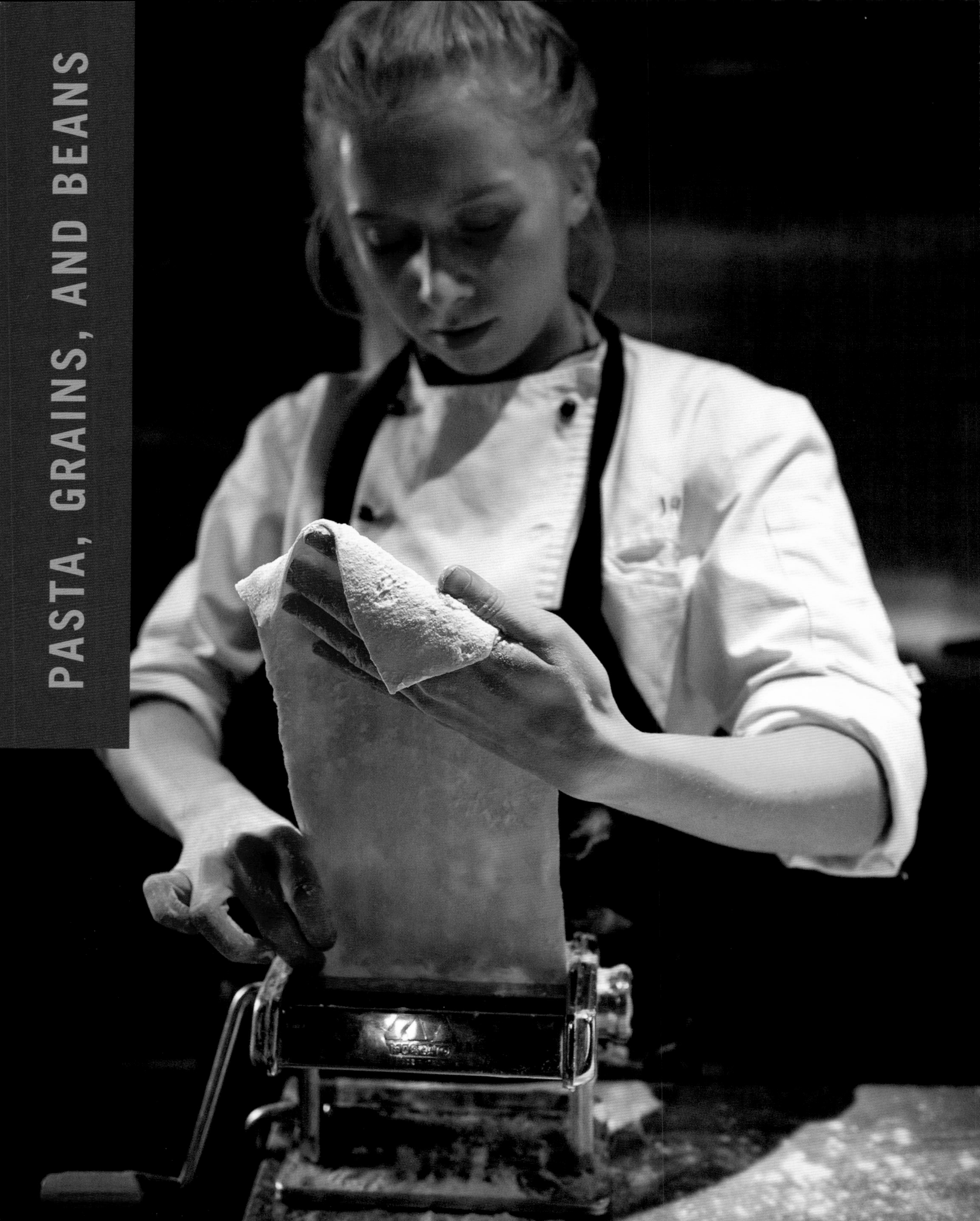

PARALLEL POST

The last thing you might expect inside the Trumbull Marriott is a rockin' contemporary farm-to-table restaurant. Prepare for plenty of surprises from Parallel Post, named for the rustic old parallel posts that border the farms of the country hillsides of Connecticut, New York, and Vermont. The remote location allows the creative team, including consulting chef Dean James Max, executive chef Christopher Molyneux, and chef de cuisine Ali Goss, to work with the farmers and fishermen who work the land and waters along the Connecticut coast. Molyneux, who grew up near the Chesapeake Bay and worked as a longshore fisherman, first trained at Johnson & Wales in Rhode Island, and then crisscrossed the country as an executive chef for Marriott before landing on Connecticut shores.

Seeking to roll out a restaurant with "wow" factor, the brass at Marriott brought in Max's DJM Restaurants, whose niche is developing concepts based around farm-to-table, local, and sustainable cooking. At Parallel Post, Max completely reenvisioned the dining spaces, the menu, and the overall vibe, creating a cool hideaway with a happening bar scene and fare that embraces the local bounty of the Long Island Sound and small Connecticut farmers.

The seasonal foods are the stars of the show here. Max explains, "We are inspired by the deep flavors of the summer fruits and vegetables, to the sweet flavor of New England seafood, and the rich palate of the area's artisan cheese and dairy producers. Our passion is in sourcing the best flavors to bring to our table for you.

"Our menus are a labor of love—a love of the finest foods. We proudly serve a large array of local artisan products. Organic is important to us, but more important, we believe in all-natural products without the use of steroids and growth hormones, and with animals raised responsibly. As well as our preference for products and practices that are sustainable, we try to embrace the idea of localism to strengthen our community."

To this end, the team shops locally and gets involved with community food issues and events, hosting Taste of the Nation, farm dinners and recently, participating in a Bridgeport Food Summit, a program to increase healthy food access to the underserved in the city of Bridgeport, where greens, fruits and farm-fresh foods are hard to come by.

Homemade Tagliatelle Pasta with Norm Bloom & Son CT Lobster

SERVES 6

"The inspiration for the pasta comes from finding fresh, off-the-boat lobster harvested by our local clam guys. Chris, Ali, and I discovered this extra catch while on a clam farm tour, and wanted to be the ones to grab up all the supersweet fresh lobster we could get. Any New Englander can tell you there is a huge difference in fresh-caught lobster.

"The dish reminds me of the time I took my mom to Italy before she had passed from cancer. We both sat on the coast of Cinque Terre and had a very simple lobster dish with the spiny lobster right off the boat, sautéed in olive oil right in its shell . . . only simply sliced to expose the meat, but capturing all the luscious fat and juice. The sauce was the grated flesh of vine-ripe tomatoes, basil, and olive oil, and it was served with fresh artisan spaghetti. I wanted to repeat that flavor for our guests with Connecticut lobster. To this day, it is my favorite lobster dish." —Dean James Max

Note: The pasta can be made ahead and frozen for up to three months in an airtight container.

Tagliatelle Pasta Dough (see note)

2 1/2 cups Italian "00" flour, plus more for dusting

4 large eggs

Pinch of sea salt

1/2 teaspoon extra-virgin olive oil

Tomato Sauce (makes 5 cups; see note)

6 large red tomatoes (about 4 pounds)

3 tablespoons extra-virgin olive oil

3 garlic cloves, thinly sliced (about 1 1/2 tablespoons)

1 medium-size whole shallot, minced (about 5 tablespoons)

1 Calabrian chile pepper, drained and minced (see note), or 1 teaspoon crushed red pepper flakes

1 teaspoon granulated sugar, plus more as needed

Lobster Sauce (makes about 2 cups)

4 (6- to 8-ounce) lobster tails with shells

3 tablespoons unsalted butter, chilled

1/4 cup extra-virgin olive oil

2 cups dry white wine

3 cups water

1 1/2 teaspoons kosher salt

2 cups packed fresh basil leaves, thinly sliced

Juice of 1 Meyer lemon (see note)

1. To make the pasta dough: Sift the flour into a large bowl and make a well in the center of the flour. Break the eggs into the well and add the salt. With a fork, mix the egg mixture into the flour. Continue mixing together by hand until a firm dough forms. If the dough is too dry, add a few drops of water. Turn out the dough onto a lightly floured surface and massage lightly with olive oil. Wrap the dough in plastic wrap and refrigerate for at least 1 hour.

2. To make the tagliatelle pasta: On a lightly floured surface, knead the dough with your fingers until soft but not sticky wet. If the dough feels too wet, add a little flour. Divide the dough into four equal pieces and dust with flour, keeping the pieces you are not working with covered with plastic. Feed a dough piece into the widest setting of a pasta machine (usually marked "1"). Pass the dough through this setting four times. Feed the pasta dough through the machine again, lightly dusting with flour as needed, starting at the widest setting and gradually reducing the setting, one pass at a time, until you are at #3 on the roller. Feed the pasta sheet through

the tagliatelle cutter; drape the pasta over a pasta rack or clean coat hangers. Repeat with the remaining dough pieces and let the pasta air dry on the coat hangers until almost brittle, about 15 minutes.

3. Lightly dust a baking sheet with flour. Coil the pasta into six nests and place on the prepared baking sheet. Place in the freezer and chill until completely frozen. Place in an airtight container and freeze for up to 3 months.

4. To make the tomato sauce: Score each tomato by cutting an X on the underside. Set aside. Bring to a boil in a large pot just enough water to cover the tomatoes. Fill a large bowl halfway with ice water. Working in batches if necessary, with a slotted spoon, carefully place the tomatoes in the boiling water and blanch until the skins begin to crack, about 20 seconds. Carefully remove the tomatoes and place them in the ice water for 1 to 2 minutes. Remove the tomatoes from the water and peel off the skins. Slice the tomatoes in half, remove the seeds, and place the tomatoes on baking sheets to cool. Working in batches, transfer them to a blender or food processor and crush.

5. Heat the olive oil in a medium-size saucepan over low heat. Add the garlic and shallot and cook until just fragrant, about 2 minutes. Add the tomatoes, chile pepper, and the sugar. Increase the heat to medium-low and simmer down to a thickness that can be pushed to one side of the saucepan, about 55 minutes. Season with additional sugar and salt to taste, and set aside.

6. To make the lobster sauce: Cut the lobster tails in half, from head to tail; remove the meat, and discard the black vein (digestive system). Cut the meat into large chunks, reserving the shells. Melt the butter and heat the oil in a large skillet over medium-high heat. Add the lobster shells and cook for 2 minutes. Add the wine and cook stirring frequently, until the liquid is almost evaporated, about 35 minutes. Add the water and salt and continue to simmer until the mixture is reduced by half, about 30 minutes. Strain the lobster sauce, discarding any solids. Add the lobster meat (about 2 cups) and cook until just opaque, about 4 minutes. Add the lobster meat and lobster sauce to the tomato sauce and cook over medium heat until the sauce is heated through. Stir in the basil and Meyer lemon juice.

7. To cook the pasta: Bring 6 quarts of water and 1 tablespoon of salt to a boil in a large stockpot. Add the tagliatelle and cook until al dente, about 3 minutes. Drain the pasta in a colander and transfer to the pasta sauce. Adjust the seasonings with salt and olive oil to taste.

Notes:

In a pinch, you can substitute a good-quality store-bought fresh pasta for the homemade.

You can also substitute about 5 cups of good-quality spicy tomato pasta sauce; just combine with the lobster sauce.

Calabrian chile peppers are fiery. Cutting back on the amount of pepper can reduce the heat.

If you cannot find a Meyer lemon, substitute equal parts lemon juice and orange juice.

Parallel Post

G. W. TAVERN

Once a circa 1850 Colonial home, the quaint red G. W. Tavern, tucked away in a rural hamlet of Litchfield County, has been operating since 1996 on Bee Brook Road. A few years back, it was purchased by John and Julia VandenBosch, who kept the period charm, and the menu, which offers some lighter fare in addition to the heartier mainstays.

The cuisine, executed by chef-owner Julia VandenBosch and executive chef Lawrence Feola, is based on classic New England comfort foods, with daily specials changing with the season using local ingredients.

To complement the traditional setting (hand-painted murals of old town and farms, and portraits of good ol' George Washington himself), and to keep long-time patrons happy, the cuisine here is not about molecular gastronomy or modern riffs. Rather, you'll find an update on classics, such as local and Kobe beef, and locally raised venison, pork, quail, and duck. As the weather warms and seasons change, the menu reflects the area's wide range of local crops, such as tomatoes, arugula, and basil, which expands the variety of daily specials. Shad roe and soft-shell crabs are available in season, as well as swordfish from the Grand Banks and day boat striped bass from Cape Cod.

The setting is just as cozy as one might imagine, with a floor-to-ceiling wood-burning fireplace, and vistas of the Shepaug River from the flagstone patio. Locals flock here for weekly special dinners in the old-style tradition, including Mom's Roasted Turkey Dinner on Mondays, Calves Liver on Thursdays, and Wiener Schnitzel on Saturdays.

Pasta with Beef and Veal Bolognese

MAKES ABOUT 9 CUPS PASTA; SERVES 10

Nothing says comfort food like a dish of pasta with homemade Bolognese sauce. This version incorporates both locally farmed beef and veal, as well as local tomatoes, onions, garlic, and even red wine from a nearby vineyard.

28 ounces whole cooked, peeled tomatoes with juice (cooked canned San Marzano tomatoes are a good substitute)

1/4 cup extra-virgin olive oil

1 medium-size onion, diced (about 1 1/2 cups)

1 medium-size carrot, peeled and diced (about 3/4 cup)

1 celery rib, diced (about 1/4 cup)

6 medium-size garlic cloves, peeled, crushed, and chopped

1 1/2 pound ground beef

3/4 pounds ground veal

1 cup dry red wine

1/4 cup tomato paste

Freshly grated nutmeg

1/4 cup heavy cream

2 teaspoons fresh oregano leaves

1/4 cup packed thinly sliced fresh basil

1/4 cup grated Parmigiano-Reggiano cheese, plus more as needed

1 1/2 pounds good-quality pasta, such as penne, rigatoni, fusilli, or orecchiette (The G.W. Tavern uses homemade fettuccine.)

1. Puree the tomatoes with juice in a blender or food processor until smooth. Set aside.

2. Heat the oil in a large pot over medium heat. Add the onion, carrot, and celery, and cook, stirring occasionally, until soft and just browned, about 15 minutes. Add the garlic and cook, stirring frequently, for 2 minutes. Add the beef and veal and season with salt and pepper to taste. Increase the heat to medium-high and cook, breaking up with a fork, until the meat begins to brown, about 10 minutes. Carefully pour off any excess fat. Add the wine and bring to a boil, scraping up the brown bits from the bottom of the pot. Continue cooking, stirring frequently, until most of the wine has evaporated, about 5 minutes. Add the tomato paste and cook, stirring constantly, for 1 minute. Stir in the tomato puree and nutmeg and lower the heat to low. Simmer, uncovered, stirring occasionally, until the sauce is very thick, about 1 1/4 hours. Stir in the cream and continue to cook until completely absorbed, about 3 minutes. Stir in the oregano, basil, and cheese, and season with salt and pepper to taste.

3. When Bolognese is almost done, bring a large pot of salted water to a boil, add the pasta, and cook until al dente. Drain, reserving 1/4 cup of the pasta water, and return the pasta to the pot. Add half of the sauce and toss to coat well, adding more sauce to taste. If the sauce seems too dry, stir in the reserved pasta water as needed. Serve with Parmigiano-Reggiano cheese.

Note: Freeze the extra Bolognese sauce and serve over polenta or use as filling for Bolognese cannelloni crepes.

G. W. Tavern

Spicy Rabbit Ragù with Pappardelle Pasta

MAKES ABOUT 4 1/2 CUPS OF SAUCE; SERVES 8

1 whole rabbit (about 3 pounds)

3/4 tablespoon smoked picante paprika

1/2 tablespoon kosher salt, plus more as needed

1/4 cup extra-virgin olive oil

1 small onion, coarsely chopped

1 medium-size carrot, peeled and coarsely chopped

1 celery rib, coarsely chopped

4 garlic cloves, crushed

2 tablespoons all-purpose flour

1 tablespoon harissa paste

2 tablespoons honey

2 tablespoons red wine vinegar

1 cup dry white wine

3 fresh medium-size to large tomatoes, coarsely chopped (about 2 pounds)

1 quart veal or low-sodium chicken stock

3 sprigs thyme

2 fresh bay leaves

Freshly ground black pepper

....

2 pounds pappardelle pasta

1 bunch rainbow Swiss chard, thick stems removed and reserved for another dish, coarsely chopped

1 tablespoon olive oil

Kosher salt and freshly ground black pepper

4 ounces Parmigiano-Reggiano cheese shavings

1. Cut the rabbit into six pieces. (You can also ask your butcher to do this for you.)

2. Combine the paprika and salt in a small bowl. Season the rabbit with the paprika mixture.

3. Heat 2 tablespoons of the oil in a Dutch oven over medium-high heat. Add the rabbit and brown on all sides, about 15 minutes. Remove the meat and set aside. Discard any excess grease in pan. Add the remaining 2 tablespoons of oil, onion, carrot, and celery, and cook, stirring often until soft and translucent, about 4 minutes. Add the garlic and cook, stirring often, until fragrant, about 1 minute. Sprinkle with the flour and cook, stirring often, for 1 minute. Stir in the harissa paste and honey and continue to cook for 2 minutes. Stir in the vinegar, scraping up the brown bits from the bottom, and cook until reduced by three-quarters, about 3 minutes. Stir in the wine and reduce by half, about 5 minutes. Return the rabbit to the pan; add the tomatoes, stock, thyme, bay leaves, and pepper. Bring to a boil. Cover and simmer until the meat is tender and pulling away from the bone, about 1 hour.

4. Transfer the rabbit to a cutting board and when cool enough to handle, remove the meat from the bones and chop to a uniform size. Set aside.

5. Strain the cooking liquid in a fine-mesh strainer, pressing on the vegetables to release as much flavor as possible, then transfer the liquid back to the pot. Bring to a simmer over medium-high heat and reduce by half (about 4 1/2 cups), about 45 minutes. Adjust the seasonings with salt and pepper to taste. Add the meat to the sauce and keep warm.

6. Cook the pappardelle according to the package directions.

7. While waiting for the pasta water to boil, start the Swiss chard. Heat the oil in a large skillet over medium-heat. Add the Swiss chard and cook until just wilted, about 3 minutes.

8. To assemble: Combine the pasta and Swiss chard in a large bowl. Add the ragù to taste. Toss until well combined. Adjust the seasonings with salt and pepper to taste. Garnish with cheese shavings. Serve at once.

Artisan Restaurant

DARLING FARM

Nestled at the base of West Rock Park on the grounds of the historic Thomas Darling House in Woodbridge, Darling Farm is a small and diverse vegetable farm with about an acre of land currently under cultivation. Aaron and Caitlin Taylor started Darling Farm in 2012 when they became the caretakers at the Thomas Darling House and were given the opportunity to return the long-neglected fields surrounding the house to small-scale agricultural production. Prior to starting Darling Farm, and throughout the startup phase, Aaron trained and worked at Massaro Community Farm, also in Woodbridge. Caitlin is a recent graduate of the Yale School of Architecture, and also works as a practicing architect at a firm in Essex.

As of 2014, the Darling Farm team has expanded to include farmer Rachel Berg, who worked with Aaron at Massaro Community Farm and is a graduate of the University of Vermont Farmer Training Program.

As the farm is a signatory to the Connecticut NOFA Farmer's Pledge, all the produce at Darling Farm is grown without the use of synthetic pesticides or synthetic fertilizers, and every effort is made to use sustainable growing practices, such as cover-cropping, composting, and crop rotation. Darling Farm focuses on growing a wide array of specialty crops, including baby salad greens, Asian cooking greens, numerous hot pepper and eggplant varieties, herbs, garlic, and heirloom tomatoes.

During the 2013 season, Darling Farm provided produce to a few local restaurants and markets, and attended the weekly Edgewood Park Farmers' Market in New Haven. As we speak, it is working to expand both its market presence and restaurant sales.

Autumn Pasta Sauce of Cauliflower and Apples

SERVES 2 TO 3

When the temperatures drop, try this unique sauce, with cauliflower and orchard-fresh apples, over penne for a hearty fall entrée.

2 tablespoons pine nuts
12 ounces whole wheat or tricolored penne
1/4 cup extra-virgin olive oil
12 large garlic cloves, peeled and slightly crushed
6 oil-packed anchovy fillets, drained and minced
1 small (about 1 1/2 pounds) cauliflower head, trimmed, cored and cut into 1-inch florets
2 medium-size apples, such as McIntosh or Braeburn, unpeeled, cored and cut into 1/4-inch-thick slices
1/4 cup chopped fresh sage leaves
Kosher salt and freshly ground black pepper

1. To toast the pine nuts: Heat a small, nonstick skillet over medium heat. Add the pine nuts, and toast, stirring frequently, until fragrant and golden brown, about 4 minutes. Set aside.

2. While the pine nuts are toasting, bring a large pot of salted water to a boil, add the pasta, and cook until al dente. Drain, reserving 3/4 cup of the pasta water, and return the pasta to the pot.

3. While the pasta is cooking, in a large, heavy skillet or saucepan with a tight-fitting lid, heat the oil over medium heat. Add the garlic and anchovies and cook, stirring frequently, until the garlic is lightly golden brown and the anchovies have mostly disintegrated into the oil, about 5 minutes. Add the cauliflower and continue to cook, stirring until ingredients are fully incorporated, about 5 minutes. Add the apples and 1/4 cup of the reserved pasta water. Cover and steam until cauliflower is fork tender, 5 to 7 minutes.

4. Uncover and increase the heat to medium-high. Continue to cook, stirring often, until most of the water has evaporated. (If the sauce seems too dry, stir in some of the reserved pasta water, as needed.) Add the sage and season with salt and pepper to taste. Cook for 2 more minutes and then remove from the heat. Adjust the seasonings with salt and pepper to taste. Spoon over individual bowls of pasta and garnish with the toasted pine nuts.

Darling Farm

Macaroni and Cheese

SERVES 10 TO 12

"My mom knew how much we loved her macaroni and cheese, and she leveraged that fondness to get us to do just about anything—from mowing the lawn to peeling a couple of bushels of apples in canning season. The dish was an indulgence for us because of the expense of the cream. One of our chores was bringing in the milk left by the milkman and storing it in the refrigerator. I remember how happy we would be when we spied a small bottle of cream with the milk. Macaroni and cheese day!"

—Michel Nischan

1 pound good-quality semolina or semolina/
    legume-based short, chunky pasta, such
    as penne or ziti

6 cups heavy cream

2 tablespoons grapeseed oil

1/2 pound cured, braised pork belly or thick-cut
    bacon (see note)

1 cup fresh bread crumbs or panko bread crumbs

2 cups grated cheese, such as Gouda (4 ounces)
    or Pecorino Romano (4 1/2 ounces) or a
    mixture of the two, divided

1 1/2 tablespoons fresh chopped thyme,
    plus more for garnish

2 tablespoons unsalted butter

Sea salt and freshly ground black pepper

1. Preheat the oven to 350°F. Lightly grease a 9 1/2 x 13 1/2 x 2-inch baking dish with butter or coat with nonstick cooking spray; set aside.

2. Bring 5 quarts of salted water to a boil in a large pot over medium-high heat. Add the pasta and cook until al dente, about 9 minutes. Drain the pasta in a colander. Spread out the pasta in a single layer on a baking sheet to dry slightly.

3. Meanwhile, in a medium-size saucepan, bring the cream to a simmer over medium-high heat. Lower the heat to medium-low and simmer until the cream is reduced by half. Cover and set aside to keep warm.

4. While the cream is simmering, heat a medium-size, heavy skillet over medium heat. When hot, carefully pour the oil into the pan. Add the pork belly and cook until lightly browned but still tender in the center, about 5 minutes. Do not cook until fully crisp. With a slotted spoon, transfer the pork belly to a paper towel–lined plate and allow to drain. Cut the pork belly into 1/2-inch cubes and set aside.

5. To make the bread crumb topping: Discard all but 2 tablespoons of the pork belly fat in the skillet. Add the bread crumbs and 1/4 cup of the cheese and toss until well combined. Set aside.

6. Meanwhile, bring the cream back to a simmer over medium heat. Stir in the remaining 1 3/4 cups of cheese and the thyme until the cheese has melted. Stir in the butter. Remove the saucepan from the heat and stir in the reserved pasta and pork belly. Season with salt and pepper to taste. Transfer the pasta mixture into the prepared baking dish; if the sauce is too thick, add cream as needed. Sprinkle the bread crumbs over the top. Bake until hot and bubbly and the top is crisped and golden brown, about 30 minutes. Let rest for 5 minutes, garnish with thyme and serve.

Note: If using bacon, you will not need the grapeseed oil. Cook the bacon until lightly browned but still tender in the center. Do not cook until fully crisp.

The Dressing Room Restaurant & Wholesome Wave

Caseus Mac' N Cheese

SERVES 10 TO 12

Homemade Bread Crumbs

1 (12-ounce) loaf brioche or challah bread,
  cut into 3/4-inch cubes (8 cups)

1 1/2 tablespoons extra-virgin olive oil, or
  2 1/2 tablespoons unsalted butter, melted

Kosher salt and freshly ground black pepper

Pasta and Cheese

1 pound orecchiette pasta

1/4 pound (4 ounces) fresh goat cheese,
  crumbled, softened (about 3/4 cup)

1/3 pound (5.3 ounces) extra-sharp Vermont
  Cheddar cheese, shredded (about 1 1/3 cups)

1/3 pound (5.3 ounces) Dutch Gouda cheese,
  shredded (about 1 1/4 cups)

1/3 pound (5.3 ounces) Comte or Cantal cheese,
  shredded (about 1 1/2 cups)

1/3 pound (5.3 ounces) Swiss Raclette cheese,
  shredded (about 1 1/3 cups)

1/4 pound (4 ounces) provolone cheese, shredded
  (about 1 1/3 cups)

1/3 cup unsalted butter

1/3 cup all-purpose flour

1 quart whole milk

1/2 teaspoon freshly grated nutmeg

Kosher salt and freshly ground black pepper

Chopped fresh parsley, for garnish (optional)

1. To make the bread crumbs: Preheat the oven to 300°F. In a large bowl, toss the bread cubes with the olive oil and season with salt and pepper to taste. Spread out the bread cubes in a single layer on a baking sheet and bake, stirring occasionally, until golden brown and crisp, about 20 minutes. Let cool to room temperature. Working in batches, if necessary, pulse the bread cubes in a food processor until coarse crumbs form. Set aside.

2. To make the pasta and cheese: Raise the oven temperature to 350°F. Lightly grease a 9 1/2 x 13 1/2 x 2-inch baking dish with butter or coat with nonstick cooking spray; set aside. Bring 5 quarts of salted water to a boil in a large pot over medium-high heat. Add the pasta and cook until al dente, about 9 minutes. Drain the pasta in a colander and set aside.

3. In a medium-size bowl, combine all the cheeses; set aside.

4. Melt the butter in a medium-size saucepan over medium-low heat. Add the flour and cook, whisking constantly, until the mixture has thickened and the flour is a pale golden color, about 4 minutes. Whisk in the milk gradually until well combined. Stir in three-quarters of the cheese mixture, in batches, whisking frequently, until the cheese has melted and incorporated. Season with nutmeg, and salt and pepper to taste. Remove the pan from the heat and stir in the reserved pasta. Transfer the pasta mixture into the prepared baking dish. Lightly coat the dull side of a sheet of foil with nonstick cooking spray or butter and cover the baking dish.

5. Bake the pasta and cheese until hot and bubbly, about 20 minutes. Remove the dish from the oven and sprinkle 1 1/2 cups of the bread crumbs and the remaining cheese over the top. Return to the oven, uncovered, and bake until the cheese has melted, about 10 minutes. Let rest for 10 minutes, sprinkle with parsley, if desired, and serve.

Notes:

Save the extra bread crumbs for meatballs or as a fish topping. You can store the remaining bread crumbs in an airtight container for up to 30 days or in the freezer for up to 3 months. In a pinch, you can substitute store-bought bread crumbs, preferably panko.

This recipe is delicious with other types of cheeses, such as grated fresh Parmesan or shredded Monterey Jack.

The Farmer's Cow

Ricotta Gnocchi

SERVES 4 (30 TO 40 GNOCCHI EACH)

Making light and fluffy gnocchi takes a deft hand. Once mastered, this ricotta gnocchi recipe will become a go-to favorite.

1 pound whole-milk ricotta cheese

1 large egg, lightly beaten

1/2 cup freshly grated Parmigiano-Reggiano cheese, plus more for serving

1/4 teaspoon freshly grated nutmeg

1/8 teaspoon red pepper flakes

Kosher salt

1 cup all-purpose flour, plus extra for dusting

Olive oil, for sprinkling

1. Place the ricotta in a fine-mesh strainer lined with a double layer of cheesecloth, set over a large bowl, for about 1 1/4 hours. Squeeze out any excess moisture.

2. Place the ricotta in a standing mixer. While the motor is running on medium speed, add the egg and mix until just combined. Add the cheese, nutmeg, red pepper flakes, and 1/8 teaspoon of salt and mix until combined, then add the flour. Cover and refrigerate for 1 1/2 hours.

3. Lightly oil a baking sheet and set aside. Bring 4 quarts of water and 1 tablespoon of salt to a simmer in a large stockpot.

4. Lightly flour your hands and a clean work surface and cut the dough into tennis ball–size pieces. Roll each piece of dough into a 3/4-inch-thick rope. Using a sharp, floured knife, cut each rope into 3/4-inch pieces. Transfer the gnocchi to prepared baking sheet and repeat the process with the remaining dough.

5. Add the gnocchi in batches, to the simmering water and cook until the pasta has floated to the surface, about 3 minutes. Place a colander in the sink. Remove the gnocchi with a slotted spoon, transfer to the colander, and drizzle with olive oil. Repeat with the remaining gnocchi.

6. To serve, the toss gnocchi with your favorite sauce and serve immediately.

Note: Gnocchi freezes well. Spread out gnocchi in a single layer on a lightly oiled baking sheet; place in the freezer until firm. Transfer into a resealable plastic freezer bag and freeze for up to 1 month. To cook, simply add the frozen gnocchi to boiling water and cook until the pasta has floated to the surface. No thawing needed!

Winvian Relais & Chateaux

TRUELOVE FARMS

Truelove Farms is a small, sustainable farm nestled in the Litchfield hills, raising pork, beef, eggs, and poultry without growth hormones or antibiotics. The farm's agricultural origins date back to the mid-1700s.

Its pigs are raised exclusively outdoors, in both a shagbark hickory grove and a second-growth hardwood forest. Gregarious and social, the pigs are kept in herds and rotated through their woodlot "pastures" via electric fence and portable solar chargers. The pigs naturally aid decomposition and fertilize the ground as they return to each area on only an annual basis.

This method of hog husbandry produces happier and healthier animals. In addition to eating a grain-based diet, they forage for hickory nuts and earthworms (and in the fall enjoy apples, corn, pumpkins, and acorns from local farms and forest). Truelove relies on heritage breed Berkshire and Tamworth hogs, old breeds out of favor industrially but which produce fantastic pork when raised on pasture.

Perhaps most crucial, the pigs lead happy lives. They sleep in the shade and wallow in the mud, and behave in a perfectly piggy fashion. In their woodlots, the hogs are truly at home, raised in a millennial-old tradition in sync with the land, the seasons, and their nature.

When it comes to cattle, Truelove adheres to pasture-based husbandry. Its cattle get fresh water, a trace mineral block, organic hay in the winter, small amounts of supplemental grains, and access to all the various grasses the from the fields. By using rotational grazing, Truelove ensures the fitness of its herd and the soundness of its pastures. Manure becomes a valuable fertilizer, spread evenly on the fields as the cattle graze. The cattle have sun and shade and the sky overhead; they have space and fresh air and contentment.

The beef, from Black Angus and White-Faced Hereford cattle, is leaner than industrial meat, and the fat it does contain is higher in healthy omega-3 fatty acids, a direct product of the sun-grass-cow relationship. The flavor is robust and "beefy."

Truelove Farms also raises poultry on pasture, utilizing Great Pyrenees guard dogs to protect laying hens, Red Ranger and Cornish Cross roasting chickens, and heritage-breed turkeys. The birds and canine guardians roam in concert with the cattle.

You can find Truelove meats and eggs at a range of Connecticut farmers' markets, as well as at a number of top local restaurants.

Millet and Lacinato Kale with Dried Sour Cherries, Pistachios, and Chèvre

SERVES 6

"When chef John Naughright joined Caseus in 2013, he brought with him a love of grain salads. Since then, different grain salads have been featured on the menu just about daily. They work beautifully with cheeses, as fat and richness pairs well with earthy, nutty grains. This simple recipe can be made ahead and served the next day."
—Jason Sobocinski

Note that the dried sour cherries must be started at least five hours or up to one day in advance.

Dried Sour Cherries

1 cup dried tart cherries
1 cup cider vinegar

Millet

1 1/2 cups uncooked millet, rinsed
    and drained
4 1/2 cups water
1/4 teaspoon kosher salt

Dressing

1/4 cup pure maple syrup, or to taste
1/2 cup extra-virgin olive oil
Kosher salt and freshly ground black pepper
1 large bunch green kale, such as lacinato,
    stemmed and cut into 1-inch strips
3/4 cup unsalted, shelled pistachios
4 ounces fresh chèvre, crumbled

1. To rehydrate the dried sour cherries: Place the cherries in a medium-size bowl. Pour the vinegar over the fruit and let sit, covered, for at least 5 hours or up to 1 day.

2. To make the millet: Bring the water and salt to a boil in a medium-size saucepan over medium-high heat. Add the millet in a slow, steady stream and cook, stirring constantly, until the water is almost absorbed, about 15 minutes. Remove from the heat and let sit for 10 minutes. Fluff with a fork and set aside.

3. To make the dressing: Drain the cider vinegar from the cherries into a small bowl and reserve. Coarsely chop the cherries and place in a separate bowl.

4. In a medium-size bowl, combine 1/2 cup of the reserved vinegar and the maple syrup. Whisking vigorously, add the oil in a slow, steady stream. Season with salt and pepper to taste.

5. In a large bowl, combine the kale and half of the dressing. Using tongs, massage the kale until it is bright green and slightly softened, 2 to 3 minutes. Add the millet, pistachios, cherries, and chèvre, tossing until well combined, adding more dressing to taste. Adjust the seasonings with additional maple syrup and/or reserved vinegar, if desired. Season with salt and pepper to taste. Serve warm or at room temperature.

Chef John Naughright and Jason Sobocinski for Caseus Fromagerie Bistro

WINVIAN RELAIS & CHATEAUX

When you're seeking an escape from reality, venture to Winvian, the ultimate getaway, set on a pastoral 113-acre Litchfield Hills property, sited amidst meadows, ponds, stone walls and hemlock groves. With 18 architecturally unique and whimsical private cottages dotting the property, a Zenlike spa, and an award-winning restaurant, Winvian is an oasis of nature and serenity.

Then there's the food. No Spartan spa cuisine here! The Restaurant at Winvian features the five-diamond cuisine of Executive Chef Chris Eddy, who uses the freshest possible ingredients year-round, many of which are seasonally harvested from the property's bountiful garden in season. The kitchen garden is often the centerpiece the fresh and spontaneous offerings that were likely gathered from the farm a few hours before appearing on your plate.

The nightly menu is presented in a prix-fixe format—allowing the meal to unfold over an array of courses—which can be paired with wine selections from their extensive cellar. A recent menu's choices included a starter of tender grilled octopus served with Ortiz anchovies, potatoes, haricots verts, Graffiti eggplant and red peppers (all from the garden), quail eggs, and virgin olive oil. The second was butter-poached Maine lobster and local trout cannelle in a light ragout of garden peas and favas, fresh tarragon and lemon-scented lobster jus. The entrée was tender roasted lamb chop from Latella Farm with fresh minted raita, crispy samosa, and summer couscous.

Having trained under Daniel Boulud and Alain Ducasse, Chef Eddy has done his mentors proud.

Lentils with Chorizo and Bacon

SERVES 5 (1 1/2 CUPS EACH)

This is a great make-ahead dish that is served the second day. To serve, reheat the lentils until warmed through, skimming any fat off the surface.

Bouquet Garni

1/2 garlic bulb, halved horizontally

2 bay leaves

Lentils

2 cups lentils, preferably beluga or green du Puy, picked over

1 tablespoon duck fat, oil, or butter

3 slices bacon

2 small or 1 large spicy chorizo sausages, thickly sliced

1 cup finely diced onion

1/2 cup finely diced celery

3/4 cup finely diced carrot

1/2 cup finely diced celery root

2 teaspoons minced garlic

4 cups chicken stock, or as needed

1 cup water

Kosher salt and freshly ground black pepper

Olive oil, for serving (optional)

Fresh parsley

1. To make the bouquet garni: Place the garlic bulb half (bottom root part) and bay leaves in a piece of cheesecloth and tie into a bundle with kitchen twine. Set aside.

2. Place the lentils in heavy-bottomed saucepan and cover with cold water 2 inches above the lentils. Bring to boil, strain, and repeat the process two more times. Drain the lentils and set aside.

3. Meanwhile, heat the duck fat in a large, heavy stockpot over medium-high heat. Add the bacon and fry, rendering the bacon of its fat and until just browned, about 5 minutes. Add the chorizo and sauté until browned, about 5 minutes longer.

4. Drain the fat from pan, reserving 1 tablespoon in the pot. In the same stockpot, add the onion, celery, carrot, and celery root and cook over medium heat, stirring often, until soft and translucent, about 5 minutes. Add the garlic and cook for 2 minutes.

5. Add the lentils to the stockpot. Stir in the chicken stock, water, and bouquet garni. Increase the heat to medium-high, cover, and bring to a boil. Lower the heat to a simmer and cook for 10 minutes. Lower the heat to medium-low, partially cover, and simmer, skimming and discarding the fat from the top occasionally, until tender, about 20 minutes. Remove from the heat, season with salt and pepper to taste, then set aside to cool. Cover and let the lentils marinate in the refrigerator for 2 days.

6. To serve, with a slotted spoon, remove the bacon and chorizo and dice into small pieces, then return them to the pot of the lentil mixture. Remove and discard the bouquet garni. Reheat the lentil mixture over medium heat until heated through. Drizzle olive oil over the top, if desired, and sprinkle with parsley. Serve.

Note: You may also leave the lentils in the liquid and store for up to 1 week and/or freeze.

Winvian Relais & Chateaux

SUGAR & OLIVES

Foodies and lovers of all things organic and local have ferreted out the orange door that opens into Sugar & Olives, an industrial-chic spot tucked away on a side street in Norwalk. Part coffee/tea/espresso bar, part breakfast/lunch/dinner spot, part after-movie cocktails spot, part entertaining space, and part cooking school, Sugar & Olives is a hip and comfy respite from the hustle-bustle.

Opened by Jennifer Balin, a Westport mother of four and a classically trained French chef, Sugar & Olives is the manifestation of Jen's desires to create a unique and relaxed gathering spot that celebrates local food and community.

Sugar & Olives also seeks to educate its diners and cultivate the relationship between farms and families. Nearly all menu items come from the Nutmeg State or close by—including milk, cheese, eggs, fruit, vegetables, beef, pork, and poultry— in addition to wine, beer, and spirits.

Jen not only shops the farmers' market in Westport and Black Rock (Bridgeport), she sells her baked goods and other prepared foods there, and keeps her finger on the pulse of the local green foods move-

ment. The restaurant's grass-fed beef hails from upstate New York farms. Its eggs and poultry are organic and free-range and local. Their food uses whole grains and is trans-fat free. They even use non-GMO cooking oils and other products that often slip through the cracks. Recently, the restaurant began hosting a series of its own Friday night farmers' markets with an array of sustainable purveyors.

This three-star Certified Green restaurant serves brunch, dinner, and holds cooking classes, as well as parties for up to 250 people, with two smaller spaces for more intimate gatherings. Built inside a retired airplane parts factory, the space boasts a 22-foot "old soul" oak bar with southern roots and lots of hospitality.

Jen says, "We believe that good health and happiness are a product of a wholesome diet. Who has time to figure out healthy food? We do. We promise to give you what you love—and make sure it's good for you, too. Our offerings are first based on what we can find that's grown locally, and every attempt is made to source organic products whenever they are available."

Quinoa Paella

**MAKES 6 CUPS PAELLA;
SERVES 4 AS A SIDE DISH**

Dried Currants

1/4 cup dried currants

1/8 teaspoon kosher salt

2 tablespoons brandy

2 tablespoons water, warmed to a simmer

Quinoa

1/2 cup organic white quinoa

2 1/2 cups plus 1 tablespoon cold water, divided

Kosher salt and freshly ground black pepper

1/2 cup organic red quinoa

2 tablespoons extra-virgin olive oil, divided,
    plus more as needed

2 large carrots, peeled and cut into small dice

1 medium-size to large fennel bulb, cored, or 3 to
    4 fennel stalks, fronds removed and reserved
    for garnish, cut into small dice

1/4 cup toasted walnuts, coarsely chopped

4 large kale leaves, cut into thin strips

1 tablespoon ground turmeric

1. To rehydrate the currants: Place the currants and salt in a small bowl. Pour the brandy and water over the fruit and let sit, covered, for 1 hour before making the recipe. Strain the currants and set aside.

2. Using a fine-mesh strainer, rinse the quinoas separately, under cold running water.

3. Place the white quinoa in a small pot with the 1 cup of water and bring to a boil. Cover, lower the heat to low and simmer until tender, about 7 minutes. Drain in a fine-mesh strainer. Return the quinoa back to the pot, cover, and let sit for 15 minutes. Fluff with a fork and season with salt and pepper to taste. Set aside.

4. Place the red quinoa in separate small pot with 1 1/2 cups of water and bring to a boil. Cover, lower the heat to low and simmer until tender, about 9 minutes. Drain in a fine-mesh strainer. Return the quinoa back to the pot, cover, and let sit for 15 minutes. Fluff with a fork and season with salt and pepper to taste. Set aside.

5. Heat 1 tablespoon of the oil in a large sauté pan over medium heat. Add the carrots and cook, stirring frequently, until soft and translucent but not browned, about 3 minutes. Add the fennel and cook, stirring often, until tender but not browned, about 5 minutes. Salt to taste. Add the remaining 1 tablespoon of olive oil and the quinoas, walnuts, kale, turmeric, and 1 tablespoon of water and cook until the kale starts to wilt, about 3 minutes. Fold in the strained currants. Season with salt and pepper to taste. Spoon into bowls and drizzle with olive oil, if desired, and garnish with fennel fronds. Serve immediately.

Sugar & Olives

SPECKLED ROOSTER FARM

Speckled Rooster Farm is located on a residential road lined with stately old (and massive new) homes. It's a wonder the high-value Westport land (formerly an onion farm) has resisted development. But as of this writing, matriarch Irina Pabst, 98, had held tight to her overgrown one-and-a-half-acre parcel until agreeing to lease it to two eager young dreamers in 2011.

Now in its fourth year, Speckled Rooster continues to flourish, thanks to the sweat equity put in by Matt Oricchio and Jessica van Vlamertynghe, a dynamic duo who almost look too fresh-faced to know their way around the rigors of a gritty farming operation.

These two energetic rookies are living their dream. Though Matt's grandfather owned a farm, the two first lived off the land as students at UConn's Sustainable Living Community at Spring Valley Farm, where they lived in a farmhouse and cultivated an organic, sustainable lifestyle growing their own produce and selling it to local markets.

They've recreated a similarly unique oasis in Westport, upon which grows a variety of organic vegetables, focusing recently on leafy greens and small roots.

In addition to a B.S. in Horticulture, Matt is also passionate about Animal Science and Ecology. Speckled Rooster raises pigs, rabbits, and chickens for meat, as well as ducks and chickens for eggs. Recently, they introduced bees. Because the farm is small, they sell through a weekly email. They also supply some Westport restaurants and food markets, including The Whelk, Barcelona, Craft Butchery and Double L Market, as well as Sugar & Olives in Norwalk.

COMMUNITY FARM OF SIMSBURY

There's always a flurry of activity at Community Farm of Simsbury (CFS), a working farm and collaborative organization that promotes education and local agriculture, while practicing sound environmental stewardship, preserving the Town Farm, and benefiting those in need.

One of the great ways Community Farm helps the community is by feeding area families. In 2013, CFS donated more than 8,500 pounds of healthy, certified organic produce to families through partnerships with Simsbury Social Services, Gifts of Love, Hartford Food System, Foodshare, and Billings Forge Community Works.

Additionally, CFS introduced the concepts organic gardening to more than 2,000 students in Simsbury, Hartford, and the entire Farmington Valley, through hands-on, farm-based school programs and summertime camps, and provided need-based financial aid and scholarships to all who qualified. It also hosts an incubator program that provides aspiring farmers with hands-on training with CT NOFA (Northeast Organic Farming Association of Connecticut) and UConn, teaching them how to plant crops, use a hoophouse, set up irrigation systems, safely control weeds and pests, and use farm equipment.

Seasonal Quinoa Salad

SERVES 4 AS A MAIN DISH
OR 6 TO 8 AS A SIDE

Students at the farm created this quinoa recipe during a summer camp program teaching entrepreneurship. The challenge was for the students to create their own small business that sold a value-added product at a farmers' market.

1 1/2 cups quinoa, rinsed and drained

2 1/4 cups water or vegetable stock

1 pound green beans, trimmed, cut crosswise into 1-inch pieces

1 tablespoon unsalted butter

2 cups chopped fresh spinach, stems removed

1/4 cup plus 2 tablespoons extra-virgin olive oil

Kosher salt and freshly ground black pepper

1/4 cup plus 1 1/2 teaspoons white wine vinegar

1/4 cup plus 2 tablespoons raw hulled sunflower seeds

1/2 cup chopped green onions

1/4 cup chopped fresh cilantro leaves

1/4 cup chopped fresh parsley leaves

1. Fill a large bowl with ice water and set aside.

2. Combine the quinoa and water in a medium-size saucepan and bring to a boil over high heat. Cover, lower the heat, and simmer until the quinoa is tender and the little tails are visible, about 15 minutes. Uncover, fluff with a fork, and set aside.

3. Meanwhile, bring a medium-size pot of salted water to a boil. Add the green beans and cook until bright green and crisp-tender, about 4 minutes. Drain the beans in a colander, transfer to the bowl of ice water, and immerse, stirring occasionally, until completely cooled, about 4 minutes. Drain in a colander, then pat dry with paper towels; set aside.

4. Melt the butter in a medium-size skillet over medium heat. Add the spinach and cook, stirring occasionally, until just wilted, 2 to 3 minutes. When cool enough to handle, transfer the spinach to a paper towel and squeeze out any excess water. Set aside.

Whisk together the oil and vinegar until well combined. Season with salt and pepper to taste. Set aside.

5. Toast the sunflower seeds in a small, nonstick skillet over medium-high heat, stirring frequently, until the seeds are dry and fragrant, about 30 seconds.

6. Transfer the quinoa to a large bowl and add the green beans, spinach, sunflower seeds, green onion, cilantro, and parsley. Stir in the oil mixture and toss to coat. Season with salt and pepper to taste. Serve at once.

Note: This dish can be made ahead; just combine ingredients, then cover and refrigerate for up to 6 hours. Drizzle with the oil mixture just before serving.

Community Farm of Simsbury

EKONK HILL TURKEY FARM, LLC

Ekonk Hill Turkey Farm is owned and operated by the Hermonot family in Moosup. If you stop by to pick up a holiday turkey, your CSA share, an ice cream, or other local treats, you're bound to run into at least one of the Hermonot flock.

Elena, the matriarch, says, "We've had a family tradition of raising everything that is served on our Thanksgiving table. Of course, that starts with the turkey. In 1998, we raised 15 turkeys for family and friends. We have grown to 2,800 pasture-raised turkeys today. We are now the largest grower of pasture-raised turkeys in Connecticut!"

She adds, "We are having fun helping lots of folks develop the tradition of experiencing a locally grown holiday! We are very excited that our children are also interested and have supported the growth of the farm. Our many wonderful friends, who gather at the farm to help us process the turkeys, have been critical to our success as well."

Elena and her husband, Rick, started as dairy farmers. Now, Elena runs Ekonk's Milkhouse Bakery, and can be found waiting on customers in the farm's store seven days a week; that is, after her early start baking the day's pies, muffins, cookies, and breads. Rick works offsite as a farm consultant, and helps out on the farm wherever needed, even making homemade cider donuts on weekends.

All the Hermonot children are involved in one way or another on the Connecticut agricultural scene and at Ekonk Hill.

Slow Cooker Turkey Chili

SERVES 6 TO 8

Turkey chili is a Hermonot favorite after a long day on the farm. In addition to garnishing it with cilantro, they like to serve this chili with an assortment of toppings, such as sour cream or Greek yogurt, sliced avocado, and shredded cheese.

1 tablespoon olive oil

1 small red onion, diced

1 medium-size green bell pepper, stemmed, seeded, and diced

2 jalapeño peppers, stemmed, seeded (if desired), and minced

3 garlic cloves, minced

1 pound ground turkey

Kosher salt and freshly ground black pepper

1 (28-ounce) can crushed tomatoes with juice

1 (15-ounce) can kidney beans, drained and rinsed

1 (15-ounce) can black beans, drained and rinsed

2 cups fresh or frozen and thawed corn kernels

2 cups low-sodium chicken stock

1 (6-ounce) can tomato paste

1 tablespoon chili powder

1 tablespoon ground cumin

1 bay leaf

2 1/2 tablespoons fresh lime juice, plus lime wedges for garnish

Honey (optional)

Chopped fresh cilantro, for garnish

1. Heat the oil in a large skillet over medium heat. Add the onion and bell pepper and cook, stirring occasionally, until soft and translucent, about 10 minutes. Add the jalapeño and garlic and cook for 1 minute. Add the turkey and season with salt and pepper. Increase the heat to medium-high, and cook, breaking up the turkey with a fork until the meat is just browned.

2. Transfer the meat mixture to a 4-quart slow cooker. Stir in the tomatoes with juice, beans, corn, stock, tomato paste, chili powder, cumin, bay leave, lime juice, and 1 1/2 teaspoons of salt. Cover and cook on LOW for 5 hours. Remove and discard the bay leaf. Adjust the seasonings with honey, if using, and salt to taste. Sprinkle with cilantro and serve with lime wedges on the side.

Ekonk Hill Turkey Farm, LLC

BILLINGS FORGE COMMUNITY WORKS & FIREBOX RESTAURANT

Imagine a forgotten urban area where jobs are scarce and healthy foods are scarcer, an area suffering from poverty, homelessness, lack of opportunity, and disinvestment. Then, imagine that a grassroots group decides to turn things upside down, creating a model complex that offers housing, job training and hope.

At Billings Forge Community Works in Frog Hollow, just steps from the state capital, you'll find a vibrant hub where local farmers hawk their wares at a weekly farmers' market, an oasis with 48 garden beds, a farm-to-table job-training café, a bakery, a professional catering company, and a teaching kitchen where local residents, some battling such barriers as incarceration or addiction, learn job skills.

In 1990, the Melville Charitable Trust spearheaded an investment in Billings Forge, setting its sights on transforming a former factory complex into a vibrant mixed-use community where 280 residents (including 75 children) live in affordable and supportive housing, and enjoy a roster of community based programs, many centered around food.

At the core of this effort is the Firebox Restaurant, an award-winning eatery that anchors the Billings Forge complex, run by executive chef Sean Farrell. The Firebox goes beyond the notions of "locavore" by making a deeper commitment to community: One-third of the staff at Firebox resides in the surrounding community, and the team sources mainly from local farms.

Since opening its doors in 2007, the 125-seat restaurant has received accolades from *Gourmet* magazine and the *New York Times*, and was named Best Hartford Restaurant of 2009 by *Connecticut Magazine*. The restaurant continues to draw visitors into Frog Hollow (80,000 in 2013), emerging as the area leader in the farm-to-table movement.

For some, the farm-to-table philosophy is a trend. For Firebox, it's a way of life.

Cast-Iron Duck Breast

SERVES 4

This dish has a variation of colors, textures, and flavors from the sweet caramelized corn and crispy yet fork-tender roasted potatoes, to the savory, duck slices and the acidic basil vinaigrette.

4 (8-ounce) skin-on duck breasts, trimmed

1 pound fingerling potatoes, such as banana, unpeeled and cut in half lengthwise

5 tablespoons duck fat, divided

3 tablespoons minced fresh rosemary leaves

Kosher salt and freshly ground black pepper

1 tablespoon canola oil

2 cups fresh kernels cut from cobs (from about 4 ears) or frozen corn, such as butter-sugar

1 tablespoon butter

1 1/2 bunches kale, such as lacinato, tough stems removed, leaves cut into thin strips

1 1/4 cups halved cherry tomatoes, such as Sun Gold

Basil Vinaigrette (makes 1 1/8 cups)

1 1/4 cups packed fresh basil leaves

1 medium-size garlic clove, crushed

2 tablespoons chardonnay vinegar (see note)

1/2 cup extra-virgin olive oil

Kosher salt and freshly ground black pepper

1. Rinse the duck breast and pat dry with paper towels. Place the breasts on a cutting board and score the skin in several places with a sharp knife.

2. Preheat the oven to 350°F. Lightly oil a baking dish or rimmed baking sheet and set aside. Place the potatoes in a medium-size bowl. Add 1/4 cup of the duck fat, the rosemary, and salt and pepper to taste, and toss to combine, making sure to coat all the potatoes.

3. Spread the potatoes onto the prepared baking dish. Roast, stirring every 15 minutes, until the potatoes are fork-tender and golden brown, about 40 minutes. Set aside.

4. Heat the canola oil in a medium-size skillet over medium-high heat. Add the corn kernels and cook, stirring often, until light golden brown, about 8 minutes. Remove from the heat and set aside.

5. To make the basil vinaigrette: Fill a small bowl with ice water and set aside. Meanwhile, fill a small saucepan with water and bring to a boil over medium-high heat. Add the basil and blanch for 30 seconds. Using a slotted spoon, transfer the basil to the prepared ice-water bath and let cool completely, about 3 minutes. Drain the basil thoroughly and pat dry with paper towels.

6. Process the basil, garlic, and vinegar in a food processor until well blended. With the food processor running, slowly add the olive oil in a steady stream until smooth. Season with salt and pepper to taste. Set aside.

7. To make the duck: Season the breasts with salt and pepper to taste. Heat a 14-inch cast-iron skillet over medium-low heat. Add the duck breasts, skin side down, and cook until the fat is rendered and the skin is golden brown and crisp, about 20 minutes. Carefully flip the breasts over and cook until an internal temperature of the meat reaches 135°F (for medium-rare), about 14 minutes, or until the desired doneness is reached. Drain the duck fat from the pan and reserve. Transfer the meat to a carving board and let rest for 15 minutes.

8. While the duck is resting, heat the remaining 1 tablespoon of duck fat and the butter in the same cast-iron skillet used for the duck, over medium-high heat. Add the potatoes and cook until golden brown; adding additional reserved duck fat as needed, about 3 minutes. Add the kale, stirring to coat. Cook until wilted, stirring frequently, about

5 minutes. Add the corn, stirring frequently, and cook for another 2 minutes. Remove from the heat and add the tomatoes. Season with salt and pepper to taste.

9. To serve, cut the breasts into thin slices. Spoon some of the potato mixture onto each plate. Place the meat slices on top of the potato mixture, then spoon the vinaigrette over the dish to taste. Drizzle with additional vinegar, if desired.

Note: If you can't find chardonnay vinegar, champagne vinegar is a good substitute.

Firebox Restaurant

THE MAX RESTAURANT GROUP

Talk about the Midas touch. In the early '80s, restaurateur Richard Rosenthal launched his now ubiquitous brand of Hartford-centric restaurants and bars bearing the Max moniker, with Max on Main, which eventually moved into its primo Downtown digs in City Place in the heart of the business district. It is still the original and standard bearer.

The "crown jewel in the Max group," Max Downtown is lauded for outstanding service, beautiful decor, and first-class cuisine and wines, sweeping numerous "Best of" awards from *Zagat*, *Hartford Magazine* (winning 10 awards), *Wine Spectator*, and others. Executive chef Hunter Morton wows guests with his creative take on all-natural steaks, sustainable seafood, and other trend-setting dishes, with an eye toward local purveyors.

The thing about the Max restaurants is that there is one for every mood. With eight distinct eateries—all with unique menus, ambience, bar scenes, and personalities—Rosenthal and partners have cornered the market, building gorgeous yet comfortable mainstays and offering foods people really want to eat. In the mood for Italian-inspired cuisine or a crispy "stone pie"? There's Max Amore and Max a Mia. Craving superfresh local seafood and craft cocktails? There's Max Fish and Max's Oyster Bar. Looking for a more globally eclectic menu, hop over to Trumbull Kitchen, and for more casual American comfort food and a first-rate burger, head to Max Burger and Max's Tavern in Springfield, Massachusetts.

On top of eight über-successful restaurants, there's Max's Catering, the exclusive caterer at the Bushnell, Connecticut's premier performing arts center, and the Basketball Hall of Fame, serving legendary ball players, coaches, and sports fans. Max's Catering also runs the Chef to Farm summer dinner series held at local farms, including Rosedale Farms in Simsbury, Graywall Farm in Lebanon, and Nathan Hale Homestead in Coventry. With live bands, local, organic wines, and fresh farm fare prepared by chef Scott Miller, they are a huge summer draw.

COVENTRY REGIONAL FARMERS' MARKET

There's good reason 80,000 visitors a year converge on the Coventry Regional Farmers' Market. It's a regional treasure, held at the Nathan Hale Homestead in Coventry, abutting 500 acres of forest. Against this rural backdrop, the market is like a country fair *every* Sunday, June through October, and well worth the trip. Visit once, and you'll know why it was voted New England's best farmers' market by *Yankee Magazine* and selected as one of *USA Today's* "Top 10 great places to shop at a farmers' market."

With 50 to 75 vendors each Sunday, the market teems with action—the old-fashioned kind—with stand after stand displaying a colorful smorgasbord of organic produce, freshly baked pies, preserves and pickles, and handmade goods. Here, wee ones frolic, fiddlers fiddle, puppies romp, and chefs and consumers chat up their farmers and sample their wares.

It's a huge and diverse market, so plan on staying for lunch and making an afternoon out of it. Just about every week, there is something new and novel to discover, such as the annual Dog Day event, where attendees bring their dogs to mingle with other four-legged friends, or the preseason offsite pop-up markets. The team is always whipping up fun seasonal events. To find out what's happening on any given week, visit: www.coventryfarmersmarket.com.

The market masters do a bang-up job of vetting the vendors, who specialize in organic, heirloom, ethnic, and gourmet varieties of fruits and vegetables, as well as grass-fed beef, free-range eggs, milk, yogurt, smoked bacon, rustic breads, farmstead cheeses, European pastries, salsa, pesto, fresh herbs, cut flowers, chocolate fudge, honey, maple syrup, and more.

The market also features the work of local artists and artisans. Live entertainment and food trucks makes shopping at the market an opportunity to visit, lunch, and unwind. Sustainable living programs, such as Homesteading Boot Camp and Summer in a Jar, are a fun way to learn something new. Pet a goat, have lunch in a grassy spot under the maple trees, or give your little one a ride in a red wagon. If you are looking for the quintessential Connecticut family outing, this is it.

MarWin Farm's Duck with Corn Bread Stuffing and Strawberry Sauce

SERVES 4

This delicious recipe is a novel spin on a traditional turkey dinner, substituting locally raised duck and strawberry sauce for roast turkey and cranberry sauce.

Corn Bread Stuffing

About 1 pound (2 day-old) corn bread, cut into 1-inch cubes (about 6 cups)
2 tablespoons unsalted butter
1/2 cup diced onion
1/2 cup diced celery
4 fresh sage leaves, finely chopped
4 sprigs thyme, finely chopped
1 ear fresh corn, kernels removed
1 cup duck stock or low-sodium chicken stock
Kosher salt and freshly ground black pepper

Duck

2 duck breast halves (about 1 pound each)
1 tablespoon olive oil
Kosher salt and freshly ground black pepper

Strawberry Sauce

1 tablespoon local honey
1/2 cup port wine
8 local strawberries, hulled and cut in half
1 cup duck or low-sodium chicken stock
1 tablespoon unsalted butter
Kosher salt and freshly ground black pepper

1. To make the corn bread stuffing: Preheat the oven to 400°F. Place the bread cubes in a single layer on a baking sheet and bake until just golden brown, about 15 minutes (depending on the density of the bread). Set aside to cool completely. Place in a food processor and pulse until coarse crumbs begin to form. Transfer the crumbs to a large bowl.

2. Melt the butter in a medium-size skillet over medium heat. Add the onion and celery and cook, stirring occasionally, until soft and translucent, about 10 minutes. Stir in the sage, thyme, and corn and cook for another minute. Fold the onion mixture into the bread crumbs and stir in the stock. Season with salt and pepper to taste. Set aside to cool completely.

3. To make the duck: Pat the duck breasts with paper towels. Place the duck breast, skin side up, on a cutting board and, with a sharp knife, score the skin in a crosshatch pattern, piercing through the skin and fat, about 1/2 inch deep. Season both sides with salt and pepper. Cut four pieces of kitchen twine long enough to wrap around the breasts with extra length to tie a knot. Place the four pieces of twine on a cutting board with equal spacing between each truss. Place one duck breast half, skin side down, crosswise over the twine. Place 1/2 cup of stuffing on top of the duck and top with a second breast half, skin side up. Wrap the kitchen twine around the breasts and tie into knots.

4. Place the remaining stuffing (about 5 1/2 cups) in an 8 x 8-inch buttered baking dish and cover with foil.

5. Preheat the oven to 375°F. Heat the oil in a large, ovenproof skillet over medium heat. Add the breasts, skin side down, and cook, turning once, until golden brown, about 6 minutes per side. Drain the fat from the skillet. Transfer the skillet to the oven and bake for 35 minutes, or until a meat thermometer inserted into the center of a duck half reads 130°F. Transfer to a cutting board, tent with foil, and allow to rest for 15 minutes. Transfer the remaining stuffing to the oven and bake until the top is lightly golden brown, about 20 minutes.

6. To make the sauce: While the stuffing is baking, place the honey in a medium-size saucepan and bring to a simmer over low heat. Increase the heat to medium-high, add the port, and cook, stirring often, until the port has been reduced by half, about 6 minutes. Add the strawberries and stock and continue to simmer, stirring often, until the sauce coats the back of a spoon, about 20 minutes. Whisk in the butter and season with salt and pepper to taste.

7. To serve: Slice the duck and arrange over the stuffing. Drizzle with the sauce to taste and serve at once.

Max Downtown

GOURMAVIAN FARMS, LLC

Buying conventional chicken has become a dicey proposition, with salmonella outbreaks a regular occurrence and new, drug-resistant strains of bacteria becoming more difficult to treat.

But poultry lovers, never fear. The good folks at GourmAvian Farms LLC, a growing family business headquartered in Bolton, slowly grows heritage colored-feather chickens in an organic, free-range way up in the "Quiet Corner" of Connecticut. The result is healthy birds whose taste and texture is highly coveted by local chefs and, increasingly, by local families concerned about where their chicken is coming from.

These hardy birds are bred from old-world chickens originating in France and Italy, and raised by methods learned over the years by owner Gary Proctor, a Vietnam vet who has over 35 years of experience in the poultry business, establishing and operating breeding facilities on three continents in six countries.

Proctor is committed to responsible animal care and environmental protection, and seeks to engage the community while producing a safe, wholesome, high-quality, Connecticut-grown product. "The farm's mission goes beyond raising superior birds," says Proctor. "We are passionate about connecting people to agriculture through farmers' markets, agricultural fairs, the Ag in the Classroom Initiative, 4-H, and other educational venues."

GourmAvian birds are proudly served at top restaurants and eateries across the state, including at many of the venues within this book.

THE MILL AT 2T

The Mill at 2t, in the tiny town of Tar-iffville, is a charming, seasonally inspired restaurant, set in a reclaimed historic textile mill dating back to the 1800s, close enough to the Farmington River to hear the gurgles. This cozy 1,000-square-foot dining spot offers a mere nine tables, so make an early reservation and expect to wait with a drink if the table ahead of you decides to linger.

The exposed-brick room is complemented with exposed beams, hardwood floors, high-back leather chairs, and a prime view into the tiny open kitchen where chef Ryan Jones takes center stage.

When you dine here, owners Ryan and Kelleanne Jones make you feel as if you are dining in their home. Kelleanne dotes on each table, while Ryan cooks and mingles with the lucky few who score front-row seats at the chef's counter.

The Mill at 2t offers an ever-changing menu of local fare and fine wines. If you're feeling flush, put yourselves in Ryan's hands and order the five-course chef's tasting menu at $70, or $100 with wine parings. You'll enjoy signature starters, such as the pan-seared diver scallops with roasted red and yellow beets, candied fennel, tangerines, and pea tendrils, then move to decadent entrées, such as the Cowboy Steak for Two, Australian rack of lamb, or roasted cobia fillet. For dessert, you'll have a choice of the likes of homemade brioche donuts with caramel or a strawberry rhubarb cobbler, served with fresh buttermilk ice cream.

It's hard to pin down what will be available each time you visit, as the menu changes frequently with the seasons and with what is fresh at the market. Of one thing you can be sure: You will walk away telling your friends about the little culinary gem by the river.

Duck and Foie Gras Poutine

SERVES 4 TO 6

This poutine is a decadent version that tops golden French fried potatoes with local duck and foie gras.

Note: The confit duck must be started two days before it is served. The duck leg can be cooked up to four days ahead; simply cover the shredded meat with some of the duck fat to prevent it from drying out.

Confit Duck Leg

2 duck legs with thighs attached, excess fat trimmed and reserved (about 1 1/2 pounds duck)

1 large garlic clove, minced

1 1/2 teaspoons minced fresh thyme

2 bay leaves, crushed

1 1/2 teaspoons kosher salt

1/2 teaspoon fresh ground black pepper, or to taste

6 tablespoons unsalted butter, cut into pieces

1/2 gallon vegetable oil, for frying

Mirepoix

1 tablespoon extra-virgin olive oil

1/3 cup medium-dice celery (between 1/4- and 1/2-inch dice)

1/3 cup medium-dice onion (between 1/4- and 1/2-inch dice)

1/3 cup medium-dice carrot (between 1/4- and 1/2-inch dice)

1 tablespoon all-purpose flour

Poutine Sauce (makes 2 1/2 cups)

2 cups duck or chicken stock

1 cup grated Gruyère cheese

2 tablespoons pure maple syrup

1/2 teaspoon aged sherry vinegar

Kosher salt and freshly ground black pepper

3 ounces Hudson Valley foie gras, cut into medium dice (between 1/4- and 1/2-inch dice)

French Fries (makes 2 1/2 quarts)

6 large organic russet potatoes, peeled and cut into about 1/2 x 1/2 x 3-inch-long rectangular sticks (The chef prefers potatoes from Anthony Farm.)

Kosher salt and freshly ground black pepper

For Assembly

1/4 cup chopped green onion

1/4 cup grated Gruyère cheese

1. To make the confit duck leg: Place the reserved duck fat at the bottom of a small baking dish. Place the legs on top of the fat, skin side down. In a small bowl, combine the garlic, thyme, bay leaves, and salt and pepper into a paste. Press the paste evenly on the duck leg. Cover with plastic wrap and refrigerate for 12 hours.

2. Preheat the oven to 200°F. Scrape off the residual garlic, bay leaves, salt, and pepper into a medium-size ovenproof skillet. Add the trimmed duck fat. Pat the duck legs dry with paper towels, then add to skillet, skin side down. Add the butter. Cover and bake until the meat pulls away from the bone, about 10 hours (see note). Remove the duck from the fat. Strain the fat and reserve. Remove the meat from the bones (about 1 1/4 cups) and set aside.

3. Fill a 1-gallon, heavy-bottomed pot halfway up the sides with the oil. Heat the oil to 275°F for the fries.

4. While the oil is heating for the fries, start the poutine sauce. Heat the oil in a medium-size skillet over medium heat. To make the mirepoix, add the vegetables and sauté until tender, about 10 minutes. Sprinkle the vegetables with flour and

stir to coat evenly. Add 1 cup of the duck meat and the stock. Bring to a simmer over medium heat, stirring occasionally, until slightly thickened, about 30 minutes. Slowly stir in the cheese and continue to cook until cheese has melted, about 2 minutes. Whisk in the maple syrup and vinegar. Season with salt and pepper to taste.

5. Heat a cast-iron skillet until hot but not smoking. In batches, add the foie gras and sear on both sides, about 5 minutes. Using a slotted spoon, fold the foie gras pieces into the poutine sauce.

6. To make the fries: Place the fries in a large bowl of ice cold water to release some of the starch, for 15 minutes. Drain in a colander and pat the potatoes dry with paper towels. Working in batches, gently drop the fries into the hot oil to blanch for 7 minutes. Using a slotted spoon, remove the potatoes and drain on paper towels. Increase the oil temperature to 350°F. Working in batches, gently drop the fries back into the oil and fry until golden brown on all sides, about 3 minutes. Using a slotted spoon, remove the potatoes and drain on paper towels in a single layer. Season with salt and pepper to taste.

7. To assemble: Place the fries in a bowl and top with the poutine sauce. Garnish with green onions and Gruyere cheese. Serve at once.

Note: This recipe calls for a low and slow roasting technique. The oven is intentionally set at a low temperature until the meat falls off the bone.

The Mill at 2T

BISTRO SEVEN RESTAURANT

In 2012, Breno Donatti opened Bistro Seven with a seasonally changing menu. Donatti, who was born in Brazil and came to the United States at as a twenty-something, worked his way up from dishwasher to chef to restaurateur in less than 10 years. His dream to open a farm-to-fork bistro serving American comfort food was inspired on a 2011 trip to Paris with his young opera singer wife, after they stumbled upon Café Central, an alluring bistro serving American food, sourced locally and prepared with a deft hand.

When he returned from his travels, Donatti searched a spot for his dream restaurant. In 2012, Bistro Seven sprang to life in a high-traffic spot near Ridgefield, Wilton, and Redding.

He explains, "The local, seasonal concept allows us to make sure we are using the best ingredients available. It also allows us to support the farmers and producers of our surroundings as much as possible, and source wine and beer that are actually 'worth the sip.'"

In 2013, Bistro Seven planted its own sizeable garden on a nearby plot to supply a portion of its herbs and vegetables, and also teamed up with local purveyors of meats, produce, and fish, as well as local growers, to source as much produce as possible. Most of the products are sourced through Pound Ridge Organics, a company created by Donna Simons.

Part of the Slow Food movement and the Non-GMO Project, Donatti strives to create a simple, seasonal menu that is creative yet not precious. Today, two chefs share the kitchen, executing Donatti's vision.

Organic Duck Breast with Ginger-Carrot Puree and Ginger-Orange Sauce

SERVES 4

The lovely ginger-carrot puree and ginger-orange sauce provide a dash of color and zip to this classic roast duck recipe.

Sweet Potatoes and Apples

2 medium-size sweet potatoes, peeled and cut into 1-inch pieces

2 apples, such as McIntosh, cored, peeled, and cut into 1/3-inch-wide slices

2 tablespoons unsalted butter

Ginger-Carrot Puree

5 medium-size multicolored organic carrots, such as white and orange, peeled and cut into 1-inch pieces

1 ounce coarsely chopped fresh ginger
1/4 cup heavy cream, warmed, or as needed
1 tablespoon unsalted butter
Kosher salt and coarsely ground black pepper

Ginger-Orange Sauce

3 tablespoons unsalted butter, divided
1 1/2 large shallots, thinly sliced
2 ounces chopped fresh ginger
2 large garlic cloves, minced
2 organic oranges, peeled, sectioned, membranes
  and seeds removed, and chopped
1/3 gallon fresh orange juice
2 tablespoons brown sugar

Duck

4 (8-ounce) skin-on duck breasts, trimmed

For Assembly

4 sprigs rosemary, for garnish

1. Preheat the oven to 350°F.

2. To start the sweet potatoes and apples: Place the sweet potatoes in a medium-size saucepan and cover with cold, salted water. Bring to a boil over medium-high heat and cook until the potatoes are fork-tender, about 8 minutes. Drain and transfer to a medium-size bowl. Set aside.

3. To make the ginger-carrot puree: Place the carrots and ginger in a medium-size saucepan and cover with cold, salted water. Bring to a boil over medium-high heat and cook until the carrots are fork-tender, about 20 minutes. Drain and transfer to a food processor. Add the cream and butter and pulse until smooth. Season with salt and pepper to taste. Transfer to a bowl and cover with foil.

4. To make the ginger-orange sauce: Melt 2 tablespoons of the butter in a medium-size saucepan over medium heat. Add the shallots, ginger, and garlic and cook, stirring often, until the shallots

are soft and translucent, about 4 minutes. Add the oranges and sauté for 1 minute. Stir in the orange juice and brown sugar and bring to a boil over medium-high heat. Lower the heat to a simmer and cook until the sauce has reduced by two thirds, about 50 minutes. Whisk in the remaining 1 tablespoon of butter. Adjust the seasonings with salt and pepper to taste.

5. To make the duck: Rinse the duck breast and pat dry with paper towels. Place the breast on a cutting board and, with a sharp knife, score the skin in several places.

Season the breasts with salt and pepper to taste. Heat a 14-inch ovenproof skillet over medium-high heat. Add the duck breasts, skin side down and cook until the fat is rendered and the skin is golden brown and crisp, about 5 minutes. Carefully flip the breasts over and cook until golden brown and crisp, about 3 more minutes. Transfer to the oven and bake until a thermometer reads 135°F, about 15 minutes.

6. Transfer the duck to a cutting board and allow to rest for 10 minutes before thinly slicing on an angle.

7. While the meat is resting, sauté the apples and sweet potatoes: Melt the butter in a medium-size skillet over medium-high heat. Add the apples and sweet potatoes and cook, stirring often, until the apples are tender and the sweet potatoes are heated through, about 5 minutes.

8. To assemble: Reheat the ginger-orange sauce and the puree until heated through. Divide the sautéed sweet potatoes and apples among four plates. Top with duck slices. Spoon some of the puree onto each plate. Garnish with a rosemary sprig and drizzle the sauce over the duck and puree and around the plate.

Bistro Seven Restaurant

MUSE BY JONATHAN CARTWRIGHT

One cannot speak of the Mayflower Grace Hotel and Spa, set on the sprawling, idyllic grounds of a Litchfield County estate, without mentioning New England luxury: as in, four-poster beds with feather-topped mattresses and Frette linens, antique appointments, and sumptuous marble baths. *Luxe* is also the watchword for the main restaurant, Muse by Jonathan Cartwright, the ideal backdrop for any anniversary, special occasion, or lively night out.

Inside the surprisingly mod, casually elegant restaurant, featuring a serene gray palette, guests dine on a menu created by Grand Chef Relais & Châteaux Jonathan Cartwright and executed by executive chef Stephen Barc. Muse delivers ambitious seasonal cuisine, drawing on fresh local ingredients, presenting the likes of farm-raised foie gras with sautéed Gala apples, oxtail ragout, port syrup, sour cherries, and onion marmalade, or butter-poached Maine lobster and scallop mousseline with sautéed kale, fennel, lemon gnocchi, and cognac coral butter sauce. For an exquisite indulgence, there is even a caviar menu with options that range from a traditional California Transmontanus for $100 per serving to a Special Reserve osetra caviar from Russia for $600 per serving.

The Mayflower Grace features a range of simply elegant and relaxed New England dining experiences, featuring both à la carte and prix fixe menus. Whether you are stopping in for a classic Grace cocktail or full gourmet service, there are countless choices designed to satisfy. During warm weather, enjoy breakfast, lunch, or dinner alfresco on the terrace that peers over the manicured grounds. Guests seeking a low-key option will enjoy the convivial atmosphere of the Tap Room, serving lounge-style dishes, such as seasonal soups, jumbo shrimp cocktail, tuna tartare, Prince Edward Island mussels and truffle-Parmesan fries. Whichever atmosphere suits your mood, all menus offer fresh, seasonal fare that showcase the bounty from an array of Connecticut and New York State farms.

Pan-Roasted New England Pheasant Breast with Shallot-Cranberry Puree, Braised Red Cabbage, and Madeira Sauce

SERVES 4

Note: The braised cabbage can be started two days before it is served. Just reheat!

Braised Red Cabbage (makes 6 portions)

1 small head red cabbage (about 2 pounds), quartered, cored, and finely shredded

1 cup dry red wine

1/2 cup sherry vinegar

3 tablespoons honey

1 tablespoon chopped fresh thyme

Kosher salt and fresh ground black pepper

2 tablespoons unsalted butter

1 small onion, thinly sliced

Mushroom and Shallot Puree

1 tablespoon unsalted butter

2 tablespoons minced shallots

Kosher salt and freshly ground black pepper

1 cup packed coarsely chopped mixed fresh mushrooms, such as white button, oyster, porcini, or chanterelles

1/4 cup heavy cream

Cranberry and Shallot Puree

1 tablespoon unsalted butter

2 tablespoons thinly sliced shallots

1/2 cup cranberries

1/4 cup heavy cream

Kosher salt

Honey (optional)

Pheasant Breasts

1 tablespoon blended oil

4 pheasant breasts, removed from bone with skin and wing attached

Sea salt, such as Maine sea salt, and freshly ground white pepper

Madeira Sauce

1 tablespoon unsalted butter

1/2 cup minced mixed fresh vegetables, such as onion, celery, carrot, and leek

1 garlic clove, minced

1 sprig thyme

6 black peppercorns

1/2 cup port wine

1/4 cup Madeira wine

1 cup veal jus

For Assembly:

Blanched Brussels sprout leaves (optional)

Crispy sweet potato chips (optional)

1. To make the braised cabbage: Place the cabbage in a large bowl. Add the wine, vinegar, honey, thyme, and salt and pepper to taste and toss to coat. Cover and let the cabbage marinate in the refrigerator, tossing occasionally.

2. Preheat the oven to 300°F. Heat 2 tablespoons of butter in a large, oven-safe pan with lid over medium-low heat. Add the onion and sauté until soft and translucent, about 5 minutes. Add the cabbage and its marinade and bring to a boil, stirring occasionally, over medium heat. Cover, transfer to the oven and cook, stirring occasionally, for 3 hours. Set aside to reheat just before serving.

3. To make the mushroom and shallot puree: Heat the butter in a medium-size sauté pan over medium heat. Add the shallots and cook, stirring often, for 3 minutes. Add the mushrooms and cook, stirring often, for 2 minutes. Season

with salt and pepper to taste. Cover the pan and continue to cook, stirring occasionally, until the mushrooms are soft, about 3 minutes. Remove from the heat, transfer to a blender or food processor, and pulse to a puree. While the motor is running, slowly add the cream. Strain the mushroom mixture through a fine-mesh sieve; season with salt and pepper to taste. Set aside.

4. To make the cranberry and shallot puree: Heat the butter in a medium-size sauté pan over medium heat. Add the shallots and cook, stirring often, until tender, about 3 minutes. Add the cranberries and cook, stirring occasionally, for 5 minutes. Remove from the heat, transfer to a blender or food processor, and pulse to a puree. While the motor is running, slowly add the cream. Season with salt to taste. Adjust the seasonings with honey, if desired.

5. To make the pheasant: Preheat the oven to 375°F. Pat the breasts dry with paper towels and season with salt and pepper. Heat the oil in a large oven-safe skillet over medium-high heat until hot but not smoking. Add the pheasant, skin side down, and sear until golden brown and crisp, about 4 minutes. Transfer the skillet to the oven and roast until cooked through, about 8 minutes. Allow the breasts to rest for 5 minutes before plating.

6. While the breasts are searing, reheat the purees, in separate small saucepans, until heated through.

7. While the pheasant is searing, make the Madeira sauce: Heat the butter in a medium-size sauté pan over medium heat. Add the vegetables and cook, stirring often, for 3 minutes. Add the garlic and cook, stirring often, until fragrant, about 1 minute. Stir in the thyme, peppercorns, port wine, and Madeira wine. Increase the heat to a simmer and cook, stirring often, until the sauce is reduced by half; about 5 minutes. Stir in the veal jus and bring to a simmer and cook, stirring often, until the sauce is thick enough to coat the back of a spoon, about 6 minutes. Strain the sauce through a fine-mesh sieve; season with salt and pepper to taste. Set aside.

8. To assemble: Plate the cabbage in the center of a plate, drag the purees on each side, and place the pheasant breast on top of the cabbage. Spoon some of the Madeira sauce around the pheasant. Garnish with blanched Brussels sprout leaves and crispy sweet potato chips, if desired.

Note: Save the extra cabbage and use in a wrap or sandwich.

The Mayflower Grace

Buttermilk Fried Chicken

SERVES 5

This recipe is all about the brine, which is key when frying chicken for flavor and tenderness. The crispy golden brown outside complements the succulent meat inside.

Brine

2 gallons water

1 cup kosher salt

3 garlic heads, halved horizontally

1 large Spanish onion, quartered

1/4 cup brown sugar

10 fresh bay leaves

1 ounce thyme sprigs (about a handful)

1/2 ounce rosemary sprigs (about 8 sprigs)

6 lemons, halved, juice removed and reserved for brine

2 tablespoons allspice berries

2 tablespoons black peppercorns

Chicken

2 (2 1/2- to 3-pound) chickens, cut into 10 pieces each to yield 8 breast quarters (rib bones left attached), 4 wings, 4 thighs, and 4 drumsticks

Seasoned Flour

8 cups all-purpose flour

1/2 cup granulated garlic

1/2 cup granulated onion

2 tablespoons sweet smoked paprika

2 tablespoons Old Bay seasoning

1 tablespoon cayenne pepper

1 tablespoon freshly ground black pepper

4 cups buttermilk

About 2 quarts oil, preferably peanut, for frying, or as needed

12 sprigs thyme

12 sprigs rosemary

Kosher salt and freshly ground black pepper

1. To make the brine (see notes): Combine all the ingredients in a large stockpot. Bring to a simmer over medium-high heat. Remove from the heat and allow to cool completely, about 2 hours. Add the chicken, cover, and refrigerate for 12 hours.

2. Remove the chicken from the brine, rinse under cold running water, and dry thoroughly with paper towels. Set on racks with baking sheets underneath, to catch excess liquid, and allow the chicken to come to room temperature before frying, about 2 hours.

3. To make the seasoned flour: In a large bowl, combine all the ingredients, then divide the flour between two separate shallow bowls. Pour the buttermilk into a third shallow bowl.

4. Heat the oil, about 3 inches deep, to 320°F in a large, heavy-bottomed, cast-iron Dutch oven, over medium-high heat. Add the thyme and rosemary sprigs and fry until crisp, about 1 minute. Using a slotted spoon, carefully remove the herbs and drain on paper towels. Set aside for garnish.

5. Pat the thighs and drumsticks dry once more with paper towels. Dredge the thighs and drumsticks in the flour, shaking off any excess; then in the buttermilk, shaking off any excess; and then in the second bowl of flour, shaking off any excess. Working in batches, carefully drop one piece of dredged chicken at a time into the hot oil (depending on the size of pot, about three pieces at a time). Fry the chicken until golden brown and cooked through, turning occasionally to brown on all sides and to prevent the pieces from sticking together; about 12 minutes per batch (depending on the size of drumsticks and legs).

6. Using a slotted spoon, remove the chicken and drain on paper towels, skin side up. Season with salt and pepper to taste.

7. Adjust the oil temperature to 340°F and repeating the process with the breast pieces, frying until golden brown and cooked through; depending on size of breasts, about 10 minutes per batch. Finish with the wings, frying for about 8 minutes per batch. Garnish with the reserved fried herbs.

Notes:

If a 2-gallon stockpot is too big for your refrigerator, transfer the chicken pieces to large bowls with the brine solids; top off with enough of the liquid brine to cover the chicken.

Feel free to use precut chicken parts.

Cafemantic

CT VALLEY FARMS, LLC

A visit to CT Valley Farms, in Simsbury, is like being transported to the fields Cambodia or Thailand. It's a local farm that specializes in Asian and ethnic produce.

CT Valley Farms was created and tended by Vicheth Im, a former nonprofit sector health advocate, and her boyfriend, Jim Dombroski, a Connecticut Certified Master Gardener and who owned Connecticut Valley Worm Farm for 10 years.

Vicheth says, "We specialize in ethnic specially crops and have a passion for keeping traditions alive through food."

The pint-size farm grows an abundance of unique crops, including lemongrass, ginger, Asian greens, Thai basil, opo squash, shishito peppers, Laos purple and Cambodian green giant eggplant, even peanuts! Vicheth, who is Cambodian, says, "We have learned a lot about ethnic crops and how many of them cross over between cultures."

After researching way to start a farm, Vicheth and Jim found the "New Entry Sustainable Farming Project," a small farm business planning program through Tufts University in Lowell, Massachusetts. Vicheth recalls, "The class taught us how to write a farm business plan and many aspects of operating a small farm. We wanted to grow ethnic crops because we knew that it would diversify our business and there is definitely a need. We were thrilled to get our certificates when we completed the program."

Next, they were accepted into the Community Farm of Simsbury's Incubator Farm program. "It was perfect," Vicheth says. "We could lease land for a low cost and have access to a high-tunnel greenhouse, equipment, and irrigation. There is even a walk-in cooler to store our produce. We farm on about less than an acre of land."

A stint at the popular Coventry Farmers' Market helped put them on the map for growing unique items, and they were on their way. They now sell at farmers' markets in Hartford, and look forward to expanding their reach. They hope to expand their wholesale accounts and sell to ethnic grocery stores this year.

Chicken Ginger Stir-fry

SERVES 3

"Having a farm is rewarding and hard work, which does not leave you a lot of time to wait for a meal. Being Cambodian, I have had many ginger stir-fries. This one satisfies my craving for an authentic stir-fry with a marriage of something fresh and cool." —Vicheth Im

1 cup cherry tomatoes, cut in half

4 red bunching onions or green onions, chopped

3 tablespoons red wine vinegar

1/2 teaspoon freshly ground black pepper

3 tablespoons vegetable oil, divided

3 tablespoons thinly sliced fresh ginger, chopped

3 garlic cloves, minced

1 1/2 pounds boneless, skinless chicken breasts, cut into thin strips

1 teaspoon granulated sugar

2 tablespoons oyster sauce (see note)

3 to 4 cups jasmine rice, cooked according to the package directions

1. Combine the tomatoes, onions, vinegar, and pepper in a small bowl. Allow the tomatoes to marinate at room temperature for 15 minutes.

2. Heat 1 tablespoon of the oil in a large skillet or wok over medium-high heat. The oil should be almost smoking. Add the ginger and cook, stirring constantly, until the ginger is crispy and brown. With a slotted spoon, remove the ginger and set aside.

3. Carefully add the remaining 2 tablespoons of oil. Add the garlic and cook, stirring frequently, until light golden brown. Add the chicken and cook, stirring constantly, until chicken is lightly browned. Add the sugar, oyster sauce, and ginger, and continue to cook, stirring continually, until the chicken is cooked through. Remove from the heat. Serve the chicken over the hot rice, topped with the tomato mixture.

Note: Oyster sauce can be found in many grocery stores, in the Asian food section, as well as at specialty Asian markets.

CT Valley Farms, LLC

MOUNTAINTOP MUSHROOMS

Restaurateurs seeking unique and hard-to-find specialty mushrooms have made Mountaintop Mushrooms in Waterbury a gourmand's go-to resource. Owner Gregg Wershoven says, "We plant a variety of gourmet mushrooms that you can't normally find in a typical grocery or gourmet market, including golden, blue, and pink oyster; jumbo shiitake, trumpet, and shimeji, as well as Lion's Mane, maitake, and reishi." Although Mountaintop sells mainly to wholesale clients, Wershoven says, "We enjoy offering our naturally grown "wild-type" mushrooms to everyone who enjoys the best. For the retail customer, it's best to call ahead to see what is available before visiting."

Wershoven says Mountaintop has cultivated about 14 different strains in the last seven years, and continues to develop these unique varieties to suit the demands of local chefs, serving a clientele with a sophisticated palate that gets more global and sophisticated every year. He says that growing new mushrooms is much like a science: "We use a laboratory for our strain culture work and an incubation room for our spawn runs. Our mushrooms grow in three large underground grow rooms on the farm." The result is an array of specialty mushrooms that transform a simple dish into an extraordinary meal.

Chicken and Blue Oyster Mushrooms with Sherry Cream Sauce

SERVES 3 TO 4

Serve this dish with mashed potatoes or over egg noodles.

1 tablespoon extra-virgin olive oil
1/2 pound blue oyster mushrooms (see note), trimmed, stemmed, and cut into 1-inch strips
1 1/2 tablespoons minced shallot
1 tablespoon minced garlic
1/3 cup dry sherry
1/2 cup low-sodium chicken stock
1 cup heavy cream
1 teaspoon chopped fresh rosemary, plus more for garnish
1/8 teaspoon freshly grated nutmeg, plus more for garnish
1 1/2 pounds boneless, skinless chicken breasts or thighs, cooked, trimmed, and cut into 1-inch strips
3 tablespoons diced smoked ham
1 1/2 teaspoons cornstarch
2 tablespoons water

1. Heat the oil in a large sauté pan over medium heat. Add the mushrooms and cook, stirring frequently, until the mushrooms are soft, about 6 minutes. Add the shallot and garlic and cook, stirring often, for 2 minutes.

2. Increase the heat to medium-high, add the sherry, and bring to a boil, stirring frequently, until most of the sherry has evaporated, about 2 minutes.

3. Whisk in the chicken stock, cream, rosemary, and nutmeg. Add the chicken and ham, lower the heat to a simmer, and cook until the chicken and ham are heated through, about 4 minutes.

4. Combine the cornstarch and water in a small bowl, then whisk the cornstarch slurry into the cream mixture. Simmer until the sauce thickens, stirring often, about 1 minute. Season with salt and pepper to taste.

5. Serve garnished with rosemary and nutmeg.

Note: You can substitute white, portobello, or stemmed shiitake mushrooms for the blue oyster mushrooms.

Mountaintop Mushrooms

THE SPREAD

The Spread in South Norwalk is such a party that one might overlook the fact that the food is so darned good. Hats off to executive chef Carlos Baez, who is firing on all cylinders—and garnering the respect of the culinary elite along the way. In fact, the Spread won or placed in five of *Connecticut Magazine*'s 2014 Reader's Choice Awards: Best New Restaurant, Best in Overall Excellence, Best Brunch, Best Appetizers, and Best Cocktails. More recently, the Spread bagged Best American and Best New Restaurant from Moffly Media's Gold Coast Awards.

Hailing from Mexico, Baez brings a global perspective to bear in his sophisticated cuisine, from American farmhouse to French, Italian, and Spanish. Baez will catch your attention with such entrées as duck breast with ginger-carrot puree and fennel pollen; bacon-wrapped local scallops with a mushroom farrotto and shallot jam; or Hudson Valley foie gras or perfect lamb saddle. Mix in a few of his lighter bites, such as fiery shishito peppers; crispy Brussels sprouts; truffle risotto balls; and a mean roasted beet salad with mandarin orange, pistachios, and mascarpone, and you'll see why The Spread is garnering such good buzz.

Served on kitschy, mismatched vintage china, Baez's creations, which come in a range of plate sizes depending on your appetite, are pretty as a picture and full of locally sourced veggies, eggs, meats and seafood, when available. Clearly, Carlos' training on the line at La Panetière (Rye, New York) and Napa & Co. (Stamford), has served him well, catapulting this relative newcomer to the top of the food chain in Fairfield County.

If you're into a nice quiet meal, opt for a weeknight visit or brunch, or plan to dine before the DJ starts to pump up the jams, typically after 11 on weekends.

Chicken Under a Brick

SERVES 4

Chef Carlos Baez served this recipe at Westport's Wakeman Town Farm Harvest Fest Dinner, where it was a runaway hit. Cooking the chicken under a brick is a nice departure from the traditional roast chicken method. The key to this dish is using a high-quality chicken. If you have the opportunity, go for a sustainably raised chicken whenever possible.

Lemon-Garlic Dressing

1/4 cup extra-virgin olive oil, or to taste
1 tablespoon fresh lemon juice
1 small garlic clove, minced
1/2 teaspoon finely grated lemon zest (optional)
1/2 teaspoon kosher salt
1/4 teaspoon freshly ground black pepper
1/4 teaspoon dry mustard

Chicken

1 (3 1/2-pound) chicken (fryer), backbone and
    keel bones removed
1/4 cup canola oil
Kosher salt and freshly ground black pepper
2 tablespoons dry white wine
Juice of 1 medium-size lemon
1/4 cup chopped fresh parsley
1 tablespoon unsalted butter (optional)

Polenta

1/2 cup fine yellow or white polenta, such as
    Anson Mills
1 1/2 tablespoons finely grated Parmigiano-
    Reggiano cheese

Salad

1/4 pound artisan lettuce, such as Blushing
    Petite Oak, Green Gem, or Tango

1. Preheat the oven to 450°F. Wrap two clean bricks with a couple of layers of aluminum foil. Set aside.

2. To make the lemon-garlic dressing: Whisk together all the ingredients in a small bowl. Adjust the seasonings with additional oil, salt, and pepper to taste. Set aside.

3. To make the chicken: Cut in half and rinse under cold running water. Pat dry with paper towels, and set aside.

4. Heat the canola oil in a large cast-iron or oven-proof sauté pan over medium-high heat until hot but not smoking. Season the chicken generously with salt and pepper. Place the chicken halves, skin side down, in the pan. Top each half with a prepared brick. Lower the temperature to medium heat and cook until the skins are a deep golden brown, about 15 minutes. Remove the bricks, and using a thin metal spatula, carefully turn the chicken over so as not to tear the skin. Replace the bricks on top of chicken pieces and bake in the oven until juices run clear and the internal temperature of the meat reaches 165°F, about 25 minutes. Let rest for 10 minutes before carving into pieces.

5. While the chicken is browning, prepare the polenta according to the package directions. When the polenta grains are soft, stir in the cheese.

6. To make the sauce: Using the same pan to roast the chicken, stir in the wine, lemon juice, and parsley, and bring to a simmer over medium-high heat. Deglaze the pan, stirring frequently and scraping up the bits from the bottom, until the liquid is reduced by half, about 3 minutes. Whisk in the butter, if using, until well incorporated. Adjust the seasoning with salt and pepper to taste.

7. To make the salad: In a medium-size bowl, combine the lettuce and half of the dressing. Toss until well combined, adding more dressing to taste.

8. To assemble: Spoon the polenta in the center of four individual plates. Top with the chicken pieces and drizzle the sauce to taste over the top. Serve with the salad on the side.

Oven-Roasted Chicken with Stuffing-Style Frittata, Pickled Green Beans, and Poached Cranberries

SERVES 4 TO 5

This is the quintessential fall meal with a twist. The chef takes succulent roast chicken pieces and arranges them over the top of the stuffing, then garnishes with tangy pickled green beans, and tart cranberries.

Note: You will need to pickle the green beans and poach the cranberries the day before you intend to serve the chicken.

Pickled Green Beans

1 pound green beans, trimmed and cleaned
6 tablespoons cider vinegar
1/4 cup water, plus more as needed
2 tablespoons kosher salt
1/4 cup granulated sugar
1 teaspoon red pepper flakes
1 teaspoon freshly ground black pepper
6 garlic cloves

Poached Cranberries

1 pound fresh or frozen cranberries
1/2 cup red wine
1 cup water
1/2 cup granulated sugar, or to taste (see note)

Roasted Roots

4 carrots, cut into 1-inch pieces
4 parsnips, cut into 1-inch pieces
20 Brussels sprouts, trimmed and halved lengthwise
5 garlic cloves

2 shallot bulbs, cut into 1-inch pieces
5 sprigs thyme, leaves removed and stems discarded
2 sprigs rosemary, leaves removed and stems discarded
2 tablespoons extra-virgin olive oil
Kosher salt and freshly ground black pepper

Roast Chicken

1 (3 1/2-pound) whole chicken, giblets and neck discarded
2 tablespoons unsalted butter, at room temperature
Kosher salt and freshly ground black pepper

Stuffing

8 large eggs, lightly beaten
3/4 cup heavy cream
1 1/2 teaspoons chopped fresh sage leaves
4 cups toasted bread cubes (about one-third of a large loaf of Italian bread)
Kosher salt and freshly ground black pepper

1. To make the pickled green beans: Place the green beans in a 1-quart jar with a tight lid. Combine the cider vinegar, water, salt, sugar, red pepper flakes, black pepper, and garlic in a saucepan and bring to a boil over medium-high heat. Cook, stirring frequently, until the sugar is dissolved. Pour the brine over the green beans, add additional water to cover the beans fully, and seal the jar. Let cool to room temperature, then refrigerate overnight.

2. To make the poached cranberries: Combine the wine, water, and sugar in a saucepan and bring to a boil over medium-high heat. Cook, stirring frequently, until the sugar is dissolved. Lower the heat to medium-low, add the cranberries, and cook for 9 minutes. Transfer the cranberries and liquid to a bowl and let cool to room temperature, then refrigerate overnight.

3. To make the roasted roots: Preheat the oven to 375°F. Lightly oil a 9 x 13-inch baking dish and set aside. Place the carrots, parsnips, Brussels sprouts, garlic cloves, shallots, thyme, and rosemary in a large bowl. Drizzle the olive oil over the vegetables and season with salt and pepper to taste. Toss to combine, making sure to coat all the vegetables well. Spread the vegetable mixture into the prepared baking dish.

4. To make the chicken: Rinse the chicken and pat dry with paper towels. Using your fingers, smear the butter all over the chicken and under the skin. Season generously inside and out with salt and pepper. Place the chicken, breast side up, in the roasting pan with the vegetable mixture. Roast the chicken, basting every 20 minutes and occasionally stirring the vegetables, until the skin is golden brown, the juices run clear, and the chicken breast reaches an internal temperature of 160°F, about 1 hour 25 minutes. Transfer the chicken to a carving board and let rest for 20 minutes. Transfer the roasted roots to a food processor and puree until smooth; set aside to cool. Place the pan juices in a container; set aside to cool.

5. To make the stuffing: While the chicken is resting, preheat the oven to 325°F. Lightly butter a 9 x 13-inch baking dish and set aside. Place the bread cubes and vegetable puree in a large bowl. In a separate large bowl, whisk together eggs, cream, sage, and reserved pan juices. Add the egg mixture to the bread cubes. Gently mix all the ingredients together; do not overmix. Season with salt and pepper. Spoon the stuffing into the prepared baking dish and bake until the center has just set, about 40 minutes.

6. While the stuffing is cooking, carve the chicken into eight pieces (two drumsticks, two thighs, two breasts (then cut in half again), and two wings). Cut the breasts into thick slices. Remove the stuffing from the oven; arrange the chicken on top, and continue to bake for 10 minutes. Remove from the oven and allow to rest for 5 minutes. Garnish with the pickled green beans and poached cranberries (about 1/4 cup of each per person). Serve at once.

Notes:

For the poached cranberries, use more or less sugar depending on your taste.

Save the extra cranberries and use in your favorite bread recipe or as a sandwich topping. Save the extra pickled green beans and use in your favorite salad.

Terrain Westport Garden Café

INFINITY MUSIC HALL & BISTRO

Infinity Bistro, located inside the historic Infinity Music Hall, is a full-service bistro and bar serving progressive American cuisine, created by executive chef Dan Fortin. Though the bistro, which has won "Best Place for Dinner and a Show" for several years, is the natural choice to dine before a reggae, rock, or blues concert in the music hall (with a pretty outdoor dining terrace in summer), diners don't need to wait for their favorite musical act to stop to sample the small plates (try the Lobster Hushpuppies or the Papadum Crusted Sea Scallops), salads, flatbreads, pastas, steaks, and other casual, seasonally inspired fare. At both lunch and dinner, the menu incorporates ingredients from local farms and foragers, and the specialty cocktails are named for hit songs, such as the Werewolves of London (a combination of Bulldog gin, Massimo sauvignon blanc, elderflower liqueur, and a splash of homemade sour mix).

Headed by owner Dan Hincks, Infinity Hall opened its second venue in the heart of the state capital. Like the Norfolk location, Hartford's hall provides an intimate music, entertainment and dining experience, where every seat in the house feels like the front row, and the farm-to-table fare is refreshingly authentic and homey, with decadent desserts and a good-times vibe.

Quail with Yam Puree and Microgreens

SERVES 4

Quail is a small and delicate bird that is big on flavor. This version calls for one quail per person. Some butchers and poultry vendors sell quail that is already deboned—a true time-saver. To do it yourself, we like chef Jacques Pépin's, "How to Debone a Quail" tutorial on YouTube.

Yam Puree

2 medium-size yams or sweet potatoes, peeled and diced
2 tablespoons brown sugar
1 tablespoon balsamic vinegar
1 1/2 teaspoons unsalted butter
1 teaspoon minced fresh ginger
Kosher salt and freshly ground white pepper

Quail

4 quail, deboned (about 1/2 pound each)
Kosher salt and freshly ground black pepper
1 tablespoon grapeseed oil
....
2 cups microgreens

1. To make the yam puree: Place the sweet potatoes in a medium-size saucepan and cover with cold, salted water. Bring to a boil over medium-high heat and cook until the potatoes are fork-tender, about 10 minutes. Drain and transfer to a medium-size bowl. Add the sugar, vinegar, butter, and ginger. Mash with an old-fashioned masher or immersion blender until smooth, then season with salt and pepper to taste. Cover the bowl to keep the puree warm; set aside.

2. To make the quail: While the potatoes are cooking, heat the oil in a large skillet. Season the quail with salt and pepper. When the pan is hot

but not smoking, add the quail, skin side down, and sear until golden brown, 5 to 7 minutes. Carefully flip the quail over and cook until the breasts feel both firm and a little springy to the touch and juices run clear, 5 to 7 minutes more. Let the quail rest for 5 minutes before serving.

3. To serve, divide the yam puree among four individual plates, place a quail on top of each portion of puree, and scatter about 1/2 cup of microgreens on top and around each quail.

Infinity Bistro Hartford

CORIANDER CAFÉ & COUNTRY STORE

Coriander is a cozy, red clapboard café in the center of charming Eastford. Regulars stop in for a cup of java and breakfast on the patio, grab a quick lunch to go, take home tonight's dinner, or bring a bottle of wine and dine on the premises. Chef Brett Laffert says, "Our goal is to make great food utilizing local farms and producers from the region according to the season. We try and create everything in-house, from our baked goods to our fresh soups and weekly changing dinner menu." Here, you'll find hearty meals, comfort food, and vegetarian options to desserts from its own in-house bakery. Laffert offers a sophisticated summer menu that includes fresh Atlantic cod with wild rice and corn griddle cakes.

Atlantic Cod with Wild Rice and Corn Griddle Cakes and Garlicky Kale

SERVES 4

Cod loin is a tasty, meaty white fish, plucked from the deep waters of the Atlantic. Although it is surprisingly easy to prepare with a simple pan searing, it makes an impressive dinner for guests, particularly when paired with Chef Laffert's griddle cakes and sautéed Garlickly Kale.

Wild Rice and Corn Griddle Cakes (makes 18)

1 cup wild rice
2 cups all-purpose flour
1 tablespoon baking powder
1 teaspoon baking soda
1 teaspoon kosher salt
1 teaspoon freshly ground black pepper
3 large eggs
1 to 1 1/4 cups whole milk, or as needed
1 tablespoon unsalted butter, melted
2 cups fresh corn kernels (cut from 2 to 3 large ears of corn)
1 small sweet onion, diced
1 large garlic clove, minced
2 tablespoons chopped scallions
1/2 cup grated Asiago cheese

Garlicky Kale

4 cups (10 ounces) kale, stemmed and chopped
1 tablespoon salted butter
1 large garlic clove, chopped
Kosher salt and freshly ground black pepper

Cod Loin

1 tablespoon canola oil, or as needed

2 pounds thick-cut Atlantic cod loin, cut into
    4 equal pieces

Kosher salt and freshly ground black pepper

2 ripe tomatoes, thickly sliced

1 lemon, cut into 8 wedges

1. To make the wild rice: Bring 4 cups of water,
the rice, and 1/2 teaspoon of salt to a boil in a
medium-size saucepan over medium-high heat.

Lower the heat to a simmer; cover, and cook until
tender and most of the liquid has been absorbed,
50 to 60 minutes. Add salt to taste, fluff the rice
with a fork, and set aside.

2. To make the griddle cakes: Preheat the oven to
275°F.

3. In a medium-size bowl, sift together the flour,
baking powder, baking soda, salt, and pepper.

4. In a second medium-size bowl, whisk together
the eggs, milk, and butter. Add the wet ingredients

to the dry mixture and fold in the cooked rice, corn kernels, onion, garlic, scallions, and cheese (the batter should have a pancake consistency). If the batter seems too thick, add additional milk as needed.

5. Preheat a griddle, then lightly spray with non-stick cooking spray. Using a 2-inch ice-cream scoop or 1/4-cup measure, drop the mixture onto the prepared griddle. Using a fork, gently flatten into griddle cakes and cook on one side until nicely browned and bubbles form on top of the cakes, about 3 minutes. Flip and cook until the griddle cakes are cooked through and golden brown, about 3 minutes.

6. Transfer the griddle cakes to an ovenproof dish and keep warm in the oven. Repeat with the remaining batter.

7. To make the garlicky kale: Fill a large bowl with ice water and set aside. Meanwhile, fill a 6-quart stockpot halfway with water and bring to a boil over medium-high heat. Add the kale and blanch for 2 minutes. Using a slotted spoon, transfer the kale to the prepared ice-water bath and let cool completely, reserving 1 tablespoon of the blanching water. Drain the kale thoroughly and pat dry with paper towels.

8. Heat the butter in a medium-size skillet over medium heat. Add the garlic and cook until fragrant but not browned, about 2 minutes. Add the kale with the 1 tablespoon of reserved blanching water and cook over medium-high heat until dark green and crispy and the water has evaporated. Season with salt and pepper to taste. Set aside.

9. To make the cod loin: Heat the oil in a large skillet over medium-high heat. Season the cod with salt and pepper. When the oil is hot, add the cod and sear until golden brown, 4 to 5 minutes. Using a large spatula, carefully flip the fish over

and cook until the loins are cooked through and golden brown, about 4 more minutes.

10. Place a griddle cake on each plate and top with kale. Arrange the cod, tomato wedges, and green beans, if desired, on the side. Garnish with lemon wedges and serve.

Note: The extra cakes make great snacks and also pair perfectly with grilled pork or chicken.

Coriander Café

COD: LOIN OR FILLET?

Cod is a popular fish with a mild flavor and a dense, flaky white flesh. Atlantic cod (*Gadus morhua*) lives in the colder waters and deeper sea regions throughout the North Atlantic. Once abundant, the mighty Atlantic cod has been overfished, which is why it can be so pricey.

When shopping for Atlantic cod, there are a few ways to buy it. "It all depends on how you plan to prepare it," says Tony Norado, the owner of Bon Ton Fish Market in Greenwich, a local purveyor of quality seafood, serving restaurateurs and the public since 1902. Norado outlines the differences below:

Cod loin: The cod is a large fish, and the cod loin—a choice cut—is a meaty, boneless fillet cut from a section just below the head of the fish. Like a thick beef filet mignon, this cut stands up well to a quick pan sear, and then finishing in the oven. It can also be breaded and baked or dredged in flour and deep fried (fish and chips).

Cod fillet: The fillet is a medium-thick boneless cut that is taken from the fattier midsection of the fish. Due to its higher fat content, this cut is ideal for sautéing.

Cod steak: This large, bone-in cut is best prepared like a steak: Pop it on the grill or into the oven.

MATCH RESTAURANT

If you ask chef-owner Matt Storch the secret of Match's longevity (celebrating 15 years in South Norwalk in 2015), he says, "Our mission from the beginning was to provide a complete dining experience, which includes an innovative menu, a wood-burning oven, and a warm, friendly and well-trained staff, all brought together in a space that exudes energy and comfort."

In 2014, he gave the restaurant a facelift, modernizing the decor with mod white leather seats and splashes of signature purple, and shaking up the menu to make it more flexible and alluring to different states of mind. Changes start with the addition of well-priced bar nibbles, including China Wings, Poppers, Tacos du Jour, and Bistro Fries, and moving to Matt's riffs on Tuna and Steak Tartare, Baked Clams, and Fresh Fish Crudo to the Classic Cravings (house favorites, such as Wasabi Tuna and "Kisses from Angels" [Matt's airy ricotta gnocchi], oxtail broth–based pho, osso buco, and steak frites), to Market Finds (local and seasonal inspirations), all the way to the more decadent choices, such as caviar, foie gras, and truffles. To kick up the action in the already hot bar, he brought in Adam Patrick, a pedigreed local mixologist who rolled out an inventive cocktail program.

Matt says, "The place wasn't broke, so why fix it? I just wanted to make a few changes to bring Match into the 21st century to keep things fresh."

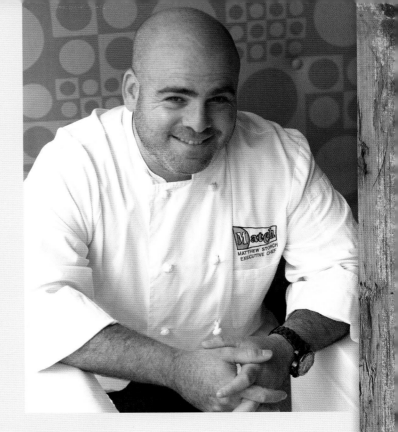

As other SoNo eateries have come and gone, Match has held its perch a top local and regional "Best of" lists, and continues to be favorite where quality trumps pretense. On Matt's seasonal menu, Asian and Mediterranean flavors are married with more classic American concepts. The international wine list has earned *Wine Spectator*'s Award of Excellence for the past 10 years in a row. All of this explains why Match was listed in the *New York Times* best-selling book *1,000 Places to Eat Before You Die.*

A frequent farmers' market shopper, Matt relies on what's fresh as his inspiration. He says, "Start with beautiful, raw, local food. And taste as you shop." In this recipe, the freshness of the Copps Island oysters spoke to Matt, and will speak to you.

Bacon-Jalapeño Oysters

SERVES 6
(THIS RECIPE CAN BE SCALED DOWN EASILY.)

Matt says, "I will be honest. I'm not a huge fan of raw oysters (bad experience) but, cooked, I will eat them all day long. This is a little take on casino-style clams using oysters. They are buttery, spicy, and delicious. Just be careful: They tend to talk back to you when they get hot on the grill!"

2 ounces (about 2 slices) smoked bacon, minced
1 cup (2 sticks, 8 ounces) unsalted butter, at
    room temperature
1 large jalapeño, halved, stemmed, seeded and
    minced
Finely grated zest and juice of 2 limes
1/3 teaspoon hot sauce, plus more as needed
1/4 cup panko bread crumbs, toasted
3 tablespoons minced fresh chives
2 teaspoons freshly ground black pepper
6 dozen oysters
Rock salt or fresh seaweed

1. Cook the bacon in a small skillet over medium-high heat until crisp, about 3 minutes. Transfer to paper towels to drain. Set aside.

2. In a small bowl, stir together all the ingredients, except the oysters and rock salt, until fully combined. Transfer the butter mixture to the refrigerator and chill until just firm, about 2 hours.

3. Shuck all the oysters, making sure to release the muscle from the shell, and place them on a sheet tray lined with rock salt or seaweed. This steadies the oysters and prevents them from wobbling.

4. Place a ball of butter, the diameter of a nickel, on top of each oyster.

5. Heat a gas, electric, or charcoal grill to medium-high heat (see note). Place the entire sheet tray on the grill and cook until the butter melts and starts to bubble and the oysters are just cooked through, about 5 minutes. Serve immediately.

Note: If you do not own a grill, preheat the oven to 450°F and bake until the butter melts and oysters are just cooked through, about 5 minutes.

Match Restaurant

THE WORLD IS THEIR OYSTER

The mighty oyster is enjoying a renaissance with trendy oyster bars opening across the country and top chefs giving the humble mollusk star billing. In fact, oysters remain the largest seafood product in Connecticut.

Since the '40s, Norm Bloom & Son, based in Norwalk, has been sustainably farming oysters in beds in the Long Island Sound, filling the demand for the plump, briny bivalve known as the Copps Island oyster. Fans say the Copps Island oyster tastes better than oysters from anywhere else, due, in part, to the Sound's fluctuating water temperatures.

Although Norm Bloom & Son owns and tends several beds off the islands near Norwalk and Westport, it leases the other beds from the state; some have been cultivated since before the American Revolution. After carefully dredging and sorting, only about 15 to 20 percent makes the grade and lands on menus at restaurants throughout the state and as far as California; the rest, mainly shells and undersized oysters, are tossed back to decompose or mature.

Norm Bloom is a stickler for sustainability. He fought to keep the oyster sizes to 3 inches or larger to allow oysters to mature and reproduce, and he will only take out what he sells that day, to ensure peak freshness. He notes, "After I fill my orders, that's it for the day."

Oyster are farmed on designated grounds. The oyster farmers pick only what they need, then reseed the beds, as they would with greens. The effort takes the patience of a farmer, as oysters take up to four years to mature to full size. The result is far more oysters along the Eastern Seaboard than would be reproduced without reseeding.

The team at Norm Bloom & Son works with Harborwatch and other organizations to monitor the water quality and conditions of water sources and their grounds. They actively support efforts to protect and restore the Sound and create a new generation of stewards to carry on the venerable oyster farming tradition into the future.

LEFARM AND THE WHELK

Chef Bill Taibe is a force of nature. In Connecticut, he's a culinary rock star, known for creating not one—but three—perennially packed and buzz-worthy Westport eateries, LeFarm, the Whelk, and Kawa Ni, and for doing it his way. Bill's way includes getting out and visiting the Norwalk docks where Norm Bloom & Sons' oysters and clams are hauled onto shore, and for taking his team on "field" trips to Millstone and Sport Hill farms to get their hands dirty, pulling plants from the ground and learning firsthand just what it takes to grow a healthy organic crop, despite deer, drought, and other obstacles.

By the age of 33, Taibe had earned bragging rights at a number of top Connecticut restaurants, including Relish Food & Wine in South Norwalk and Napa in Stamford, and received three "Excellent" ratings from the *New York Times*. He is counted among the new generation of chefs supporting local farms and distributors.

In the summer of 2009, Taibe left his prestigious post at Napa to create the iconic LeFarm. This rustic, cozy, 34-seat restaurant opened to unprecedented success. It is home to an ever-changing menu that reflects the season's freshest produce, fish, and meat, which is now executed by chef Arik Bensimon. LeFarm's accolades include a 27 rating from the *Zagat* guide, Best Overall Restaurant and Best Chef from *Fairfield County Weekly*, and Best American Restaurant, statewide winner,

Connecticut Magazine. In 2011, 2012, and 2013, Taibe was named a semifinalist for Best Chef: Northeast by the James Beard House. And he has created a series of underground dining events he calls "Souterrain."

In 2012, Taibe joined with Massimo Tullio to open the Whelk, a 45-seat oyster bar and seafood restaurant. The Whelk, with chef Geoff Lazlo in the kitchen, follows the same principles established at LeFarm, utilizing the freshest ingredients from local purveyors. Sought-after for reserva-

tions, the Whelk snapped up its fair share of accolades, such as "Don't Miss" from the *New York Times*, and a triple play from *Connecticut Magazine*, including "Superior-Extraordinary," Best New Restaurant—2013 and Best Seafood—2013.

Taibe can be found chatting up the vendors and fellow chefs at the weekly Westport Farmers' Market. He generally sports a scruffy beard and a black T-shirt, but don't let his casual vibe fool you. He is serious in the kitchen. Not in the haughty, perfectionist vein. He's serious about fresh-

ness and bold flavor combinations, and letting the raw ingredients do the talking. He's serious about provenance, creativity, and seasoning. About using what was pulled out of the Sound this morning or creating a new dish using mother lode of peppers brought in by the bushel from an Easton farmer.

Bill Taibe's on a roll, just back from a tasting tour of Japan opening an Asian pub around the corner from the Whelk with brother Jeff, a sustainable chef best known for putting Oak + Almond in Norwalk on the map. The atmosphere at Kawa Ni is similar to that of an *izakaya*, a Japanese pub, serving up small plates, donburi bowls, and noodle bowls, among other options.

Deviled Eggs with Cornmeal Fried Oysters and Pickled Red Onion

SERVES 12 (2 EGGS EACH)

In his 2013 *GQ Magazine* roundup of the "50 Best Things to Eat and Drink Right Now," reviewer Alan Richman rated his No. 1 choice as the Green-Goddess Deviled Eggs from the Whelk in Westport. In Richman's words:

"This has been the breakout year for deviled eggs, forgotten except in southern and midwestern kitchens. I ate them across the country, but none came close to this complex and captivating variation." Chef Bill Taibe shares his recipe below.

Note: The pickled red onions must be started one day before being served.

Pickled Red Onion

1 firm medium-size red onion, peeled and thinly sliced into 1/4-inch half-moons (about 1 1/4 cups)

3 cups rice vinegar

1 cup granulated sugar

Blackening Spice

1 teaspoon black peppercorns

1 teaspoon mustard seeds

1 teaspoon fennel seeds

1/2 teaspoon coriander seeds

1/2 teaspoon cumin seeds

2 teaspoons Old Bay seasoning

2 teaspoons cayenne pepper

2 teaspoons crushed red pepper flakes

1 teaspoon smoked paprika

1 teaspoon Aleppo chile pepper

Deviled Eggs

1 dozen large eggs

1/4 cup chopped mixed fresh herbs, such as dill, tarragon, or parsley

1/2 teaspoon anchovy paste

1/2 teaspoon chopped garlic

1 tablespoon fresh lemon juice

1 teaspoon capers, drained and rinsed

1/4 cup pickled red onion

1/4 cup plus 2 tablespoons mayonnaise

2 teaspoons whole-grain mustard

2 teaspoons Dijon mustard

Kosher salt

Oysters

7 cups canola oil, or as needed

24 oysters, shucked

3 cups cornmeal, or as needed

Kosher salt

1. To make the pickled red onion: Place the onion in a 32-ounce glass mason jar with a tight lid. Combine the vinegar and sugar in a small saucepan. Bring to a boil over medium-high heat, stirring often, until sugar has dissolved. Remove from the heat, pour over the onion, and gently stir to evenly distribute the vinegar. Allow onion to cool to room temperature; then seal and store in the refrigerator.

2. To make the blackening spice: Place the peppercorns and seeds in a small, dry sauté pan. Lightly toast over medium-low heat, shaking the pan often, until fragrant, about 3 minutes. Remove from the heat and let cool completely. Transfer the toasted seed mixture to a spice grinder, coffee grinder, or mortar and grind into fine powder. Place the powder in a small bowl and stir in the Old Bay seasoning, cayenne, red pepper flakes, paprika, and chile pepper until well combined.

3. To make the eggs: Fill a large bowl with ice water and set aside. Place the eggs in a large pot and cover with cold water. Bring the water to a boil over medium-high heat; then add 1 tablespoon of kosher salt. Bring to a boil, cover, and cook the eggs for 7 minutes; remove from the heat. Using a slotted spoon, transfer the eggs to the prepared ice-water bath and let cool completely, about 3 minutes. Remove the eggs, carefully peel, and slice in half lengthwise. Remove the yolks and set aside for the filling. Place the whites, hollow side up, on a platter and reserve.

4. Combine the herbs, anchovy paste, garlic, lemon juice, capers, 1/4 cup pickled red onions, mayonnaise, and mustards in a food processor. Process until well combined. Add the egg yolks and puree until mixture is smooth. Season to taste with kosher salt. Using two teaspoons or a piping bag, evenly fill the centers of the egg whites with the yolk filling.

5. Fill a deep, heavy-bottomed pot with about 4 inches of canola oil. Heat the oil to 350°F, using a candy thermometer. Working in batches of about 12 at a time, dredge the oysters in cornmeal, making sure they are well coated, then carefully drop into the hot oil. Fry the oysters for about 45 seconds. Using a slotted spoon, remove the oysters and drain on a paper towels. Season the fried oysters with 4 teaspoons of blackening spice, or to taste, and kosher salt.

6. Place one fried oyster on top of each deviled egg and garnish with one onion slice.

Notes:

Pickled onions will keep for several weeks in the refrigerator but are best eaten in the first week.

The blackening spice will make more than needed. Store the remaining blackening spice in an airtight container in the refrigerator.

The Whelk

Seared Scallops with Corn and Purslane

MAKES 2 APPETIZERS

Charring your onions before adding them to the vinaigrette will create a blackened texture on the outside and a rich caramelization on the inside.

Burnt Onion Vinaigrette

3 tablespoons extra-virgin olive oil

2 tablespoons minced onion

Kosher salt

1 tablespoon white or red vinegar

1/4 teaspoon Dijon mustard

Scallops

1 tablespoon canola oil

Kosher salt

6 large sea scallops, tough muscles removed

1 tablespoon unsalted butter

Corn

2 tablespoons unsalted butter

1/2 cup corn kernels

1/4 teaspoon thinly sliced green cayenne pepper

Purslane and Arugula

1/2 cup purslane (see note), radish sprouts, watercress, or young dandelion leaves

1/2 cup arugula

2 teaspoons fresh lemon juice

2 teaspoons extra-virgin olive oil

Chopped chives or fennel fronds, for garnish

1. To make the burnt onion vinaigrette: Heat the oil in a small sauté pan over medium-high heat. Add the onion and season with salt. Cook stirring frequently, until the onion begins to brown, about 1 minute. Lower the heat to medium and continue to cook, stirring often, until the onion is blackened in spots and becomes dry, about 2 minutes. Remove from the heat and stir in the vinegar and mustard. Set aside.

2. To make the scallops: Heat the oil in a small sauté pan over medium-high heat. Pat the scallops dry with a paper towel and season with salt. Add the scallops, making sure they are not touching, and let sear on one side, until a golden crust forms, about 4 minutes. Using tongs, turn the scallops. Add the butter and baste until the second side is well browned and just firm to the touch, about 4 minutes. Remove from the heat and set aside.

3. While the scallops are searing, make the corn. Heat the butter in a small sauté pan over medium heat. Add the corn and cayenne and cook, stirring often, until the corn is warmed through. Remove from the heat and set aside.

4. To make the purslane and arugula: Combine the greens in a small bowl. Add the lemon juice and oil, tossing until well combined. Pour the corn mixture over the greens and gently toss to combine.

5. To assemble: Place the purslane mixture into the center of a serving bowl. Arrange the scallops on top. Drizzle with 1 tablespoon of the vinaigrette, or to taste, and season with salt and pepper to taste. Garnish with chives and/or fennel fronds, if desired. Serve at once.

Note: Purslane is a nutritious, broad-leafed weed with a mild lemon flavor.

Geoff Lazlo for The Whelk

Mystic River Oysters with Grace Cocktail Mignonette

SERVES 8

Local oysters served with a bracing mignonette. Nothing beats a classic!

Grace Mignonette

1 cup champagne vinegar

1/4 cup apple juice

Juice of 1/2 lemon

1 1/2 teaspoons honey

1/2 ripe pear, such as Bosc or Anjou, unpeeled, cored, and diced

1/2 stalk lemongrass, trimmed, tough outer layers discarded, minced

1 1/2 tablespoons minced shallot

Kosher salt and freshly ground pepper

....

24 fresh oysters

1. In a medium-size bowl, whisk together all the ingredients except the oysters. Cover with plastic wrap and refrigerate for 24 hours. Whisk again just before using.

2. Just before serving, shuck the oysters. Drizzle the sauce over the oysters or serve on the side.

The Mayflower Grace

Grilled Tuna with White Bean and Arugula Salad

SERVES 6

If you prep the dressing and white beans in advance, you can serve this beautiful and very aromatic grilled tuna dish in under 10 minutes.

Dressing

6 tablespoons fresh lemon juice, divided
2 teaspoons minced fresh garlic
1 1/2 teaspoons chopped fresh thyme
1 teaspoon kosher salt
1/4 teaspoon freshly ground black pepper
3/4 cup extra-virgin olive oil

White Bean Salad

3 (15-ounce) cans cannellini beans, drained and rinsed
6 fresh plum tomatoes, seeded and cut into thin strips
1 cup red onion, cut into small dice
15 pitted Kalamata olives, halved
Kosher salt and freshly ground black pepper

Tuna

Oil as needed, for grill
2 pounds fresh tuna steak
1 tablespoon soy sauce
Kosher salt and freshly ground black pepper

1/2 pound fresh arugula, torn into bite-size pieces
Kosher salt and freshly ground black pepper

1. To make the dressing: In a small bowl, whisk together 1/4 cup of the lemon juice and the garlic, thyme, salt, and pepper. Whisking vigorously, add the olive oil in a slow, steady stream. Reserve 1/4 cup of the dressing for the tuna steaks and set aside.

2. To make the white bean salad: In a large bowl, combine the beans, tomatoes, onion, and olives and toss with 3/4 cup of the dressing. Season with salt and pepper to taste. Place the salad in the refrigerator for 2 to 4 hours, stirring occasionally to marinate evenly.

3. To make the tuna: Place the tuna in a large resealable plastic bag, pour the remaining 1/4 cup of the dressing and soy sauce over the tuna, seal, and let sit at room temperature for 45 minutes, turning the bag over at least once to marinate evenly.

4. Heat a gas or electric grill (see note) to medium-high heat and generously brush the cooking grate with oil. Remove the tuna from the dressing and season with salt and pepper; grill, turning once, until seared on the outside but still pink in the center, 2 minutes per side. Remove and let rest for 3 minutes, then slice on the bias into 1/3-inch-thick slices.

5. Divide the arugula among six plates and evenly mound the bean salad on top. Arrange the tuna slices on top and drizzle with the remaining 2 tablespoons of lemon juice. Season with salt and pepper to taste, and serve at once.

Note: If you do not own a grill, heat 1 tablespoon of canola oil in a large, nonstick skillet over medium-high heat. Add the tuna and cook, turning once, until seared on the outside but still pink in the center, 2 minutes per side.

Thompson Street Farm, LLC

MAMA'S BOY SOUTHERN TABLE & REFUGE

A child of the south, Greer Fredericks drew on her earliest memories when she and partner Amiel Dorel hatched the concept for Mama's Boy, named for Greer's son Jax, who, she jokes, is "the original Mama's Boy." She says, "We call ourselves a 'southern table and refuge' because that's exactly what we are." It's a place to enjoy casual, yet refined country cuisine (such as Little Yardbird: fried game hen atop a corn bread waffle with collard greens; Shrimp and Grits; Low Country Bouillabaisse; Redneck Edamame), where you're treated like family and can seek respite in a relaxed Southern home away from home.

Building out the space themselves, the team used reclaimed wood from a South Carolina water tower, authentic Alabama railroad ties, and repurposed garden tools, furnishings, and mirrors to add warmth and character. The kitchen galley was built out of an old tobacco barn from Knoxville, Tennessee; windows from Al Capone's summer hideaway hang in the parlor; liquor lockers in the bar are from a Gentleman's Gym in Alabama. The massive bar and a communal table in the front of the house set the stage for a rollicking cocktail hour, featuring handcrafted cocktails; an intimate parlor toward the rear is reserved for quieter dining.

The food is fabulously fresh, locally sourced, and authentically prepared by executive chef Chaz Mazas, who was brought in to carry on the traditions created by founding chef Scott Ostrander. Ostrander expanded his relationships with local farms and fishermen and cooked in top venues throughout the south, including Town (Jacksonville, Florida), a farm-to-table eatery named Best New Restaurant in Florida in 2011.

On the bottom of the Mama's Boy's menu, Fredericks declares her support of small artisanal purveyors "here at home and throughout the Southern States" by listing them there.

If you manage to make room after dinner, this is a destination for desserts, chiefly the sky-high coconut layer cake, classic red velvet cake, and moist carrot cake—all made on the premises and perfect for sharing.

Sunday brunch is party time, featuring live music and an indulgent stick-to-your-ribs feast that will tip your scale over the edge.

Low Country Bouillabaisse

SERVES 6

"This recipe is our version of Frogmore Stew, which is a traditional shrimp boil indigenous to John's Island, South Carolina, just south of Charleston. Traditionally, shrimp, smoked sausage, potatoes, and corn are boiled with bay leaves in water and served family style. For Mama's Boy, we jazzed it up a bit by adding additional locally caught shellfish and fish, fresh herbs, and steaming in an aromatic stock made from the shells of the shrimp."
—Greer Fredericks

1 pound uncooked shrimp, peeled and deveined, shells reserved

Shrimp Stock

1 tablespoon olive oil

1 small onion, coarsely chopped

1 small carrot, coarsely chopped

1 celery rib, coarsely chopped

1 teaspoon fennel seeds

1 teaspoon red pepper flakes

1 tablespoon sweet smoked paprika

1/2 cup white wine

5 cups water

Bouillabaisse

1 pound red-skinned potatoes, quartered and roasted

3 tablespoons olive oil, or as needed, divided

Kosher salt and freshly ground black pepper

3 ears fresh corn

1 pound littleneck clams, scrubbed

1 pound mussels, scrubbed and debearded

1/2 pound lean, white-fleshed fish fillets, such as red snapper or cod, cut into 1-inch pieces

1/2 pound smoked sausage, such as Andouille, cut into 1/4-inch rounds

1/2 cup (1 stick, 4 ounces) unsalted butter

2 tablespoons chopped fresh parsley

6 slices crusty bread, toasted

1. To make the shrimp stock: Heat the oil in a 14-inch skillet over medium heat. Add the onion, carrot, and celery and cook, stirring frequently, until the onion is soft and translucent, about 10 minutes. Add the reserved shrimp shells and cook, stirring often, until the shells turn opaque, 2 to 3 minutes. Add the fennel seeds, red pepper flakes, and paprika and stir until well combined. Add the wine and bring to a gentle boil over medium-high heat until the liquid is reduced by half, about 2 minutes. Add the water, bring to a simmer, and cook for 30 minutes. Strain the stock into a saucepan, discarding any solids, and reserve.

2. To make the roasted potatoes: Preheat the oven to 400°F. Place the potatoes in a small bowl with 1 tablespoon of the olive oil and toss until the potatoes are well coated. Transfer the potatoes to a sheet pan in one layer. Season with salt and pepper to taste. Roast, stirring occasionally, until fork-tender, about 45 minutes. Set aside for the bouillabaisse.

3. Cook the corn in the microwave on HIGH for 2 minutes. When cool enough to handle, cut into 1-inch rounds. Set aside.

4. Reheat the reserved stock in saucepan until hot. Heat the remaining 2 tablespoons of oil in a medium-size stockpot or Dutch oven over medium-high heat. When the oil is hot, add the clams, cover, and cook, shaking the pot occasionally, for 3 minutes. Add the mussels, cover, and cook, shaking the pot occasionally, for 3 minutes. Season the fish with salt and pepper. Add the hot stock, fish, shrimp, sausage, roasted potatoes, and butter and bring to a simmer. Add

the corn and parsley, cover, and steam over medium-high heat until the shellfish open and the shrimp are opaque throughout, about 5 minutes. Season with salt and pepper to taste. Discard any shells that do not open.

5. Divide the fish mixture evenly among six large bowls, ladle over the broth, and serve with crusty bread.

Mama's Boy

ESTIA'S AMERICAN

Since 1991, Estia, on the main drag of Amagansett, was a required pit stop on the East End, for Colin Ambrose's casual American and Mexican-inspired eats. It was also one of the region's first farm-to-fork kitchens, harvesting home-grown vegetables from a 2-acre garden before it was trendy. In 1998, Colin purchased Estia's Little Kitchen in a shingled cottage along the highway in Sag Harbor, New York, and ran both restaurants simultaneously until 2006. Although you could blink and miss the place, fans know where to find it. Retaining its cult status for two decades, fans still line up for a killer breakfast and brunch (breakfast burritos, Robbie's Gringo Hash, whole wheat pancakes), as well as fish tacos, Mexican sweet corn soup, and fresh salads—with produce often harvested directly from Colin's half-acre garden shortly before service. Colin, who has built relationships with farmers over the past 20 years, recently opened a new venue in Connecticut, focusing on the same principles.

Estia's American, in downtown Darien, is a small, full-service American restaurant serving weekend breakfast, as well as lunch and dinner. The bartender puts a fresh spin on Bloody Marys, margaritas, and specialties, such as the 888 Nantucket Salty Dog and Blueberry Lymanaide made with blueberry vodka.

Sourcing sustainably, Colin says, has made all the difference. "For me it has always been a responsible and wholesome way of running my restaurant. And at the end of the day, the most important thing is that it all tastes great."

During the growing season, specials at both locations are inspired by the "Little Kitchen" garden harvest. Colin has also been an active member of the farmers' market community in the Hamptons since its inception in the late '90s and he is now a regular at Darien's Farmers' Market on Wednesdays in the Goodwives Shopping Plaza, a short hop from Estia's.

Fairfield County diners have embraced Estia's in Darien, making it a regular stop for freshly prepared, authentic American cuisine in a relaxed atmosphere.

Cioppino Verde

SERVES 4 TO 6

Colin Ambrose's Cioppino Verde (fish stew with green sauce) is the quintessential summer meal. Made with a fresh herbs and poblanos, pulled from Estia's garden, as well as fresh shrimp, cod and littleneck clams, the light, yet flavorfully spicy stew is wonderful paired with a crusty baguette and a simple garden salad.

Verde Sauce (makes 2 cups)

1/2 cup loosely packed fresh cilantro leaves

1/2 cup loosely packed fresh parsley leaves

1/4 cup loosely packed fresh mint leaves

1 cup loosely packed fresh arugula leaves

4 garlic cloves, chopped

1 poblano pepper, halved, stemmed, seeded, and coarsely chopped

1/2 jalapeño pepper, stemmed, seeded, and coarsely chopped

1/4 cup dry white wine

1/4 cup olive oil

1/4 cup fresh lime juice

Sea salt

Cioppino

1/2 cup (1 stick, 4 ounces) unsalted butter

1/2 cup minced onion (about 1 medium-size onion)

1/2 cup minced carrot (about 2 medium-size carrots)

1/2 cup minced fennel bulb, stalks removed and trimmed (about 1/2 large bulb)

1/2 cup minced celery (about 2 medium-size ribs)

1 cup dry white wine

2 cups clam juice

12 littleneck clams, scrubbed

16 mussels, scrubbed and debearded, or 12 sea scallops, tough muscles removed

1 pound fresh cod, cut into 2-inch pieces

1 pound uncooked shrimp, peeled and deveined

2 ripe tomatoes, diced

Sea salt and freshly ground black pepper

4 to 6 slices baguette, toasted and buttered

Fresh lemon juice

1. To make the verde sauce: Fill a medium-size bowl with ice water and set aside. Meanwhile, fill a 2-quart pot halfway with water and bring to a boil over medium-high heat. Add the herbs and arugula and blanch for 2 minutes. Using a slotted spoon, transfer the herbs and arugula to the prepared ice-water bath and let cool completely, about 3 minutes. Drain the herbs and arugula thoroughly and pat dry with paper towels.

2. Process the garlic and peppers in a food processor. With the processor running, slowly add the wine in a steady stream until well blended. Add the herbs, arugula, olive oil, and lime juice and blend until smooth. Pour into a bowl and season with salt to taste. Cover and refrigerate until ready to use.

3. To make the cioppino: Heat the butter in a stockpot or Dutch oven over medium-high heat. Add the onion, carrot, fennel, and celery and cook, stirring occasionally, until the onion is soft and translucent, about 6 minutes. Whisk in the wine and clam juice and bring to a boil over medium-high heat. Lower the heat to a gentle simmer, add the clams and mussels, if using, and cook for 5 minutes. Add the cod, shrimp, and scallops, if using, cover, and continue to simmer until the shellfish open and the shrimp and scallops are opaque throughout, about 5 minutes. Add the tomatoes and cook for 1 minute. Discard any shells that do not open.

4. Meanwhile, in a medium-size saucepan, warm the verde sauce over medium heat, stirring occasionally, until heated through. Do not bring sauce to a boil.

5. Divide the seafood evenly among four to six warmed bowls and ladle the heated broth over the seafood. Stir in 2 to 4 tablespoons of the verde sauce into each bowl, or to taste. Season with salt and pepper to taste. Top each serving with a baguette slice and a splash of lemon juice, and serve.

Note: Save the extra verde sauce and serve with chicken or pork.

Estia's American

FIGS WOOD FIRED BISTRO

Figs Wood Fired Bistro, a neighborhood eatery featuring a local, seasonal mix of traditional American foods with global influences, is located in the charming Sandy Hook village. Customers come here to relax, feel at home, and dine on home-made organic food that is sourced locally.

Figs fuses New England eclectic, historic colonial English charm, and urban atti-tude. Inside, you'll find a bustling metro-style restaurant, warmed by a reclaimed floor and antique bar, cozy banquettes, a wood-fired brick oven, and an open kitchen. Outside, the circa-1782 white clapboard Colonial is framed by lovely trees and flowers.

Before opening Figs, owners Joe and Kris-tina Tartaglia, local residents, owned Tarta-glia's Restaurant (Bridgeport) and Twisted Vine Restaurant (Derby), and ran the catering at the Westport Inn (Westport).

At Figs, they strive to bring guests food and drink from Connecticut farm fields, when available, in their effort to support the organic local economy and the sustain-ability of local farming.

Maple-Glazed Salmon

SERVES 4

"I have always loved the taste of real maple syrup. The crisp seared salmon, topped with the natural sweetener; melts in your mouth. That is why it is one of our customers' favorite dishes here at Figs" —Joe Tartaglia

Serve this dish with brown rice and a steamed vegetable.

1/2 cup vegetable stock
1 tablespoon balsamic vinegar
2 tablespoons fresh lemon juice
1 1/2 teaspoons chopped fresh thyme leaves
1 1/2 tablespoons extra-virgin olive oil
4 (7-ounce) wild Alaskan salmon fillets, skin-on
1/4 cup pure maple syrup
1 tablespoon unsalted butter
Kosher salt and freshly ground black pepper

1. In a small bowl, whisk together the vegetable stock, vinegar, lemon juice, and thyme. Set aside.

2. Heat the oil in a large sauté pan over medium-high heat. Meanwhile, pat the salmon fillets dry with paper towels. Add the salmon, skin side up, and sear for 2 minutes. Using a large spatula, carefully flip the fillets over and cook for 1 min-ute. Pour in the vegetable stock mixture, lower the heat to low, bring to a simmer, and cook for 4 minutes. Transfer the fillets to a platter and set aside.

3. Whisk in the maple syrup and butter, stirring constantly, until smooth. Season with salt and pepper to taste.

4. Spoon the maple sauce over the fillets and serve.

Figs Wood Fired Bistro

Connecticut River Shad

SERVES 2

It's a sure sign of spring when shad start running in the Connecticut River. Once considered a "poor man's" food, shad's reputation as a delicacy has increased as the annual catch has dwindled. Here's a great way to prepare them.

1 pound asparagus, trimmed

Sorrel Sauce

1 cup dry white wine

1 tablespoon minced shallot

1/2 cup heavy cream

6 tablespoons unsalted butter

1 bunch sorrel (see note), washed, thick stems discarded, and chopped into bite-size pieces

Kosher salt and freshly ground black pepper

....

3 tablespoons extra-virgin olive oil, divided

2 (6-ounce) shad fillets (see note), skin removed, deboned

Kosher salt and freshly ground black pepper

1. To make the asparagus: Cut the asparagus into 4-inch lengths. Blanch in salted boiling water for 1 minute. Strain and place in ice water.

2. To make the sorrel sauce: Place the wine and shallot in a medium-size saucepan, and bring to a boil over low heat, about 15 minutes. Increase the heat to medium and reduce until most of the wine has evaporated, whisking frequently. Slowly whisk in the cream and reduce by half, whisking frequently. Lower the heat to low and slowly whisk in the butter. Add the chopped sorrel and season with salt and pepper to taste.

3. Preheat the oven to 375°F. Heat 2 tablespoons of the oil in a 12-inch ovenproof skillet over medium heat. Add the fish and season with salt and pepper. Place the skillet in the oven and cook for about 3 minutes (the fish should be slightly undercooked). Remove from the oven, cover with foil, and allow to rest for 5 minutes.

4. To finish: Heat the remaining 1 tablespoon of oil in a medium-size skillet over medium heat. Add the asparagus and sauté until heated through, about 5 minutes. Season with salt and pepper to taste.

5. To serve, divide the asparagus between two plates, arranging them in the center of each plate. Place the shad on top of the asparagus and drizzle the sauce over the fish and asparagus, to taste. Serve at once.

Notes:

You can substitute herring (smaller) or mackerel or freshwater bass for the shad.

You can substitute spinach plus lemon zest or arugula for the sorrel.

Union League Cafe

Calamari
with Eggplant Chutney

MAKES 6 CUPS CHUTNEY; SERVES 6 TO 8

This fiery eggplant chutney is the ideal way to perk up grilled calamari. The sweetness from the golden raisins and squid balances the heat from the harissa paste. The green color from the micros makes a striking contrast with the red chutney.

1 1/2 pounds eggplant, unpeeled and cut into medium dice (about 8 cups)

Kosher salt

1/4 cup plus 3 tablespoons extra-virgin olive oil, divided

1 medium-size onion, diced

1/2 pound fennel, diced

3 1/2 tablespoons sliced garlic

1/3 cup golden raisins

1 tablespoon harissa paste

2 tablespoons Chermoula blend spice, homemade or store-bought

2 tablespoons packed dark brown sugar

3/4 cup champagne vinegar

1/2 cup cooked chickpeas

3 medium-size to large organic tomatoes, diced

3 bay leaves

Zest from 1 lemon

1/3 cup pumpkin seeds

3 pounds fresh calamari, bodies only, cleaned and sliced

Freshly ground black pepper

2 ounces microgreens

1. Presoak bamboo skewers for 30 minutes or have ready metal skewers.

2. Place the eggplant in a medium-size bowl and sprinkle with salt, tossing to coat well. Set aside

for 20 minutes. Place the eggplant in a colander and wash well under cold running water. Wrap the eggplant in a clean dish towel or paper towels and squeeze out any excess moisture. Set aside.

3. Heat 1/4 cup of the oil in a 12-inch skillet over medium heat. Add the eggplant and sauté until golden brown, about 10 minutes. Using a slotted spoon, remove the eggplant and drain on paper towels.

4. Add 2 tablespoons of oil to the same skillet. Add the onion and fennel and continue to cook, stirring often, until the onion is soft and translucent, about 6 minutes. Add the garlic and cook for 1 minute. Add the raisins and cook for 1 minute. Stir in the harissa, Chermoula spice, and brown sugar and cook, stirring often, for 1 minute.

5. Stir in the champagne vinegar and bring to a boil, scraping up the brown bits from the bottom of the skillet. Continue to cook until most of the vinegar has evaporated, about 5 minutes.

6. Add the eggplant, chickpeas, tomatoes, bay leaves, and lemon zest. Bring to a simmer and cook for 15 minutes.

7. Meanwhile, toast the pumpkin seeds in a small, dry skillet over medium heat until fragrant and light golden brown, about 7 minutes.

8. Wrap the calamari in paper towels and pat dry. Toss the calamari with the remaining 1 tablespoon of oil in a large bowl. Slide the precut calamari rings on two skewers each. Season with salt and pepper to taste.

9. Heat a grill (see note) to medium-high and grill the calamari until just opaque throughout and golden, about 3 minutes per side.

10. Place microgreens in a small bowl and drizzle with olive oil.

11. To serve: Place the chutney in a decorative bowl and fold in the pumpkin seeds. Season with salt and pepper to taste. Arrange the calamari around the bowl and top the calamari with microgreens.

Note: This recipe can also be made indoors, by sautéing the calamari in a skillet.

L'Escale Restaurant

Swordfish Pizzaioli

SERVES 4

A house favorite at the Max restaurants for many years, this Swordfish Pizzaioli delivers on a classic.

4 (8-ounce) swordfish steaks

2 tablespoons extra-virgin olive oil, plus more for the grill, swordfish, and drizzling

4 medium-size garlic cloves, chopped

1 medium-size onion, sliced 1/4 inch thick

2 medium-size bell peppers, 1 red and 1 yellow, sliced 1/4 inch thick

2 fresh Italian hot peppers or 2 jarred, such as pepperoncini, drained and thinly sliced (see note)

1 pint heirloom cherry tomatoes, quartered

1 cup dry white wine

1 tablespoon minced fresh flat-leaf parsley

2 tablespoons chopped fresh basil

Kosher salt

1. Pat the swordfish dry with paper towels. Set aside. Heat a gas or electric grill to medium-high heat and generously brush the cooking grate and both sides of steaks with oil. Season the steaks with salt and grill until grill marks appear, about 2 minutes each side. Using a large spatula, carefully remove the steaks and place on a platter. Set aside.

2. Heat the 2 tablespoons of oil in a large sauté pan over medium heat. Add the garlic, stirring often, cook until fragrant, about 1 minute. Add the onion and bell peppers, stirring occasionally; cook until the onion is soft, about 6 minutes. Add the hot peppers and tomatoes; stirring occasion-ally, cook for 5 minutes. Stir in the wine and cook for 5 minutes. Stir in the parsley. Season with salt to taste.

5. Add the swordfish, cover, and cook until opaque in the center, 8 to 10 minutes, depending on the thickness of the steaks.

6. Transfer steaks to a platter. Garnish with the basil and drizzle with oil. Top with the vegetable mixture. Season with salt to taste. Serve.

Note: Cutting back on the number of hot peppers will reduce the spiciness to your preferred level.

Max Amore Ristorante

MAPLE LANE FARMS KEEPS IT "CURRANT"

From the hilltop perch of his front porch, farmer Allyn Brown III surveys his picturesque 120-acre farm property in Preston, which has been drawing visitors for a classic pick-your-own experience since the '80s. For more than 30 years, families have flocked to this idyllic spot to experience the thrill of the harvest in berry season and at the holidays.

Back in the early '80s, PYO places were just taking off, and Brown imagined that his old dairy farm would be a great spot to make the switch from land-scaping to growing. He planted strawberries, and people across southeastern Connecticut found their way to his berry fields. To keep visitors coming back, he added a virtual fruit salad of PYO fruits.

To supplement the seasonal trade, Brown raises and sells Oyster Shell mushrooms to local restaurants and black currants to juice manufacturers. Recog-nizing the health benefits of black currants, Brown launched A Currant Affair, a line of black currant juice and blends, now sold through retailers in the Northeast. As the largest grower of black currants in North America, Maple Lane Farms grows, har-vests, crushes, bottles, and distributes all its own black currants—from the Preston fields to the store shelves. It doesn't get any fresher.

LA BELLE AURORE

La Belle Aurore is a charming bistro located in the seaside village of Niantic, serving farm-to-table cuisine, simply prepared and beautifully presented. The word *homey* aptly describes chef-owner Dawn Bruckner's tasty bistro fare, which relies as much as possible on local and organic products. Even the tabletop flowers come from Hungs Brook Farm in Quaker Hill.

Dawn says, "Our menu changes often to reflect the best of what our local farmers and the seasons have to offer. Ninety percent of your dinner this evening has been grown or raised within a 100-mile radius—the majority of that 90 percent, within 50 miles."

Dawn, who owns the restaurant with her husband, sports reporter Wally Bruckner, says she lets fresh herbs, fresh vegetables, and other seasonal market foods inspire her *bonne femme* ("good wife") cuisine, making simple dishes spectacular with items sourced daily at the market. "The way I cook is the way French women cook at home," she explains.

Here, farm-to-table grab-and-go dinners are available on weeknights, dinner is served Friday and Saturday nights (with a nice selection of locally brewed beers and a well-edited and well-priced wine list), and a much-lauded brunch is served Saturday and Sunday. La Belle Aurore is also known for hosting farm dinners, cheese tastings, and other foodie events.

Stonington Royal Red Shrimp over Root Vegetable Cakes

SERVES 4

Using root vegetable cakes as a base, the boiled Royal Red shrimp from local waters provide a nice textural contrast to the cakes.

Beets

1 red beet (about 4 ounces), trimmed and cut into 1/2-inch pieces

Olive oil, for drizzling

Kosher salt and freshly ground black pepper

Mashed Rutabaga, Turnip, and Parsnip

1 small rutabaga (about 8 ounces), peeled and cut into medium dice

1 purple-top turnip (about 6 ounces), peeled and cut into medium dice

1 small parsnip (about 2 ounces), cut into 1-inch pieces

Cabbage and Leeks

1 tablespoon extra-virgin olive oil, plus more for frying vegetables

1/2 cup shredded sweet cabbage

1/2 small leek, cleaned, white part only, thinly sliced into 1/2-inch pieces

1 1/2 teaspoons fresh minced herbs, such as rosemary or thyme

Kosher salt and freshly ground black pepper

Shrimp

2 pounds shrimp, shells on, preferably large Stonington Royal Red shrimp

1 1/2 teaspoons extra-virgin olive oil

2 tablespoons unsalted butter

Fresh lemon juice (optional)

1 radish, such as watermelon, scrubbed, sliced into rounds, then cut into matchsticks

Fresh parsley, minced

1. Preheat the oven to 375°F. Lightly oil a small baking dish and set aside. Lightly grease a baking sheet with cooking spray; set aside.

2. To make the beets: Spread the beets in a single layer into the prepared baking dish. Drizzle oil over the beets and toss to combine. Season with salt and pepper to taste. Roast, stirring occasionally, until the beets are fork-tender, about 40 minutes. Set aside to cool. Lower the oven temperature to 200°F.

3. To make the rutabaga, turnip, and parsnips: While the beets are roasting, place other root vegetables in a medium-size saucepan and cover with salted water. Bring to a boil over medium-high heat and cook until the vegetables are fork-tender, about 12 minutes. Drain in a colander. Transfer the vegetables to a medium-size bowl and mash with an old-fashioned potato masher or ricer until the mixture has the consistency of the inside of a baked potato. Set aside to cool.

4. To make the cabbage and leeks: While the rutabaga mixture is cooling, heat 1 tablespoon of olive oil in a medium-size sauté pan over medium heat. Add the cabbage and leeks and sauté until just tender and still slightly crisp, about 3 minutes.

5. In a large bowl, mix together the beets along with any reserved juice, the rutabaga mixture, the cabbage mixture, herbs, and salt and pepper to taste. Heat 1 tablespoon of oil in a large skillet over medium heat. Working in batches, drop about 1/3 cup of the vegetable mixture into the skillet. Using a fork, flatten into pancakes and cook on one side until crispy and golden brown, about 3 minutes. Flip the pancakes and cook until crispy and golden brown, about 3 minutes more, adding additional oil as needed. Transfer the pancakes to an ovenproof dish and keep warm in the oven.

6. To make the shrimp: While the oil is heating for the cakes, bring a large saucepan of generously salted water to a boil. Boil the shrimp until pink and opaque, about 3 minutes. Drain in a colander. When cool enough to handle, peel the shrimp and set aside. Heat 1 1/2 teaspoons of oil and the butter in a large sauté pan over medium-high heat. Add the shrimp and sauté for 2 minutes.

7. To assemble: Place one or two root vegetable cakes in the center of four plates. Divide the shrimp evenly among the cakes and drizzle with butter sauce and lemon juice, if desired. Garnish with radish sticks and parsley. Serve at once.

La Belle Aurore

WALRUS + CARPENTER

Would an oddly named Texas-style barbecue joint pass muster in the hip and burgeoning Bridgeport dining scene? That's the gamble Joe Farrell took when he set up his custom smoker and opened Walrus + Carpenter, a smokehouse and gastropub named for an obscure Alice in Wonderland reference, serving up an array of slow-cooked barbecue and an eclectic assortment of great American craft beers.

Since firing up the smoker, Walrus + Carpenter has won a slew of awards, most notably, First Place: Best Barbecue, Second Place: Best New Restaurant and Best American, and Third Place: Best Cocktail from *Connecticut Magazine*.

As much as we're fans of the smoky, dry-rubbed meats and the seriously crispy fried chicken, it's chef Adam Roytman's small plates and sides that draw the buzz—everything from Fried Oysters to Shaved Fennel and Cherry Pepper Salad to Braised Veal and Dumplings to Seared Foie Gras to pickled veggies and southern collards—are unexpected little culinary surprises with an emphasis on fresh and local ingredients.

The best way to attack so many inventive offerings is to bring friends. Plenty of friends. You can work your way down the Small Plates side of the menu, split a couple of smoker options, such as the Maple-Bourbon Baby Backs or the Spice-Rubbed Beef Brisket, or go the whole hog (pun intended), and order the Notorious P.I.G., a three-course extravaganza that starts out with oysters, poutine, smoked Andouille sausage, and maple pork belly, moves to the ribs, brisket, pork shoulder, mac and cheese, corn bread, coleslaw and mashed potatoes, and ends with a bacon-chipwich and chocolate bread pudding. This feast is not for the faint of heart, but it's available for $120, at press time, and is ideal for four intrepid carnivores.

Wash it all down with an icy brew from a fairly impressive craft beer menu, or take a walk on the wild side with an inspired cocktail, a smooth single malt or small batch bourbon.

Stonington Royal Red Shrimp and Heirloom Grits with Smoked Tasso Pork

SERVES 4

Note: The Tasso pork must be started three days before it is served; the grits must be started one day before it is served.

Tasso Pork

2 tablespoons paprika

1 1/2 tablespoons kosher salt

1 tablespoon minced fresh garlic

1 tablespoon freshly ground black pepper

1 1/2 teaspoons brown sugar

1 1/2 teaspoons freshly ground white pepper

1 teaspoon cayenne pepper

1/2 teaspoon ground cinnamon

1 (1 3/4-pound) boneless pork shoulder or butt, cut into four equal pieces

Grits

1 cup coarse white grits, preferably Anson Mills Antebellum

2 1/2 cups water

2 cups whole milk

3 tablespoons unsalted butter

Sea salt and freshly ground black pepper

Shrimp

4 green onions, minced

1 tablespoon fresh lemon juice

2 garlic cloves, minced

3 tablespoons extra-virgin olive oil, divided

2 teaspoons sea salt

1 teaspoon freshly ground black pepper

1 pound Stonington Royal Red Shrimp, peeled, deveined, and tails removed

Sauce

3 tablespoons unsalted butter, chilled, cut into small pieces, divided

4 ounces Tasso pork, diced small (recipe above)

4 green onions, sliced

2 garlic cloves, sliced

1/4 cup dry white wine

1 tablespoon hot sauce, such as Crystal or Tabasco

Sea salt

1. To make the Tasso pork: Place a meat rack on a baking sheet and set aside. In a medium-size bowl combine the paprika, salt, garlic, black pepper, sugar, white pepper, cayenne, and cinnamon. Pat the pork pieces dry with paper towels. Dredge the pork pieces into the spice mixture, making sure to coat the meat completely. Place the meat on the rack, cover, and let sit in the refrigerator for 3 days.

2. Set up a smoker (see note) according to the manufacturer's directions, using apple wood. Place the meat in the smoker and smoke slowly, turning once halfway through, while maintaining a temperature of 200°F, until the internal temperature of the meat reaches 150°F, 4 to 6 hours, depending on your smoker.

3. To make the grits: In a medium-size bowl, cover the grits with the water. Stir once and skim the top of the water of any debris floating on the surface. Cover and refrigerate overnight. Pour the grits and water into a medium-size, heavy-bottomed saucepan and bring to a simmer over medium heat, stirring constantly, 5 to 8 minutes.

4. Meanwhile in a separate saucepan, heat the milk over medium heat until hot but not boiling. Pour 1/4 cup of the milk into the grits at 5-minute intervals until well absorbed. Cook the grits until creamy and tender, but not mushy, 30 to 50 minutes, depending on the grit variety used. Remove

from the heat and stir in the butter. Season with salt and pepper to taste. Set aside.

5. While the grits are simmering, start the shrimp: In a medium-size bowl, combine the green onions, lemon juice, garlic, 2 tablespoons of the oil, salt, and pepper. Add the shrimp and toss to coat well. Let marinate at room temperature for 1 hour.

6. While the shrimp is marinating, make the sauce: In a small saucepan, melt 1 tablespoon of the butter over medium-high heat. Add the pork and sauté until the fat begins to render, about 4 minutes. Add the green onions and sauté until soft, about 8 minutes. Add the garlic and sauté for 1 minute. Stir in the wine and hot sauce and cook until most of the wine has evaporated, about 4 minutes. Lower the heat to low and whisk in the remaining 2 tablespoons of butter one piece at a time. Remove from the heat. Set aside.

7. Heat the remaining 1 tablespoon of olive oil in a large, cast-iron grill pan until hot but not smoking, over medium heat. Add the shrimp, in batches, and grill until firm and opaque, about 3 minutes per side. Spoon the grits into individual bowls. Evenly divide the shrimp on top. Drizzle with sauce to taste. Serve.

Notes:

If you don't own a smoker, you can use a gas or charcoal grill. Some gas grills come with a metal smoker box that sits atop a dedicated burner. Just turn on the burner, and add damp wood chips. Control the smoke level by turning the burner higher or lower. Or, you can purchase a heavy-gauge stainless-steel smoker box that sits right on top of your grill's cooking grate. Holes in the lid direct the fragrant smoke over your food.

Save the extra rub and use on chicken or steak.

Save the extra pork and add to green beans or baked bean dishes.

Walrus + Carpenter

GUILFORD LOBSTER POUND

The Long Island Sound once teemed with lobsters, which were abundant and cheap. Although their populations aren't what they used to be, there are still plenty of down-and-dirty lobster shacks dotting the Connecticut coastline where you can make a quick pit stop and enjoy a fresh-caught lobster with a first-rate view of the Sound.

Nothing beats wolfing down a fresh lobster roll al-fresco at a New England lobster shack.

The Connecticut lobster roll is an institution. It does not involve celery or onion, or heaven forbid, mayonnaise. The classic contains only hunks of freshly cooked lobster meat, dunked generously in butter, and served on a toasted, steamed or grilled soft roll, split down the middle. The lobster roll originated at Perry's, in Milford, as early as 1929, according to the *Encyclopedia of American Food and Drink*.

Craving a lobster roll? Guilford Lobster Pound is an old-school lobster haven, run for three decades by the Mansi family. Boaters and beachgoers flock to this down-home, family-owned seafood shack in season for bowls of steaming chowder and lobster rolls—succulent lobster meat, piled into toasted, buttered rolls. These babies are fresh off the boat, hauled in that day by Capt. Bart Mansi, who has been lobstering in Long Island Sound since the mid 1970s.

Capt. Bart leaves the docks at 4:00 a.m. every morning aboard the *Erica Page*, his 42-foot vessel, and returns every afternoon to weigh and sorted his catch by size and then put the feisty critters into ice-cold, 38°F water to ensure freshness.

Bart says, "Not only can you pick up just-caught lobster to bring home, you can also enjoy the freshest lobster rolls around. You will taste the difference."

So, when you have a hankering for a warm lobster roll slathered in drawn butter, go to the dock at the Guilford Lobster Pound. Snag a waterfront table, and enjoy your feast fresh off the boat, while taking in the vistas of Faulkner Island, Grass Island, and acres of protected Salt Marsh teeming with shore birds.

Spicy Littleneck Clams

SERVES 2 TO 3

The rich broth for this spicy littleneck clams recipe is addictive. Be sure to have a loaf of crusty bread handy for dunking.

24 littleneck clams
2 tablespoons extra-virgin olive oil, divided
4 ounces Spanish chorizo sausage (see note), minced
1/2 cup canned white beans (cannellini), drained and rinsed
1 jalapeño pepper, halved, stemmed, seeded, and minced
1 teaspoon minced fresh garlic
2 cups dry white wine
3 tablespoons unsalted butter
1 teaspoon minced flat-leaf parsley
Kosher salt and freshly ground black pepper
Crusty bread

1. Rinse and scrub the clams under cold running water. Discard any clams that may be broken or do not close when tapped.

2. Heat 1 tablespoon of the oil in a large pot over medium heat. Add the sausage, stirring frequently, until the sausage is lightly browned, about 5 minutes. Add the beans, jalapeño pepper, and garlic, stirring often, and cook until the jalapeño is tender, about 2 minutes. Season with salt and pepper to taste.

3. Add the clams, cover, increase the heat to medium-high, and cook for 1 minute.

4. Add the wine, the remaining 1 tablespoon of olive oil, and the butter, stirring gently to coat. Cover the pot and simmer until all the clams have opened, about 10 minutes, shaking the pot occasionally. Remove from the heat and discard any clams that do not open. Stir in the parsley. Season with additional salt and pepper. Place the clams in a serving bowl and serve with the broth and crusty bread.

Note: If you can't find Spanish chorizo sausage, a Portuguese linguiça sausage (sweeter) or chouriço sausage (spicier) are suitable substitutes. Both are available in specialty food stores and some supermarkets.

The Wharf at Madison Beach Hotel

MEAT

Local Lamb Burgers with Wasabi Aioli

**MAKES 2 LARGE
OR 4 SMALLER BURGERS**

Although he could have chosen to show off one of his more sophisticated offerings, Joseph Tartaglia instead shares the juicy local lamb burger, a house favorite, enhanced by a spicy topping of wasabi aioli and arugula. Stone-ground mustard, cumin, and scallions give a fresh flavor to the lamb.

Wasabi Aioli

1 tablespoon water
1 1/2 teaspoons wasabi powder
1/8 teaspoon granulated garlic
2 tablespoons fresh orange juice
1/2 cup mayonnaise
Kosher salt

Lamb Burgers

1 pound ground lamb
2 teaspoons stone-ground mustard
1 teaspoon minced scallion
1/4 teaspoon ground cumin
3 garlic cloves, minced
Kosher salt and freshly ground black pepper
3 1/2 tablespoons extra-virgin olive oil, divided
4 thin slices (about 2 ounces) smoked cow's milk Gouda cheese
2 teaspoons fresh lemon juice
2 cups loosely packed baby arugula leaves
2 ciabatta rolls, sliced in half and toasted

1. To make the wasabi aioli: In a small bowl combine the water, wasabi powder, garlic, and orange juice to form a paste. Let stand for about 4 minutes. Whisk in the mayonnaise until well combined. Add salt to taste; set aside.

2. To make the lamb burgers: In a medium-size bowl, mix the lamb, mustard, scallion, cumin, garlic, and salt and pepper until just combined. Using your hands, form into two 3/4-inch-thick patties (see note). Set aside.

3. Heat a gas or electric grill (see note) to medium-high heat and generously brush the cooking grate with 1 tablespoon of the oil. Season the burgers with salt and pepper. Grill the burgers for 5 minutes. Using a large spatula, carefully flip the burgers over and grill for about 5 minutes for medium-rare, or until the desired doneness is reached. Lay two slices of cheese on top of each burger and cover the grill. Cook until the cheese has just melted. Remove the burgers from the grill and let rest for 4 minutes.

4. In a small bowl, combine the remaining 2 1/2 tablespoons of olive oil and the lemon juice; drizzle to taste over the arugula and toss until well combined. Season with salt and pepper to taste.

5. To assemble: On each bun, spread about 1 tablespoon of the wasabi aioli, divided between the top and bottom of the bun. Place each burger on the bottom half and top each with the arugula mixture to taste. Top with the bun tops and serve at once.

Notes:

If you are making four burgers, the patties will be thinner and will cook faster, 2 to 3 minutes per side.

If you do not own a grill, heat 1 tablespoon of olive oil in a large, nonstick skillet over medium-high heat. Add the burgers, and cook, turning once, about 5 minutes per side for medium-rare. Lay two slices of the cheese on top of each burger and cover the pan. Cook until the cheese has just melted.

Figs Wood Fired Bistro

Polpette alla Napoletana (Meatballs)

MAKES ABOUT 24 MEATBALLS; SERVES 4 TO 6

When you're seeking an authentic, go-to meatball recipe, look no further. You'll make these meatballs in batches, so if you freeze a batch in a resealable plastic freezer bag, you can pop out a few meatballs whenever the mood strikes.

Soaking the stale bread in warm water will create moist and tender meatballs.

1 (2-day-old) loaf sourdough bread, cut in half, center removed and crust discarded (about 5 ounces crust-less)
1 cup plain bread crumbs
3 pounds ground pork
2 large eggs, lightly beaten
1 cup finely grated Parmigiano-Reggiano cheese, plus more for serving
1/2 cup chopped fresh parsley
4 garlic cloves, minced
3/4 tablespoon kosher salt
3/4 tablespoon freshly ground black pepper
2 tablespoons olive oil
6 cups good-quality tomato pasta sauce
Rustic bread or cooked pasta, for serving

1. Place the white center of the bread in a medium-size bowl and pour enough cold water over the bread to moisten. Let the bread soak for 10 minutes. Using your hands, squeeze out any excess liquid until the bread is just damp, about 3 minutes, then coarsely chop.

2. In a large bowl, combine the chopped sourdough bread, bread crumbs, pork, eggs, Parmigiano-Reggiano, parsley, garlic, salt, and pepper until just combined. Do not overmix.

Spoon or scoop about 1/4 cup of the meat mixture for each meatball. Using your hands, form into 25 meatballs.

3. Heat 1 tablespoon of the oil in a Dutch oven over medium-high heat until hot, but not smoking. Add half of the meatballs and cook, turning gently with tongs, until browned on all sides, about 12 minutes. With a slotted spoon, transfer the meatballs to a plate. Repeat with the remaining oil and remaining meatballs. Drain off the excess oil. Return all the meatballs to the Dutch oven. Add the pasta sauce and simmer until the sauce is heated through and the meatballs have reached an internal temperature of 140°F, about 15 minutes. Season with salt and pepper. Serve with rustic bread, if desired, or atop pasta.

Tarry Lodge Enoteca Pizzeria

COMMON GROUND HIGH SCHOOL, URBAN FARM & ENVIRONMENTAL EDUCATION CENTER

New Haven's Common Ground is on a mission to put city dwellers in touch with fresh foods and the farm experience, offering hands-on farm experiences, farm stands, and educational programs that connect people of all ages with the natural world and the sources of their food.

The working farm boasts flourishing production and educational gardens, as well as a variety of farm animals. Located at the base of West Rock Ridge State Park, the site also includes 20 acres of forest with hiking trails, wildlife, and diverse natural habitats.

You can find Common Ground produce June through November at CitySeed Farmers' Markets in New Haven and on the Common Ground campus. During the winter, the harvest goes to school lunch programs.

COMMUNITY TABLE

Chef Joel Viehland is passionate about sustainability and the interplay of flavors on the plate. After stints at Chez es Saada, Quilty's, and Gramercy Tavern in New York; Bayona, Emeril's, and Herbsaint in New Orleans; and Noma, the famed two-star restaurant in Copenhagen, Viehland was lured up to the Litchfield countryside with the chance to run his own show at Community Table.

The Scandinavian-chic locavore restaurant in Washington has drawn foodies, celebs, and critics from far and wide. Diners often plan a weekend in the hills around a dinner reservation and, recently, the restaurant was overhauled to feature a beautiful new dining room and bar, as well as an outdoor patio space, to complement the rustic-modern space.

With Community Table, Viehland's inventive local cuisine has earned him a place among *Food & Wine*'s picks for the Top 10 Up-and-Coming Chefs in New England and status as a semifinalist for a James Beard Award for Best Chef New England in 2013 and 2014.

Viehland credits mentor Katy Sparks for teaching him to taste, and his stint at Noma for his mastery of ages-old food preservation techniques, such as pickling, curing, and preserving, which allow him to wake up sleepy winter palates to the fresh tastes of spring and summer, with root-cellar specialties, such as Cherry Preserves with Almond and Ginger and Coffee-

Cured Ham in a celery root–Parmesan broth, topped with a local farm egg.

In the warmer months, Viehland turns to farmers who dot the surrounding hills for inspiration. In addition, outside the back door, you'll spy raised vegetable garden beds and beehives that provide extra honey for use in the restaurant. With local bounty all around him, Viehland continues to up the ante, turning simple, honest ingredients into wholly innovative taste sensations that you won't try anywhere else. Crispy duck confit, accented with fennel puree, arugula, and a medley of tangy local berries is just one such a dish that showcased Viehland's deft and restrained hand, leaving you lusting after another piquant bite.

Celebrating? Book the actual "community table," a 12-seat communal table and the centerpiece of the dining room, made from a black walnut tree that fell 30 years ago.

Swedish Meatballs
G. Swenson Style
(G. Swenson's Köttbullar)

**MAKES ABOUT 33 MEATBALLS;
SERVES 6**

Meatballs made at G. Swenson's, a restaurant in Torekov, Sweden, inspired this dish. *This* is how Swedish meatballs are meant to taste.

Note: Brine the cucumbers two days before you intend to serve the meatballs.

Pressed Cucumbers

2 English cucumbers, peeled and sliced paper thin
2/3 cup white vinegar
1/2 cup granulated sugar
6 tablespoons water
1/4 teaspoon freshly ground white pepper
1/4 cup fresh parsley, finely chopped
3/4 teaspoon kosher salt

Sugar-Marinated Lingonberries
(Rårörda lingon; see note)

1 pound fresh or frozen lingonberries
1 cup granulated sugar, or to taste

Meatballs

1 cup bread crumbs
1/2 cup + 1 tablespoon water
1 tablespoon olive oil
1 medium-size onion, minced
3 pounds ground beef
2 large eggs, lightly beaten
1 tablespoon veal or beef stock
1 tablespoon kosher salt
3/4 tablespoon freshly ground black pepper
2 tablespoons unsalted butter, or as needed

Cream Sauce (Gräddsås)

1 tablespoon unsalted butter
1 medium-size yellow onion
3 cups beef stock
1/2 cup heavy cream
2 tablespoons cornstarch combined with 1/4 cup
    broth to make a paste
Kosher salt
Chopped fresh dill, for garnish

1. To make the pressed cucumbers: Place the cucumbers in a colander, cover with plastic, then weigh it down with a heavy can or brick for 10 minutes. Remove the weight and pat dry with paper towels. Combine the rest of the ingredients in a small bowl. Place the cucumbers in a clean quart-size jar with a canning or plastic lid. Pour the vinegar mixture over the cucumbers and place in the refrigerator for 2 days.

2. To make the sugar-marinated lingonberries: In a medium-size bowl, combine the berries and sugar. Cover with plastic wrap and place in the refrigerator. Chill, stirring occasionally, for 2 days.

3. To make the meatballs: Place the bread crumbs in a small bowl and pour enough cold water (about 1/2 cup) over the crumbs to moisten. Let the bread crumbs soak for 15 minutes. Drain. Using paper towels, squeeze out any excess liquid until the bread crumbs are just damp.

4. Heat the oil in a medium-size sauté pan over medium heat. Add the onion and a pinch of salt and cook, stirring occasionally, until soft and translucent, about 6 minutes. Set aside.

5. In a large bowl, combine the bread crumbs, olive oil, onion, ground beef, eggs, remaining water, stock, and salt and pepper until just combined. Do not overmix. Spoon 1 heaping tablespoon of the meat mixture to form into golf ball–size meatballs. Using your hands, form into about 33 meatballs.

6. Preheat the oven to 200°F. Melt 1 tablespoon of the butter in a Dutch oven over medium-high heat. Add the meatballs in batches and cook, turning gently with tongs, until browned on all sides, 6 to 8 minutes. With a slotted spoon, transfer the meatballs to an ovenproof dish and place in the oven to keep warm. Repeat with the remaining butter and remaining meatballs. Transfer the meatballs to the oven to keep warm.

7. To make the cream sauce: Lower the heat beneath the Dutch oven to medium, add the butter, and onion, and sauté, stirring often, until the onion is soft and translucent, about 6 minutes. Gradually whisk in the beef stock and cream and bring to a simmer. Whisk in the cornstarch paste and continue to cook, whisking often, until the sauce reaches the desired consistency, about 8 minutes. Season with salt to taste. Add the meatballs and continue to cook until heated through, about 1 minute. Garnish with dill. Serve with the pressed cucumbers, lingonberries, and boiled potatoes on the side, if desired.

Note: If you cannot find fresh or frozen lingonberries, lingonberry preserves make a fine substitute.

Chef Joel Viehland for Community Table

Grass-Fed Beef and Root Vegetable Meat Loaf

SERVES 8

Meat loaf, well made, is one of America's triumphs, and demonstrates what resourceful home cooks can do. The glory of a good meat loaf is that it's as tasty cold as it is hot—as anyone who has ever tasted a meat loaf sandwich knows only too well. When it's made with outstanding meat and local vegetables, nothing beats it!

"Because meat loaf is seasonless, I serve it with a simple tomato and herb salad dressed with extra-virgin olive oil and sea salt in the summer. In cold weather, I often serve it will caramelized onion gravy." —Chef Michel Nischan

2 to 3 tablespoons olive oil

1 cup peeled, medium-dice parsnip (about 1 large)

3/4 cup peeled, medium-dice carrot (about 1 large carrot)

1/2 cup peeled, medium-dice celery root (about 2 ounces)

1/3 cup diced onion (about 1 1/2 ounces)

Kosher salt and freshly ground black pepper

2 cups soft, fresh bread crumbs (about 4 slices)

1 cup whole milk

2 large eggs, lightly beaten

1/3 cup ketchup (3 ounces)

3 pounds high-quality pasture-raised ground beef

Congrats! The James Beard Foundation awarded Michel Nischan, acclaimed leader in the sustainable food movement, the 2015 James Beard Foundation Humanitarian Award. The award is given to an individual or organization whose work in the realm of food has improved the lives of others and benefited society at large.

Topping

1 teaspoon olive oil
1 medium-size onion, diced
2 large heirloom tomatoes, seeded and cut into
   1-inch cubes
3 tablespoons unsalted butter, chilled
3 tablespoons freshly sliced chives
Kosher salt and freshly ground black pepper

1. Preheat the oven to 375°F. Lightly coat a
9 x 13-inch baking dish with cooking spray. Set
aside.

2. Heat the oil in a large skillet over medium-
high heat. When hot but not smoking, add the
parsnip, carrot, celery root, onion, and salt and
pepper to taste and sauté, stirring often, until the
onion is soft and translucent, about 8 minutes.
Set aside to cool slightly, about 10 minutes.

3. In a large bowl, mix together the bread
crumbs, milk, eggs, ketchup, 1 tablespoon of
salt, and 1/4 teaspoon of pepper. Add the meat
and cooked vegetables and mix well, using a
wooden spoon or your hands.

4. Transfer the meat mixture to the prepared baking dish and form into a 6 x 10-inch oval loaf.

5. Bake until the internal temperature reaches
150°F, about 1 1/2 hours. Let rest for 15 minutes,
then carefully drain off the liquid fat and discard.

6. To make the topping: While the meat loaf is
resting, heat the oil in a medium-size skillet over
medium-high heat. Add the onion and sauté, stirring often, until soft and translucent, about 6 minutes. Add the tomatoes and butter and bring to a
simmer and cook, stirring often, until the sauce
thickens, about 6 minutes. Stir in the chives and
season with salt and pepper to taste. Spread the
topping over the top to the edges of the meat loaf.
Cut into 1-inch-thick slices, and serve.

The Dressing Room Restaurant & Wholesome Wave

FOUR MILE RIVER FARM

Nunzio and Irene Corsino started Four Mile
River Farm in Old Lyme in 1985, raising
beef, pigs, and chickens. For a quarter of a
century, the Corsinos have raised Angus
and Hereford cattle and Yorkshire pigs, as
well as a flock of chickens, which provides a
regular supply of fresh eggs to their on-site
farm stand.

Their cattle are raised on open pasture and,
in the cold winter months, when grasses
are sparse, they feed on hay from the fields
(which are fertilized naturally without pesticides) as well as on all-vegetarian corn
silage, both milled in Connecticut. Their
pigs are housed in open pens and are grain-
and milk-fed. The eggs come from free-range
chickens that enjoy a rich, natural diet.

The Corsinos do not use pesticides, antibiotics, growth stimulants, or hormones at the
farm. Taking things one step further, they
have a clean, locally inspected, modern processing facility right at the farm where they
age, cut, vacuum-pack and fast-freeze their
meats. Four Mile River Farm sells various
cuts of steak, kebabs, short ribs, and all
manner of bones and organ meats, as well
as quarter-sides of beef and bacon. Their
prepared foods include all-beef meatballs,
farm burgers, BBQ beef, beef stock, chili,
stews, and even meat loaf.

The farm participates in various farmers'
markets as well as supplies meats to a number of restaurants profiled in this book.

Four Mile River Farm Burgers

SERVES 4

This is Four Mile River Farm's signature hamburger. The owners like to refer to it as the lazy man's burger because everything is *inside* the burger—no need to waste time adding toppings—just grill and enjoy!

1 1/2 pounds ground beef chuck (80% lean)
1/2 cup shredded Cheddar cheese
4 slices bacon, cooked and crumbled
1 garlic clove, minced
2 scallions, chopped
2 tablespoons ketchup
2 tablespoons Dijon mustard
1 tablespoon Worcestershire sauce
Kosher salt and freshly ground black pepper
1 tablespoon safflower oil
4 artisan rolls, sliced in half and toasted
1 cup loosely packed baby spinach (optional)

1. In a medium-size bowl, mix the beef, cheese, bacon, garlic, scallions, ketchup, mustard, Worcestershire sauce, and salt and pepper, until just combined. Using your hands, form into four 1-inch-thick patties. Set aside.

2. Heat a gas or electric grill (see note) to medium-high heat and generously brush the cooking grate with oil. Season the burgers with salt and pepper. Grill the burgers for 3 minutes. Using a large spatula, carefully flip the burgers over and grill for about 4 more minutes for medium-rare, or until the desired doneness is reached. Remove the burgers from the grill and let rest for 4 minutes.

3. Place each burger on the bottom half of a roll and top each with the spinach, if desired. Top with the buns and serve at once.

Note: If you do not own a grill, heat 1 tablespoon of safflower oil in a large nonstick skillet over medium-high heat. Add the burgers, and cook, turning once, about 4 minutes per side for medium-rare.

Four Mile River Farm

Skirt Steak over Roasted Butternut Squash, Rainbow Swiss Chard, Topped with Caramelized Onions

SERVES 4

This rustic dish has a wide variation of flavors. It has an earthiness from the caramelized onions, coupled with the roasted butternut squash to the juicy skirt steak. The rainbow Swiss chard adds a savory depth and slightly bitter taste.

Butternut Squash

1 medium-size butternut squash, peeled, seeded, and cut into 1-inch cubes (about 2 pounds)
1 1/2 tablespoons extra-virgin olive oil
Kosher salt and freshly ground black pepper

Caramelized Onions

2 medium-size onions, thinly sliced
2 tablespoons extra-virgin olive oil
Kosher salt

Steaks

2 pounds skirt steak
1 1/2 tablespoons extra-virgin olive oil, plus more for grill
Kosher salt and freshly ground black pepper

Rainbow Swiss Chard

3 tablespoons extra-virgin olive oil, or as needed

2 medium-size garlic cloves, minced

2 bunches rainbow Swiss chard, washed, dried, thick stems discarded, cut into 1-inch-wide ribbons

Kosher salt and freshly ground black pepper

1. To make the squash: Preheat the oven to 375°F. Lightly grease a baking sheet. Arrange the squash in a single layer on the prepared baking sheet. Drizzle with olive oil and season with salt and pepper to taste. Roast in the oven, turning occasionally, until fork-tender, 25 to 30 minutes.

2. While the oven is preheating, make the caramelized onions. Heat the oil in a large skillet over medium-low heat. Add the onions and cook, stirring occasionally, for 20 minutes. Lower the heat to low and continue to cook, stirring occasionally, until the onions begin to brown, about 20 more minutes. Season with salt. Set aside.

3. To make the steaks: When the onions are halfway done, heat a gas or electric grill or cast-iron skillet to/over medium-high heat and brush generously with oil. Brush the meat with 1 1/2 tablespoons of olive oil and season with salt and pepper. Grill the steaks for 3 minutes. Using a large spatula, carefully flip the steak over and grill for 3 more minutes. Let the steaks rest for 5 minutes.

4. While the steaks are cooking, make the Swiss chard. Heat 1 tablespoon of the oil in a large sauté pan over medium heat. Add the garlic and cook, stirring frequently, until fragrant, about 1 minute. Add the remaining 2 tablespoons of oil. In batches, add the Swiss chard leaves, ribs, and stalks, allowing each batch to slightly wilt before adding the next batch. Season with salt and pepper. Cook until the leaves are wilted and the stalks are slightly tender, about 5 minutes.

5. To serve: Thinly slice the meat across the grain at an angle. Place the squash on four plates, top with some of the Swiss chard, add the steak slices over the squash and Swiss chard, then top with caramelized onions. Serve at once.

La Belle Aurore

SAUGATUCK CRAFT BUTCHERY (THE KITCHEN)

Saugatuck Craft Butchery was launched at a terrific time. Not only was the there a hole in the market for a quality local butcher featuring grass-fed and local meats, but the riverfront Saugatuck section of Westport was undergoing a major renaissance.

Ryan and Katherine Fibiger, owners of Saugatuck Craft Butchery, were among the first to set up shop in the new Saugatuck Center, a mixed retail-residential development, launching their new butcher shop in a riverfront space and shortly thereafter moving across the street to a larger storefront and kitchen.

With executive chef Mark Heppermann behind the scenes, Ryan says, "The Kitchen at Craft is an extension of the butcher shop. We have a nose-to-tail philosophy, bringing in only whole, naturally raised animals, so the Kitchen provides an outlet for parts of the animal that may not be used in the shop, such as bones for stocks, ground meats for chilis, soups, meatballs, in-house hams, bacons, and charcuterie."

In addition to trying to use every part of the animal, they try to source as many local items as possible. The rest come from right outside their doors, provided to by their organic kitchen gardens, which were built for them by Homefront Farmers in Ridgefield, a company that specializes in designing, building, and maintaining custom gardens to help people produce their own food organically.

Ryan says, "Our menu changes weekly, and we try to keep it fun and interesting, focusing on the seasons and what is available to us from our own gardens."

The Saugatuck Craft Butchery staff strives for a community vibe, and can be frequently found doing live butchering demos at local festivals or hosting fun events, such as Porktoberfest, an Oktoberfest party with an emphasis on pork, featuring whole Berkshire pig roasts, pulled pork, sausages and sides, as well as keg beer and a local Austrian band.

Dry-Aged Steak Tartare Crostini with Pickled Garden Turnips

MAKES ABOUT 27 BREAD ROUNDS; SERVES 9 (3 ROUNDS EACH)

When using raw eggs, use only fresh, clean, properly refrigerated eggs with intact shells.

Note: Pickle the turnips one day before you intend to serve the crostini.

Pickled Turnips

1/2 cup cider vinegar

1 tablespoon granulated sugar

2 whole allspice berries

1 teaspoon coriander seeds

1 teaspoon fine sea salt

1/2 teaspoon freshly ground black pepper

2 small or 1 medium-size turnip, thinly sliced and then cut into thin julienne

Dry-Aged Steak Tartare

1 1/2 pounds dry-aged steak (tender cuts, such as top sirloin, NY strip, or tenderloin)

2 tablespoons extra-virgin olive oil

3 tablespoons finely cut garden chives

2 tablespoons finely minced fresh flat-leaf parsley

1 teaspoon sriracha hot sauce

1 large egg yolk (optional)

Sea salt and freshly ground black pepper

Crostini

1 crusty baguette, cut into 1/2-inch-thick rounds

Extra-virgin olive oil

Sea salt and freshly ground black pepper

Chopped fresh chives, for garnish (optional)

1. To make the pickled turnips: In a medium-size bowl, whisk together the vinegar, sugar, allspice berries, coriander seeds, salt, and pepper until the sugar has dissolved. Adjust the seasonings with vinegar and sugar. Add the turnips and toss until well coated. Set aside and let rest at room temperature overnight.

2. To make the steak tartare: Using a sharp knife or a meat grinder fitted with a small-grind plate, finely mince the meat. In a large bowl, combine the oil, chives, parsley, sriracha, egg yolk, if using, and the meat. Season with salt and pepper to taste and mix until well combined.

3. To make the crostini: Preheat the oven to 350°F. Arrange the bread slices in a single layer on a baking sheet. Drizzle the slices with olive oil, season with salt and pepper to taste, and bake until golden brown, about 10 minutes. Set aside.

4. To assemble: Just before serving, spread about 1 tablespoon of the tartare, or to taste, onto each bread slice and garnish with the pickled turnips and chives, if desired. Serve at once.

Saugatuck Craft Butchery (The Kitchen at SCB)

Slow-Roasted Porchetta with Cilantro and Smoked Paprika

SERVES 6 TO 8

This recipe is a great party dish that needs very little fuss to get onto the table. The meat is tender and flavorful with crispy fatty bits.

4 pounds pork belly, skin on

Spice Mix

2 tablespoons Spanish smoked sweet paprika

1 tablespoon ground cumin

1/4 cup dark brown sugar

1 teaspoon ground ginger

1 1/2 teaspoons chipotle powder

Garlic, Scallion, and Cilantro Rub

2 1/2 tablespoons plus 1/2 teaspoon coarsely chopped garlic

1 bunch scallions, trimmed, white and green parts, coarsely chopped (about 1 1/2 cups)

1 bunch fresh cilantro, coarsely chopped (about 2 cups)

Fine sea salt and freshly ground black pepper

1. Pat the pork belly dry with paper towels. Place the pork belly, skin side up, on a cutting board and score the skin with a sharp knife in a cross-hatch pattern, piercing about 1 inch deep through the tough skin. Season both sides generously with salt.

2. In a small bowl, combine the paprika, cumin, brown sugar, ginger, and chipotle powder. Rub the pork belly all over with the spice mix.

3. Mix together the rub ingredients in a medium-size bowl. Place the pork belly, skin side down, in a baking dish. Coat the meat side with 2 cups of the rub. Roll the pork, and using butcher's twine, tie the pork belly tightly at 2-inch intervals. Allow to chill, uncovered, in the refrigerator overnight.

4. Preheat the oven to 275°F. Roast the pork on a rack on a baking sheet, skin side up, uncovered, until the meat pulls apart easily, about 3 1/2 hours. Increase the oven temperature to 400°F and continue to roast until the skin is crisp, about 30 minutes. Remove from the oven and allow to rest for 20 minutes. Season with salt and pepper. Slice and serve.

Note: Save the extra spice mix in an airtight container and use on chicken.

Saugatuck Craft Butchery (The Kitchen at SCB)

MOHAWK BISON

Bison once roamed North America in numbers estimated at over 60 million. These majestic beasts were the lifeblood of the ecosystem, thriving on wild grasses, native shrubs and other plants. Bison, or the American Plains Buffalo, were the economic and spiritual heart of the Plains Indians, supplying food, clothing and shelter. But the revered relationship between the Native Americans and the buffalo forever changed with the arrival of white settlers, who virtually wiped out the population through slaughter and introduced diseases.

Across the country, conservation efforts have brought the bison back from the brink of extinction. And in sleepy Goshen, CT, there's a small local bison revival afoot. In 2007, Peter Fay established Mohawk Bison on his family's former dairy farm. Preserving his ancestors' dedication to sustainability and in harmony with the bison's natural genetic make-up, the animals are raised the way nature intended, grazing out on some 60-acres of open pasture and fields in the Litchfield Hills. They are never subjected to questionable drugs, chemicals or hormones.

OX HOLLOW FARM

Ask around about a superior source for fresh, farm-raised Connecticut meats, and you'll hear the name Ox Hollow Farm. Ox Hollow is a diversified, family-operated farm in Roxbury, at the gateway of Litchfield County. Mark Maynard established the farm in 1994, with the mission of providing hormone- and antibiotic-free products to consumers. Over the years, Mark has produced all-natural, pasture- raised Angus beef, as well as high-grade pork, lamb, and poultry. Underlying Mark's 20-plus years of experience is his belief in conservation and obtaining maximum crop yields.

Mark's parents taught their children all-natural livestock practices at an early age. Then, Mark went on to study at the University of Connecticut's Department of Animal Science while laying the groundwork for Ox Hollow Farm. Through educational and professional experiences, Mark broadened his network with other farmers nationwide, integrating innovations and new practices into his own operations.

All stock is raised on Ox Hollow lands, using rotational grazing to expose the animals to full pasture, from spring through fall. During the winter, the animals live and move about freely in open housing, offering hay and corn silage, all grown and processed at the farm.

You will find Ox Hollow Farm's all-natural Angus beef, high-grade Duroc and Hampshire pork, free-range chickens, seasonal turkeys, and brown eggs at local restaurants and at several local area farmers' markets, as well as various local natural food markets. Ox Hollow Farm's products are available year-round via CSA meat share, as well as through online/phone orders.

THE CONNECTICUT FARMERS' MARKET TRAIL

For the ultimate agricultural day trip, the Connecticut Farmers' Market Trail is your guide to more than a dozen of hand-selected farmers' markets across the state— fun community markets that are well stocked with farm-fresh foods made and grown with passion, where you'll meet people who enjoy creating things that matter.

When you visit the website, you can click through the map to get directions to one of the farmers' markets you've always wanted to visit. You'll also find descriptions of each market on the trail, as well as information about winter markets, vendors, PYO farms, nearby local sustainable restaurants and attractions, and seasonal special events, so you can chart your own course to discover our region's agricultural bounty and have a blast while you're at it!

The interactive website was created as a project of Bridges Healthy Cooking School, a registered 501(c)(3) dedicated to teaching about healthy food preparation, the importance of consuming locally grown foods, nutrition, and eating habits.

Oxen Driver's Short Ribs

SERVES 6

Serve with mashed potatoes, polenta, buttered noodles, or crusty bread.

Herb Bundle

2 sprigs thyme

2 sprigs rosemary

6 sprigs flat-leaf parsley

1 fresh bay leaf

5 pounds bone-in beef short ribs, trimmed of excess fat

Kosher salt and freshly ground black pepper

1/4 cup extra-virgin olive oil

1 small fennel bulb, stems removed, fronds reserved, cut into medium dice

1 medium-size leek, white and light green parts only, coarsely chopped

4 large carrots, peeled and cut into medium dice

3 celery ribs, cut into medium dice

5 large garlic cloves, crushed and chopped

2 tablespoons tomato paste

1 (750-ml) bottle dry red wine, such as cabernet sauvignon

6 cups low-sodium beef stock

1 tablespoon Worcestershire sauce

1 tablespoon brown sugar

1. To make the herb bundle: Place the thyme, rosemary, parsley, and bay leaf in a piece of cheesecloth and tie into a bundle with kitchen twine. Set aside.

2. Position a rack in the center of the oven and preheat the oven to 400°F. Pat the ribs dry with paper towels. Place the ribs on a baking sheet and generously season on all sides with salt and pepper. Bake for 15 minutes. Set the ribs and any juices that have accumulated aside. Lower the oven temperature to 300°F.

3. While the ribs are baking, heat the oil in a Dutch oven over medium heat. Add the fennel, leek, carrots, and celery and cook, stirring occasionally, until the vegetables are tender, about 15 minutes. Stir in the garlic and tomato paste and cook until fragrant, about 1 minute. Pour in the wine and stir, scraping up the brown bits from the bottom of the pot. Increase the heat to medium-high and bring to a gentle boil. Cook, stirring occasionally, until the liquid is reduced by half, about 8 minutes. Stir in the stock, Worcestershire sauce, brown sugar, and 1 teaspoon each of salt and pepper.

4. Transfer the ribs along with any juices that have accumulated back into the pot. Add the herb bundle and bring to a gentle simmer over medium-high heat. Cover, carefully transfer to the oven and cook, until the meat is fork-tender, about 2 hours.

5. Allow the ribs to sit in liquid for 15 minutes. With a slotted spoon, transfer the ribs to a large bowl and tent with foil. Remove and discard the herb bundle. Skim the fat off the surface of the sauce. Transfer half of the vegetables and liquid to a food processor and puree until smooth. Transfer the puree back to the pot with the remaining vegetables and liquid. Stir until well combined. Bring the sauce to a simmer over medium-high heat, and simmer until the liquid is reduced by almost half, about 15 minutes. Return the ribs to the pot and cook until heated through. Season with salt and pepper to taste.

6. Transfer the ribs to individual bowls. Spoon the sauce over the ribs and garnish with the reserved fennel fronds.

Ox Hollow Farm

BAILEY'S BACKYARD

Chef Forrest Pasternack relishes his days "off," driving to picturesque farms dotting the upper Connecticut countryside in search of ingredients for his next "tasting" menu. Pasternack is the executive chef at the re-imagined Bailey's Backyard, an American farm-to-table restaurant located in the charming town of Ridgefield, where local sourcing reigns supreme.

In 2013, Forrest, owner Sal Bagliavio, and their team brought freshness, locality, and a modern take on American regional cuisine to the spiffed up new eatery. As a true farm-to-table venue, Bailey's is committed to delivering a changing menu based on the freshest and finest local food sources as well as fresh seafood from New England waters. On the menu, Forrest pays homage to his myriad farm suppliers, listing them by name next to their ingredients.

At the local farmers' market, all the vendors know Forrest by first name. "I was thrilled to connect with Forrest," recalls Sal. "He has worked with some of the best modern chefs in the country, and his knowledge and relationship with the local farms is invaluable. In Forrest, I have found someone I can stand with and carry out my goal."

Forrest's love of local foods goes back to his childhood in western Connecticut, where he and his family would often spend their days at local farms, picking vegetables for the supper table. Summers were spent on Cape Cod, fishing the waters off Nantucket Sound and the National Seashore, as well as digging clams in Chatham, Massachusetts.

Balsamic-Glazed Short Ribs with Gilfeather Turnip Puree and Rainbow Carrots with Orange-Blossom Honey and Fresh Sage

SERVES 4 TO 5

This hearty fall/winter meal dresses up beef short ribs with a rich balsamic glaze, a rustic whipped turnip puree, and a colorful take on glazed carrots.

Short Ribs

4 pounds bone-in beef short ribs, trimmed of excess fat

1/4 cup extra-virgin olive oil

2 pounds onions, such as Spanish, coarsely chopped

1/2 pound carrots, peeled and coarsely chopped

1/2 pound celery, coarsely chopped

6 sprigs thyme

2 fresh bay leaves

2 2/3 cups red wine, such as merlot

1 cup balsamic vinegar

Turnip Puree

3 pounds Gilfeather turnip or a 1 1/2 pounds each turnip and rutabaga, peeled and cut into 1-inch pieces

2 cups whole milk

2 cups water

1/4 cup (1/2 stick, 2 ounces) unsalted butter, cut into pieces, at room temperature

Kosher salt and freshly ground black pepper

Rainbow Carrots

1 pound rainbow carrots, peeled and thinly sliced on a diagonal

1 1/2 teaspoons chopped fresh sage, or to taste, plus more for garnish

2 tablespoons honey, such as orange blossom, or to taste

1 tablespoon extra-virgin olive oil, or to taste

1. Preheat the oven to 325°F.

2. To make the short ribs: Heat the oil in a Dutch oven over medium-high heat until hot, but not smoking.

3. Meanwhile, pat the ribs dry with paper towels and season generously on all sides with salt and freshly ground black pepper. Add the ribs, in batches, to the pot and sear on one side, 3 to 4 minutes. Using tongs, turn the ribs and sear until well browned, about 3 minutes. Remove from the heat and set aside on a large plate.

4. Add the onions, carrots, and celery to the pot, and cook, stirring often, until the onions are soft and translucent, about 5 minutes. Stir in the wine and vinegar and bring to a boil. Transfer the ribs, along with any juices that have accumulated, back into the pot. Add the thyme and bay leaves. Cover, carefully transfer to the oven, and cook until the meat is fork-tender, about 3 1/2 hours. With a slotted spoon, transfer the ribs to a large plate and tent with foil. Strain the liquid through a fine-mesh strainer. Transfer the liquid back to the pot and bring to a simmer over medium-high heat, and simmer until the liquid is reduced by almost half. Return the ribs to the pot and cook until heated through. Season with salt and pepper to taste.

5. Start the turnip puree 30 minutes before the short ribs are ready. Place the turnip in a medium-size saucepan and cover with the milk and water. Bring to a boil over medium-high heat and cook until the turnip is fork-tender, about 10 minutes. Drain and reserve 1/2 cup of the cooking liquid. Transfer the turnip to a food processor along with a 1/3 cup of the reserved cooking liquid and butter and pulse, adding more

liquid as needed, until smooth. Season with salt and pepper to taste. Transfer to a bowl and cover with foil.

6. While the sauce is simmering, place the carrots in a medium-size saucepan and cover with cold, salted water. Bring to a boil over medium-high heat and cook until the carrots are fork-tender, about 5 minutes. Drain and transfer to a medium-size bowl. Add the sage, honey, and olive oil and toss until well coated. Adjust seasonings with honey and/or olive oil and salt and pepper to taste.

7. To assemble: Place some of the turnip puree in the center of individual plates; top with carrots and ribs. Spoon the sauce over the ribs and garnish with sage.

Bailey's Backyard

Nutmegger's Lamb Chops

SERVES 2

These petite chops have a rich flavor and tender texture. The mild tangy lemony flavor from the ground sumac brightens the rub, while the ground nutmeg adds a sweet but slightly bitter flavor, offering a balance of tangy, sweet, and bitter to these chops.

4 large garlic cloves, crushed
1 teaspoon ground sumac (see note)
1 teaspoon ground nutmeg
1 teaspoon sea salt
1 teaspoon white pepper
4 lamb loin chops, about 3/4 inch thick
2 tablespoons extra-virgin olive oil

1. Combine the garlic, sumac, nutmeg, and salt and pepper in a small bowl. Rub the spice mixture evenly over the lamb chops, and refrigerate for 1 hour. Remove from the refrigerator and allow the chops to come to room temperature, about 15 minutes.

2. Preheat the oven to 400°F.

3. Heat the oil in a medium-size, ovenproof skillet over medium-high heat until hot but not smoking. Add the lamb chops and brown, about 3 minutes per side. Cover the skillet with aluminum foil, transfer to the oven, and roast until an instant-read thermometer registers 145°F (medium-rare), about 4 minutes.

4. Transfer the lamb chops to a plate and serve.

Note: What makes this rub unique is the sumac-nutmeg blend. Sumac is a Middle Eastern herb that can be found in specialty food markets.

Farming 101

Sepe Farm Lamb Meat Loaf with Goat Cheese

SERVES 6

This versatile meat loaf is delicious hot for dinner or cold for lunch as the ultimate meat loaf sandwich.

1 cup stale torn-up bread pieces
1/2 cup whole or 2% milk
2 tablespoons extra-virgin olive oil
1 small onion, minced
1 small carrot, minced
1 small celery rib, minced
1 garlic clove, minced
1 1/2 teaspoons minced fresh rosemary
1 tablespoon chopped fresh mint
2 pounds ground lamb
1 large egg, lightly beaten
1/2 cup fresh goat cheese, crumbled, about 2 3/8 ounces
1 teaspoon kosher salt
1/2 teaspoon freshly ground black pepper
1/2 cup ketchup or other sauce, to coat (optional)

1. Preheat the oven to 325°F. Line a baking dish with aluminum foil. Set aside.

2. In a medium-size bowl, combine the bread and milk and let stand until the bread is completely mushy, about 20 minutes.

3. Meanwhile, heat the oil in a medium-size sauté pan over medium heat. Add the onion, carrots, and celery and cook, stirring occasionally, until onion is soft and translucent, about 10 minutes. Add the garlic, rosemary, and mint and cook for 1 minute. Set aside to cool slightly.

4. In a large bowl, mix the bread mixture, vegetable mixture, lamb, egg, cheese, and salt and pepper.

5. Transfer the lamb mixture to the prepared baking dish and shape into 9 x 5-inch loaf. Spread 1/4 cup of the ketchup or other sauce, if using, over the top to the edges of the meat loaf. Bake for 60 minutes, then spread the remaining 1/4 cup of ketchup over the top to the edges, and bake until the meat loaf has reached an internal temperature of 155°F, about 15 minutes. Let the loaf rest for 15 minutes, then carefully drain off the liquid fat and discard. Transfer the meat loaf to a cutting board, cut into thick slices, and serve.

Dish Bar & Grill

TRUCK

Chef-owner Nancy Allen Roper grew up in New Mexico and began sharing her love for the Southwest nearly 20 years ago at her restaurant, Boxcar Cantina, in Greenwich. She was one of the first on the Connecticut food scene to stake her claim to run a restaurant guided by the principles of using local, organic ingredients, which were not always easy to source.

After 20 years in Greenwich, Nancy has taken her act on the road, just over the Connecticut border, to Bedford, New York. On the site of a former truck stop, she opened Truck, a casual, southwestern eatery and gathering spot evoking an old general store with plenty of rustic charms, including an historic front counter and salvaged wood paneling baring original antique wallpaper and marks left from generations past. A museum-quality Texas Longhorn skull hangs overhead. Outside, there's an edible garden with pear and fig trees, herbs, rhubarb, and even blueberry bushes.

The menu, which is close to Nancy's heart, is packed with casual fare, such as tacos, enchiladas, and signature salads made with grass-fed beef, sustainably raised pork, and salad greens straight from local farms. You'll find more sophisticated offerings as well, such as the Salmon Burrito, which uses wild sockeye salmon from Bristol, Bay Alaska, and Connecticut chèvre from Beltane Farm. The flavors are inspired by the down-home cooking traditions of Nancy's youth in northern New Mexico, and you can't go wrong with the killer margaritas, made with top-quality, 100% agave tequila, fresh-squeezed lime, and all-natural Triple Sec.

Ironically, Truck was once a truck stop along scenic Route 22, a rural, two-lane road that weaves through small villages and hamlets. To this day, this route is still used to transport fresh produce, dairy and meats from pastoral upstate New York farmlands straight into the bustling restaurants of New York City. But, first, they make a pit stop to deliver to Truck.

Green Chile Stew

SERVES 6 TO 8

This stew is a great make-ahead dish that is best served the second or third day. To serve, reheat the stew until meat is warmed through, skimming any fat off the surface.

3 plum tomatoes, halved

2 medium-size green bell peppers, stemmed, halved, and seeded

1 medium-size red bell pepper, stemmed, halved, and seeded

5 tablespoons olive oil, divided

3 1/2 to 4 pounds pork butt or shoulder, lightly trimmed and cut into 1-inch pieces

Kosher salt freshly ground black pepper

1 medium-size red onion, chopped (about 2 cups)

2 medium-size carrots, peeled and diced (about 2 cups)

2 medium-size parsnips, peeled and diced (about 2 cups)

1 medium-size rutabaga, peeled and diced (about 2 cups)

1 1/2 tablespoons minced fresh garlic

1 tablespoon ground cumin

2 cups fresh or frozen and thawed New Mexican green chile pepper, such as Hatch or Anaheim, stemmed, seeded and coarsely chopped (see note)

4 cups vegetable stock or water

4 new potatoes, cut into 1-inch pieces

Chopped fresh cilantro

6 to 8 (8-inch) flour or corn tortillas, warmed

1. Adjust an oven rack to the top position and heat the broiler.

2. Place the tomatoes and bell peppers on a baking sheet, drizzle with 2 tablespoons of the olive oil, and season with salt and pepper to taste. Roast, cut side down, rotating the baking sheet often, until charred on all sides, about 15 minutes. Let sit for 10 minutes. Remove and discard the skins from the tomatoes and bell peppers, coarsely chop, and set aside.

3. Heat the remaining 3 tablespoons of oil in a large Dutch oven over medium-high heat until hot but not smoking. Season the pork with salt and pepper. Working in batches, lightly brown the pork in spots, 3 to 4 minutes. With a slotted spoon, transfer the pork to a large plate and set aside.

4. Lower the heat to medium and add the onion, carrots, parsnips, and rutabaga; cook, stirring often, until the onion is soft and translucent, about 7 minutes. Add the garlic and cumin and cook for 1 minute. Add the tomatoes, peppers, chile pepper, and stock, scraping the bottom of the pot to loosen any brown bits.

5. Return the pork to the pot along with any accumulated juices. Bring to a simmer over medium heat. Cover, lower the heat to low, and cook, stirring occasionally, until the meat is fork-tender, about 1 hour. Add the potatoes 40 minutes before the stew is done and cook until fork-tender. Season with salt and pepper.

6. Ladle into bowls, garnish with the cilantro, and serve with tortillas on the side.

Note: We recommend wearing rubber gloves when handling the chile peppers.

Truck

Grilled Berkshire Pork Chops Topped with Braised Pork Belly and Baked Asian Pear Stuffed with Blue Cheese

SERVES 4

This multidimensional recipe is a show-stopper, served on a bed of whipped parsnips and sautéed rainbow Swiss chard with an apple cider–sage sauce. It takes time to prep all the elements, so, if you're under the gun, you can cut out the two-day braised pork belly and still have a dish that draws raves.

Note: Start the braise the day before you intend to serve the pork chops.

Bouquet Garni

2 sprigs thyme
4 sprigs parsley
1 fresh bay leaf
4 black peppercorns

Pork Belly

1 pound pork belly
2 tablespoons canola oil
Kosher salt and coarsely ground black pepper
1 small onion, diced
1 large carrot, peeled and diced
1 celery rib, diced
1 quart beef stock

Pears

4 small, firm Asian pears
1 tablespoon unsalted butter, melted
4 ounces blue cheese, such as Cato Corner Farms Black Ledge Blue
Kosher salt and coarsely ground black pepper

Garlic Chips

1 teaspoon olive oil
2 elephant garlic cloves, thinly sliced

Whipped Parsnips

1 pound parsnips, peeled and coarsely chopped
8 ounces white round potatoes, peeled and coarsely chopped
1/4 cup heavy cream, warmed
1/4 cup (1/2 stick, 2 ounces) unsalted butter, at room temperature
1/8 teaspoon ground nutmeg
Kosher salt and coarsely ground black pepper

Pork Chops

1 1/2 tablespoons olive oil
4 (8-ounce, 1 1/4-inch-thick) bone-in pork chops, trimmed
Sea salt and freshly ground black pepper

Apple Cider Sauce

2 cups apple cider
1 tablespoon thinly sliced purple sage, plus more for garnish (see note)

Rainbow Swiss Chard

1 tablespoon unsalted butter
1 1/2 pounds rainbow Swiss chard, stems and leaves separated, stems diced and leaves cut into 1-inch strips

1. To make the bouquet garni: Place the thyme, parsley, bay leaf, and black peppercorns in a piece of cheesecloth and tie with butcher's twine. Set aside.

2. To make the pork belly: Preheat the oven to 325°F. Pat the pork belly dry with paper towels. Place the pork belly, skin side up, on a cutting board and score the skin with a sharp knife in a crosshatch pattern, piercing about 1-inch deep through the tough skin (see note).

3. Place the pork belly, skin side up, in a Dutch oven and drizzle with the oil. Season the skin side with salt and pepper and roast in the oven until the belly starts to bubble and turn a deep golden brown, about 18 minutes. Using a large spatula, carefully flip the pork belly over and continue to cook until golden brown, about 30 minutes. Remove from the pan and set aside, reserving the oil in pan.

4. Heat the reserved oil in the same Dutch oven over medium heat. Add the onion, carrot, and celery, stirring often, and cook until the onion is soft and translucent, about 8 minutes. With a slotted spoon, remove the vegetable mixture and place in a bowl. Drain the fat from the Dutch oven. Return the vegetable mixture and pork belly to the pot. Add the beef stock and bouquet garni, and braise in the oven for 2 hours.

5. Transfer the pork belly to a clean pan and let cool for 30 minutes. Wrap the belly in plastic wrap, return to pan, and weight the pork down with another pan or dish and refrigerate for 24 hours. Strain the braising liquid into a bowl, cover with a lid or plastic wrap, discarding the vegetables, and place in the refrigerator overnight.

6. The next day, remove the pork belly and cut into four equal cubes.

7. To make the pears: Preheat the oven to 325°F. Cut the tops off each pear and set aside. Working from the stem end, use a melon baller or small spoon to carefully remove the inner core of the pears, cutting to within 1/2 inch of the bottom of each pear and creating a well roughly 1 inch wide. Place the pears in an 8-inch square baking pan. Brush the inside and outside generously with butter and season with salt and pepper to taste. Bake for 12 minutes. Remove from the oven and set aside to cool.

8. Using an electric mixer on medium speed, beat the cheese until light and fluffy, about 3 minutes, scraping down the sides of the bowl as needed. Season with salt and pepper to taste and beat until combined. Spoon about 1 1/2 tablespoons of the cheese mixture into each pear and cover each with pear top.

9. To make the whipped parsnips: Place the parsnips and potatoes in a medium-size pot of cold salted water. Bring to a boil over medium-high heat, then lower the temperature and simmer until the potatoes are fork-tender, about 20 minutes. Drain thoroughly in a colander and place in a medium-size bowl. Add the cream, butter, and nutmeg. Mash with an old-fashioned masher or immersion blender until smooth, then season to taste. Cover and set aside.

10. To make the garlic chips: While the parsnips are simmering, heat the oil in a small skillet over medium heat. Add the garlic and fry until golden brown on both sides, about 1 minute per side. Using a slotted spoon, remove the garlic and set aside on paper towels.

11. To make pork chops: Preheat the oven to 375°F. Heat the oil in a large, ovenproof skillet over medium-high heat until hot but not smoking. Add the pork chops and brown, about 6 minutes per side. Cover the skillet with aluminum foil, transfer to the oven, and roast until an instant-read thermometer registers 150°F, about 8 minutes. Transfer the pork to a plate and tent with foil, reserving the jus for the apple cider sauce.

12. To make the apple cider sauce: While the pork chops are browning, skim any visible fat from the reserved braising liquid. Combine the cider and braising liquid in a medium-size saucepan over medium heat and simmer until the sauce is reduced by half, about 25 minutes. Add the reserved jus from the pork chops and continue to cook until heated through. Stir in the sage and season with salt and pepper to taste.

13. While the pork chops are resting lower the oven temperature to 350°F. Place the stuffed pears and pork belly on a lightly greased baking

sheet and bake for 6 minutes. (Depending on their ripeness, the pears may need to cook a bit longer than the pork belly.)

14. To make the rainbow Swiss chard: While the pears and pork belly are baking, melt the butter in a large skillet over medium heat. Add the chard leaves, stirring to coat. Cover and cook until wilted, stirring occasionally. Add the stems and the salt and pepper to taste and cook until tender, about 5 minutes. Sprinkle with the reserved garlic chips.

15. To assemble: Place equal amounts of whipped parsnips, then chard in the center of four warmed dinner plates. Place a pork chop on each portion of Swiss chard, and top each pork chop with one pork belly cube. Place a stuffed pear on the side of each pork chop and drizzle with the apple cider sauce. Garnish with fresh sage and serve.

Notes:

If you are purchasing your pork belly from a local butcher, ask the butcher to score the pork belly for you.

The dish works just as well with common or garden sage.

Stuffed Pear Variation: Cut in half lengthwise, core, and spoon the mixture into each pear half.

Chamard Vineyards Farm Winery Bistro

CONNECTICUT WINE TRAIL

Can't make it to Napa? Visit the Connecticut Wine Trail website, an interactive site that lets you peruse 25 local wineries and plan the perfect Connecticut day trip. The site allows you to click on wineries and create your own customized wine tour itineraries. Not only will you enjoy tastings and tours at the state's most picturesque vineyards, at some, you can dine like royalty, so be sure to stick around for lunch or dinner.

Celebrating one of the fastest-growing wine regions in the United States, the Connecticut Wine Trail offers a tremendous variety of wine styles and stunning scenery as you traverse the hills, valleys and coastline of this beautiful state. In addition to a handy winery map and itinerary, blue Wine Trail signs will help guide you to the wineries on the trail. Regardless of where your trip takes you, you will experience a common theme of dedicated farmers, passionate winemakers, and timeless New England charm.

Although it has long been customary to enjoy a cheese or charcuterie plate, or even picnic on the grounds at local vineyards, more Connecticut wineries are now offering a complete food and wine experience. For instance, Chamard Vineyards, in Clinton, and Sharpe Hill Vineyard,

in Pomfret, have award-winning, full-service restaurants where you'll enjoy delicious meals that incorporate ingredients from neighboring farms (paired with local wines, naturally).

You'll also find more wineries hosting casual outdoor dining, themed food tastings, music on weekends, cooking classes, food trucks, and seasonal culinary festivals that showcase the marriage between local wines and locally farmed foods.

To find out what's happening, check the Connecticut Wine Trail website's winery profiles.

Pork-Belly—Stuffed Tomatoes

SERVES 4

Serve this dish with a nice, crusty baguette.

1 pound uncured fresh pork belly

1 teaspoon canola oil

4 large heirloom tomatoes, such as Brandywine

2 1/2 tablespoons extra-virgin olive oil, divided

2 tablespoons panko bread crumbs

2 cups arugula, washed, dried, and torn into
   bite-size pieces

1 1/2 tablespoons fresh lemon juice

2 ounces Parmigiano-Reggiano cheese

1. To make the pork belly: Preheat the oven to
250°F. Pat the pork belly dry with paper towels.
Place the pork belly skin side up on a cutting
board and score the skin with a sharp knife in a
crosshatch pattern, piercing about 1-inch deep
through the tough skin. Place the pork belly, skin
side up, in an 8 x 11-inch baking dish and drizzle
with the canola oil. Season the skin side with salt
and pepper, and roast until the meat pulls apart
easily, about 4 hours. Cut the pork belly into four
equal pieces.

2. Increase the oven temperature to 350°F. Cut
out and discard a cone-shaped section (big
enough to fit the pork pieces) from the stem end
of each tomato, being careful not to go all the way
through. Place the tomatoes, cut side up, in an
8 x 11-inch baking dish. Brush the cavity of each
tomato with 1 1/2 teaspoons of the olive oil; season with salt and pepper to taste.

3. Place one pork belly piece into each tomato.
Fill each tomato with 1 1/2 teaspoons of bread
crumbs. Drizzle with 1 tablespoon of the olive oil
and roast in the oven until the skin on the tomatoes just begin to blister, about 35 minutes.

CONNECTICUT WINE FESTIVALS

Connecticut wine season kicks into high gear in
May/June, but most local wineries don't release
event details on their fall harvest events until later
in the year. These festivals are a great way to visit
the wineries in September and October—the perfect
leaf-peeping and sweater weather. In addition to
wine tasting, you can expect music, arts-and-crafts
vendors, food trucks, grape-stomping competitions,
kids' activities. Some wineries will even allow you to
help harvest the grapes!

The most well-known and largest wine festival,
hosted by the Connecticut Vineyard and Winery
Association, is the Connecticut Wine Festival at the
Goshen Fairgrounds, held the last weekend in July.

Visit the Connecticut Wine Trail's website for events
and information.

4. Place the arugula in a medium-size bowl and
drizzle with the remaining 1 tablespoon of olive oil
and the lemon juice, tossing until well combined.
Season with salt and pepper to taste. Using a
vegetable peeler, shave the cheese into eight thin
pieces. Set aside.

5. To assemble: Place a tomato in the center of
four plates; top each tomato with a little salad and
two cheese curls. Serve.

Plum Luv Foods

BAR SUGO

When you enter Bar Sugo, an Italian tapas restaurant/wine bar/pizzeria tucked away on a strip of Wall Street in Norwalk, your first impression is of walking into a party that's just heating up. Waiters scoot past with trays of chilled martinis, red wine, and craft beers; classic rock plays on the sound system; and pulsating energy thrums through the space.

What raises the bar at Bar Sugo? It's the rustic-meets-modern Italian fare, created by Pasquale "Pat" Pascarella, a dynamic young chef who made his bones in the kitchens of Mario Batali's Esca and Scott Conant's L'Impero, and then honed his skills as a pie master at Cortina Pizzeria in Bridgeport and Norwalk. At Bar Sugo, he and chef Paul Failla are all about sourcing the best local foods, such as eggs, greens, and dairy from Sport Hill Farm, Millstone Farm, Farah's Farm, Arethusa Farm, and other nearby purveyors.

Find your bliss in homemade pasta (cavatelli with traditional Bolognese, sage velouté, and ricotta), but the real fun lies in mixing, matching and tasting Chef Pat's bold, seasonal creations with friends. The portions are designed for sampling, so be adventurous!

You can't go wrong with a sampling of the 15-plus Italian "Chicchetti" (small bites), such as the short-rib arancini; roasted Brussels sprouts with smoked sea salt and pearl onions; asparagus with duck prosciutto and black pepper; and calamari fritti tossed with arugula, fennel, and lemon. These small bites change with the seasons and with the chefs' whimsy, and will whet your appetite for all the goodness yet to come.

Next, split a 13-inch brick-oven pie (such as the caramelized onion, sopressata, Fontina, and aged balsamic), a salad (try the beets with goat cheese, or grapefruit in pistachio vinaigrette), and a fresh mozzarella dish (there are five types: bufala, smoked, burrata, Wisconsin, and homemade); each arrives with its perfect complement of truffle honey, fig jam, or 12-year-old balsamic vinegar.

Don't forget the meatballs—Mommy's, pork, rabbit, Ox Hollow Farm, Crispy Veal and Ricotta, or Sugo's. Can't decide? Do the Meatball Tasting and sample all six.

Antipasto Platter

SERVES 4 AS AN APPETIZER OR 2 AS A MAIN DISH

For a summer cooking demonstration at Westport Farmers' Market, chef Pat Pascarella of Bar Sugo wowed the crowd with this easy-to-assemble antipasto platter, created using fresh burrata mozzarella, cubed mortadella, heirloom Zebra tomatoes, and ripe plums plucked from one of the farmers' stalls.

Note: If time is tight, simply forgo the mortadella sauce and skip to the plating steps.

Sauce (makes 1/2 cup)

1/4 pound mortadella sausage, cut into 1-inch cubes

1 tablespoon extra-virgin olive oil

2 medium-size garlic cloves, minced

2 tablespoons chopped shallot

Kosher salt and freshly ground black pepper

1 cup sherry vinegar

1 cup dry white wine

1 cup chicken stock

1/4 cup tomato puree

Salad

1/2 pint heirloom cherry tomatoes, cut into bite-size pieces

1/2 pint red and yellow plum tomatoes, cut into bite-size pieces

1/2 cup pickled peppers, thinly sliced

12 cherry-size fresh mozzarella cheese balls, or to taste

1 tablespoon extra-virgin olive oil, for drizzling

1/4 cup chiffonaded mustard greens or Swiss chard

1/4 cup chiffonaded fresh purple or green basil leaves

1 tablespoon Fig Vincotto Vinegar

1. To make the sauce: Heat the oil in a medium-size sauté pan over medium heat. Add the mortadella and cook until lightly browned, about 4 minutes. Using a slotted spoon, transfer the meat to a paper towel-lined plate. Add the garlic and shallot to the reserved fat and oil in pan. Sauté until the shallot is soft and translucent and the garlic is fragrant, about 3 minutes. Stir in the vinegar and bring to a simmer. Cook until the sauce reduces to a syruplike consistency, about 14 minutes. Whisk in the wine and cook until the sauce reduces to a syruplike consistency, about 16 minutes. Stir in the chicken stock and tomato puree. Lower the heat to low. Add the mortadella back to the pan and continue to cook, stirring occasionally, until the sauce reduces to a jamlike consistency, about 50 minutes. Transfer to a blender and pulse until the sauce is well combined. Adjust the seasonings with salt and pepper to taste. Set aside.

2. To assemble: Smear a white platter with a 1/4 cup of the mortadella sauce. Scatter the tomatoes evenly over the platter. Scatter the cheese and peppers around the tomatoes. Drizzle with olive oil. Add the mustard greens and basil. Finish by dotting the platter with vinegar. Season with salt and serve immediately or at room temperature.

Bar Sugo

OYSTER CLUB AND ENGINE ROOM

It wasn't enough for Dan Meiser and chef James Wayman to knock it out of the park with Oyster Club, a Mystic favorite for fresh local lobster, raw bar, heirloom vegetables, and changing seasonal specials. Two years after opening the popular restaurant and bar, which won Best Upscale Restaurant by the Connecticut Restaurant Association in 2013, they were at it again, this time, building out the buzzworthy Engine Room, a 150-seat eatery in a refurbished marine building with river views and al fresco seating for 30, serving up craft beers and American comfort food.

If two busy venues don't keep them ping-ponging across the river, there are future plans for a butcher shop and an oyster farm to supply their two restaurants (and the public)—and after that, Meiser is toying with finding a small farm so he and his partners can raise their own pigs.

Dan's runaway passion for local foods has struck a chord, and chef-partner James is on the same page. Not surprisingly, the two forged their culinary alliance while foraging mushrooms and fishing for blues in Long Island Sound.

For Dan and James, buying local ensures the quality of the product, and helps the local economy. "There's a pride and a security in sourcing locally and from smaller farms and fishermen who we know," Dan explains. "Our customers appreciate that our food has a story. We know where the meat and seafood came from, how it was cultivated, raised and harvested, and that means something."

Pork Ciccioli Terrine Served on Rustic Bread Topped with Soft-Boiled Duck Eggs and Mustard Pickled Ramps

MAKES 1 (9-INCH) TERRINE

Note: The pickled ramps and Italian pork spread must be started one day before the dish is served.

Pickled Ramps

16 ramps (see note), cleaned, green leaves discarded

1 cup champagne vinegar

1 cup water

1/2 cup julienned shallot (about 3 bulbs) (optional)

3 tablespoons toasted mustard seeds

2 sprigs thyme

2 bay leaves

1/8 teaspoon cayenne pepper

1/2 cup raw sugar

1 tablespoon kosher salt

Ciccioli (Italian Pork Spread)

1 3/4 pounds pork shoulder, cut into 1-inch cubes

3/4 pound reserved pork back fat (see note),
    cut into 1-inch cubes

1 cup water, or as needed

1/16 teaspoon InstaCure or pink curing salt

4 juniper berries

1 tablespoon sea salt, or to taste

3/4 tablespoon freshly ground black pepper,
    or to taste

3/4 tablespoon fresh thyme, or to taste

....

4 duck eggs

Rustic bread, cut 1/2-inch slices

1. To make the pickled ramps: Place the ramp bulbs in a 32-ounce glass jar with a tight lid. Combine the vinegar, water, shallot, mustard seeds, thyme, bay leaves, cayenne, sugar, and salt in a medium-size saucepan and bring to a boil over medium-high heat. Cook, stirring frequently, until the sugar is dissolved. Pour over the ramps and seal the jar. Let cool to room temperature, then refrigerate for 24 hours.

2. To make the ciccioli: Combine the pork, pork fat, water, InstaCure, juniper berries, and salt and pepper in a 3-quart, heavy-bottomed saucepan. Bring to a simmer, uncovered, and continue to simmer until the liquid runs clear. Cover and cook at a bare simmer for about 2 1/2 hours. Once tender, strain the fat from the solids and reserve. Mince the meat and fat finely and add the thyme. Transfer to a 9-inch loaf pan and pour the reserved liquid over the top. Gently mix and place in the refrigerator to solidify. This will take at least 2 hours and can be made a few days ahead if desired. Before turning out, run a knife along the inside edge of the terrine.

3. To make the duck eggs: Fill a medium-size bowl with ice water and set aside. Place the eggs in a medium-size pot and cover with cold salted water. Bring to a boil over medium-high heat. Cover and cook the eggs for about 7 to 8 minutes for soft boil. Remove from the heat. Using a slotted spoon, transfer the eggs to the prepared ice-water bath and let cool completely, about 3 minutes. Remove the eggs, peel carefully, then slice crosswise.

4. To make the bread: While the eggs are boiling, preheat the oven to 450°F. Skim some of the fat off the top of the ciccioli and spread a thin layer, about 1 tablespoon, onto each bread slice. Place the bread slices on a baking sheet and toast in the oven until golden brown and crisp, 8 to 10 minutes.

5. To assemble: Thinly slice or spread between 2 tablespoons and 1/4 cup of the ciccioli over the top of bread, or to taste, top the meat with two egg slices per bread slice, or to taste, and about one-quarter of the pickled ramps per slice, or to taste. Season with salt and pepper and serve at once. (Please note that these are guidelines and the amount of ciccioli will depend on the size of the bread slices.)

Notes:

Ramp substitutes: Baby leeks or green garlic.

If pork back fat can't be found, leaf lard would be a good alternative.

Oyster Club

3B RANCH

Located in Northford, 3B Ranch is a grower of certified organic fruits and vegetables, as well as naturally raised cattle, buffalo, and pigs. The ranch is owned and operated by three brothers: Andrew, Steven, and Dennis Bozzuto. The trio is committed to sustainable agricultural practices; the brothers raise their animals on their fields and on neighboring fields. Their livestock is free-range and grass-fed, as well as USDA-certified. In colder winter months, the animals feed off hay that was collected and bailed from their own natural fields during past seasons.

The Bozzutos operate a 70-acre organic farm, including about 10 acres of organically grown vegetables and small fruits, as well as herbs and some heirloom vegetables—all certified organic by the USDA and Bay State Certifiers. Their produce is grown according to organic standards, without pesticides or commercial fertilizers. Their plants owe their health and vigor to their "black gold" soil, comprised mainly of farm-generated compost and food waste (they also own a refuse and a composting company).

If a vegetable can be grown in the Northeast, the Bozzuto brothers try to grow it. They sell their produce at various organic and natural food stores, local farmers' markets, farm stands, and restaurants in New Haven County. Farm tours are available upon request.

Farmer's Pork Special

SERVES 4

Serve with roasted beets and a green salad, if desired.

1 pound organic tricolor fingerling potatoes, scrubbed and sliced into 1/8-inch-thick coins
1 tablespoon minced fresh parsley, divided
2 teaspoons minced fresh oregano, divided
Kosher salt and freshly ground black pepper
2 tablespoons extra-virgin olive oil, divided
1 small yellow onion, thinly sliced
2 medium-size garlic cloves, minced
1 1/2 teaspoons Worcestershire sauce
2 pounds grass-fed ground pork
1/4 teaspoon dried red pepper flakes, or to taste
Chopped garlic scapes, for garnish

1. Preheat the oven to 400°F. Lightly oil a baking sheet and set aside. Place the potato coins in a medium-size bowl. Season with 1 teaspoon of the parsley, 1 teaspoon of the oregano, and salt and pepper to taste. Drizzle with 1 tablespoon of the olive oil and toss to combine, making sure to coat all the potatoes well. Spread the potatoes on the prepared baking sheet in a single layer and roast until fork-tender, about 20 minutes.

2. Meanwhile, heat the remaining 1 tablespoon of olive oil in a large skillet over medium heat. Add the onion and cook until soft and translucent, about 8 minutes. Add the garlic and cook until fragrant, about 1 minute. Add the Worcestershire sauce and pork, crumbling with a fork, and cook until well browned and no longer pink in the center, about 15 minutes. Fold in the potatoes. Add the remaining 2 teaspoons of parsley, the remaining 1 teaspoon of oregano, and the red pepper flakes. Season with salt and pepper to taste.

3B Ranch

URBAN OAKS ORGANIC FARM

Located in a food desert without easy access healthy fruits and vegetables, Urban Oaks, a working organic farm, is a welcome surprise, smack dab in the middle of a city block in New Britain. Here, volunteers grow heirloom organic produce, both on the 3.5 acres of fields and in six greenhouses.

One of two urban farms in the state, this organic farm sprang up in 1999 on the sites of a commercial greenhouse operation. Its farm stand is located on the site of a former gas station and auto repair shop. Started by "Founding Farmer" Mike Kandefer, Urban Oaks is dedicated to growing top-quality, certified organic produce, year-round, to the local community as well as to Connecticut restaurants.

A proud member of the North/Oak Neighborhoods Revitalization Zone, Urban Oaks brings a hands-on organic gardening experience to school children, as well as to young adults. When we visited, volunteers working community service hours were planting winter crops in the greenhouses, home to prodigious fig trees, rosemary bushes, and flourishing Meyer lemon and grapefruit trees.

The team is also committed to the neighborhood children, and sees them as the future of urban farming. To keep greenhouses operational and educational programs alive, Urban Oaks relies on funding grants and initiatives. It also participates in many farm-to-school, farm-to-chef, and farm dinners.

Urban Oaks has taught scores of people to grow vegetables over the years. Volunteers also help clean and package vegetables for sale, and the farm offers a limited number of "work shares" for community members who exchange work hours for CSA credit, as well as summer and winter CSA shares.

Urban Oaks is known for its broad variety of greens—kales, collards, sorrels, mustard greens, chicory, and so forth, as well as several lettuce varieties, endive, escarole, lamb's-quarter, purslane, radicchio, and nasturtium leaves and blossoms (edible flowers abound in the farm's salad mixes). It also produces heirloom tomatoes (sauce, paste, slicing, and cherry), as well as cucumbers, tomatillos, eggplant, squash, okra, rhubarb, and beans.

For many years, Urban Oaks has supplied top Connecticut restaurants with herbs, peppers, lemongrass, and shiso leaves grown in the greenhouses.

Arugula and Sunflower Seed Pesto over Sliced Heirloom Tomatoes

SERVES 5 AS AN APPETIZER
OR 4 AS A MAIN DISH

Few things are as satisfying as the perfect tomato accompanied by the sharp, rich tang of pesto. Here, arugula adorns heirloom tomato slices, interspersed with sliced fresh mozzarella, accompanied by chunks of artisanal bread and sliced olives.

Pesto (makes about 2 cups)

2 cups packed arugula
1/2 cup finely grated Pecorino Romano cheese
1/2 cup finely grated Parmesan cheese
1/3 cup sunflower seeds
2 garlic cloves, chopped
3 tablespoons fresh lemon juice (see note)
1 cup extra-virgin olive oil, or more as needed
Sea salt and freshly ground black pepper

2 large, firm heirloom tomatoes, such as Cherokee Purple, Arkansas Traveler, beefsteak, or Brandywine, cut into 1/4-inch-thick slices
8 ounces fresh mozzarella cheese, sliced 1/4 inch thick
10 Kalamata olives or other brined-cured black olives, pitted and cut in half
1 loaf artisanal bread, cut into large chunks
Sea salt and freshly ground pepper

1. To make the pesto: Combine the arugula, cheeses, sunflower seeds, garlic, and lemon juice in a food processor and pulse to a puree. While the motor is running, slowly add the oil. Season with salt and pepper to taste and continue to pulse to reach the desired consistency.

2. Alternate the tomato and mozzarella slices on a platter, overlapping the slices. Arrange the olives between the tomato and mozzarella slices. Drizzle the pesto over the top of the salad. Season with salt and pepper to taste. Serve with crusty bread and additional pesto for dipping.

Note: Lemon juice is used both to balance the richness and create a lighter texture. For use on pasta, feel free to use less lemon juice to preserve a tighter consistency.

Urban Oaks Organic Farm

FORT HILL FARM

Fort Hill Farm, located in southwestern Connecticut, grows 40 to 50 types of certified organic vegetables for 300 CSA shareholders and customers at the New Milford and Westport Farmers' Markets. The farm regularly supplies produce to a number of Connecticut and New York restaurants.

The farm, run by farmers Paul Bucciaglia and Rebecca Batchie, is situated on a terrace above the Housatonic River, operating on land leased from Sunny Valley Preserve, a project of the Nature Conservancy. The farm focuses heavily on soil nutrition through the growth of cover crops, and the application of compost and rock powders. It offers a full-season apprenticeship program for individuals interested in learning how to farm.

Bucciaglia, an ag school grad who used his life savings to start the farm, said, "There's a lot of demand for this type of leased-land farming in the state. It works because in Connecticut, there are people interested in local and organic produce very close to good farmland. We could have dozens of farms like this across the state. There are invaluable pieces of agricultural land that we need to preserve. If we don't preserve quality farmland now, we'll have no place to farm in the future."

Garlic Scape and Basil Pesto

MAKES 3 CUPS PESTO

This pesto is a versatile summer standby that keeps well, so make some when scapes are in season and keep some on hand. It is delicious tossed with pasta, on grilled corn, on pizza, or as a sandwich spread. It also provides a nice kick as a condiment to complement simple summer poultry and fish dishes. The pesto keeps well in the refrigerator, covered, for up to one week, or in the freezer for one month.

2 cups garlic scapes, whips removed, chopped into 1-inch pieces (about 27 scapes)
2 cups packed fresh basil leaves
3 tablespoons pine nuts or walnuts
2 teaspoons fresh lemon juice
2/3 cup extra-virgin olive oil, plus more for drizzling (optional)
1 cup freshly finely grated Parmigiano-Reggiano cheese
Salt and freshly ground pepper

Combine the garlic scapes, basil, pine nuts, and lemon juice in a food processor and pulse to a puree. While the motor is running, slowly add the oil. Add the cheese, and salt and pepper to taste, and pulse until well blended. Drizzle with olive oil, if desired, and serve.

Fort Hill Farm

AVERILL FARM

Averill Farm is one of the few farms in the country that has been operated by the same family since it was purchased from Native Americans in 1746. Currently, it is primarily run as a fruit orchard, though the family also grows hay and Christmas trees on the farm's 260 hilltop acres.

Sam Averill, of the ninth generation, runs the farm and market with his wife, Susan, son Tyson, and several employees. Averill Farm is best known for its more than 100 varieties of apples, along with several types of pears and quinces.

Much of the fruit is handpicked by customers, and some is sold to local stores and restaurants. Recently, Tyson, a tenth-generation Averill, launched a new enterprise, the Cidery at Averill Farm, LLC, producing an excellent, dry hard cider.

Quince Paste (Membrillo)

MAKES 1 HALF SIZE SHEET PAN

In Spain, this delicacy is called *membrillo*, and is served with Manchego cheese as a snack or appetizer. In New England, we like it with extra-sharp Cheddar cheese. It can also be cut into small cubes, dusted with confectioners' sugar and served as a dessert.

5 pounds ripe quince
1 vanilla bean
Zest of 1/2 lemon, cut into strips
Granulated sugar, as needed

1. Wash and remove the stems and cores from the quinces, but do not peel. Coarsely chop the quinces. Place the quinces into a large stockpot. Add the vanilla bean, lemon zest, and just enough water to cover the fruit, and bring to a boil over medium-high heat. Lower the heat to a simmer, cover, and cook until the fruit is fork-tender, about 1 hour. Let the fruit cool slightly. Using a slotted spoon, transfer the fruit to a food mill, reserving the liquid for another use, if desired. Transfer the vanilla bean to a work surface. Discard the lemon zest. Pass the fruit mixture through the mill, discarding any skins and leftover seeds.

2. Using a measuring cup, measure the puree and combine with equal amounts of sugar. Return the quince mixture to the saucepan. Split the vanilla bean in half lengthwise using a paring knife. Scrape the seeds into the saucepan with the puree. Cook over low heat, stirring often, to keep the paste from burning, until very thick, about 2 1/2 hours. The color will be a jewel-like red.

3. Preheat the oven to 200°F. Line a rimmed half sheet pan with enough parchment paper to come up the sides and grease with butter. Pour the paste into the prepared sheet pan, spreading it about 1 1/2 inches thick.

4. With the oven door open a crack, let the paste dry in the oven for about 2 hours on your lowest oven setting. (The baking time will vary depending on the cooking temperature used.) Remove from the oven and allow the quince paste to cool completely. The paste will continue to thicken as it cools. Invert onto a separate baking sheet. Remove the parchment paper. Cut into slices and store in an airtight container in the refrigerator. The quince paste will keep for up to 1 month.

Averill Farm

Since its first dinner in California in 1999, Outstanding in the Field has taken its moveable feast across the country—and, more recently, throughout Europe—creating magical, one-of-kind dining experiences smack in the middle of verdant farm fields. Founding chef Jim Denevan and his crew, who operate out of a renovated red-and-white 1953 Flxible bus, set one of the longest communal tables you've ever seen, then present an "outstanding" family-style meal paired with fine wines and sometimes locally crafted beers and spirits. To ramp up the excitement, a celebrated regional chef whips up the memorable, multicourse feast using hyperlocal ingredients, often harvested just a few feet from your seat.

Over the years, Denevan and the OITF team have served dinners on islands and coastal beaches, at ranches and vineyards, and occasionally inside a refurbished barn, cool greenhouse, or stately museum.

Connecticut host farmer Dina Brewster of the Hickories in Ridgefield explains what makes this collaboration so special: "I eat off this farm every day, and so I know a fair amount about the tastes that come from our soil, our grass, our water, and our sunshine here at the Hickories. And yet being able to experience our food through the creative work of these chefs and the OITF staff was an altogether new experience for me.

"Being chosen to host an OITF farm dinner is undoubtedly an honor. But the honor that is far greater is being able to share our farm lifestyle with our community—the guests. . . . My favorite part of the collaboration among OITF founder and staff and chefs and farmers is that it celebrates the artistry of our work in addition to the nourishment. Professional farmers and artists are both species on the brink of extinction in our society—and the OITF dinners recognize our common mission in a way I find deeply inspiring."

Tickets go on sale in mid-March on the first day of spring and sell like hotcakes.

Green Tomato Salsa Verde

MAKES ABOUT 2 CUPS SALSA

Who doesn't like a great salsa verde? Spicy, smoky, sweet, and perfect for eating with chips or served over meat, fish, or tofu.

4 medium-size green tomatoes, halved
2 medium-size chile peppers, such as serrano or jalapeño
1/4 cup extra-virgin olive oil, divided
Kosher salt and freshly ground black pepper
2 medium-size garlic cloves
2 tablespoons chopped fresh cilantro or oregano leaves
Juice of 1/2 lime, or to taste

1. Adjust an oven rack to the top position and heat the broiler.

2. Place the tomatoes and chile peppers on a baking sheet and drizzle with 2 tablespoons of the olive oil. Season with salt and pepper to taste. Roast, cut side down, until lightly charred on all sides, about 7 minutes. Let sit for 10 minutes. Remove and discard the skins from the tomatoes and coarsely chop; reserving the oil and juices from the tomatoes. Cut the peppers in half, removing the stems and seeds, and coarsely chop.

3. Heat the garlic and the remaining 2 tablespoons of oil in a large saucepan over medium heat until garlic is fragrant, about 3 minutes. Add the tomatoes and peppers and sauté, stirring often, for 10 minutes. Stir in 1/2 cup of water and the cilantro, and cook for 5 minutes.

4. Puree in a blender or food processor, until smooth, adding the reserved oil and juice from the tomatoes and the lime juice. Return to the saucepan and cook until heated through.

Note: This can be made one day ahead; just reheat before serving or serve cold with corn chips.

Waldingfield Farm

CATO CORNER FARM

Cato Corner Farm is a small family farm in Colchester, Connecticut, where the mother-son team of Elizabeth and Mark Gillman raises 50 free-range Jersey cows without the use of hormones or antibiotics. We asked Mark what he considers a pretty darn good cheese plate, and he was happy to oblige. Naturally, it features a few of the aged farmhouse cheeses made from the raw milk of Cato Corner cows, ranging from mild and milky to runny and pungent to sharp and firm. To order any of these lovely cheeses, visit Cato Corner's website.

Fondue with Farmstead Cheeses

MAKES 1 QUART MELTED CHEESE; SERVES ABOUT 8 (1/2 CUP EACH)

Fondues have made a comeback. Who can resist the communal experience sitting around a table with friends, dipping bits of bread and cut-up fruits, meats, or veggies into a bubbling urn of melting cheese? Add a chilled Riesling or chenin blanc, and it's a party!

1 pound Vivace cheese, or 8 ounces Gruyère plus 8 ounces Italian provolone cheese, shredded

3/4 pound Dairyere or Comte cheese (for a more pungent, full-bodied flavor, Hooligan cheese), or fontina, Beaufort or Emmentaler shredded

1 1/2 tablespoons cornstarch

1 garlic clove, halved crosswise

1 cup dry white wine, such as sauvignon blanc

1 tablespoon cherry brandy, such as kirsch, or Poire William

Freshly grated nutmeg

Kosher salt and freshly ground white pepper

Assorted dippers, such as 1-inch cubes of crusty bread; blanched vegetables, such as carrots, broccoli florets, asparagus, raw mushrooms, or cherry tomatoes; roasted potatoes; cured meat; or pickled gherkins

Combine the cheeses and cornstarch in a medium-size bowl. Set aside. Rub the inside of a fondue pot or heavy, enameled casserole dish with the cut sides of garlic, then discard the garlic. Pour in the wine into the pot, and bring to a simmer over medium-low heat, about 6 minutes. Gradually add the cheese mixture by the handful, stirring frequently, until melted, creamy, and well combined, about 9 minutes. Stir in the brandy and bring to a simmer, stirring frequently, until thickened, about 1 minute. Adjust the seasonings with nutmeg, salt, and pepper to taste. Spear assorted dippers with fondue forks or wooden skewers. Serve the mixture over a low flame to keep the cheese warm.

Cato Corner Farm, LLC

Pesto, Condiments, and Sauces 269

Chef Scott Quis's Kimchee

MAKES ABOUT 1 1/2 QUARTS KIMCHEE

Note: The kimchee must be started one month before it is served.

1 1/2 heads napa cabbage (1 1/2 to 2 pounds)
1/2 cup kosher salt
1/2 cup dried Grindilla peppers, seeds and stems removed
1/2 quart fresh cherry peppers, stems and seeds removed
1/2 quart fresh cayenne peppers, stems and seeds removed
2 tablespoons grated fresh ginger
1/2 cup peeled garlic cloves
3/4 cup rice vinegar

1. First, cut the cabbage lengthwise into quarters and then cut crosswise into 2-inch-wide strips, removing the tough inner cores and root ends. Place the cabbage in a large bowl. Add the salt, cover with plastic wrap, and let sit at room temperature for 24 hours. Drain thoroughly in a colander; then rinse under cold running water. Gently squeeze out the excess water from the leaves and pat dry with paper towels. Transfer the cabbage to another large bowl.

2. Combine the peppers, ginger, garlic, and rice vinegar in a food processor and puree until smooth. Add to the cabbage and toss until well combined.

3. Pack the kimchee, along with the brine, into a clean 4-quart jar with a canning or plastic lid, leaving 1 inch of headspace, and seal. Place the jar in a bowl to catch any overflow.

4. Transfer to the refrigerator and let sit for 1 month. Gently shake the jar occasionally during that time.

Barcelona Wine Bar & Restaurant

NORTHFORDY FARM

Since 1975, Northfordy Farm has been striving toward a more sustainable way of life by growing vegetables and raising animals without chemical pesticides or fertilizers. On this small family farm located in Northford, Peter Rothenberg grows more than a dozen varieties of heirloom tomatoes, as well as ginger and interesting perennial fruits, like hardy kiwi and paw-paw—a tropical-type fruit, native to North America, which resembles a mango. You will also find wool, free-range lamb, free-range eggs, and maple syrup year-round at the farm's stand at the Wooster Square Farmers' Market in New Haven. Additionally, Northfordy sells to local restaurants.

Fresh Pickled Ginger

MAKES ABOUT 3/4 PINT PICKLED GINGER

"When you see pickled ginger in the supermarket, check the ingredients: It is usually loaded with aspartame and food dye. For a healthier version, you will find that pickling a jar or two of fresh ginger at home is far easier than you might imagine, plus it lasts for about a month in the refrigerator. With a steady supply on hand, you'll find yourself adding it to everything from Asian rice bowls and stir-fries to soups, grilled fish, and poultry and so much more." —Peter Rothenberg

Ginger

1 mounded cup peeled, thinly sliced fresh ginger, no thicker than 1/16 inch thick (see note) (about 4 5/8 ounces peeled ginger)
1 teaspoon organic cane sugar
1 1/2 teaspoons kosher salt

Brine

1/2 cup plus 2 tablespoons rice vinegar or white vinegar
1/2 cup water
1/4 cup organic raw cane sugar

1. To make the ginger: In a medium-size, nonreactive bowl, toss together the ginger, sugar, and salt. Set aside and let sit at room temperature for 1 hour, stirring occasionally. Drain thoroughly in a colander; then rinse under cold running water. Gently squeeze out any excess water, then pat dry with paper towels. Transfer to a clean 1-pint jar with a canning or plastic lid.

2. To make the brine: Combine the vinegar, water, and sugar in a small saucepan and bring to a boil over medium-high heat. Pour the brine over the ginger, add additional water to cover the ginger fully, and seal the jar. Let cool to room temperature, about 1 hour 40 minutes, then refrigerate overnight.

Note: Peel the ginger with a vegetable peeler before slicing.

Northfordy Farms

DRINKS

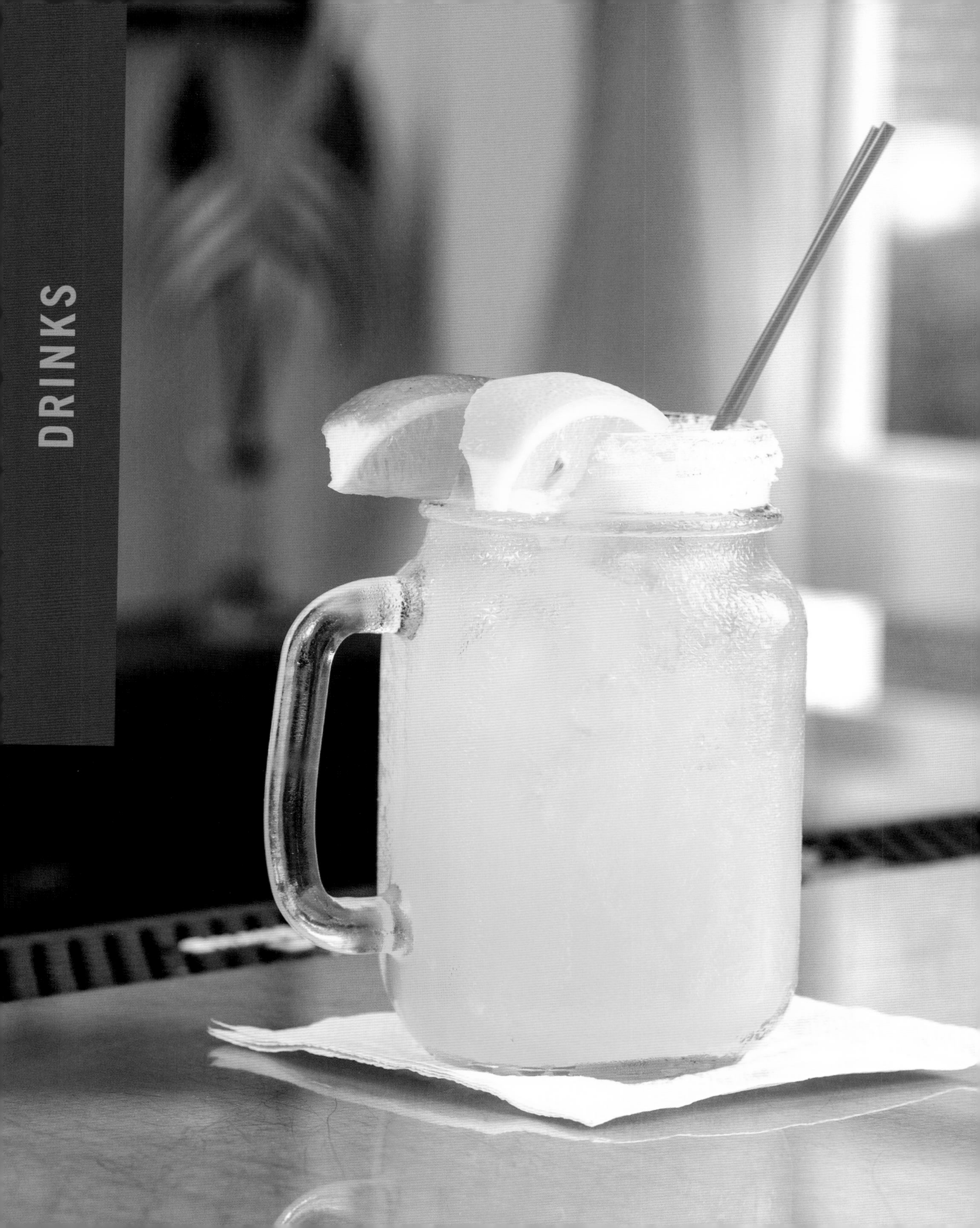

Hidden Vegetable Smoothie

SERVES 4 (8 OUNCES EACH)

When it's time for a break, students at the farm follow this recipe to create a healthy, tasty snack after picking some of the ingredients directly from the garden. The berries, fruit juice, yogurt, and honey are the flavors that rise to the top; they mask the nutrient-rich greens, which pack a nutritional punch.

1 cup frozen strawberries, coarsely chopped

1 cup frozen raspberries

1/2 cup chopped kale leaves, stems removed

1/2 cup packed baby spinach leaves

1 cup vanilla nonfat yogurt, preferably organic

1 cup 100% pure berry juice, such as raspberry, blueberry, or blackberry

Honey (optional)

Crushed ice (optional)

Blend the strawberries, raspberries, kale, spinach, yogurt, and berry juice in a blender until smooth. Divide the mixture among four tall glasses, add honey and/or crushed ice, if desired, and serve.

Community Farm of Simsbury

Green Pear Smoothie

SERVES 2 (10 OUNCES EACH)

This smoothie is especially good in late September or early October, when you've got an excess of greens. It's also a perfect way to take advantage of the season's sweet pears.

1 large or 2 small ripe pears, such as Bartlett, cored and chopped, plus more for garnish

1 cup tightly packed chopped Swiss chard leaves, tough stems removed, or baby spinach leaves

1 cup cold unsweetened almond or soy milk

1 tablespoon honey, or to taste

1/2 cup frozen berries, such as blueberries, raspberries or blackberries plus more for garnish

1 1/2 teaspoons chia seeds (optional)

1 tablespoon hulled hemp seeds or maca powder (optional)

Crushed ice (optional)

Blend the pear, Swiss chard, almond milk, honey, berries, and chia seeds and hemp seeds, if using. Blend until smooth, adding extra milk if needed. Garnish with fresh raspberries or a slice of pear. Add crushed ice, if desired. Serve immediately.

Notes:

Chia seeds, hulled hemp seeds, and maca powder can be found in the natural foods section of large grocery stores or in natural foods stores.

If you are having trouble finding unsweetened almond milk you can use sweetened instead; just cut back on the honey to compensate.

Massaro Community Farm

THE STAND JUICE COMPANY

Mike Hvizdo and Carissa Dellicicchi Hvizdo started making fresh organic juice in their rental cottage in 2005, and quickly outgrew the space. They then launched the Stand on Wall Street in Norwalk, and their following grew, with more folks seeking out organic juices, cleanses, and raw foods. After seven years, they opened their Fairfield location, and in October 2014, they moved their flagship location into the Ironworks Building in SoNo, a bustling part of town undergoing a major renaissance.

Carissa says, "Seeing the growing popularity in the green foods movement has been incredible. We are often overwhelmed with gratitude to be part of it. When we started this, we had to explain to people what kale was. Oh, and collards. What the heck were those? Now our customers educate *us*."

At the Stand, the Hvizdos are dedicated to promoting a healthy lifestyle through wholesome products made from organic, sustainably and ethically sourced (no animal products, no GMOs) goods from farmers and producers they believe in. In 2013, they launched a more personal labor of Love: Hideaway Farm in East Haddam, where they raise chickens, five goats, and a black Galloway cow, and grow carrots, beets, kale, collards, beans, pumpkins, salad greens, tomatoes, potatoes, peppers, okra, Brussels sprouts, Swiss chard, and garlic.

Summer Garden Mojito Smoothie

MAKES ABOUT 3 CUPS SMOOTHIE

1/2 medium-size cucumber, peeled, and cut into 1/2-inch-thick rounds
1/2 ripe avocado
1 large kale leaf
1 large Swiss chard leaf
1 1/2 teaspoons chopped mint, or to taste
Juice of 1/2 medium-size lime, or to taste
1 tablespoon pure maple syrup, or to taste
1 1/4 cups water
1/2 cup crushed ice

Blend the cucumber, avocado, kale, Swiss chard, mint, lime juice, maple syrup, water, and ice in a blender until smooth. Adjust the seasonings with mint, lime juice, and maple syrup. Pour into glasses and serve immediately.

The Stand Juice Company

Sweet Curry Juice

MAKES ABOUT 2 1/2 CUPS JUICE

1 large apple, such as Cortland or Honeycrisp, cored and cut into chunks
4 medium-size carrots, ends removed
1 large golden beet, ends removed, peeled, and cut into chunks
1 (1/2-inch) piece fresh ginger, peeled, or to taste
Curry powder

Feed all the vegetables into a juicer, according to the manufacturer's instructions. Add the curry powder to taste and mix well. Pour into glasses and serve.

The Stand Juice Company

THE WILLOWS

If you scoff at the idea of fine dining inside a hotel, there are plenty of Connecticut venues to change your mind. Across the state, top eateries are serving stellar cuisine amid stylish hotel backdrops.

The Bristol DoubleTree is a welcome surprise. Recently, it underwent a multimillion-dollar facelift that one might expect to find in LA. Upon entering, a chic hostess leads you into this über-modern oasis, encased in a $20-million glass cube, cozied up with leatherette chairs, banquettes, and screen-star lighting effects.

Living up to its surroundings, the farm-inspired New American cuisine is expertly turned out by Certified Master Chef Dale L. Miller, a Culinary Institute of America graduate and rising star on the Connecticut dining scene. Raised in a farming family in the small town of Tribes Hill, New York, he spent time planting and harvesting vegetables in his mother's garden and helping her around the kitchen. His father introduced him to hunting for wild game, fishing, and foraging in the wild for mushrooms, fiddlehead ferns, and ramps. This upbringing instilled in him a respect for the land, its bounty, and the love that goes into food preparation and cooking

His menu at the Willows showcases his dedication to the local farm community through his use of seasonal ingredients and local products. It is updated regularly to feature foods of the season, paired with an extensive wine list showcasing boutique selections from around the world.

Local ingredients permeate all aspects of the dining experience, from the bar through the desserts—from the Garden Fresh Bloody Mary to the Honey Black Walnut Tart (page 284).

Garden Fresh Bloody Mary

SERVES 5 (12 OUNCES EACH)

Bloody Mary Mix (makes about 7 cups)

12 to 14 large celery ribs with leaves (see note)

1 quart fresh tomato juice, or good-quality bottled

1/2 cup green olive juice, strained from jarred green olives

Juice of 1 large lemon

1 1/2 tablespoons freshly grated horseradish, or to taste

1/4 teaspoon Worcestershire sauce, or to taste

1/2 teaspoon hot sauce, such as Louisiana

1/2 teaspoon freshly cracked black pepper

To Serve:

3 ounces garlic-infused vodka, store-bought or homemade (recipe follows)

4 ounces cucumber-infused vodka, store-bought or homemade (recipe follows)

Ice

Black sea salt or coarse salt, for rimming glasses

1 large lemon cut into 5 wedges

5 sprigs celery leaves

5 green olives, such as Spanish Queen, stuffed with hot cherry peppers, skewered

1. To make the Bloody Mary mix: Feed the celery through a juice maker, according to the manufacturer's directions.

2. Place the tomato juice, celery juice, olive juice, lemon juice, horseradish, Worcestershire sauce, hot sauce, and black pepper in a large container with a tight-fitting lid. Shake vigorously until well combined. Refrigerate for 2 hours before serving.

3. To serve: In a large pitcher, mix together the Bloody Mary mix and the vodkas.

4. Pour the salt onto a plate. Dampen the rims of five glasses and dip them in the salt. Fill with ice

5. Pour the Bloody Mary mixture into the five prepared glasses and garnish with celery leaves, lemon wedges, and olive skewers. Serve immediately.

Note: In a pinch, you can substitute organic cold pressed juices, such as carrot or beet, for celery juice.

The Willows Bristol DoubleTree by Hilton

Infused Vodka

MAKES 1/2 PINT VODKA EACH

Note that these recipes require some advance planning: The infused vodkas must be started five to seven days before they are served. For a quick version of this recipe, you can use a good-quality store-bought garlic-infused and cucumber-infused vodkas.

Garlic-Infused Vodka

4 garlic cloves, crushed, skins discarded

1/2 pint vodka

Cucumber-Infused Vodka

1/2 cup peeled, seeded, and thinly sliced cucumber

1/2 pint vodka

1. To make the garlic-infused vodka: Place the garlic in a pint-size mason jar with a tight-fitting lid. Add the vodka and seal. Shake well. Let sit in a cool, dark place, shaking the jar once a day, for 7 days. Strain the vodka through a fine-mesh strainer into a sterilized mason jar; discard the garlic.

2. To make the cucumber-infused vodka: Place the cucumber slices in a pint-size mason jar with a tight-fitting lid. With a wooden spoon, lightly crush the cucumber. Add the vodka and seal. Shake well. Let sit in a cool, dark place, shaking the jar once a day, for 5 days. Strain the vodka through a fine-mesh strainer into a sterilized mason jar; discard the cucumber.

Sarah Strauss

SERVING CONNECTICUT'S UNDERSERVED

Where do urbanites go to learn about and purchase healthy, local foods on a limited income?

CitySeed

CitySeed provides urbanites with greater access to local, healthy food. The first producer-only farmers' market was started by four residents who lived in the Wooster Square neighborhood, where it was easy to find pizza, but next to impossible to locate a fresh tomato—never mind one grown locally.

With support from the City of New Haven and key funding from the Community Foundation for Greater New Haven), CitySeed rolled out three additional producer-only markets: Downtown, Fair Haven, and Edgewood Park. By 2010, CitySeed had opened a fifth in the Hill neighborhood.

By enabling residents to eat fresh, locally grown food, these markets have an immediate, positive effect on the health of low-income community members, who are at greater risk for obesity and other diet-related illnesses. The markets also promote sustainable farming and the local economy, as well as the spirit of community.

What's more, all five markets accept Farmers' Market Nutrition Program coupons for nutritionally at-risk women, infants, children and senior citizens, as well as Supplemental Nutrition Assistance Program benefits (SNAP, formerly known as Food Stamps).

Wholesome Wave: Nourishing Neighborhoods Across America

Even after many farmers' markets started springing up in urban pockets across the state, Michel Nischan observed that many city dwellers desperately couldn't afford to purchase the healthy fruits and vegetables on display. Nischan decided to change that.

He spearheaded Wholesome Wave, now a national 501(c)(3) organization that is helping to reshape the American food system by partnering with farmers, farmers' markets, community leaders, health-care providers, likeminded nonprofits, and government entities to implement programs that increase affordability and access to healthy, locally grown fruits and vegetables for single moms, veterans, and families of all stripes.

Wholesome Wave's innovative programs—the Double Value Coupons, the Fruit and Vegetable Prescription, Healthy Food Commerce Investments, and the Innovations Lab—all address issues of food security, farm viability, economic vitality and diet-related health issues, such as diabetes, obesity, and heart disease.

MIYA'S SUSHI

Chef Bun Lai is a James Beard Foundation Award Nominee, an Ivy League lecturer (on food as it relates to climate change and child development), a Seafood Watch Ambassador, an Olympic trials wrestling coach, and the founder of the world's first sustainable sushi restaurant. He is on the vanguard of the worldwide sustainable food movement and has appeared on television and in publications in more than two dozen countries. He has been named as one of the ten most influential chefs in America by EcoSalon and has been teased on *Saturday Night Live* for his use of cicadas in sushi.

While his recipes are emulated all around the world, he may be best known for using a variety of jaw-dropping local ingredients foraged from the land and the water in his New Haven sushi restaurant, Miya's. He's not a farm-to-table restaurateur in the conventional sense, but a visionary chef who turns out cuisine from wild flora and fauna sourced on his own farm in Woodbridge and his shell-fishing grounds in Branford.

From Lai's terrestrial farm, he harvests wild edible plants, such as ramps, pokeweed, garlic mustard, wild lettuce, wild amaranth, dandelion, and burdock. But he doesn't stop there. He explains, "We also grow vegetables, too, and harvest the insects that infest them. Insects are supertasty and nutritious, and harvesting them allows us not to use pesticide in a world where 5 billion pounds of it are used each year. We catch fish, and use their bones to trap whelk on our grounds. We also go diving for clams, oysters, and seaweed. All of our most experienced chefs and servers at Miya's are scuba divers who are fisherman and foragers, too. We specialize in types of flora and fauna that are abundant, underutilized, nutritious and delicious."

On top of all of this, Lai believes in educating the community about healthy, sustainable eating. He is the former director of nutrition and cooking for New Haven Farm, a CSA that provides 16 weeks of vegetables, cooking and nutrition classes, and clinical testing, to low-income pre-diabetics from New Haven. What is more, Miya's (in partnership with Dr. David Ross and the Yale Psychiatry Department) also hosts an internship program for the students at New Haven's Common Ground High School which specializes in farming and environmental education see sidebar, page 235).

Knot Your Mother's Lemonade

MAKES 3 1/2 CUPS LEMONADE

Japanese knotweed grows quickly in clusters and crowds out other herbaceous species. It was named one of the world's 100 worst invasive species by the World Conservation Union and is thriving in 39 states. The taste is crunchy, juicy, and tart—not unlike a Granny Smith apple. This is a twist on Bun Lai's mother's lemonade.

2 1/2 young Japanese knotweed shoots or thick rhubarb stalks, trimmed and chopped (about 2 cups)

2 cups mineral water

1/2 cup honey, or to taste

5 fresh kaffir lime leaves or mint leaves

1 cup fresh lemon juice (from about 5 lemons)

1. In a medium-size saucepan, combine the Japanese knotweed, water, honey, and lime leaves and bring to a boil over medium heat. Lower the heat to low and allow to simmer for 5 minutes. Remove from the heat and allow to steep for 30 minutes.

2. Strain the mixture through a fine-mesh sieve, discarding any solids, and refrigerate until cold. Stir in the lemon juice and adjust sweetness with honey, if desired. Serve over ice.

Note: Fresh kaffir lime leaves are sold fresh in the produce section of Asian and Chinese stores and markets.

Bun Lai, Miya's Sushi

THE CONNECTICUT BEER TRAIL

Connecticut's craft brewing industry has enjoyed tremendous growth since early 2011, says Bryon Turner, director of the Connecticut Beer Trail, expanding from about five production breweries and four brewpubs to about 30 distinct breweries, brewpubs, and contract brewers in 2014, with more still under development.

As the state's breweries and brewpubs continue to impress local beer fans, they also have earned recognition in formal competitions, within industry publications and from the greater craft beer community. Connecticut breweries and brew pubs have become destinations, with organized bus tours, guided bicycle rides, and other special events along the Connecticut Beer Trail.

Beer fans can enjoy beer dinners, brew fests, tours and a wide array of other craft beer-related events and activities all year or visit in October for the Connecticut Beer Week. The annual week-long event, started in 2013, was such a success it returned in 2014 as two separate week-long celebrations of the state's craft beer industry through a partnership between craft brewers, restaurants, and retailers.

DESSERTS

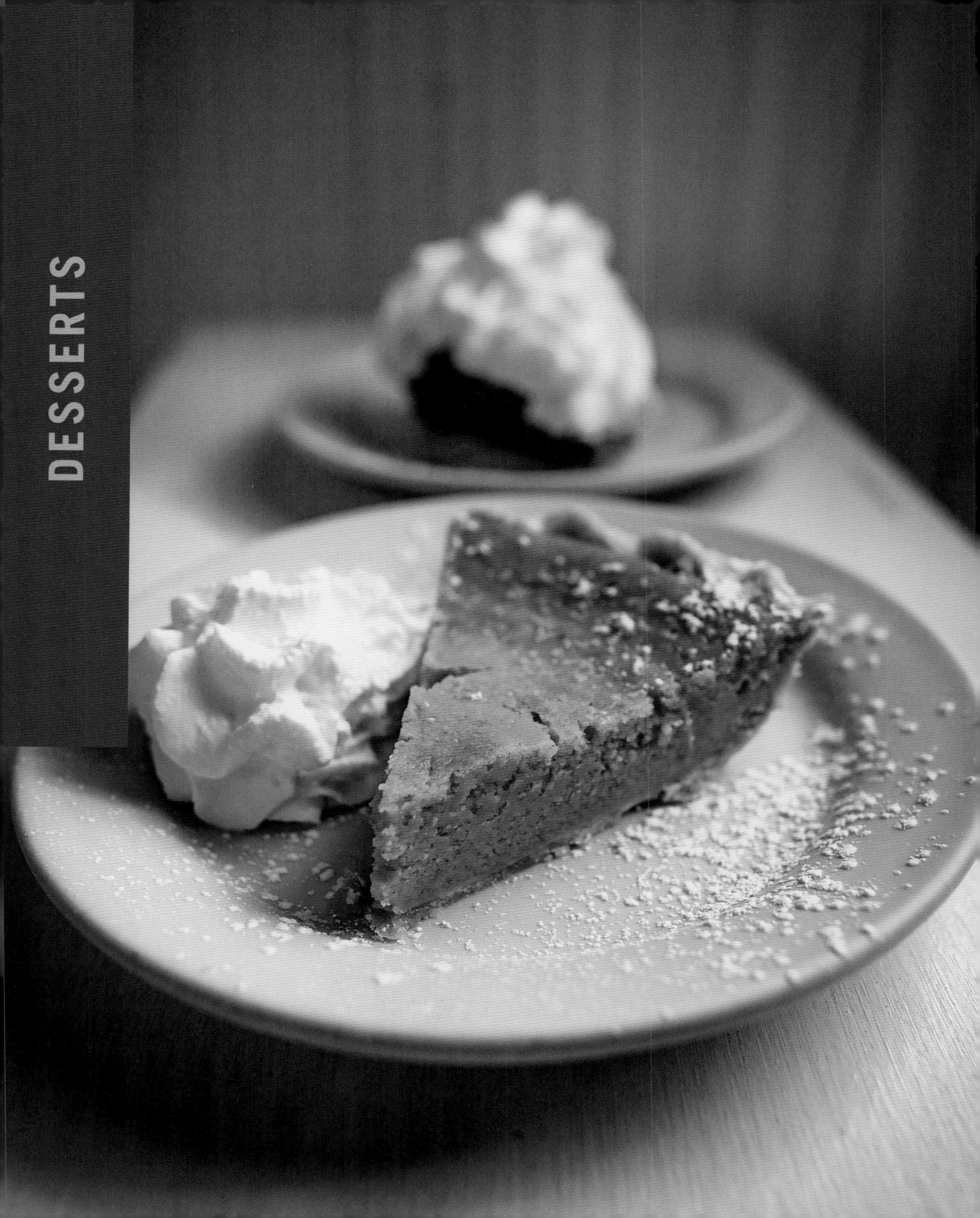

WAVE HILL BREADS BAKERY

It was no surprise to us when Wave Hill Breads Bakery was selected by the editors of Connecticut Magazine as makers of the "Best Bread" in Connecticut in 2013 and 2014. Top local restaurateurs, like Tim Labant (The Schoolhouse at Cannondale) and Michel Nischan (The Dressing Room) were loyalists way before Wave Hill Breads became a cult classic in Connecticut and New York, drawing fans at farmers' markets and specialty stores.

It's easy to root for owners Margaret Sapir and Mitch Rapoport, the duo behind Wave Hill Breads, the artisan bakery started in 2005 in Wilton. They've never done things the easy way, for years hand-making only one kind of bread—the Pain de Campagne—until it was perfection, using organic spelt and rye berries that they mill themselves daily, as well as King Arthur flour. Though they are now baking a variety of breads, including the addictive olive and roasted red pepper ciabatta and a multi-grain loaf, they are still employing the age-old techniques that were passed on to them by Gerard Rubaud, a master French baker based in Westford, Vermont. He taught them to respect the sensory process, which involves time, temperature and touch. To this day, the loaves taste and feel as though they are made with love.

From humble beginnings, the breads can now be found at 13 farmers' markets in Connecticut and Westchester County, New York, as well as local grocery and specialty stores, and even chain supermarkets eager to offer true artisan breads to their customers. Wave Hill Breads are now sold in more than 35 stores and 40 restaurants.

This recipe comes from Kay Carroll, of Brookside Farm II, located in Litchfield CT. It is a relatively small and very high-quality maple syrup operation.

Maple Bread Pudding

SERVES 4 TO 6

Using local maple syrup and day-old bread, this tasty pudding can be served as a dessert with ice cream or as a breakfast treat.

1 tablespoon unsalted butter, at room temperature

2/3 cup pure maple syrup

4 cups day-old bread, such as ciabatta, brioche, or challah, buttered and cut into 1-inch cubes

1/2 cup packed golden raisins or nutmeats

2 large eggs

1 1/4 cups whole milk

1 teaspoon fresh lemon juice

1/4 teaspoon pure vanilla extract

1/4 teaspoon ground cinnamon

1/4 teaspoon kosher salt

Vanilla ice cream or whipped cream (optional)

1. Grease the bottom and sides of the top pan of a 2-quart double boiler with butter.

2. Pour the maple syrup into the double boiler. Add the bread cubes on top of the maple syrup. Top with raisins and gently press them into the bread.

3. In a small bowl, whisk together the eggs, milk, lemon juice, vanilla, cinnamon, and salt. Pour the egg mixture evenly over the bread and raisins, and gently press on the bread to allow it to absorb the liquid. Do not stir.

4. Set the pan over simmering water, cover, and cook, until the pudding has set in the center, about 1 hour (see note).

5. Remove the top pan from the simmering water. Let rest, uncovered for 10 minutes. Spoon the pudding into small bowls. Drizzle the sauce over the pudding. Serve warm with scoops of vanilla ice cream, if desired.

Note: You may need to add additional simmering water to pan.

Kay Carroll of Brookside Farm II
for Wave Hill Breads Bakery

Honey Black Walnut Tart

SERVES 8 TO 10

Tart Crust

1 1/2 cups all-purpose flour, plus more for rolling

1 teaspoon granulated sugar

1/4 teaspoon sea salt

1/2 cup (1 stick, 4 ounces) unsalted butter, chilled, cut into small cubes

1 large egg, lightly beaten

3 tablespoons ice water, or as needed

Honey Black Walnut Filling

4 large eggs, lightly beaten

1 cup honey

1/4 cup (1/2 stick, 2 ounces) unsalted butter, melted and slightly cooled

1/2 teaspoon pure vanilla extract

2 cups coarsely chopped black walnuts

Whipped cream or vanilla ice cream (optional)

1. To make the tart crust: Lightly coat a 9-inch, removable-bottom tart pan with cooking spray. Set aside. Pulse the flour, sugar, salt, and butter in a food processor until mixture is crumbly and forms pea-size lumps. Add the egg and mix until the dough just comes together. Add the water, 1 tablespoon at a time, until the dough holds together. Turn the dough out onto a lightly floured surface and form into a disk. Wrap the disk in plastic wrap and refrigerate for 25 minutes.

2. On a lightly floured surface, roll out the dough disk into a 1/4-inch-thick 12-inch round. Transfer to the prepared tart pan and gently press the dough into the bottom and up the sides of pan; trimming any overhanging dough. Place the pan in the freezer and chill for 15 minutes.

3. While the dough is chilling in the freezer, pre-heat the oven to 375°F.

4. Line the tart shell with parchment paper and enough pie weights or beans to fill the bottom of the shell. Bake the dough for 15 minutes, remove the parchment paper and weights, and continue to bake until lightly golden brown, about 12 minutes. Transfer the pan to a cooling rack and let cool completely.

5. While the crust is cooling, lower the oven temperature to 350°F.

6. To make the filling: Whisk together the eggs, honey, butter, and vanilla until smooth.

7. Place the prepared tart shell, in its pan, on a baking sheet. Evenly line the bottom of tart with the walnuts. Pour the filling over the walnuts and rake with a fork to evenly distribute. Bake until the filling is set in the center, about 40 minutes.

8. Transfer the pie to a cooling rack and let cool completely. Serve with a dollop of whipped cream or a scoop of ice cream, if desired.

Notes: If the crust is done before the filling is set, loosely cover the tart edges with foil and continue to bake.

The Willows Bristol DoubleTree by Hilton

Blueberry Tea Cake with Crumble Topping

SERVES 16 (2 X 2-INCH PIECES)

Serve this cake for breakfast with a steaming pot of tea, as an afternoon snack, or for dessert when you are craving something sweet!

Cake

2 cups all-purpose flour

2 teaspoons baking powder

1/2 teaspoon kosher salt

1/2 cup (1 stick, 4 ounces) unsalted butter, at room temperature

3/4 cup granulated sugar

1 large egg, lightly beaten

1/2 cup whole milk

1/2 teaspoon pure vanilla extract

1 1/2 teaspoons fresh lemon juice

1 pint (about 2 cups) fresh blueberries

Crumble Topping

1/2 cup all-purpose flour

1/2 cup granulated sugar

1/2 teaspoon ground cinnamon

1/4 cup (1/2 stick, 2 ounces) unsalted butter, chilled, cut into pieces

1/2 pint vanilla ice cream (optional)

1. Preheat the oven to 350°F. Spray an 8-inch square pan with nonstick cooking spray. Set aside.

2. To make the cake: In a medium-size bowl, sift together the flour, baking powder, and salt.

3. Using an electric mixer on medium speed, in a large bowl, cream together the butter and sugar. Add the egg, milk, vanilla, and lemon juice, scraping down the sides of the bowl as needed, and beat until just smooth. Add the flour mixture and beat until smooth. Fold in the blueberries and with a rubber spatula, scrape the batter into the prepared pan, and distribute evenly.

4. To make the crumble topping: In a medium-size bowl, combine the all-purpose flour, sugar, and cinnamon. Using your fingers, work in the butter until the mixture is crumbly and forms pea-size lumps.

5. Sprinkle the crumble evenly over the batter. Bake for 30 minutes; rotate the pan by a half-turn, and bake until the top is golden brown and a toothpick inserted into the center of the cake comes out clean, about 30 minutes. Let cool for 10 minutes; serve warm with scoops of vanilla ice cream, if desired.

Anastasia March of March Farm

Blueberry Sour Cream Coffee Cake

SERVES 8

"Teresa Scaglia Rose, one of Rose's Berry Farm's original owners, was an avid baker. This coffee cake was one of her favorites, and we are thrilled to be able to share it with anyone who loves blueberries and much as we do." —Sandra Rose, Rose's Berry Farm

Topping

1/2 cup packed brown sugar

1/2 cup chopped nuts, such as pecans or walnuts

1/2 teaspoon ground cinnamon

Cake

2 cups fresh blueberries

2 cups plus 1 1/2 teaspoons all-purpose flour, divided

2 teaspoons baking powder

1/2 teaspoon kosher salt

1/2 cup (1 stick, 4 ounces) unsalted butter, at room temperature

1 cup granulated sugar

3 large eggs

1 cup sour cream

1 teaspoon pure vanilla extract

Confectioners' sugar

1. Preheat the oven to 350°F. Lightly grease an 8 x 11-inch baking dish and set aside.

2. To make the topping: In a medium-size bowl, combine the brown sugar, nuts, and cinnamon and set aside.

3. To make the cake: In a medium-size bowl, combine the blueberries with 1 1/2 teaspoons of flour, set aside. In a separate medium-size bowl, sift together the remaining 2 cups of flour, baking powder, and salt.

4. Using an electric mixer on medium speed, in a large bowl, beat the butter until creamy. Add the granulated sugar and beat until smooth. Add the eggs, one at a time, and the sour cream and vanilla, scraping down the sides of the bowl as needed and beating until just smooth. Add the flour mixture and beat until smooth. Fold in the blueberries. Pour half of the batter into the prepared pan and sprinkle half of the topping evenly on top. Repeat with the remaining batter and topping. Bake until a toothpick inserted into the center of the cake comes out clean, about 45 minutes.

5. Let the cake cool in the pan for 20 minutes. Cut into squares, dust with confectioners' sugar, and serve.

Rose Berry Farm, LLC

Strawberry Shortcake

SERVES 8

Here's what you can do with that bumper crop of ripe strawberries you scored at the farm.

Note: The biscuits can be made ahead.

Biscuits

2 cups all-purpose flour
1 tablespoon baking powder
1 teaspoon kosher salt
1/4 cup (1/2 stick, 2 ounces) unsalted butter, cut into pieces, chilled
3/4 cup cold whole milk

Strawberries

2 pounds strawberries, hulled and sliced
2 tablespoons granulated sugar
1 1/2 to 2 cups whipped cream

1. Preheat the oven to 450°F.

2. To make the biscuits: In a large bowl, sift together the flour, baking powder, and salt. Using a fork or your fingertips, cut in the butter until the flour mixture resembles crumbs.

3. Make a well in the center of the flour mixture and slowly pour in the milk. Stir until the dough just starts to come together. Do not overmix.

4. Spoon or scoop about 1/4 cup of dough for each biscuit onto ungreased baking sheet. Press down gently on each biscuit. Bake until golden brown, about 15 minutes.

5. Toss the strawberries with the sugar and refrigerate 30 minutes before serving.

6. To serve: Cut the biscuits in half horizontally and spoon the strawberries and their juice over each shortcake bottom. Top each with whipped cream and then the shortcake top. Spoon more strawberries over the top and serve immediately.

Barberry Hill Farm

Fresh Peach Tart

SERVES 12

Nothing says summer like a ripe, juicy peach—unless it's a bushel of them. When local peaches make the scene, Chef Malcarney snaps them up by the case so he can turn out this scrumptious peach tart. "I have a good relationship with Rose's Berry Farm, in Glastonbury. I will frequently take all their overripe peaches and make sorbet with it."

Shortbread Crust

1 cup all-purpose flour
1/2 cup granulated sugar
1/8 teaspoon salt
3/4 cup (1 1/2 sticks, 6 ounces) unsalted butter, melted

Crème Patissière

1 cup milk
4 large egg yolks
1/4 cup granulated sugar
2 tablespoons bourbon
1 teaspoon pure vanilla extract
1 1/2 tablespoons cornstarch

Almond Crème

1 1/4 cups (2 1/2 sticks, 10 ounces) unsalted butter
1 1/4 cups granulated sugar
2 1/4 cups almond flour
6 large eggs, lightly beaten

About 7 large or medium-large ripe peaches, pitted and cut into 1/2-inch-thick slices

1. Preheat the oven to 350°F. Grease a 9 x 13-inch baking dish. Set aside.

2. To make the shortbread crust: In a medium-size bowl, sift together the flour, sugar, and salt. Stir in the butter until the dough starts to come together. Press the dough firmly into the prepared baking dish. Cover the top tightly in plastic wrap and freeze for 20 minutes. Remove the plastic wrap and line the dough with foil, then fill with dried beans. Bake for 20 minutes. Remove the foil and beans and continue to bake until the crust is golden brown, about 17 minutes. Set aside to cool.

3. Meanwhile, make the crème patissière: In a small saucepan, bring the milk to just a boil over medium-high heat. In a medium-size bowl, whisk together the egg yolks, sugar, bourbon, vanilla, and cornstarch. In a slow and steady stream, whisk the milk into the egg mixture. Transfer the egg mixture back into the saucepan and cook over low heat, stirring constantly, until the mixture nears the consistency of a pudding or custard, about 4 minutes.

4. To make the almond crème: Using an electric mixer on medium speed, in a medium-size bowl, cream the butter until light and fluffy, scraping down the sides of the bowl as needed. Beat in the sugar until well blended, scraping down the bowl. Beat in the almond flour until just blended, scraping down the bowl. Do not overmix. Mix in the eggs. Fold the almond crème into the crème patissière; then pour over the shortbread dough, about halfway up the sides of the pan. Tuck the peaches evenly into the crème, cut side down, so that only their furry backs are sticking up over the tart. The tops of the peaches should be just visible. Add a bit more crème, if necessary. Bake until the top is golden brown and the filling is set, about 70 minutes. Let rest for 15 minutes.

Blue Lemon Restaurant

BLOODROOT RESTAURANT

Tucked away on a residential block in Bridgeport with views of the Long Island Sound, Bloodroot is an iconic 37-year-old vegan/vegetarian restaurant that has stood the test of time. Founded by Selma Miriam and Noel Furie, Bloodroot has always served up globally inspired cuisine—from seasonal soups to pilafs to fruit tarts—for customers looking for something a little different.

Furie says, "Our menus are seasonal in nature, based upon what's growing in our garden, what's available in the market, and what we think our diners will enjoy."

Miriam explains, "We are interested in exploring and promoting ethnic foods from around the world. We work to reproduce them as authentically as possible, using local farm produce."

Over the years, Bloodroot has attained a loyal following, publishing several cookbooks and even a popular annual calendar. Every day, visitors stop in for a self-serve bite and, on sunny days, enjoy it from an outdoor perch overlooking the water. The influx of new fans affirms the duo's desire to open a friendly neighborhood gathering spot and feminist bookstore almost four decades ago. Miriam and Furie are pioneers in the movement to eat sustainably, healthfully, and deliciously from the bounty provided by local farms—they introduced the concept of sustainable cuisine decades before it became *de rigueur*.

Selma recalls, "When Urban Oaks, in New Britain, began delivery to restaurants (around 2000), we were delighted to have local organic produce brought to us. Then, a farmers' market opened in Westport on Thursdays, and it became a great pleasure to shop there each week . . . Currently, Patti, of Sport Hill Farm, participates in the Saturday market right in our Black Rock neighborhood. How wonderful! Hopefully, other farms will join her."

Macerated Summer Fruit Tart

SERVES 8

Note: You will need to macerate the berries one day before you intend to bake the pie.

Berry Filling

Zest and juice of 1 lime

3 tablespoons Demerara or brown sugar, plus more as needed

1/2 teaspoon ground cardamom

1/2 teaspoon kosher salt

1 tablespoon gin

2 pounds mixed berries, such as strawberries, quartered; blueberries; raspberries; pitted cherries, halved; or peaches, pitted and cut into 1/2-inch slices

2 tablespoons cornstarch

Coconut Oil Piecrust

1 cup all-purpose flour, plus more for rolling

1 tablespoon granulated sugar, plus more as needed

1/2 teaspoon ground cardamom

1/2 teaspoon kosher salt

1/3 cup coconut oil

2 tablespoons water

....
Whipped cream (optional)

Mint leaves, for garnish

1. To macerate the fruit: In a medium-size bowl, combine the zest and lime juice, sugar, cardamom, salt, and gin. Stir in the fruit and combine well. Cover with plastic wrap and refrigerate overnight.

2. Preheat the oven to 375°F.

3. To make the crust: Combine the flour, sugar, cardamom, and salt in a medium-size bowl. In a small saucepan, heat the coconut oil over medium-low heat until the oil liquefies, then stir in the water. Add the oil to the flour and stir with a floured fork until a sticky ball of dough begins to form.

4. Place a 14-inch piece of parchment paper on a clean work surface and sprinkle with flour. Turn out the dough onto parchment paper and sprinkle with additional flour. Top with another sheet of parchment paper, roll out the dough into a 12-inch round, and then carefully slide the dough onto a rimless cookie sheet or pizza peel. Carefully remove the top piece of parchment paper and invert a 9-inch pie plate over the dough and baking sheet. (Using your fingers, press back into the crust any pieces of dough that may have fallen off.) Carefully turn over the baking sheet and pie plate so the is dough right side up. Remove the baking sheet and the remaining piece of parchment paper on top of the dough. (Using your fingers, press back into the crust any pieces of dough that may have fallen off.) Trim the excess dough just at the level of the edge of the pie pan. Lightly sprinkle the crust with flour, place in the refrigerator, and chill for 20 minutes.

5. Line the crust with parchment paper and enough pie weights or beans to fill the bottom of the shell. Bake the dough for 10 minutes; remove the parchment paper and weights, and continue to bake until golden brown, about 20 minutes. Transfer the tart shell to a cooling rack and let cool completely.

6. While the crust is baking, make the filling: Place a strainer over a large bowl. Place the macerated berries in the prepared strainer and let drain at room temperature for 30 minutes.

7. Place the fruit juice in a small saucepan and bring to a simmer over medium heat. In a small bowl, whisk together 1 teaspoon of the fruit juice with the cornstarch. Whisk the cornstarch mixture into the saucepan with the juice and continue to simmer, stirring occasionally, until the liquid is clear and thickened, about 2 minutes. Adjust the tartness with sugar to taste. Using a rubber spat-

ula, spread the fruit filling evenly over the bottom of the crust. Let the pie rest until the juice has fully absorbed into the berries, about 20 minutes, and serve at room temperature or refrigerate overnight and serve cold. Slice into eight wedges and serve with a dollop of whipped cream, if desired. Garnish with mint leaves.

Note: The berry filling is also delicious served over ice cream or cake, or mixed with yogurt.

Bloodroot Restaurant

CONNECTICUT FARMLAND TRUST

Connecticut Farmland Trust (CFT) is the only land trust in the state dedicated to the protection of family farms. Since 2002, CFT has protected over 31 farms and 2,650 acres of farmland, and has helped its partners protect nearly 1,000 additional acres. In spite of public and private efforts, Connecticut loses more farmland than it saves every year. If we hope to have a vital regional food economy in the years to come, that pace is unsustainable. For more information on what you can do to help, visit the CFT website. A portion of the proceeds from the sale of this book will be donated to the Connecticut Farmland Trust.

THE SONO BAKING COMPANY & CAFÉ

Fans of the SoNo Baking Company & Café in South Norwalk cheered the opening of the Westport store located at A&J's Farm Market on the Post Road. With a few small tables and initially geared for takeout, the little coffee bar has become a go-to gathering spot, with outdoor tables in warm weather. Buoyed by this success, a third location opened in Darien in August 2014.

The SoNo Baking Company & Café is the creation of chef John Barricelli, who had a vision of creating artisan breads, European-style pastries, and specialty cakes in a warm, inviting bakery and café environment. John's philosophy is: "If you start with the best possible ingredients, techniques and equipment, you can't help but produce the best possible results." He has found that the key to "best possible ingredients" is farm-fresh fruit, eggs, butter, and milk.

At his café, you can enjoy breakfast or lunch with a gourmet coffee. Breakfast offerings include the SoNo Egg Sandwich, Ham & Cheese Croissants, and an assortment of sweet croissants and Danishes; Chocolate Croissants, Almond Croissants, Raspberry Crumb Danish, Cheese Danish, and Apricot Danish are just a few of your options. At lunch you can enjoy baguette sandwiches: ham, apple, and Swiss cheese with Dijon mustard or the Caprese with tomato, mozzarella, pesto, and fresh basil. Really hungry? Opt for a panino. We're partial to the Cubano (slow-roasted pork,

baked Virginia ham, Swiss, and pickles on country white bread) or the Prosciutto di Parma (mozzarella, tomato, and pesto on focaccia). All are even tastier with a cup of SoNo Blend coffee, a robust cappuccino, or latte (beans are roasted expressly for the SoNo Baking Company by Unique Coffee Roasters of Staten Island, New York). The café also offers teas from Harney & Sons; enjoy them hot all year long or, during the summer, try the flavored iced teas: peach, mango, and raspberry are brewed throughout the season.

John appeared regularly on *The Martha Stewart Show*, and is the author of two cookbooks: *The SoNo Baking Company Cookbook* and *The Seasonal Baker*.

Caramel-Apple Tart

MAKES 1 (9-INCH) TART; SERVES 8

"This rustic apple tart is something I like to make in the fall. The kids like it because it tastes like caramel apples. The sliced apples are cooked in a hazelnut Linzer shell lined with a smear of caramel pastry cream. The cream keeps the apples moist and a dusting of confectioners' sugar encourages the apples to caramelize during baking." —Chef John Barricelli

Linzer Crust

1 1/2 cups (6 ounces) hazelnuts

1/2 cup plus 1 1/2 tablespoons granulated sugar, divided

1 cup plus 2 tablespoons all-purpose flour

1/2 teaspoon baking powder

1/2 teaspoon ground cinnamon

1/4 teaspoon grated nutmeg

1/2 cup (1 stick, 4 ounces) unsalted butter, at room temperature

1/2 teaspoon coarse salt

1 large egg, at room temperature

3/4 teaspoon vanilla paste or pure vanilla extract

Caramel Pastry Cream

2 large egg yolks

1/4 cup plus 1 tablespoon granulated sugar

2 tablespoons cornstarch

1/8 teaspoon coarse salt

1 cup whole milk, divided

3 tablespoons water

1/4 teaspoon vinegar

1 teaspoon pure vanilla extract

1 1/2 tablespoons unsalted butter, chilled, cut into pieces

Apples

2 to 2 1/2 Granny Smith apples, cored, peeled, and cut into 1/4- to 1/3-inch wedges (cut each quarter into 4 slices)

2 tablespoons unsalted butter, melted

1/2 teaspoon ground cinnamon

Confectioners' sugar

1. To make the crust: Preheat the oven to 350°F. Place the hazelnuts in a single layer on a rimmed baking sheet and bake until they are lightly colored and the skins are blistered and cracking, 10 to 15 minutes. Wrap in a kitchen towel and let steam for 1 minute. Rub the nuts in the towel to rub off as many of the skins as possible, but don't worry about the skins that stick; set aside to cool completely.

2. In a medium-size bowl, whisk together the flour, baking powder, cinnamon, and nutmeg; set aside.

3. In a food processor, pulse the toasted hazelnuts with 1 1/2 tablespoons of the sugar until finely ground. (Be careful not to overprocess, as the nuts will turn into an oily paste.) Transfer to the bowl of a standing mixer fitted with the paddle attachment. Add the butter, the remaining 1/2 cup of sugar, and the salt, and beat on medium-high speed until light and fluffy, about 2 minutes, scraping down the sides of the bowl halfway through. Beat in the egg and vanilla.

4. Add the flour to the hazelnut mixture and beat on low speed until the flour is absorbed. Scrape the dough onto a sheet of plastic wrap, flatten into a disk, and wrap in plastic wrap. Refrigerate until firm, at least 2 hours.

5. To make the pastry cream: In a medium-size, heatproof bowl, whisk together the egg yolks, 1 tablespoon of the sugar, the cornstarch, and salt. Whisk in the 1/4 cup of the milk in a slow, steady stream until smooth. Set aside.

6. In a medium-size saucepan, combine the remaining 1/4 cup of sugar, 3 tablespoons of water, and the vinegar. Bring to a boil over medium-high heat, swirling the pan to dissolve the sugar, about 5 minutes. Boil until the mixture turns a deep amber color, about 8 minutes. Remove the pan from the heat, and slowly and carefully whisk in the remaining 3/4 cup of milk. Return the pan to medium heat and stir until the caramel melts and the mixture is smooth, about 3 minutes.

7. Whisking constantly, gradually pour the hot caramel into the egg yolk mixture to temper, about 1 minute. Set a strainer over the saucepan; strain the mixture back into the pan. Bring to a boil over medium heat whisking constantly, about 6 minutes. Let boil (in the center of the pan, not just around the sides) for 10 seconds, still whisking. The mixture should thicken to a pudding-like consistency (see note). Transfer the mixture to the bowl of a standing mixer fitted with the paddle attachment (see note). Beat the cream on medium speed for 2 to 3 minutes to cool it slightly. Beat in the vanilla, then the butter. Beat until cooled, 5 to 10 more minutes. Press a piece of plastic wrap directly on the surface to prevent a skin from forming, and refrigerate.

8. On a lightly floured work surface, roll the chilled dough to a 12-inch round about 1/8 inch thick. Fit the dough into a 9-inch fluted tart pan with a removable bottom and trim the dough so that it comes slightly above the rim of the tart pan (see note). Then, with the heel of your hand, press the excess dough against the sharp edge of the rim of the pan to cut it level with the pan. Chill until firm, about 30 minutes.

9. Arrange the oven rack in the lower third of the oven. Preheat the oven to 375°F. Line a baking sheet with parchment paper or a nonstick silicone baking mat.

10. Spread the pastry cream over the bottom of the pie shell. Arrange the apple wedges on top in concentric circles. Brush the apples with the melted butter and sprinkle with the cinnamon. Sift confectioners' sugar generously over the top.

11. Bake, rotating the baking sheet about two-thirds of the way through the baking time, until the pastry is cooked through, and the apples are bubbling, tender, and caramelized, about 40 minutes. Transfer to a cooling rack to cool.

Notes:

During step 7, watch the caramel carefully: Don't let it get too dark or it will scorch.

If you find it difficult to transfer the dough to the tart pan, press as many pieces of the dough into the pan and use a floured base of a cake pan to press it into place.

At the bakery, the pastry cream is beaten in a standing mixer to cool as quickly as possible. If you don't have a standing mixer, turn out the cream into a large bowl and refrigerate quickly.

SoNo Baking Company & Cafe

Strawberry Frangipane Tartlets

MAKES 6 (3 1/2-INCH) TARTLETS

"These tartlets remind me of the individual Table Talk fruit pies my brothers and I loved as kids. (Except they're a lot better!) The filling is soft and the strawberry jam echoes the flavor of the fresh strawberries on top. They're easy to make because the filling cooks along with the pastry, and the kids love having their own tartlet. You will need six 3 1/2-inch fluted molds with removable bottoms (see note), and a 4 1/2-inch-diameter round cutter (the lid of a standard quart-size deli container works perfectly). It's a very pretty presentation and you can vary the tart with whatever berries are available. The important part is to not overbake the filling." —Chef John Barricelli

1/2 recipe Pâte Sucrée, chilled (recipe follows)

Almond Cream

1/4 cup blanched whole almonds,
      or 6 tablespoons almond flour

3 tablespoons granulated sugar

1/2 teaspoon coarse salt

3 tablespoons unsalted butter

1 large egg, at room temperature

3/4 teaspoon almond extract

1 1/2 tablespoons all-purpose flour

1/4 cup strawberry jam

24 medium-size strawberries, hulled

1 tablespoon confectioners' sugar, for dusting

1. On a lightly floured surface, roll the dough about 1/8 inch thick. Cut as many 4 1/2-inch-diameter rounds as possible. Press the scraps together in a ball; chill. Reroll the scraps as necessary to make six rounds. Fit the dough rounds into six 3 1/2-inch fluted tartlet pans with removable bottoms, and trim the dough so that it

comes slightly above the rim of the pan. Then press the excess dough against the sharp edge of the rim of the pan with the heel of your hand to cut it level with the pan. Chill until firm, about 30 minutes.

2. To make the almond cream: In a food processor, pulse the almonds with the sugar and salt for about 10 seconds, until finely ground. Add the butter and process to blend. Add the egg, processing until blended and scraping the bowl. Add the almond extract. Add the all-purpose flour and process until combined.

3. Set the oven rack in the lower third of the oven. Preheat the oven to 375°F.

4. Use the back of a spoon to spread each tartlet shell with 1 teaspoon of the strawberry jam. Spread 2 tablespoons of the almond cream on top of the jam in each shell. Place the tartlet shells on a baking sheet and chill for 5 minutes.

5. Bake, rotating the baking sheet about two-thirds of the way through the baking time, until the pastry is cooked through and golden brown and the almond cream is puffed and golden, 22 to 26 minutes. Transfer the tartlets to a cooling rack. Let cool completely. Remove the tartlets from the molds. Spread the top of each with a thin layer of the remaining strawberry jam.

6. Stand a strawberry, pointed side up, in the center of each tartlet. Cut the remaining strawberries in half. Arrange four to six strawberry halves, depending on size, over the top of each tartlet, standing them on the wide end and leaning them against the center berry. Dust with confectioners' sugar.

Note: If you do not own tartlet pans with removable bottoms, you can use disposable foil pie plates that have a base that measures 3 1/2 inches across. The tartlets are easy to remove from the plates; just bend the foil away from the crust to release them.

SoNo Baking Company & Cafe

Pâte Sucrée

MAKES ENOUGH FOR 1 DOUBLE-CRUST OR 2 SINGLE-CRUST (9-INCH) PIES OR 12 TARTLETS

This sweet, rich dough is delicious in dessert tarts and pies. It tastes just like a butter cookie, so any scraps can be rolled, cut into cookie shapes, and baked.

2 cups all-purpose flour
1 cup (2 sticks, 8 ounces) unsalted butter, at room temperature
1/4 cup granulated sugar
1 teaspoon coarse salt
1 large egg
1 large egg yolk

1. In a bowl, whisk the flour to aerate it (see note); set aside.

2. In the bowl of a standing mixer fitted with the paddle attachment, beat the butter, sugar, and salt on medium-high speed until light and fluffy, about 3 minutes, scraping down the sides of the bowl halfway through. Add the whole egg and the yolk, and mix to combine. Add the flour and beat until it has been absorbed, about 3 minutes. There will still be streaks of butter visible.

3. Scoop about half of the dough onto a sheet of plastic wrap, flatten into a disk, and wrap in plastic wrap. Do the same for the other half. Refrigerate until firm, at least 2 hours.

Notes:

Instead of sifting the flour, John Barricelli whisks it in a bowl. Whisking is simpler and it also removes any lumps.

Store any remaining dough in the freezer for several months.

SoNo Baking Company & Cafe

SIMON PEARCE RESTAURANT

Tracey Medeiros lives in Vermont and penned two cookbooks celebrating the artisanal foods of the Green Mountain State. In each, she paid homage to Simon Pearce, one of Vermont's most lauded creators of fine handmade glassware, ceramics, and handcrafted home goods.

Naturally, her books featured recipes from the Simon Pearce Restaurant, a don't-miss destination for local New American cuisine in a jaw-dropping natural setting.

Stop in for a tour of the glassblowers and potters working their magic at the flagship location in Quechee, Vermont, and stay for a fine meal served in a 19th-century woolen mill with front-row seats by the waterfall, which juts precariously over the rushing falls of Quechee River.

The country dining room features French doors, exposed brick, pine floorboards, and tables set with fine pottery and twinkling stemware made next door in the studios.

When the restaurant first opened in 1983, Simon and Pia Pearce made a decision to serve simple, satisfying, garden-fresh food of the highest quality. Long before farm-to-table became a catchphrase, the restaurant relied strongly on the abundance of local edibles.

Today the Simon Pearce Restaurant, a member of the Vermont Fresh Network, proudly partners with local establishments across northern New England, from Quechee to New Haven, Vermont, to local brewers and cheese-makers and other nearby food artisans.

Authors' note: Why a Vermont restaurant in a Connecticut cookbook? Before we embarked on this cookbook collaboration, we met for the first time at Simon Pearce's retail stores in Connecticut during a day of promotional touring. Tracey was hosting a book signing for her first cookbook, *Dishing Up Vermont* and Christy was promoting her artisanal foods delivery company. We spent the day together talking about local farms, and restaurants. Wouldn't it be great to collaborate on a cookbook celebrating the best local farmers and chefs in Connecticut? If not for Simon Pearce, *The Connecticut Farm Table Cookbook* may not have made it into your hands.

Individual Pumpkin Cheesecakes with a Gingersnap Cookie Crust and Citrus-Cranberry Compote

SERVES 8

This recipe has a nice balance of sweet and tart. It has a creamy tang from the nutmeg Chantilly and a sweet spiciness from the gingersnap cookie crust combined with a tart, mildly sweet compote.

Gingersnap Cookie Crust

3/4 cup (1 1/2 sticks, 12 ounces) unsalted butter, at room temperature

1 cup packed dark brown sugar

1 large egg, lightly beaten

1 1/2 teaspoons grated peeled fresh ginger

3/4 teaspoon grated lemon zest

1 3/4 cups plus 2 tablespoons all-purpose flour

1 tablespoon ground ginger

1 1/2 teaspoons ground cinnamon

3/4 teaspoon baking powder

1/4 teaspoon ground white pepper

1/8 teaspoon ground cloves

1 tablespoon turbinado (raw) sugar

1/4 cup (1/2 stick, 2 ounces) unsalted butter, melted

Cheesecake

1 1/2 pounds cream cheese, softened

2 cups packed light brown sugar

6 large eggs

1 tablespoon pure vanilla extract

2 cups pure pumpkin puree (see note)

1/4 teaspoon ground cloves

1/4 teaspoon ground nutmeg

1/2 teaspoon ground cinnamon

Citrus-Cranberry Compote
(makes 3 cups; see note)

1/2 vanilla bean
2 cups fresh cranberries
2 cups dried cranberries
2 cups pure cranberry juice
1 cup granulated sugar
Zest and juice of 1 lemon
Zest and juice of 1 orange

Nutmeg Chantilly

1 cup crème fraîche
1/2 teaspoon ground nutmeg
1/4 teaspoon confectioners' sugar, or to taste

1. Spray eight 4-inch mini springform pans with nonstick cooking spray and set aside.

2. To make the gingersnap cookie crust: Using an electric mixer on medium speed, cream the butter and dark brown sugar together, scraping down the sides of the bowl as needed. Add the egg, ginger, and zest and beat until well blended, scraping down the sides of the bowl as needed. In a separate large bowl, sift together the flour, ground ginger, cinnamon, baking powder, white pepper, cloves, and turbinado sugar. Gradually add the dry ingredients to the butter mixture and beat until well combined. Turn the dough out onto a lightly floured surface and form into a disk. Wrap in plastic wrap and refrigerate until firm, at least 1 hour.

3. Preheat the oven to 350°F. Place two large pieces of parchment paper on a clean work surface and sprinkle with flour. Turn onto the disk out one piece of parchment paper and sprinkle with additional flour. Top with another sheet of parchment paper, roll out the dough to 1/4 inch thick, then carefully place the dough, along with the parchment paper, on a lightly greased baking sheet. Carefully remove the top piece of parchment paper, leaving the bottom piece under the

dough. Bake the gingersnap cookie until crisp and deep golden brown, about 28 minutes. Let the cookie cool for 2 minutes, then transfer to a cooling rack for 15 minutes. When cool enough to handle, place the gingersnap cookie, in batches, in a food processor and pulse into crumbs. Add the melted butter and mix until well combined.

4. To make the cheesecake: With an electric mixer on medium speed, cream together the cream cheese and sugar, scraping down the sides of the bowl as needed. Add the eggs, one at a time, beating until just combined. Gradually add the vanilla, pumpkin puree, cloves, nutmeg, and cinnamon and beat until smooth, scraping down the sides of the bowl as needed.

5. To assemble the cheesecake: Press about 1/4 cup of the gingersnap cookie crumbs gently into the bottom of each mini springform pan. Pour about 1 cup of the cheese filling evenly over each crust and smooth the tops with a rubber spatula. Wrap the bottoms of the pans with foil up the sides. (This will prevent the water getting into the little cracks in the bottom.) Set the springform pans in a roasting pan, in batches, if necessary, and add enough hot water to come halfway up the sides of the springform pans. Bake for 25 minutes; rotate the pan with a half-turn, and bake for an additional 25 minutes. Remove from the hot water bath and let cool to room temperature, then cover with plastic wrap and refrigerate for at least 8 hours or overnight.

6. To make the citrus-cranberry compote: Place the vanilla bean on a work surface and split it in half lengthwise, using a paring knife. Scrape the seeds into a medium-size saucepan. Add the fresh cranberries, dried cranberries, cranberry juice, sugar, and citrus zest and juice and bring to a boil, stirring occasionally, over medium-high heat. Lower the heat to medium-low and simmer, stirring occasionally, until the fresh cranberries have popped and the sauce has thickened, about 40 minutes. Transfer the compote to a bowl,

cover, and refrigerate until cold. Return the compote to room temperature before serving.

7. To make the nutmeg Chantilly: With an electric mixture beat the crème fraîche until stiff peaks form. Whisk in the nutmeg and sugar until well combined.

8. To unmold the cheesecakes, run a hot knife around the edge of the pans to loosen, and gently release the sides of the pans. Set the cakes, supported by their springform base, onto dessert plates. Spoon a little of the compote on and around each cheesecake, top with a dollop of nutmeg Chantilly, and serve.

Notes:

Save the extra gingersnap cookie crumbs and use as a crisp crust for fish, such as salmon or Chilean sea bass, or as a piecrust for a dark chocolate tart, Key lime pie, or fruit tart.

Make sure not to use pumpkin pie filling, which is spiced and sweetened.

The citrus-cranberry compote can be made up to 3 days ahead.

Simon Pearce Restaurant

Maple Pecan Bourbon Pie

**MAKES 2 (9-INCH) PIES
(8 SLICES EACH)**

The flavor of pure Connecticut maple syrup is highlighted in this moist, nutty pie. The bourbon adds a complementary vanilla, oak, and caramel flavor profile.

Crust (makes enough for 2 piecrusts)

2 1/2 cups unbleached flour, preferably King Arthur

1/4 teaspoon kosher salt

1 cup (2 sticks, 8 ounces) salted butter, frozen, cut into 1/2-inch cubes

1/2 cup ice water

Maple Filling

1/2 cup (1 stick, 4 ounces) unsalted butter, melted and slightly cooled

2 tablespoons all-purpose flour

1 vanilla bean

8 large eggs, lightly beaten

1 cup packed dark brown sugar

2 cups pure Connecticut dark maple syrup

1/4 cup bourbon, chilled

1/4 teaspoon kosher salt

....

2 cups pecan halves

Vanilla ice cream or whipped cream (optional)

1. To make the crust: Process the flour and salt in a food processor for 10 seconds. Add the butter and pulse until small lumps form. While the food processor is running, slowly drizzle in the ice water until the dough just comes together. The dough should still be crumbly. Turn the dough out onto a lightly floured surface and form into two disks. Wrap the disks in plastic wrap and refrigerate for at least 1 hour.

2. On a lightly floured surface, roll out one disk of dough into a 12-inch round. Transfer to a 9-inch pie plate, trim the excess dough, leaving a 1/2-inch overhang, and crimp the edges. Repeat with second disk. Place the crusts in the refrigerator and chill for at least 30 minutes.

3. To make the maple pecan filling: Preheat the oven to 375°F. Place the melted butter in a small bowl and whisk in the flour. Place the vanilla bean on a work surface and split it in half lengthwise using a paring knife. Scrape the seeds into the flour mixture and stir until well combined. In a large bowl, whisk together the eggs, sugar, maple syrup, bourbon, and salt until smooth. Add the flour mixture and whisk together until smooth.

4. Place the crusts on a baking sheet. Evenly line the bottom of the crusts with the pecans. Pour the mixture over the nuts and rake with a fork to evenly distribute. Bake for 25 minutes. Rotate the baking sheet and bake until the pie filling is puffy and beginning to crack on the surface, about 25 minutes longer. (If necessary, cover the perimeter of the crust with a foil collar to prevent it from overbrowning.)

5. Transfer the pie to a cooling rack and let cool completely. Serve with a scoop of ice cream, if desired.

Sixpence Pie Company

DIRT ROAD FARM

Dirt Road Farm is a small farm located on a homestead dating back to the 1830s in Weston. Phoebe Cole-Smith, a farm-to-table private chef, and her husband, Mike Smith, a hockey consultant, keep chickens and bees, grow vegetables, herbs, flowers, and fruit, and harvest maple syrup from their 5 1/2 rocky, hilly acres.

Phoebe adds value to the farm business through the sale of fresh eggs, honey, and maple syrup, as well as homemade pickles and preserves. Beyond what Dirt Road Farm supplies for Phoebe's cooking jobs, she also sources directly from nearby farms, farmers' markets, and purveyors of locally grown, raised and crafted goods, supporting local farmers and producers like herself.

Maple-Cardamom Pots de Crème with Crème Fraîche and Fleur de Sel

SERVES 6

Cardamom lends an exotic note to this creamy, dreamy maple concoction. A garnish of crème fraîche and sea salt balances the sweetness.

1 tablespoon green cardamom pods, or to taste
1 1/4 cups heavy cream
1 cup whole milk
3/4 cup pure maple syrup, preferably Grade B
1/4 teaspoon kosher salt

7 large egg yolks, beaten
Crème fraîche
Sea salt flakes, such as Maldon
Ground cinnamon

1. Preheat the oven to 300°F. Coat six 6-ounce ovenproof ramekins with butter or nonstick cooking spray. Place the rame-kins in a small roast-ing pan and set aside.

2. Place the carda-mom pods on a clean work surface, and using the bottom of a small skillet or rolling pin, crush the pods to split them open. Place the cardamom pods into a large saucepan and add the cream, milk, maple syrup, and salt. Bring to a simmer over medium-low heat. Remove from the heat and let stand for 30 minutes. Strain the mixture through a fine-mesh strainer into a bowl.

3. Whisk the egg yolks in a large bowl until pale yellow but not frothy. Add the cream mixture a little at a time, whisking continually. Ladle the mixture into the prepared ramekins. Skim off any foam. Add enough hot water to the roasting pan to come halfway up the sides of the ramekins.

4. Cover the pan with foil, poking two holes in two opposite corners. Bake until the custards are set but still wiggly in the center when gently shaken, about 45 minutes. Remove the pan from the oven and let the custards sit in the hot water bath for about 10 minutes. Remove the foil and ramekins from the pan and refrigerate for at least 40 min-utes. Garnish with a dollop of crème fraîche and a sprinkle of sea salt flakes and cinnamon.

Dirt Road Farm

Baked Bishop's Orchard Gala Apples with Whipped Caramel Cream and Apple Cider Sauce

MAKES AN 8-INCH SPRINGFORM SIZE

Apples

8 Gala apples
1/2 cup plus 1/4 cup granulated sugar
2 tablespoons organic corn syrup
2 tablespoons honey
2 tablespoons butter
Pinch of salt
1 1/2 cups heavy cream, divided
1 teaspoon unflavored gelatin

Sauce

2 cups apple cider
2 tablespoons granulated sugar

1. Preheat the oven to 325°F. Place a medium-size metal mixing bowl in the freezer.

2. To make the apples: Peel and core the apples. Reserve the peels for sauce.

3. Cut the apples in half and slice about 1/8 inch thick. Arrange the apples slices in multiple layers in a deep cast-iron cocotte (such as Le Creuset brand) and sprinkle with 1/2 cup of the sugar.

4. Cover the pot tightly and bake in the oven until the apple slices are golden and soft, 1 1/2 hours. Remove from the oven and allow the apples to cool. When the apples have cooled, strain away any excess juices, making sure not to squeeze the apples. Reserve the juice for the caramel mousse.

6. Fill an 8-inch springform pan with the apples. Gently pack down, leaving 1/4 inch at the top of the ring.

7. To make the caramel mousse: In a small saucepan, cook the corn syrup, honey, reserved apple juice, and remaining 1/4 cup of sugar, over medium heat until dark amber in color, (the cooking time will vary depending on the amount of reserved apple juiced used), about 19 minutes. Remove from the heat. Whisk in the butter and salt. Slowly whisk in 1/2 cup of the cream, warming slowly. Whisk until all the caramel has melted. Stir in the gelatin, and allow to cool for 20 minutes. Strain the mixture through a fine-mesh sieve and set aside.

8. To make the whipped cream: Remove the mixing bowl from freezer. Whip the remaining 1 cup of cream in the chilled mixing bowl until firm peaks form. Fold whipped cream into the caramel until fully incorporated.

9. Top the apple-filled springform pan with the caramel mousse, smoothing the top with a rubber spatula. Refrigerate until firm, about 6 hours or overnight.

10. To make the sauce: Place the reserved apple peels in a saucepan. Stir the apple cider and 2 tablespoons of sugar. Reduce the sauce, stirring occasionally, over medium heat until slightly syrupy, about 45 minutes. Strain the liquid through a fine-mesh strainer. Set aside.

11. To serve: To unmold, gently release the sides of the pan. Set the dessert, supported by the springform base, on a cake plate. Spoon the sauce around the plate. Serve with your favorite shortbread cookie.

Note: This recipe works as individual desserts—just adjust the pan size.

Union League Cafe

ASHLAWN FARM COFFEE AND LYME FARMERS' MARKET

What's better than an old-school farmers' market? One held on the bucolic grounds of a 300-year-old family farm set on 100 picture-perfect acres in backcountry Lyme. When you drive up to Lyme Farmers' Market at Ashlawn Farm, you'll pass cows and goats grazing, and feel like you've been transported back in time to a country bazaar, where families sold homespun wares and neighbors caught up on local news.

Like most farmers' markets, Lyme Farmers' Market sells all manner of locally raised vegetables and meats, as well as fresh-baked breads, handmade cheeses, fresh-cut flowers and a variety of artisan crafts. But more than supporting an array of cottage businesses, the market at Ashlawn Farm is a place for families to while away an hour or two on Fridays and Saturdays and get in touch with the land. In June through October, black Labs frolic in the grass and wee ones giggle over the antics of the feisty goats, while grown-ups sample gourmet cheeses, reconnect with friends, and stock up on provisions.

Carol and Chip Dahlke are one of only three families who have owned the property over three centuries. To keep up with the times, the Dahlkes transformed the former dairy into Ashlawn Farm Coffee, both a coffee roastery and a popular local café, pouring coffee made from fine Arabica green beans from coffee farms on every coffee-growing continent, then roasted onsite at their farm.

In 2013, they opened Ashlawn Farm Coffee's first offsite venture at the Old Saybrook Train Station, serving their signature fresh-roasted coffees from the roastery in Lyme. The cafe features homespun sandwiches, pastries, and other breakfast and lunch fare, created by Sarah Boone, the former pastry chef at Robert Redford's Zoom restaurant at the Sundance Resort in Utah.

The Dahlkes didn't start out as farmers; they stepped in and bought the farm when Chip's uncle, Sam, getting on in years, was about to lose it. Now, they're raising their family here. And the market—along with their coffee-roasting business—generates income to keep the farm's agricultural history alive, sparing the much-beloved farmland from development in the process.

Cold Brew Infused Irish Coffee Cupcakes with Bittersweet Whiskey Ganache

MAKES ABOUT 15 CUPCAKES

If you enjoy the flavors of Irish coffee, you're going to love these "adult" cupcakes with the sophisticated flavors of cold-brewed coffee and a dash of Irish whiskey.

Cupcakes

1 1/2 cups all-purpose flour

1 1/2 teaspoons baking powder

1/2 teaspoon baking soda

1/4 teaspoon kosher salt

3/4 cup brewed coffee, such as Ashlawn Farm, chilled

1/2 cup heavy cream

1/4 teaspoon pure vanilla extract

1/2 cup (1 stick, 4 ounces) unsalted butter, at room temperature

1 cup granulated sugar

2 large eggs

Bittersweet Whiskey Ganache

6 ounces high-quality dark chocolate, finely chopped (about 1 cup)

1/3 cup heavy cream

1 1/2 teaspoons whiskey

15 chocolate-covered espresso beans

1. Preheat the oven to 350°F. Spray about 15 muffin wells generously with nonstick cooking spray or line with muffin paper liners. Set aside.

2. In a medium-size bowl, sift together the flour, baking powder, baking soda, and salt. In a separate medium-size bowl, whisk together the coffee, cream, and vanilla. Set aside.

3. Using an electric mixer on medium speed, cream together the butter and sugar until fluffy. Add the eggs, one at a time, and beat until well combined. While the mixer is running, alternately add the flour mixture and coffee to the butter mixture until just smooth. Do not overmix. Fill the prepared muffin wells three-quarters full with batter.

4. Bake the cupcakes, rotating the pan halfway through, until the tops are golden brown and a toothpick inserted into the center of a muffin comes out clean, about 25 minutes. If not using paper liners, let muffins cool in the pan for 15 minutes before unmolding. Transfer the muffins to a cooling rack to cool completely.

5. To make the ganache: Place the chocolate in a medium-size bowl.

6. Combine the cream and whiskey in a small saucepan over medium-high heat and bring to a simmer. Remove from the heat and pour over the chocolate and allow to sit for 1 minute. Whisk until smooth and the chocolate has melted. Allow the ganache to completely cool at room temperature, about 30 minutes. Once completely cooled, place the ganache in the bowl of a standing mixer and beat on high speed until the frosting starts to become fluffy and thicken, about 1 minute.

7. Using a pastry bag or a spatula, spread the frosting over the tops of the cupcakes (about 4 teaspoons per cupcake). Refrigerate for 10 minutes to set. Garnish with a chocolate espresso bean on top of each cupcake. Serve.

Ashlawn Farm Old Saybrook Cafe

FORT HILL FARMS

Kristin and Peter Orr started Fort Hill Farms as a nursery 23 years ago, with 320 acres. "Farming is woven into the fabric of our lives," says Kristin. "Peter and I met in a Soils class at UConn—and now we take good care of a lot of soil—and plants and animals. We have two girls who want to continue farming, both majoring in Dairy Science and Dairy Nutrition."

At first, Kristin grew perennials and unusual trees. Peter grew blueberries and strawberries. Today, the farm grows lavender, and an educational corn maze and labyrinth, plus all the feed for their 400 cows for milk that is part of the Farmer's Cow Co-op of six farms. As Kristin jokes, "One of my friends told me, 'It took you 23 years to become an overnight sensation!'"

Peter is in charge of planting the Corn Maze Adventure, and Kristin is the maze-master, using the maze to attract thousands from across New England and to educate the public on the importance of farmland preservation. Visitors receive a game sheet as they enter, and search for clues among the cornstalks, learning about such issues as farmland preservation and sprawl.

In addition to growing lavender, blueberries, currants, and corn, the Orrs were at the ground floor of the Farmer's Cow, a Connecticut dairy cooperative (see page 127). They purchased Kristin's parents' 92 dairy cows and, not wanting to become a "commodity farmer," they joined with

five other family farmers in a consortium whose goal is to farm with heart (and without the ills of factory farming). First, they rolled out their line of fresh Connecticut milk, and then ice cream, made with the Farmer's Cow milk. Today, the Farmer's Cow, with an illustrated Holstein on the carton, is one of the most recognizable local milk brands in the state.

All the while, Kristin has been planting lavender and growing it organically for Connecticut chefs. She thought up the idea of growing lavender in "designed gardens" as a way to use her barn foundation wisely—and organically—without chemicals. Now, she has 1,500 lavender plants, planted in labyrinths and triple spirals. She uses the lavender in lemonade, tea, cookies, and cakes. She says, "If you want to get lost, come to the maze; if you want to be found, come to the labyrinth."

Kristin shares her recipe for lavender cookies here. Naturally, they go great with a cold glass of Farmer's Cow milk.

The Quintessential Lavender Cookies

MAKES ABOUT 90 COOKIES

"Lavender is related to rosemary—it is an herb, not a perfume, when it is grown organically. We hope you like the taste of the lavender cookies. It's the flavor you've been waiting your whole life for." —Kristin Orr

1 tablespoon plus 1/2 teaspoon fresh organic lavender buds, or 3/4 teaspoon dried
1/2 cup granulated sugar
3/4 cup (1 1/2 sticks, 6 ounces) unsalted butter, at room temperature
1/2 teaspoon pure vanilla extract
1/4 teaspoon fine sea salt
1 3/4 cups all-purpose flour

1. Preheat the oven to 350°F. Line baking sheets with parchment paper and set aside.

2. Grind the lavender buds, using a spice grinder, clean coffee grinder, or mortar and pestle.

3. In a large bowl, cream together the sugar, butter, and 1/2 teaspoon of the fresh lavender (or 1/4 teaspoon of the dried) until light and fluffy. Add the vanilla and salt, and beat to combine.

4. Slowly add the flour, 1/2 cup at time, and the remaining 1 tablespoon of fresh lavender (or 1/2 teaspoon of dried), stirring until the mixture forms a soft dough.

5. Turn out the dough onto a lightly floured surface and form into a disk. Wrap the disk in plastic wrap and refrigerate for 30 minutes.

6. On a lightly floured surface, working in small batches, roll out the dough pieces 1/4 inch thick. Using a 1 1/2-inch-diameter cookie cutter (see note), cut out circles of dough. Place the dough on the prepared baking sheets. Using a fork,

prick the dough. Bake until crisp and golden brown on the bottom, about 12 minutes. Allow the cookies to cool on the baking sheets for 5 minutes, then transfer to a cooling rack to cool completely.

Note: Feel free to supersize these diminutive cookies by using bigger cookie cutters.

Fort Hill Farms

ZEST FRESH PASTRY

Zest Fresh Pastry is an artisanal bakery located along the picturesque shoreline of southeastern Connecticut, tucked into a renovated historic mill, born from the shared dream of Gabriella Withrow and Erin Morris, two pastry chefs working in Stonington. Their vision was to combine their professional training in California and France with the high-quality local produce available from nearby farms.

As is the case with so many of our favorite artisanal bakers, they began selling their pastries at a few local farmers' markets. Their baked treats were so well received that they decided to open their own bakery in the former American Velvet Mill in Stonington, also the site of a popular farmers' market. Inspired by all the other artists, artisans and small businesses who have called the mill home, Erin and Gabriella take pleasure in experimenting with new recipes, surprising loyal fans with an ever-changing menu, which can include anything from French macarons, to seasonal cakes and cupcakes, to fresh fruit scones. You can expect to find an array of baked goods on a daily basis, from savory pastry to sweet desserts, American classics to old-world European delights.

Chocolate-Orange Five-Spice Bundt Cake

MAKES 1 (10-INCH) BUNDT CAKE

The humble Bundt cake is making a comeback, and Zest's version gives us good reason to break out the trusty Bundt pan, which gained popularity in the '60s. The orange and spices add a "zesty" kick to the moist chocolate cake, which is so good on its own that it needs just a dusting of confectioners' sugar to finish it.

2 cups all-purpose flour, plus more for dusting
1 1/2 cups granulated sugar
3/4 cup unsweetened cocoa powder
2 1/2 teaspoons baking powder
1 1/2 teaspoons baking soda
Zest of 1 medium-size orange
1 tablespoon Chinese five-spice powder
1/8 teaspoon kosher salt
1 cup buttermilk
3 large eggs, lightly beaten
2 teaspoons pure vanilla extract
6 tablespoons unsalted butter, melted and cooled
1 cup brewed coffee, cooled
Confectioners' sugar, for dusting

1. Preheat the oven to 325°F. Generously grease and lightly flour a 10-inch Bundt pan with non-stick cooking spray or butter. Tap out any excess flour. Set aside.

2. In a bowl of a standing mixer on medium speed, using the whisk attachment, whisk the flour, sugar, cocoa powder, baking powder, baking soda, zest, Chinese five-spice powder, and salt until well combined.

3. In a large separate bowl, whisk together the buttermilk, eggs, vanilla, butter, and coffee. While the mixer is running on low speed, slowly pour

the buttermilk mixture into the flour mixture, scraping down the sides of the bowl as need, until just smooth. Do not overmix. Pour the batter into the prepared cake pan and smooth top with a rubber spatula. Bake for 20 minutes; then rotate the pan and continue to bake until a toothpick inserted in the center of the cake comes out clean, about 20 more minutes. Let the cake cool in the pan for 30 minutes; then turn out onto a cooling rack. Let the cake cool completely before dusting with confectioners' sugar.

Zest Fresh Pastry, LLC

Lemon-Lavender Coconut Macaroons

MAKES ABOUT 20 COOKIES

Delicious with a cup of tea, these addictive coconut macaroons become a tad sophisticated when you add a fragrant dash of lemon and lavender. You might as well make an extra batch.

1 (14-ounce package) sweetened shredded coconut
1 cup granulated sugar
Zest of 1 lemon
1 1/2 teaspoons dried organic lavender buds
3 large egg whites, at room temperature

1. Preheat the oven to 325°F. Line a baking sheet with parchment paper. Set aside.

2. In a medium-size bowl, mix the coconut, sugar, zest, and lavender together until well combined. Add the egg whites to the dry ingredients and mix until well incorporated.

3. Scoop 20 tablespoon–size mounds onto the prepared baking sheet. Bake for 10 minutes, then rotate the pan and continue to bake until the macaroons are golden brown, about 15 more minutes. Transfer the parchment along with the macaroons to a cooling rack and allow to cool completely.

Zest Fresh Pastry, LLC

LAMOTHE'S SUGAR HOUSE

The Lamothe family started farming in 1971 with a few pigs and a vegetable garden. Their initial foray into maple syrup was a lark, with seven taps, producing liquid gold for family and friends. Before long, people kept asking to buy the syrup, and they knew they were onto something. As demand became greater, and with the help of family and close friends, they've expanded over the years to collect the sap from more than 5,500 taps and turn it into maple deliciousness in their state-of-the-art Sugar House. They are now the largest pure maple syrup producer in the state.

The sap is gathered in the spring from a pipeline system, which collects fresh sap from maple trees using 25 miles of plastic tubing strung through the forest. From there, the sap is pumped into a tank onto their truck and is brought back to the Sugar House to be boiled and processed into maple syrup.

In 2003, they converted an old woodshed into modern packing room for bottling maple syrup and products. In 2008, they completely renovated their country gift store, which now sells syrup, candies, kettle corn, and coated nuts, as well as pancake mix, sauces, preserves, and more.

Lamothe's is open daily year-round, but weekends are busy during the sugaring season, when you can also take a Sugar House tour and inhale the sweet aroma of syrup steam wafting from the giant evaporator.

Connecticut Farm Table Cookbook Directory

A

Ambler Farm
Wilton, CT
203-834-1143
www.amblerfarm.org

Arethusa al Tavolo
Bantam, CT
860-567-0043
arethusaaltavolo.com

Artisan Restaurant
Southport, CT
203-307-4222
artisansouthport.com

Ashlawn Farm Coffee & Lyme
Farmers' Market
Lyme, CT
860-434-3636
www.farmcoffee.com

Ashlawn Farm Old Saybrook
Café
Old Saybrook, CT
860-339-5663
www.farmcoffee.com

Averill Farm
Washington Depot, CT
860-868-2777
www.averillfarm.com

B

Bailey's Backyard
Ridgefield, CT
203-431-0796
www.baileysbackyard.com

Barberry Hill Farm
Madison, CT
203-245-2373
www.barberryhillfarm.com

Barcelona Wine Bar &
Restaurant
South Norwalk, CT
203-899-0088
barcelonawinebar.com

Bar Sugo
Norwalk, CT
203-956-7134
www.barsugo.com

Beltane Farm
Lebanon, CT
860-887-4709
www.beltanefarm.com

Beriah Lewis Farm
North Stonington, CT
860-599-1110

Billings Forge Community Works
Hartford, CT
860-548-9877
billingsforgeworks.org

Bistro Seven
Wilton CT
203-587-1287
www.bistro7wilton.com

Blackberry River Baking Co.
Canaan, CT
860-824-8275
blackberryriver.com

Bloodroot Restaurant
Bridgeport, CT
203-576-9168
bloodroot.com

Blue Lemon Restaurant
Westport, CT
203-226-2647
www.bluelemonrestaurant.com

Bricco Trattoria (Grants)
Glastonbury, CT 06033
860-659-0220
www.billygrant.com

Brookside Farm II
Litchfield, CT
860-567-3890

C

Cafémantic
Willimantic, CT
860-423-4243
www.cafemantic.com

Carole Peck's Good News Café
Woodbury, CT
203-266-4663
www.good-news-cafe.com

Caseus Fromagerie Bistro
New Haven, CT
203-624-3373
www.caseusnewhaven.com

Cato Corner Farm, LLC
Colchester, CT
860-537-3884
www.catocornerfarm.com

Chamard Vineyards Farm Winery
Bistro
Clinton, CT
860-664-0299
www.chamard.com

CitySeed
New Haven, CT
203-773-3736
Cityseed.org

Claire's Corner Copia
New Haven, CT
203-562-3888
www.clairescornercopia.com

Common Ground High School,
Urban Farm & Environmental
Education Center
New Haven, CT
203-389-4333
www.commongroundct.org

Community Farm of Simsbury
Simsbury, CT
860-217-0453
www.giftsoflovect.org/community
-farm-of-simbury

Community Table
Washington, CT
860-868-9354
www.communitytablect.com

Connecticut Beer Trail
www.CTBeerTrail.net

Connecticut Farmers' Market
Trail
www.farmersmarkettrail.com

Connecticut Pick-Your-Own
Farms
pickyourown.org/CT

Connecticut Sugar Shacks
(Maple Syrup Producers)
www.ctmaple.org

Connecticut Wine Trail
www.ctwine.com

The Copper Beech Inn
(The Oak Room)
Ivoryton, CT
860-767-0330
www.copperbeechinn.com

Coriander Café
Eastford, CT
860-315-7691
www.coriandercafeeastford.com

Coventry Regional Farmers'
Market
Coventry, CT
coventryfarmersmarket.com

Cushman Farms
North Franklin, CT
860-642-4600
(See Farmer's Cow)

CT Valley Farms, LLC
Simsbury, CT
860-941-8223
ctvalleyfarms@gmail.com

D
Darling Farm
Woodbridge, CT
860-550-1122
www.darlingfarm.net

Dinners at the Farm
860-526-8078
www.dinnersatthefarm.com

Dish Bar & Grill
Hartford, CT
860-249-3474
www.dishbarandgrill.com

Dirt Road Farm
Weston, CT
203-221-0845

The Dressing Room Restaurant
Westport, CT
(Closed, but our book wouldn't be
complete without an homage to
Michel Nischan. See Wholesome
Wave.)

E
Ekonk Hill Turkey Farm, LLC
Moosup, CT
860-564-0248
www.ekonkhillturkeyfarm.com

Engine Room
Mystic, CT
860-415-8117
engineroomct.com

Elm Restaurant
New Canaan, CT
203-920-4994
www.elmrestaurant.com

Estia's American
Darien, CT
203-202-7052
estiasamerican.com

F
Fairvue Farms
Woodstock, CT
860-928-9483
www.fairvuefarms.com
(See Farmer's Cow)

Falls Creek Farm
Moosup, CT
860-564-5554
www.fallscreekfarm.com

Farah's Farm
Wilton, CT
512-431-1515
facebook.com/farahsfarm

Farm to Hearth
Haddam, CT
860-554-5543
www.farmtohearth.com

The Farmer's Cow
Lebanon, CT
860-642-4600
www.thefarmerscow.com

The Farmer's Cow Calfé
Mansfield, CT
860-450-8408
thefarmerscowcalfe.com

Farming 101
Newtown, CT
203-304-1451
www.101brushyhill.com

Fat Cat Pie Co.
Norwalk, CT
203-523-0389
www.fatcatpie.com

Figs Wood Fired Bistro
Sandy Hook, CT
203-426-5503
www.figswoodfiredbistro.com

Firebox Restaurant, Hartford
Hartford, CT
860-246-1222
www.fireboxrestaurant.com

Fodor Farm
Norwalk, CT
www.norwalkct.org

Fort Hill Farm
New Milford, CT
860-350-3158
www.forthillfarm.com

Fort Hill Farms
Thompson, CT
860-350-3158
www.FortHillFarms.com

Four Mile River Farm
Old Lyme, CT
860-434-2378
www.fourmileriverfarm.com

Freund's Farm Market & Bakery, LLC
East Canaan, CT
860-824-0650
www.freundsfarmmarket.com

G
Gilbertie's Herb Gardens
Westport, CT
203-227-4175
www.gilbertiesherbs.com

Gilbertie's Petite Edibles
203-452-0913
www.petiteedibles.com

Golden Lamb Buttery
Brooklyn, CT
860-774-4423
www.thegoldenlamb.com

GourmAvian Farms
Bolton, CT
860-716-9064
www.gourmavian.com

Grants Restaurant and Bar
West Hartford, CT
860-236-1930
www.billygrant.com/grants

Graywall Farms
Lebanon, CT
866-355-2697
(See Farmer's Cow.)

Green Valley Farm
Eastford, CT
860-634-2196
www.greenvalleyfarmet.com

Guilford Lobster Pound
Guilford, CT
203-453-6122
www.guilfordlobsterpound.com

Gulf Shrimp Company
Plantsville, CT
860-628-8821
www.gulfshrimpco.com

G. W. Tavern
Washington Depot, CT
860-868-6633
www.gwtavern.com

G-Zen Restaurant
Branford, CT 06405
203-208-0443
www.g-zen.com

H

Heirloom/The Study at Yale
New Haven, CT
203-503-3919
www.heirloomnewhaven.com

The Hickories
Ridgefield, CT
203-894-1851
www.thehickories.org

Holbrook Farm
Bethel, CT
203-792-0561
www.holbrookfarm.net

Holcomb Farm
West Granby, CT
860-844-8616
www.holcombfarm.org

Hytone Farm
Coventry, CT 06238
860-642-4600
(See Farmer's Cow)

I

Infinity Bistro Hartford
Hartford: 860-560-7757
Norfolk: 860-542-5531
Infinityhall.com

J

Jacques Pépin
Madison, CT
www.facebook.com
/ChefJacquesPepin

L

La Belle Aurore
Niantic, CT
860-739-6767
www.labelleaurorect.com

Lamothe's Sugar House
Burlington, CT
860-675-5043
www.lamothesugarhouse.com

L'Escale Restaurant
Greenwich, CT
203-661-4600
www.lescalerestaurant.com

LeFarm
Westport, CT
203-557-3701
www.lefarmwestport.com

Liuzzi Gourmet Market
North Haven, CT
203-248-4356
www.liuzzicheese.com

M

Mama's Boy
South Norwalk, CT
203-956-7171
www.mamasboyct.com

Maple Lane Farms
Preston, CT
860-889-3766
www.maplelane.com

Mapleleaf Farm
Hebron, CT
860-642-4600
(See Farmer's Cow.)

March Farm
Bethlehem, CT
203-266-7721
www.marchfarm.com

Massaro Community Farm
Woodbridge, CT
203-736-8618
www.massarofarm.org

Match Restaurant
South Norwalk, CT
203-852-1088
matchsono.com

The Max Restaurant Group
Max Amore Ristorante
Glastonbury, CT
860-659-2819
www.maxamore.com

Max Downtown
Hartford, CT
860-522-2530
www.maxdowntown.com

Mayapple Hill Farm
New Milford, CT

The Mayflower Grace
Muse by Jonathan Cartwright
www.gracehotels.com/mayflower

Métro Bis
Simsbury, CT
860-651-1908
www.metrobis.com

The Mill at 2T
Tariffville, CT
860-658-7890
www.themillat2t.com

Millstone Farm
Wilton CT
203-834-2605
www.millstonefarm.org

Millwright's
Simsbury, CT
860-651-5500
millwrightsrestaurant.com

Miya's Sushi
New Haven, CT
203-777-9760
www.miyassushi.com

Mohawk Bison
Goshen, CT
860-601-0206
www.mohawkbison.com

Moorefield Herb Farm
Trumbull, CT
203-377-0325

Mountaintop Mushrooms
Waterbury, CT
860-919-5264

Muse by Jonathan Cartwright
The Mayflower Grace
Washington, CT
860-868-9466
www.gracehotels.com/mayflower

N
Napa & Co.
Stamford, CT
203-353-3319
www.napaandcompany.com

Norm Bloom & Son
Norwalk, CT
203-866-7546
www.coppsislandoysters.com

Northfordy Farm
Northford, CT
203-494-8408

O
Outstanding in the Field
outstandinginthefield.com

Ox Hollow Farm
Roxbury, CT
860-354-3315
www.oxhollowfarmct.com

Oyster Club
Mystic, CT
860-415-9266
www.oysterclubct.com

P
Paci Restaurant
Southport, CT
203-259-9600
www.pacirestaurant.com

Parallel Post
Trumbull, CT
203-380-6380
parallelpostrestaurant.com

Plum Luv Foods
www.plumluvfoods.com

R
Red Bee Honey
Weston, CT
203-226-4535
www.redbee.com

Restaurant Bricco (Grants)
West Hartford, CT
860-233-0220
www.billygrant.com/bricco

Riverbank Farm
Roxbury, CT
860-350-3276
riverbankfarm.com

River Tavern
Chester, CT
860-526-9417

www.rivertavernrestaurant.com

Roìa Restaurant
New Haven, CT
203-200-7045
roiarestaurant.com

Rose's Berry Farm, LLC
South Glastonbury, CT
860-633-7467
rosesberryfarm.com

S
Saugatuck Craft Butchery
(The Kitchen at SCB)
Westport, CT
203-226-6328
craftbutchery.com

The Schoolhouse at Cannondale
Wilton, CT
203-834-9816
schoolhouseatcannondale.com

Sepe Farm
Sandy Hook, CT
203-270-9507
sepefarm.com

Simon Pearce Restaurant
Quechee, Vermont
802-295-1470
www.simonpearce.com

Sixpence Pie Company
New Haven, CT
Southington, CT
860-681-6118
www.sixpencepiecompany.com

Skinny Pines Brick Oven Caterer
203-727-8177
www.skinnypines.com

The SoNo Baking Company
& Café
Darien, CT
203-309-5401
Norwalk, CT
203-847-7666
Westport, CT
203-955-1111
www.sonobaking.com

South End (at the Station)
New Canaan, CT
203-966-5200
southendnewcanaan.com

Speckled Rooster Farm
Westport, CT
www.speckledroosterfarm.com

Sport Hill Farm
Easton, CT
203-268-3137
www.sporthillfarm.com

The Spread
South Norwalk, CT
203-939-1111
thespreadsono.com

The Stand Juice Company
Fairfield, CT
203-873-0414
South Norwalk, CT
203-956-5670
thestandjuice.com

Sub Edge Farm
Farmington, CT
subedgefarm.com

Sugar & Olives
Norwalk, CT
203-454-3663
sugarandolives.com

Sustainable Food Systems
Wallingford, CT
203-294-9683
sustainablefoodsystems.com

T

Tarry Lodge Enoteca Pizzeria
Westport, CT
203-571-1038
tarrylodge.com

Terrain Westport Garden Café
Westport, CT
203-226-2750
www.shopterrain.com

Thompson Street Farm, LLC
South Glastonbury, CT
860-657-4361
www.thompsonstreetfarm.com

3B Ranch
Northford, CT
203-410-7150
www.3branchct.com

Tracey Medeiros
www.traceymedeiros.com

Truck
Bedford, NY
914-234-8900
www.truckrestaurant.com

Truelove Farms
Morris, CT
203-217-6234
truelovefarms.org

Trumbull Kitchen
Hartford, CT
860-493-7412
www.trumbullkitchen.com

U

Union League Cafe
New Haven, CT
203-562-4299
www.unionleaguecafe.com

Urban Oaks Organic Farm
New Britain, CT
860-223-6200
www.urbanoaks.org

W

Wakeman Town Farm
Westport, CT
203-557-9195
www.wakemantownfarm.org

Waldingfield Farm
Washington, CT
860-868-7270
waldingfieldfarm.com

Walrus + Carpenter
Black Rock, CT
203-333-2733
www.walruscarpenterct.com

Wave Hill Breads Bakery
203-762-9595
www.wavehillbreads.com

Westport Farmers' Market
50 Imperial Avenue Parking Lot,
Westport, CT (May–Nov)
Gilbertie's Herb Gardens, 7
Sylvan Lane, Westport, CT
(Nov–March)

West Street Grill
Litchfield, CT
860-567-3885
weststreetgrill.com

The Wharf Restaurant at
Madison Beach Hotel
Madison, CT
203-245-1404 ext. 506
www.madisonbeachhotel.com

The Whelk
Westport, CT
203-557-0902
www.thewhelkwestport.com

White Gate Farm
East Lyme, CT
860-739-9585
www.whitegatefarm.net

Wholesome Wave
Bridgeport, CT
203-226-1112
www.wholesomewave.org

The Willows Bristol DoubleTree
by Hilton
Bristol, CT
860-589-7766
www.willowsbristol.com

Winvian Relais & Chateaux
Morris, CT
860-567-9600
www.winvian.com

Z

Zest Fresh Pastry, LLC
Stonington, CT
860-381-0771
www.zestfreshpastry.com

Zinc
New Haven, CT
203-624-0507
www.zincfood.com

Photography Credits

Courtney Apple Photography, 92
Barcelona Wine Bar & Restaurant, 13, 113
Alan Barry Photography, 50, 51
Stacy Bass Photography, 301
Noel Berry, 165
Patricia Bruhn, 265
Gus Cantavero, 147, 149
Winter Caplanson, 16, 30, 49, 79, 126, 127, 131, 146, 167 (right), 170, 171, 172, 173, 177, 180, 201, 263, 264, 279, 280, 304
Ashley Caroline Photography, 8, 44, 115, 139, 140, 143, 160, 206, 207, 209 (right), 213
Christy Colasurdo, 90
Stephane Colbert, 221
Heather Conley, 26, 114
Jeanine Dell'Orfano, 74, 89, 95, 190
Serge Detalle, 188

Diane Diederich, 194
Erb Photography, 75, 76
Trout Gaskins, 98
Elizabeth Grant, 70
Michael A. Hartel, 37
Tom Hopkins, 88
Karen Ladaney, 145
Neil A. Landino Jr., 195
Michelle K. Martin, 25, 26, 49
Carla McElroy, 144, 278
Tom McGovern, 215, 217, 258
Jane S. Meister, 260
Dominic Miguel Photography, 39
Anna Moller, 252
Susan Muldoon Images, 121
Lisa L. Nichols, 176, 179
Cara Paiuk, 55
Oliver Parini, 2, 5, 6, 14, 17, 19, 20, 24, 27, 28, 29, 33, 34, 35, 36, 38, 41, 43, 45, 47, 48, 52, 53, 56, 59, 60, 61, 62, 65, 66, 72, 80, 81, 82, 83, 84, 85, 86, 91, 96, 97, 99, 100, 102, 104, 108, 110, 116, 117, 118, 119,

120, 123, 124, 128, 129, 130, 135, 136, 138, 150, 153, 154, 157, 158, 159, 161, 162, 166, 167 (left), 168, 175, 181, 183, 186, 191, 192, 198, 200, 202, 203, 208, 209 (left), 211, 214, 218, 220, 222, 223, 227, 236, 241, 242, 243, 247, 249, 251, 256, 257, 259, 269, 270, 272, 273, 275, 277, 281, 282, 283, 285, 286, 288, 289, 291, 292, 294, 299, 300, 303, 306, 307
Michelle P. Paulson, 31, 32, 77, 78
Plum Luv/CT Chefs Challenge, 54
Anna Sawin Photography, 232, 261, 278
Christina Morse Scala, 22
Jeff Skeirik, 73
Debra Somerville, 112, back cover
Laura Stone Photography, 10, 105, 107
Mary Murphy Taylor, 233
Lindsay Vigue, 56
Stephanie Webster, 205

Index

Note: Page numbers in *italics* refer to recipe photographs.

A

Almond(s)
Roasted Carrots al Andaluz, 114
Squash Bisque, 74
Strawberry Frangipane Tartlets, 295
Apple(s)
Caramel- , Tart, 293–94
and Cauliflower, Autumn Pasta Sauce with, 154
Celeriac, Caramelized Walnuts, and Cider Vinaigrette, Arugula and Endive Salad with, 33–34, *34*
Gala, Baked Bishop's Orchard, with Whipped Caramel Cream and Apple Cider Sauce, 302, *303*
Muffins, Sugary, 18
Organic Duck Breast with Ginger-Carrot Puree and Ginger-Orange Sauce, 184–85
Smoked Chicken, and Walnut Salad, 51
Sweet Curry Juice, 274
Swiss Chard and Fresh Ricotta Cheese, 117
Arugula
Crispy Poached Egg Salad, 63
and Endive Salad with Apples, Celeriac, Caramelized Walnuts, and Cider Vinaigrette, 33–34, *34*
Roasted Fig–Olive Tapenade, "Prosciutto-Style" Duck Breast, and Goat Cheese Ricotta, Flatbread with, 137–38
Salad, Saunder's Farm, with Orange Vinaigrette and Harvest Moon Cheese, 60, *61*
and Sunflower Seed Pesto over Sliced Heirloom Tomatoes, 265
and White Bean Salad, Grilled Tuna with, 214

B

Bacon-Jalapeño Oysters, 206
Basil
Fennel, and Fresh Mozzarella, Mediterranean Pasta Salad with, 41
and Garlic Scape Pesto, 266
Pistou Soup, 32
Vinaigrette, 174
Vinaigrette, Carrots and Sunflower Sprouts Salad with, 36
Bean(s). *See also* Green Beans
Chipotle Veggie Chili, 91
Farmers' Salad, 58–59
Mediterranean Pasta Salad with Fennel, Basil, and Fresh Mozzarella, 41
Moroccan Chickpea and Carrot Salad, 46
Pistou Soup, 32
Slow Cooker Turkey Chili, 172
Spicy Littleneck Clams, 232
White, and Arugula Salad, Grilled Tuna with, 214
Beef
Balsamic-Glazed Short Ribs with Gilfeather Turnip Puree and Rainbow Carrots with Orange-Blossom Honey and Fresh Sage, 248–49, *249*
Cottage Pie, *131*, 132–33
Dry-Aged Steak Tartare Crostini with Pickled Garden Turnips, 243, *243*
Four Mile River Farm Burgers, 240
Grass-Fed, and Root Vegetable Meat Loaf, 238–39
Oxen Driver's Short Ribs, 246
Skirt Steak over Roasted Butternut Squash, Rainbow Swiss Chard, Topped with Caramelized Onions, 240–41, *241*
Swedish Meatballs G. Swenson Style (G. Swenson's Köttbullar), 237–38
and Veal Bolognese, Pasta with, 151
Beet(s)
and Carrot Slaw with Raspberry Vinaigrette, 48
Red Flannel Hash, 22
Roasted Root Vegetable and Artisan Handcrafted Sausage Stuffing, 80, *81*
Salt-Roasted, with Blood Oranges, Pistachios, and Goat Cheese Salad, 93
Stonington Royal Red Shrimp over Root Vegetable Cakes, 226–28, *227*
Sweet Curry Juice, 274
Berries. *See also specific berries*
Blackberry River Scones, 21
Hidden Vegetable Smoothie, 273
Macerated Summer Fruit Tart, 290–91
Blackberry River Scones, 21
Bloody Mary, Garden Fresh, 276
Blueberry
Muffins, 20
Sour Cream Coffee Cake, 286
Tea Cake with Crumble Topping, 285
Bouillabaisse, Low Country, 216–17, *217*
Bread(s)
Baked French Toast, 26
Flatbread with Roasted Fig–Olive Tapenade, Goat Cheese Ricotta, "Prosciutto-Style" Duck Breast, and Arugula, 137–38
Pudding, Brookside Farm Maple, 282
Pumpkin, 24
Salad, 49
Brussels Sprouts
Curried, with Honey and Bacon, 83, *83*

Jerusalem Artichokes, and Carrots, Roasted, 125
and Petite Edibles, 85

Burgers
Four Mile River Farm, 240
Local Lamb, with Wasabi Aioli, 234

C

Cabbage
Braised Red, Shallot-Cranberry Puree, and Madeira Sauce, Pan-Roasted New England Pheasant Breast with, 187–88, *188*
Chef Scott Quis's Kimchee, 270
Garlic-Cilantro Slaw, 109
Stonington Royal Red Shrimp over Root Vegetable Cakes, 226–28, *227*

Cakes
Blueberry Tea, with Crumble Topping, 285
Chocolate-Orange Five-Spice Bundt, 308–9
Coffee, Blueberry Sour Cream, 286

Calamari with Eggplant Chutney, 224–25

Carrot(s)
and Beet Slaw with Raspberry Vinaigrette, 48
and Chickpea Salad, Moroccan, 46
-Ginger Puree and Ginger-Orange Sauce, Organic Duck Breast with, 184–85
Jerusalem Artichokes, and Brussels Sprouts, Roasted, 125
Rainbow, and Gilfeather Turnip Puree with Orange-Blossom Honey and Fresh Sage, Balsamic-Glazed Short Ribs with, 248–49, *249*
Roasted, al Andaluz, 114
Soup, Vegan Cream of, 64–65
and Sunflower Sprouts Salad with Basil Vinaigrette, 36

Sweet Curry Juice, 274
Terrine and Quinoa Garnished with Soubise and Carrot Top–Cashew Pesto, 122–23, *123*
Cashew–Carrot Top Pesto, Carrot Terrine and Quinoa Garnished with, 122–23, *123*

Cauliflower
and Apples, Autumn Pasta Sauce with, 154
Country Cottage Soup, 76, *76*

Celeriac
Apples, Caramelized Walnuts, and Cider Vinaigrette, Arugula and Endive Salad with, 33–34, *34*
Grass-Fed Beef and Root Vegetable Meat Loaf, 238–39

Cheese
Antipasto Platter, 259, *259*
Artisan Italian Sausage, Onion, and Kale Frittata, 128–29
Arugula and Sunflower Seed Pesto over Sliced Heirloom Tomatoes, 265
Blue, Baked Asian Pear Stuffed with, and Braised Pork Belly, Grilled Berkshire Pork Chops with, 254–56
Duck and Foie Gras Poutine, 182–83, *183*
Farmstead, Fondue with, 269
Fennel-Parmesan Fritters with Greens in Buttermilk-Bacon Dressing, 111
Four Mile River Farm Burgers, 240
Fresh Ricotta, and Swiss Chard, 117
Goat, Beltane Farm, and Mixed Baby Greens, Salad of, 53, *53*
Goat, Lamb Meat Loaf with, Sepe Farm, 250–51, *251*
Goat, Pistachios, and Blood Oranges Salad, Salt-Roasted Beets with, 93

Goat, Ricotta, Roasted Fig–Olive Tapenade, "Prosciutto-Style" Duck Breast, and Arugula, Flatbread with, 137–38
Grilled Swiss Chard Roll-ups, 101
Grilled Violetta di Firenze Topped with Heirloom Tomatoes, Fresh Burrata, and Basil, 119
Harvest Moon, and Orange Vinaigrette, Saunder's Farm Arugula Salad with, 60, *61*
Heirloom Tomato and Burrata Salad, 40
Heirloom Tomato Pie, 134–35, *135*
Homemade Whipped Ricotta Crostini with Local Honey and Sage, 145
Individual Pumpkin Cheesecakes with a Gingersnap Cookie Crust and Citrus-Cranberry Compote, 297–99, *299*
Lobster, Tomato, and Burrata Salad, 44
Macaroni and, 155
Mac 'N, Caseus, 156, *157*
Mediterranean Pasta Salad with Fennel, Basil, and Fresh Mozzarella, 41
Millet and Lacinato Kale with Dried Sour Cherries, Pistachios, and Chèvre, 161, *161*
Raclette, Roasted Potatoes with, 97, *97*
Ricotta Gnocchi, 158, *159*
Roasted Potato and Heirloom Tomato Tower, 104
Spinach and Feta Frittata, 127
Tomme, Cinnamon Chicken with a Mashed Potato Crust Topped with (Shepherd's Pie Style), 133

Cherry(ies)
Sour, Dried, Pistachios, and Chèvre, Millet and Lacinato Kale with, 161, *161*
Sour, Vinaigrette, Starlight Farm's Kale Salad with, 38

Chicken
    and Blue Oyster Mushrooms with
      Sherry Cream Sauce, 193–94
    Under a Brick, 196
    Buttermilk Fried, 189–90, *190*
    Cinnamon, with a Mashed Potato
      Crust Topped with Tomme
      Cheese (Shepherd's Pie Style),
      133
    Ginger Stir-Fry, 192
    Oven-Roasted, with Stuffing-Style
      Frittata, Pickled Green Beans,
      and Poached Cranberries,
      197–98
    Smoked, Apple, and Walnut
      Salad, 51
Chili
    Chipotle Veggie, 91
    Turkey, Slow Cooker, 172
Chocolate
    Cold Brew Infused Irish Coffee
      Cupcakes with Bittersweet
      Whiskey Ganache, 305
    -Orange Five-Spice Bundt Cake,
      308–9
Chutney, Eggplant, Calamari with,
    224–25
Cilantro
    -Garlic Slaw, 109
    and Smoked Paprika, Slow-
      Roasted Porchetta with,
      244
Clams
    Cioppino Verde, 219–20, *220*
    Littleneck, Spicy, 232
    Low Country Bouillabaisse, 216–
      17, *217*
Coconut Macaroons, Lemon-
    Lavender, 309
Cod, Atlantic, with Wild Rice and
    Corn Griddle Cakes and
    Garlicky Kale, 202–4, *203*
Coffee, Cold Brew Infused Irish,
    Cupcakes with Bittersweet
    Whiskey Ganache, 305
Collard Greens, Old South, with
    Pot Likker (a.k.a. "Mess o'
    Greens"), 106

Cookies
    Lavender, The Quintessential,
      307, *307*
    Lemon-Lavender Coconut
      Macaroons, 309
Corn
    Cast-Iron Duck Breast, 174–75
    Fresh, Soup, 72
    Low Country Bouillabaisse, 216–
      17, *217*
    and Purslane, Seared Scallops
      with, 212
    Slow Cooker Turkey Chili, 172
    and Wild Rice Griddle Cakes and
      Garlicky Kale, Atlantic Cod
      with, 202–4, *203*
Cranberry(ies)
    -Citrus Compote, Individual
      Pumpkin Cheesecakes with a
      Gingersnap Cookie Crust and,
      297–99, *299*
    Poached, Stuffing-Style Frittata,
      and Pickled Green Beans,
      Oven-Roasted Chicken with,
      197–98
    -Shallot Puree, Braised Red
      Cabbage, and Madeira Sauce,
      Pan-Roasted New England
      Pheasant Breast with, 187–88,
      188
Crostini
    Dry-Aged Steak Tartare, with
      Pickled Garden Turnips, 243,
      243
    Homemade Whipped Ricotta,
      with Local Honey and Sage,
      145
Cucumber(s)
    Bread Salad, 49
    Chilled Green Gazpacho, 67
    -Infused Vodka, 276
    Pressed, 237
    Roasted Potato and Heirloom
      Tomato Tower, 104
    Summer Garden Mojito Smoothie,
      274

Cupcakes, Cold Brew Infused
    Irish Coffee, with Bittersweet
    Whiskey Ganache, 305
Curried Brussels Sprouts with Honey
    and Bacon, 83, *83*
Curried Roasted Opo Squash, 94, *95*
Curry Juice, Sweet, 274

D
Duck
    Breast, Cast-Iron, 174–75
    Breast, Organic, with Ginger-
      Carrot Puree and Ginger-
      Orange Sauce, 184–85
    Breast, "Prosciutto-Style,"
      Roasted Fig–Olive Tapenade,
      Goat Cheese Ricotta, and
      Arugula, Flatbread with,
      137–38
    with Corn Bread Stuffing and
      Strawberry Sauce, MarWin
      Farm's, 178–79, *179*
    and Foie Gras Poutine, 182–83,
      183

E
Eggplant
    Chutney, Calamari with, 224–25
    Grilled Violetta di Firenze Topped
      with Heirloom Tomatoes, Fresh
      Burrata, and Basil, 119
    Rosa Bianca, alla Caponata, 87
Egg(s)
    Artisan Italian Sausage, Onion,
      and Kale Frittata, 128–29
    Deviled, with Cornmeal Fried
      Oysters and Pickled Red
      Onion, 210–11, *211*
    Duck, Soft-Boiled, and Mustard-
      Pickled Ramps, Pork Ciccioli
      Terrine Served on Rustic Bread
      Topped with, 260–61
    Farmers' Salad, 58–59
    "Manolo Blahnik Style," 28–29
    Oven-Roasted Chicken with
      Stuffing-Style Frittata, Pickled
      Green Beans, and Poached
      Cranberries, 197–98

Poached, Salad, Crispy, 63
Spinach and Feta Frittata, 127
Endive and Arugula Salad with
Apples, Celeriac, Caramelized
Walnuts, and Cider Vinaigrette,
33–34, *34*

F

Fennel
Basil, and Fresh Mozzarella,
Mediterranean Pasta Salad
with, 41
-Parmesan Fritters with Greens
in Buttermilk-Bacon Dressing,
111
Fig, Roasted, –Olive Tapenade, Goat
Cheese Ricotta, "Prosciutto-
Style" Duck Breast, and
Arugula, Flatbread with,
137–38
Fish
Atlantic Cod with Wild Rice
and Corn Griddle Cakes and
Garlicky Kale, 202–4, *203*
Chilled Pea and Leek Soup with
Salmon Gravlax and Pickled
Shallots, 69–70, *70*
Cioppino Verde, 219–20, *220*
Connecticut River Shad, 222,
223
Grilled Tuna with White Bean and
Arugula Salad, 214
Low Country Bouillabaisse, 216–
17, *217*
Maple-Glazed Salmon, 221
Swordfish Pizzaioli, 225
Foie Gras and Duck Poutine, 182–
83, *183*
Fondue with Farmstead Cheeses,
269
French Toast, Baked, 26
Frittata
Artisan Italian Sausage, Onion,
and Kale, 128–29
Spinach and Feta, 127
Stuffing-Style, Pickled Green
Beans, and Poached
Cranberries, Oven-Roasted
Chicken with, 197–98

Fritters
Fennel-Parmesan, with Greens
in Buttermilk-Bacon Dressing,
111
Green Tomato, 99
Fruit. *See also specific fruits*
Grilled Swiss Chard Roll-ups, 101
Summer, Macerated, Tart,
290–91

G

Garlic
-Cilantro Slaw, 109
-Infused Vodka, 276
Garlic Scape and Basil Pesto, 266
Ginger
-Carrot Puree and Ginger-Orange
Sauce, Organic Duck Breast
with, 184–85
Chicken Stir-Fry, 192
Fresh Pickled, 271
Gnocchi, Ricotta, 158, *159*
Grains. *See* Grits; Millet; Polenta;
Quinoa; Wild Rice
Grapes
Chilled Green Gazpacho, 67
Green Beans
Farmers' Salad, 58–59
Pickled, Stuffing-Style Frittata,
and Poached Cranberries,
Oven-Roasted Chicken with,
197–98
Seasonal Quinoa Salad, 168, *169*
Greens. *See also* Arugula; Kale;
Lettuce; Spinach; Swiss Chard
Arugula and Endive Salad with
Apples, Celeriac, Caramelized
Walnuts, and Cider Vinaigrette,
33–34, *34*
Bread Salad, 49
Brussels Sprouts and Petite
Edibles, 85
Collard, Old South, with Pot Likker
(a.k.a. "Mess o' Greens"), 106
Farmers' Salad, 58–59
Fennel-Parmesan Fritters with,
in Buttermilk-Bacon Dressing,
111

Mixed, with a Sherry Shallot
Vinaigrette, 56
Mixed Baby, and Beltane Farm
Goat Cheese, Salad of, 53, *53*
Quail with Yam Puree and
Microgreens, 199–200, *200*
Seared Scallops with Corn and
Purslane, 212
Grits, Heirloom, and Stonington Royal
Red Shrimp with Smoked
Tasso Pork, 230–31

H

Hash, Red Flannel, 22
Herbs. *See also* Basil; Cilantro
Cioppino Verde, 219–20, *220*
Honey Black Walnut Tart, 284

J

Jerusalem Artichokes, Brussels
Sprouts, and Carrots, Roasted,
125

K

Kale
Artisan Italian Sausage, and
Onion Frittata, 128–29
Baby, "Caesar" with Fried Capers,
Anchovies, and Herbed
Crostini, 42–43
Cast-Iron Duck Breast, 174–75
Garlicky, and Wild Rice and Corn
Griddle Cakes, Atlantic Cod
with, 202–4, *203*
Hidden Vegetable Smoothie, 273
Lacinato, and Millet with Dried
Sour Cherries, Pistachios, and
Chèvre, 161, *161*
Quinoa Paella, 165, *165*
Raspberry Balsamic Vinegar,
and Toasted Walnuts, Sautéed
Delicata Squash with, 109
Salad, Starlight Farm's, with Sour
Cherry Vinaigrette, 38
Summer Garden Mojito Smoothie,
274
Kimchee, Chef Scott Quis's, 270
Kugelis, 140

L

Lamb
Chops, Nutmegger's, 250
Local, Burgers with Wasabi Aioli, 234
Meat Loaf, with Goat Cheese, Sepe Farm, 250–51, *251*
Lavender
Cookies, The Quintessential, 307, *307*
-Lemon Coconut Macaroons, 309
Leek and Pea Soup, Chilled, with Salmon Gravlax and Pickled Shallots, 69–70, *70*
Lemonade, Knot Your Mother's, 279
Lemon-Lavender Coconut Macaroons, 309
Lentils with Chorizo and Bacon, *162,* 163
Lettuce
Chicken Under a Brick, 196
Peas à la Française, 89
Roasted Potato and Heirloom Tomato Tower, 104
Smoked Chicken, Apple, and Walnut Salad, 51
Lingonberries, Sugar-Marinated, 237
Lobster
Butter-Poached, Sandwich, 142
Eggs "Manolo Blahnik Style," 28–29
Norm Bloom & Son CT, Homemade Tagliatelle with, 148–49, *149*
Stock, 142–43
Tomato, and Burrata Salad, 44

M

Macaroons, Lemon-Lavender Coconut, 309
Maple
Bread Pudding, Brookside Farm, 282
-Cardamom Pots de Crème with Crème Fraîche and Fleur de Sel, 301
-Glazed Salmon, 221
Pecan Bourbon Pie, 300

Meat. *See* Beef; Lamb; Pork; Rabbit
Meatballs
Polpette alla Napoletana, 235
Swedish, G. Swenson Style (G. Swenson's Köttbullar), 237–38
Meat Loaf
Grass-Fed Beef and Root Vegetable, 238–39
Lamb, with Goat Cheese, Sepe Farm, 250–51, *251*
Millet and Lacinato Kale with Dried Sour Cherries, Pistachios, and Chèvre, 161, *161*
Muffins
Apple, Sugary, 18
Blueberry, 20
Mushrooms
Baked Shiitake Caps, 125
Blue Oyster, and Chicken with Sherry Cream Sauce, 193–94
Pan-Roasted New England Pheasant Breast with Shallot-Cranberry Puree, Braised Red Cabbage, and Madeira Sauce, 187–88, *188*
Mussels
Cioppino Verde, 219–20, *220*
Low Country Bouillabaisse, 216–17, *217*

N

Nuts. *See also* Almond(s); Walnut(s)
Carrot Terrine and Quinoa Garnished with Soubise and Carrot Top–Cashew Pesto, 122–23, *123*
Maple Pecan Bourbon Pie, 300
Millet and Lacinato Kale with Dried Sour Cherries, Pistachios, and Chèvre, 161, *161*
Salt-Roasted Beets with Blood Oranges, Pistachios, and Goat Cheese Salad, 93

O

Olive–Roasted Fig Tapenade, Goat Cheese Ricotta, "Prosciutto-Style" Duck Breast, and

Arugula, Flatbread with, 137–38
Onions
Peas à la Française, 89
Pickled Red, and Cornmeal Fried Oysters, Deviled Eggs with, 210–11, *211*
Orange(s)
Blood, Pistachios, and Goat Cheese Salad, Salt-Roasted Beets with, 93
-Chocolate Five-Spice Bundt Cake, 308–9
-Ginger Sauce and Ginger-Carrot Puree, Organic Duck Breast with, 184–85
Vinaigrette and Harvest Moon Cheese, Saunder's Farm Arugula Salad with, 60, *61*
Oysters
Bacon-Jalapeño, 206
Cornmeal Fried, and Pickled Red Onion, Deviled Eggs with, 210–11, *211*
Mystic River, with Grace Cocktail Mignonette, 213

P

Parsnips
Grass-Fed Beef and Root Vegetable Meat Loaf, 238–39
Pork and Green Chile Stew, 253
Stonington Royal Red Shrimp over Root Vegetable Cakes, 226–28, *227*
Pasta
with Beef and Veal Bolognese, 151
Caseus Mac 'N Cheese, 156, *157*
Homemade Tagliatelle, with Norm Bloom & Son CT Lobster, 148–49, *149*
Macaroni and Cheese, 155
Pappardelle, Spicy Rabbit Ragù with, 152
Pistou Soup, 32
Ricotta Gnocchi, 158, *159*
Salad, Mediterranean, with

Fennel, Basil, and Fresh Mozzarella, 41

Sauce, Autumn, of Cauliflower and Apples, 154

Pâte Sucrée, 296

Peach Tart, Fresh, 287–88, *288*

Pear

Asian, Baked, Stuffed with Blue Cheese and Braised Pork Belly, Grilled Berkshire Pork Chops with, 254–56

Smoothie, Green, 273

Pea(s)

à la Française, 89

and Leek Soup, Chilled, with Salmon Gravlax and Pickled Shallots, 69–70, *70*

Pecan Maple Bourbon Pie, 300

Peppers

Bacon-Jalapeño Oysters, 206

Chef Scott Quis's Kimchee, 270

Chipotle Veggie Chili, 91

Cioppino Verde, 219–20, *220*

Garlic-Cilantro Slaw, 109

Green Tomato Salsa Verde, 268

Pork and Green Chile Stew, 253

Rosa Bianca Eggplant alla Caponata, 87

Swordfish Pizzaioli, 225

Pesto

Arugula and Sunflower Seed, over Sliced Heirloom Tomatoes, 265

Garlic Scape and Basil, 266

Pheasant Breast, Pan-Roasted New England, with Shallot-Cranberry Puree, Braised Red Cabbage, and Madeira Sauce, 187–88, *188*

Pies

Cinnamon Chicken with a Mashed Potato Crust Topped with Tomme Cheese (Shepherd's Pie Style), 133

Cottage, *131,* 132–33

Heirloom Tomato, 134–35, *135*

Maple Pecan Bourbon, 300

Pistachios

Blood Oranges, and Goat Cheese

Salad, Salt-Roasted Beets with, 93

Dried Sour Cherries, and Chèvre, Millet and Lacinato Kale with, 161, *161*

Polenta

Chicken Under a Brick, 196

Pork. *See also* Sausage(s)

Bacon-Jalapeño Oysters, 206

Belly–Stuffed Tomatoes, 257

Chops, Grilled Berkshire, Topped with Braised Pork Belly and Baked Asian Pear Stuffed with Blue Cheese, 254–56

Ciccioli Terrine Served on Rustic Bread Topped with Soft-Boiled Duck Eggs and Mustard Pickled Ramps, 260–61

and Green Chile Stew, 253

Polpette alla Napoletana (Meatballs), 235

Slow-Roasted Porchetta with Cilantro and Smoked Paprika, 244

Smoked Tasso, Stonington Royal Red Shrimp and Heirloom Grits with, 230–31

Special, Farmer's, 262

Potato(es). *See also* Sweet potatoes

Cast-Iron Duck Breast, 174–75

Cottage Pie, *131,* 132–33

Duck and Foie Gras Poutine, 182–83, *183*

Farmer's Pork Special, 262

Fresh Corn Soup, 72

Kugelis, 140

Low Country Bouillabaisse, 216–17, *217*

Mashed, Crust, Cinnamon Chicken with, Topped with Tomme Cheese (Shepherd's Pie Style), 133

Pork and Green Chile Stew, 253

Red Flannel Hash, 22

Roasted, and Heirloom Tomato Tower, 104

Roasted, with Raclette Cheese, 97, *97*

Pots de Crème, Maple-Cardamom, with Crème Fraîche and Fleur de Sel, 301

Poultry. *See* Chicken; Duck; Pheasant; Quail; Turkey

Poutine, Duck and Foie Gras, 182–83, *183*

Pumpkin

Bread, 24

Cheesecakes, Individual, with a Gingersnap Cookie Crust and Citrus-Cranberry Compote, 297–99, *299*

Purslane and Corn, Seared Scallops with, 212

Q

Quail with Yam Puree and Microgreens, 199–200, *200*

Quince Paste (Membrillo), 267

Quinoa

and Carrot Terrine Garnished with Soubise and Carrot Top–Cashew Pesto, 122–23, *123*

Paella, 165, *165*

Salad, Seasonal, 168, *169*

R

Rabbit Ragù, Spicy, with Pappardelle Pasta, 152

Ramps, Mustard-Pickled, and Soft-Boiled Duck Eggs, Pork Ciccioli Terrine Served on Rustic Bread Topped with, 260–61

Raspberry(ies)

Hidden Vegetable Smoothie, 273

Vinaigrette, Beet and Carrot Slaw with, 48

S

Salads

Arugula, Saunder's Farm, with Orange Vinaigrette and Harvest Moon Cheese, 60, *61*

Arugula and Endive, with Apples, Celeriac, Caramelized Walnuts, and Cider Vinaigrette, 33–34, *34*

Baby Kale "Caesar" with Fried
  Capers, Anchovies, and
  Herbed Crostini, 42–43
Beet and Carrot Slaw with
  Raspberry Vinaigrette, 48
Blood Oranges, Pistachios, and
  Goat Cheese, Salt-Roasted
  Beets with, 93
Bread, 49
Carrots and Sunflower Sprouts,
  with Basil Vinaigrette, 36
Chickpea and Carrot, Moroccan,
  46
Farmers', 58–59
Garlic-Cilantro Slaw, 109
Heirloom Tomato, Late Summer
  CT, 54
Heirloom Tomato and Burrata, 40
Kale, Starlight Farm's, with Sour
  Cherry Vinaigrette, 38
Lobster, Tomato, and Burrata, 44
of Mixed Baby Greens and
  Beltane Farm Goat Cheese,
  53, 53
Mixed Greens with a Sherry
  Shallot Vinaigrette, 56
Pasta, Mediterranean, with
  Fennel, Basil, and Fresh
  Mozzarella, 41
Poached Egg, Crispy, 63
Quinoa, Seasonal, 168, 169
Roasted Potato and Heirloom
  Tomato Tower, 104
Smoked Chicken, Apple, and
  Walnut, 51
White Bean and Arugula, Grilled
  Tuna with, 214
Salmon
  Gravlax and Pickled Shallots,
    Chilled Pea and Leek Soup
    with, 69–70, 70
  Maple-Glazed, 221
Salsa Verde, Green Tomato, 268
Sandwich, Butter-Poached Lobster,
  142
Sausage(s)
  Antipasto Platter, 259, 259

Artisan Hand Crafted, and
  Roasted Root Vegetable
  Stuffing, 80, 81
Artisan Italian, Onion, and Kale
  Frittata, 128–29
Lentils with Chorizo and Bacon,
  162, 163
Low Country Bouillabaisse, 216–
  17, 217
Macaroni and Cheese, 155
Spicy Littleneck Clams, 232
Scallops, Seared, with Corn and
  Purslane, 212
Scones, Blackberry River, 21
Shad, Connecticut River, 222, 223
Shellfish. See also Lobster; Shrimp
  Bacon-Jalapeño Oysters, 206
  Calamari with Eggplant Chutney,
    224–25
  Cioppino Verde, 219–20, 220
  Deviled Eggs with Cornmeal
    Fried Oysters and Pickled Red
    Onion, 210–11, 211
  Low Country Bouillabaisse, 216–
    17, 217
  Mystic River Oysters with Grace
    Cocktail Mignonette, 213
  Seared Scallops with Corn and
    Purslane, 212
  Spicy Littleneck Clams, 232
Shortcake, Strawberry, 287
Shrimp
  Cioppino Verde, 219–20, 220
  Low Country Bouillabaisse, 216–
    17, 217
  Stonington Royal Red, and
    Heirloom Grits with Smoked
    Tasso Pork, 230–31
  Stonington Royal Red, over Root
    Vegetable Cakes, 226–28, 227
Slaws
  Beet and Carrot, with Raspberry
    Vinaigrette, 48
  Garlic-Cilantro, 109
Smoothies
  Green Pear, 273
  Hidden Vegetable, 273
  Summer Garden Mojito, 274

Soups. See also Stews
  Chilled Green Gazpacho, 67
  Country Cottage, 76, 76
  Cream of Carrot, Vegan, 64–65
  Fresh Corn, 72
  Pea and Leek, Chilled, with
    Salmon Gravlax and Pickled
    Shallots, 69–70, 70
  Pistou, 32
  Squash Almond Bisque, 74
Spinach
  and Feta Frittata, 127
  Hidden Vegetable Smoothie, 273
  Seasonal Quinoa Salad, 168, 169
Squash. See also Pumpkin
  Almond Bisque, 74
  Butternut, Roasted, Rainbow
    Swiss Chard, Skirt Steak over,
    Topped with Caramelized
    Onions, 240–41, 241
  Delicata, Sautéed, with Kale,
    Raspberry Balsamic Vinegar,
    and Toasted Walnuts, 109
  Opo, Curried Roasted, 94, 95
Stews
  Chipotle Veggie Chili, 91
  Cioppino Verde, 219–20, 220
  Low Country Bouillabaisse, 216–
    17, 217
  Pork and Green Chile, 253
  Slow Cooker Turkey Chili, 172
Stock, Lobster, 142–43
Strawberry(ies)
  Frangipane Tartlets, 295
  Hidden Vegetable Smoothie, 273
  Sauce and Corn Bread Stuffing,
    MarWin Farm's Duck with,
    178–79, 179
  Shortcake, 287
Stuffing
  Corn Bread, and Strawberry
    Sauce, MarWin Farm's Duck
    with, 178–79, 179
  Roasted Root Vegetable and
    Artisan Handcrafted Sausage,
    80, 81

Sunflower Seed(s)
 and Arugula Pesto over Sliced
  Heirloom Tomatoes, 265
 Beet and Carrot Slaw with
  Raspberry Vinaigrette, 48
Sunflower Sprouts and Carrots Salad
  with Basil Vinaigrette, 36
Sweet potatoes
 Organic Duck Breast with Ginger-
  Carrot Puree and Ginger-
  Orange Sauce, 184–85
 Quail with Yam Puree and
  Microgreens, 199–200, *200*
Swiss Chard
 and Fresh Ricotta Cheese, 117
 Green Pear Smoothie, 273
 Grilled Berkshire Pork Chops
  Topped with Braised Pork Belly
  and Baked Asian Pear Stuffed
  with Blue Cheese, 254–56
 Pistou Soup, 32
 Rainbow, Roasted Butternut
  Squash, Skirt Steak over,
  Topped with Caramelized
  Onions, 240–41, *241*
 Roll-ups, Grilled, 101
 Spicy Rabbit Ragù with
  Pappardelle Pasta, 152
 Summer Garden Mojito Smoothie,
  274
Swordfish Pizzaioli, 225

T
Tarts
 Caramel-Apple, 293–94
 Fresh Peach, 287–88, *288*
 Honey Black Walnut, 284
 Macerated Summer Fruit, 290–91
 Strawberry Frangipane Tartlets,
  295
Tofu Medallions, Marinated Grilled,
  141

Tomato(es)
 Antipasto Platter, 259, *259*
 Bread Salad, 49
 Garden Fresh Bloody Mary, 276
 Green, Fried, with Hot and Sweet
  Aioli, 101–2
 Green, Fritters, 99
 Green, Salsa Verde, 268
 Heirloom, and Burrata Salad, 40
 Heirloom, and Roasted Potato
  Tower, 104
 Heirloom, Fresh Burrata, and
  Basil, Grilled Violetta di Firenze
  Topped with, 119
 Heirloom, Pie, 134–35, *135*
 Heirloom, Salad, Late Summer
  CT, 54
 Heirloom, Sliced, Arugula and
  Sunflower Seed Pesto over,
  265
 Homemade Tagliatelle Pasta with
  Norm Bloom & Son CT Lobster,
  148–49, *149*
 Lobster, and Burrata Salad, 44
 Pork Belly–Stuffed, 257
Tuna, Grilled, with White Bean and
  Arugula Salad, 214
Turkey
 Chili, Slow Cooker, 172
 Old South Collard Greens with
  Pot Likker (a.k.a. "Mess o'
  Greens"), 106
Turnip(s)
 Gilfeather, Puree and Rainbow
  Carrots with Orange-Blossom
  Honey and Fresh Sage,
  Balsamic-Glazed Short Ribs
  with, 248–49, *249*
 Pickled Garden, Dry-Aged Steak
  Tartare Crostini with, 243, *243*

V
Vegetable(s). *See also specific
  vegetables*
 Farmers' Salad, 58–59
 Pistou Soup, 32
 Root, and Grass-Fed Beef Meat
  Loaf, 238–39
 Root, Cakes, Stonington Royal
  Red Shrimp over, 226–28, *227*
 Root, Roasted, and Artisan
  Handcrafted Sausage Stuffing,
  80, *81*
Vinaigrette, Basil, 174
Vodka
 Garden Fresh Bloody Mary, 276
 Infused, 276

W
Walnut(s)
 Black, Honey Tart, 284
 Caramelized, Apples, Celeriac,
  and Cider Vinaigrette, Arugula
  and Endive Salad with, 33–34,
  34
 Farmers' Salad, 58–59
 Saunder's Farm Arugula Salad
  with Orange Vinaigrette and
  Harvest Moon Cheese, 60, *61*
 Smoked Chicken, and Apple
  Salad, 51
Wild Rice and Corn Griddle Cakes
  and Garlicky Kale, Atlantic Cod
  with, 202–4, *203*

Y
Yam Puree and Microgreens, Quail
  with, 199–200, *200*

People and Places

Note: Page numbers in **bold** refer to first page of contributed recipes

A

Aitkenhead, Mike and Carrie, 90
Ambler Farm, 112
Ambrose, Colin, 218, **219**
Ancona, Mark, 103
Ancona, Stephen, 103
Ancona, Suzanne, 103, **104**
Ancona, Tony, 103
Anderson, Tyler, 120–21, **122**
Appel, Denise, 68
Arethusa al Tavolo, 27, **28**
Artisan Restaurant, **152**
Ashlawn Café Kitchen, 304, **305**
Ashlawn Farm Coffee, 304
Averill, Sam, 267
Averill, Tyson, 267
Averill Farm, 267, **267**

B

Baez, Carlos, 195, **196**
Bagliavio, Sal, 247
Bailey's Backyard, 247, **248**
Balin, Jennifer, 164
Barberry Hill Farm, 31, **32, 287**
Barcelona Wine Bar & Restaurant, 113, **114, 270**
Barricelli, John, 292, **293, 295**
Bar Sugo, 258, **259**
Batchie, Rebecca, 266
Beltane Farm, 116, **117**
Billings Forge Community Works, 173
Bistro Seven Restaurant, 184, **184**
Blackberry River Baking Co., 21, **21, 22**
Bloodroot Restaurant, 289, **290**
Bloom, Norm, 207
Blue Lemon Restaurant and Café, 33, **33, 287**
Blyn, David and Laura, 108
Bogert, Katie, 75, **76**
Boone, Sarah, 304
Booth, Bob and Virgina "Jimmie," 75

Borofsky, Jeff, 128
Bouffard, Matthew, 136
Bozzuto, Andrew, Steven, and Dennis, 262
Brewster, Dina, 268
Bricco Trattoria, 144
Brookside Farm, 281, **282**
Brown, Allyn, III, 225
Bruckner, Dawn, 226
Bruckner, Wally, 226
Bucciaglia, Paul, 266

C

Cafémantic, 94, **94, 189**
Cameron, Johnny, 124
Carbone, Bill, 134
Carole Peck's Good News Café, 66, **67, 133**
Carroll, Kay, 281, **282**
Cartwright, Jonathan, 186, **187**
Caseus Fromagerie Bistro, 96, **97, 161**
Cassar, Carlos, 42
Cato Corner Farm, LLC, **269**
Chamard Vineyards Farm Winery Bistro, 136, **137, 254**
Charlton, Craig, **91**
CitySeed, 277
Claire's Corner Copia, 71, **72**
Cochran, Lori, 130
Cole-Smith, Phoebe, 301
Common Ground High School, Urban Farm & Environmental Education Center, 235
Community Farm of Simsbury (CFS), 167, **168, 273**
Community Table, 236, **237**
Connecticut Beer Trail, 279
Connecticut Farmers' Market Trail, 245
Connecticut Farmland Trust (CFT), 291
Connecticut Pick-Your-Own Farms, 17, 18, 225
Connecticut Wine Festival, 257
Connecticut Wine Trail, 256, 257
Copper Beech Inn (The Oak Room), 42, **42, 44**

Coriander Café & Country Store, 202, **202**
Corsino, Nunzio and Irene, 239
Cosgriff, James, 55
Coventry Regional Farmers' Market, 177
Criscuolo, Claire, 71, **72**
Criscuolo, Frank, 71
CT Valley Farms, LLC, 191, **192**
Curran, Donna, 68

D

Dahlke, Carol, 304
Dahlke, Chip, 78, 304
Darling Farm, 153, **154**
Denevan, Jim, 268
DeVries, Johannes, 21
Dinners at the Farm, 31, 78
Dion, Brendan, 39
Dirt Road Farm, 301, **301**
Dish Bar & Grill, 134, **134**
Dombroski, Jim, 191
Donatti, Breno, 184
Dorel, Amiel, 215
The Dressing Room Restaurant & Wholesome Wave, **155, 238**

E

Ekonk Hill Turkey Farm, 171, **172**
Engine Room, 260
Estia's American, 218, **219**

F

Failla, Paul, 258
Farah's Farm, 115
Farming 101, 98, **99, 250**
The Farmer's Cow, 127, **127, 156**
Farm to Hearth, 25, **26, 49**
Farrell, Joe, 229
Farrell, Sean, 173
Fat Cat Pie Co., 103, **104**
Fay, Peter, 244
Febbroriello, Courtney, 82
Feola, Lawrence, 150
Fibiger, Ryan and Katherine, 242
Figs Wood Fired Bistro, 221, **221, 234**
Fila, Jessie, 110